Private High Schools of the San Francisco Bay Area

© 2009 Pince-Nez Press

Printed in the U.S.A.

ISBN 978-1-930074-20-0

Library of Congress Control Number: 2008933119

Cover design: Ana Esmee Design, Los Angeles, CA
Editor: Charles Geraci

Fonts: Didot, Futura

Pince-Nez Press
San Francisco, CA
(415) 267-5978
www.pince-nez.com
susan@pince-nez.com

PRIVATE HIGH SCHOOLS OF THE

SAN FRANCISCO BAY AREA

Betsy Little, MBA, MA
Paula Molligan, MBA, MA
Educational Consultants

www.littleandmolligan.com

Pince-Nez Press
San Francisco

Dedication

Thank you to our families for all their encouragement, patience and love. Special thanks also to all the participating schools in this book as well as to our clients who constantly make our work a joy.

CONTENTS

PART ONE: Choosing a High School and the Admission Process

PART TWO: Bay Area Private High Schools

SCHOOLS BY COUNTY

Alameda County

Bishop O'Dowd High School (Oakland)
Chinese Christian School (San Leandro)
The College Preparatory School (Oakland)
Fremont Christian School (Fremont)
The Head-Royce School (Oakland)
Holy Names High School (Oakland)
Moreau Catholic High School (Hayward)
The Quarry Lane High School (Dublin)
Redwood Day Upper School (Oakland)*
St. Elizabeth High School (Oakland)
St. Joseph-Notre Dame (Alameda)*
Saint Mary's College High School (Berkeley)

Contra Costa County

The Athenian School (Danville)
Bentley School (Lafayette)
Berean Christian School (Walnut Creek)
Contra Costa Christian Schools (Walnut Creek)
Carondelet High School (Concord)*
De La Salle High School (Concord)
East Bay Waldorf School (El Sobrante)
Orinda Academy (Orinda)
Salesian High School (Richmond)

Marin County

The Branson School (Ross)
Marin Academy (San Rafael)
Marin Catholic High School (Kentfield)
The Marin School (Sausalito)
San Domenico Upper School (San Anselmo)

San Francisco

Archbishop Riordan High School
The Bay School of San Francisco
Convent of the Sacred Heart High School
Cornerstone Academy
Drew College Preparatory School
Immaculate Conception Academy
International High School
The Jewish Community High School of the Bay
The Lisa Kampner Hebrew Academy High School
Lick-Wilmerding High School
Lycée Français La Pérouse
Mercy High School
Sacred Heart Cathedral Preparatory
St. Ignatius College Preparatory School
San Francisco University High School
San Francisco Waldorf High School
Stuart Hall High School
The Urban School of San Francisco
Woodside International School

San Mateo County

Crystal Springs Uplands School (Hillsborough)
Junipero Serra High School (San Mateo)
Menlo School (Atherton)
Mercy High School (Burlingame)
Mid-Peninsula High School (Menlo Park)
Notre Dame High School (Belmont)
Sacred Heart Preparatory (Atherton)

Santa Clara County

Archbishop Mitty High School (San Jose)
Bellarmine College Preparatory (San Jose)
Castilleja School (Palo Alto)
The Harker School (San Jose)
Kehillah Jewish High School (San Jose)
The King's Academy (Sunnyvale)
Notre Dame High School (San Jose)
Pinewood School (Los Altos Hills)
Presentation High School (San Jose)
Saint Francis High School (Mountain View)
St. Lawrence Academy (Santa Clara)
Valley Christian High School (San Jose)
Woodside Priory (Portola Valley)

Sonoma County
Cardinal Newman High School (Santa Rosa)
St. Vincent de Paul High School (Petaluma)*
Sonoma Academy (Santa Rosa)
Ursuline High School (Santa Rosa)*

BOARDING
The Athenian School (Danville) (coed)
San Domenico Upper School (San Anselmo) (girls)
Woodside Priory School (Portola Valley) (coed)

ALL GIRLS
Carondelet High School (Concord)*
Castilleja School (Palo Alto)
Convent of the Sacred Heart High School (San Francisco)
Holy Names High School (Oakland)
Immaculate Conception Academy (San Francisco)
Mercy High School-Burlingame
Mercy High School-San Francisco
Notre Dame High School (Belmont)
Notre Dame High School (San Jose)
Presentation High School (San Jose)
San Domenico Upper School (San Anselmo)
Ursuline High School (Santa Rosa)*

ALL BOYS
Archbishop Riordan High School (San Francisco)
Bellarmine College Preparatory (San Jose)
Cardinal Newman High School (Santa Rosa)
De La Salle High School (Concord)
Junipero Serra High School (San Mateo)
Stuart Hall High School (San Francisco)

*= short entries

Choosing a High School and the Admission Process

Parents and students are often overwhelmed with the myriad of high school choices available. The purpose of this Guide is to provide families with valuable information to facilitate their school search. Families can explore their options for schools with the best academic, athletic and social environment to fit their student's needs, as well as consider financial commitments and other special needs and expectations.

Approximately 9% of students in California attend private schools; in San Francisco about 30% attend private schools. Marin County has the second highest enrollment of students in private schools at 19%, followed by San Mateo County at 15% and Napa County at 13% (Source: www.sfgate.com). Private high school graduates are over represented at the country's most selective universities, making up approximately 30% of the school populations. (Source: www.greenesguides.com)

Even though there are many private high schools in the Bay Area, admission to these schools is very competitive. The information contained in this Guide is based upon (1) information provided by the schools in response to a questionnaire sent to the schools; (2) interviews with admission directors and principals; (3) visits to most of the schools (usually up to a two-hour visit per school including classroom visits); and, in some cases, (4) publicly available information on the schools. The additional schools listed in the back of the Guide, as well as any new schools between revision publications, are invited to provide full information in the next edition. Schools do not pay to be included in this Guide—it is not advertising. Should the school choose not to answer any part of the questionnaire, it is noted as "N/P" for "not provided."

No one school is best for all students; consequently, no attempt is made to rank or rate schools. Moreover, what families are looking for in a school will vary considerably. Some may be looking for a school that sends a good number of graduates to Ivy League universities; others may be interested in a spiritual environment or a good co-curricular program, and some may be looking for a well-rounded education. It is important for families to consider the fit between their student and family needs and a school's offerings.

Private Schools

In the lexicon of this Guide, "private schools" means schools established and controlled by an individual or a non-governmental entity and supported by endowment and tuition. Within this very broad category are schools that are set up as non-profit, tax-exempt corporations with boards of trustees known as independent schools; privately owned, tax-paying schools known as proprietary schools; and religiously affiliated schools. Most depend on tuition, fees and outside funding sources to finance most of their expenses. Annual fund appeals, contributions, and various fundraising activities make up the difference in a school's operating budget. Most schools look for 100% parent participation in their annual appeals as the percentage of participation makes a statement in attracting outside funding for grants and foundation support. These organizations look to the financial contributions of the school's current parents, faculty, and alumni as a reflection of satisfaction with the school.

California law requires private elementary and secondary schools to file an affidavit with the California Department of Education. Any school with an enrollment of six or more students must be registered, and a full list of these schools is available at www.cde.ca.gov/private-schools/data.html.

Independent Schools

Although any school may call itself an "independent school," members of the associations of independent schools, such as the California Association of Independent Schools (CAIS) and the National Association of Independent Schools (NAIS), are non-profit organizations governed by their own boards of trustees (as opposed to being governed by a central diocese, a church's board of trustees, or some other off-site entity). The NAIS requires that its members be "primarily supported by tuition, charitable contributions, and endowment income rather than by tax or church funds." To be eligible for NAIS membership, schools must be independently governed by a board of trustees, practice nondiscriminatory policies, be accredited by an approved state or regional association, and hold not-for-profit 501 (c)(3) tax-exempt status. For more information, see the NAIS website at www.nais.org and the CAIS website at www.caisca.org.

Generally, a board of trustees provides oversight of the school's administration. The trustees are composed of parents, community leaders, and others dedicated to the school's mission. Trustees are normally invited to serve as volunteers for terms of two to four years, and board meetings are typically closed to non-members.

Independent schools distinguish themselves as being college preparatory, offering small class size, and providing individual attention to students. Independent schools may have religious affiliations. Each independent school is responsible for its own curriculum. As tax-exempt organizations, they may be eligible for grant and/or foundation monies. Most independent schools expect that parents will make tax-deductible contributions to the school and/or be involved in fundraising activities.

High schools in the Bay Area that are members of the Bay Area Independent High Schools (BAIHS) have established "Principles of Good Practice" surrounding admissions and athletic recruitment. They also share admission forms, admission deadlines, and notification dates. They agree that members of their faculty and staff will not initiate calls or meetings with applicants except during the student's campus visit. The members of the BAIHS included in this Guide are The Athenian School, The Bay School of San Francisco, Bentley

School, The Branson School, Castilleja School, The College Prepara-
tory School, Convent of the Sacred Heart High School, Crystal Springs
Uplands School, Drew College Preparatory School, East Bay Waldorf
School, The Harker School, The Head-Royce School, Lisa Kampner
Hebrew Academy, International High School, The Jewish Community
High School of the Bay, Kehillah Jewish High School, Lick-Wilmerd-
ing High School, Marin Academy, The Marin School, Maybeck High
School, Menlo School, Mid-Peninsula High School, Orinda Academy,
Sacred Heart Preparatory-Atherton, San Domenico School, San Fran-
cisco University High School, San Francisco Waldorf High School,
Santa Catalina School, Sonoma Academy, Stevenson School, Stuart
Hall High School, The Urban School of San Francisco, and Woodside
Priory School. Some of the East Bay schools that have an elementary
and middle school also belong to the East Bay Independent School
Association (EBISA). These schools include Athenian, Bentley, and
Head-Royce. Most of the aforementioned schools are also members of
the Bay Area Admissions Directors (BAAD) group, which meets once
or twice a year to collaborate on admission issues.

Proprietary Schools

Private proprietary schools may be corporations, partnerships, or
sole proprietorships. These schools pay taxes like any other business.
Donations to them are not tax-deductible, though some schools set
up foundations to receive contributions. Generally, they do not have
boards of trustees, but they may have parent committees to advise
owners on a broad range of topics.

Religiously Affiliated Schools

Few generalities can be made about religious schools except that
they seek to instill moral values. Religiously affiliated schools, both
Christian and non-Christian, vary in degree as to the level of sectar-
ian integration of the curriculum. In addition, the percentage of the
prevailing religious affiliation varies from one school to another with
some schools requiring membership in a particular religion as an admission requirement and others welcoming students without regard
to religion. Families choose religiously affiliated schools for a variety
of reasons including: family or cultural tradition; appreciation for the
concurrent teaching of values alongside academics; and a perception
of higher academic standards, higher standards of behavior, and a
better peer group.

    Catholic: Most Bay Area Catholic high schools are not attached to
or run by parishes but draw students from the entire diocese or archdiocese. Each Catholic secondary school chooses its own curriculum
following state guidelines and/or guidelines published by the archdiocese or diocese. Schools within the same archdiocese/diocese normally
share admission deadlines and dates on which they send acceptance
notifications. A few Catholic schools choose an independent association with CAIS and NAIS, and therefore share admission deadlines

with BAIHS schools. Catholic schools may also be members of the Western Catholic Educational Association (WCEA) or the National Catholic Educational Association (NCEA). These associations advance the recognition and support of Catholic education. The high schools in the Archdiocese of San Francisco are Archbishop Riordan High School, Convent of the Sacred Heart High School, Immaculate Conception Academy, Junipero Serra High School, Marin Catholic High School, Mercy High School-Burlingame, Mercy High School-San Francisco, Notre Dame High School-Belmont, Sacred Heart Cathedral Preparatory High School, Sacred Heart Preparatory, St. Ignatius College Preparatory, San Domenico, Stuart Hall High School and Woodside Priory. The high schools in the San Jose Diocese are Archbishop Mitty High School, Bellarmine College Preparatory School, Notre Dame High School-San Jose, Presentation High School, Saint Francis High School, and St. Lawrence Academy. The high schools in the Oakland Diocese are Bishop O'Dowd High School, Carondelet High School, De La Salle High School, Holy Names High School, Moreau Catholic High School, St. Elizabeth High School, St. Joseph Notre Dame High School, Saint Mary's College High School, and Salesian High School. The Santa Rosa Diocese includes Cardinal Newman, Justin-Siena High School, St. Vincent de Paul, and Ursuline High Schools.

Christian: The term "Christian school" is used in this Guide to refer to schools that are independent and are governed by a self-perpetuating board. Some may be a ministry of a particular congregation. The Association of Christian Schools International (ACSI) provides educational assistance to Christian schools.

Jewish: Jewish day schools are designed to provide students an academic program that includes Judaic studies within a Jewish cultural environment. Students learn to appreciate and celebrate Jewish practices and philosophies. The Partnership for Excellence in Jewish Education (PEJE) is comprised of philanthropic partners whose mission is to increase Jewish day school enrollment in North America. PEJE assists schools in developing internal capacities focusing on grant making, conferences, advocating for excellence in Jewish education, and providing needed expertise in strengthening Jewish day schools.

Public Schools
The Bay Area has many excellent public high schools. Public schools are funded by local, state, and federal funding. They are controlled by the local board of education and funded by the public. Information on public schools can be obtained from each school district or from the Department of Education in Sacramento. Numerous websites provide information on Bay Area public high schools.

Charter schools are publicly funded schools that are granted a high degree of autonomy. In California there are nearly 900 charter schools. (Source: http://www.myschool.org/association/). They are unique in that they can control their own budgets, staffing, and curriculum. The charters may be granted by a local school board or the California State Board of Education. These schools must adhere to the terms of their charter involving their students and their achievement, or their charter can be revoked. Lotteries are used to determine admission with priority for enrollment based on factors such as district residency, participation in establishing the school, employee status, etc. The lottery establishes a wait list for any openings that may develop. Most districts are able to accommodate many students on the wait list by September. Families can obtain information on charter schools by calling their local school districts or visiting district websites.

College Prep or What?

Most of the schools included in this Guide offer a college preparatory curriculum aimed at fulfilling entrance standards for the University of California system. Some of the high schools allow students to choose a modified college preparatory curriculum aimed at entrance to California State universities or community colleges, and/or a general non-college prep curriculum.

In their published brochures, many private high schools describe their curriculum as a "rigorous college preparatory curriculum" and appear to be seeking the brightest students with the greatest academic potential. Other schools might emphasize a student body made up of a wide range of abilities and talents. To get a better sense of the breadth of students the school serves, each school included in this Guide was asked: What sort of student do you best serve?

On paper, it can appear that all schools cater to the "best and the brightest" and offer an extremely demanding college preparatory curriculum. Parents have commented that it seems there's no place for "average" students. The question, **"What kind of student do you best serve?"** is designed to give a sense of the "breadth" of students, in terms of abilities and varied talents/potential that the school serves. No admission director, admission committee, or parent would knowingly put a teen in an environment where he or she would not be successful.

Schools were asked if they have **minimum admission requirements** in terms of test scores and grades. This should help families focus on realistic school possibilities based on their student's individual profile. Although admission committees attribute a great deal of importance to "top factors" such as grades and test scores, they also look at "tip factors" such as essays, recommendations, interviews, extra and co-curricular activities, and potential within their school's environment. Schools are looking to complement their current population.

Although individual grade point averages are generally a good indication of a student's course performance, it may be an incomplete measure. Admission directors make distinctions among schools knowing that middle schools vary in course standards and curriculum.

Accreditation and Associations

The main accrediting agency for elementary and secondary schools in California is the Accrediting Commission for Schools, which is an arm of the Western Association of Schools and Colleges (ACS/WASC). "Accreditation certifies to other educational institutions and to the general public that an institution meets established criteria or standards and is achieving its own stated objectives." (Source: www.acswasc.org)

Accreditation serves as an indicator of the quality of the school and a tool for self-improvement. The accreditation process requires extensive documentation of a school's goals and objectives, a self-evaluation performed by the school staff and community, and an on-site visit to the school by a team of educational professionals. The evaluating team validates the internal study, evaluates its findings, and recommends a term of accreditation to the Commission. Schools that seek accreditation may apply for candidate or interim status with ACS/WASC. All schools are subject to a full review every six years. If a school has not met all ACS/WASC criteria, it may receive a shorter term of accreditation, requiring additional reports and visits. If parents have questions about accreditation, they may contact the Accrediting Commission for Schools at (650) 696-1060.

Another accrediting organization in California is the California Association of Independent Schools known as CAIS. To be a voting member of CAIS, a school must be accredited by CAIS. It is an association of over 190 college preparatory schools in California wherein each school's accountability is open for public review to assure that the school meets high standards in its quality, operations, and staff. Schools complete a self-study, which is evaluated by an on-site visit of education professionals. Schools are accredited for a maximum of six years and must complete an interim report between accreditation visits to track the school's adherence to any CAIS recommendations. CAIS is a collaborative partner with WASC and NAIS. CAIS can be reached at (310) 393-5161 or www.caisca.org.

ACSI accredits Christian schools. Christian schools may also apply for joint ACSI/WASC accreditation or be only ACSI accredited. Any questions regarding accreditation may be directed to (719) 528-6906.

Christian schools may also be members of the National Association of Street Schools (NASS). The NASS organization acts as a clearinghouse for support of Christian education for at-risk youth.

Accreditation is optional; however, certain exceptions apply for schools receiving public funds. Public schools have the option of refusing to accept credits from schools that are not accredited. Some schools, both non-profit and proprietary, choose not to go through the accreditation process because of the cost and the time involved. In addition, each school must pay the expenses—including airfare, hotel, and meals—for a team of three to four evaluators to study the school for two to three days. Schools involve parents, students, faculty, administration and board members in their self-evaluation documentation. Schools that do not seek accreditation often consider their "stamp of approval" to be satisfied parents and successful college placement, as well as the school's longevity.

The National Association of Independent Schools (NAIS) includes 1,300 independent schools in both the United States and overseas. NAIS provides Principles of Good Practice for ethical behavior and advocates broad access in affirming principles of justice and equity. It is a membership organization, not an accrediting organization, with a national voice on behalf of member schools, and it acts as a center for collective action. The voting membership comes from non-profit schools that have been established for over five years, are accredited by an independent organization recognized by NAIS, and demonstrate financially sound operations and non-discriminatory practices. For further information, call (202) 973-9700.

Waldorf schools often choose to be members of The Association of Waldorf Schools, North America (AWSNA). This organization is designed to strengthen and support independent Waldorf schools as well as Waldorf teacher education institutes.

The North American Association of Jewish High Schools (NAAJHS) was established in 1999 to act as a forum for Jewish day high schools (617-367-0001). The member schools collaborate on educational projects and discuss ideas and concerns. NAAJHS also sponsors conferences and programs for professionals, board leadership, and students. In addition, the Bureau of Jewish Education (BJE) helps to augment the impact of Jewish learning by making available collaborative opportunities for Jewish learning. Torah Umesorah is the National Society for Hebrew Day Schools. Its organization includes Orthodox Jewish day schools in the United States.

Many schools in the San Francisco area belong to the Bay Area People of Color in Independent Schools (POCIS). POCIS is a committee of NAIS and is organized to support national and regional goals for the betterment of people of color in independent schools. (Source: www.ba-pocis.org) A Better Chance (ABC) also focuses on increasing the number of minority students furthering their educational and career opportunities. Summerbridge and Making Waves serve middle school students who face limited opportunities and resources.

The National Catholic Educational Association (NCEA) is a membership organization that provides individual, affiliate, and institutional memberships to Catholic educators. It is a voluntary association of institutions and educators affiliated with religious education programs, elementary and secondary schools, colleges, and universities. It represents over 200,000 Catholic educators serving almost eight million students. The NCEA promotes the educational and religious mission of the Catholic Church, advocates Catholic education, and fosters collaboration within its membership (202-337-6232). The Western Catholic Educational Association (WCEA) works collaboratively with WASC for school improvement and accreditation of Catholic school members (714-447-9824). Jointly they review the teaching, learning, and spiritual goals of member schools.

The Secondary School Admission Test Board (SSATB) is a non-profit organization that oversees the SSAT examination and supports professional development of its members with publications and meetings. Likewise, the Independent School Management organization (ISM) is dedicated to the advancement of school management and is responsive to the needs of independent schools.

The National Coalition of Girls' School (NCGS) is an association of girls independent, private, and public day and boarding schools in the United States and abroad. The NCGS promotes the value and benefit of all-girl schools.

Boarding school associations such as The Association of Boarding Schools (TABS) and the Western Boarding Schools Association (WBSA) represent college preparatory schools and serve global student populations. Both organizations provide comprehensive support to boarding schools and provide public information and favorable publicity for the boarding school option.

The European Council of International Schools (ECIS) members are accredited schools. ECIS is a non-profit corporation that is registered in the United States but is administered in the United Kingdom.

The French Ministry of Education requires education standards to be followed in U.S. schools teaching French nationals. The Ministry sends a representative to make sure the instruction conforms to teaching programs, pedagogies, and examinations applicable in French schools.

The International Baccalaureate Organization's (IBO) diploma program was created in 1968. It is a rigorous pre-university course of study that leads to examinations to qualify for the diploma. It has earned a reputation for strict assessment and is recognized by leading universities around the world. Some schools also offer a French Baccalaureate (FB or Bac), a three-year college preparatory program that follows the curriculum guidelines of the French Ministry of Education. In the Bac program, all courses are taught in French, and students must choose a specialized program of study in the core curriculum. The diploma is awarded at the end of twelfth grade and is required for admission into any French university. The OIB (L'option internationale du baccalaureat) is not a separate diploma but a specialization within the French Baccalaureate in one of four subject areas (language, literature, history, and geography).

Blue Ribbon schools are schools that apply and are chosen in recognition of the No Child Left Behind Program, which is dedicated to ensuring every child learns. (Source: www.ed.gov/programs/nclb-brs/index.html)

Associations such as the Bay Area Learning Directors (BALD), the Bay Area Teacher Development Collaborative (BATDC), the Bay Area Independent Secondary School Counselors (BAISSC), the Bay Area Admissions Directors (BAAD), Peninsula Association of Admissions Directors (PAAD), and the Independent School Business Officers

Association (ISBOA) are collaborative associations that enhance the respective educational goals of each interest.

The California Interscholastic Federation is a "bottom up organization, and its functions are designed to ensure that new rules only come into being after having been examined and voted upon by CIF representatives throughout the state of California. Each CIF member school is assigned to a local league." (Source: http://www.cifstate.org/) These leagues are represented by the following sections: Central, Central Coast, LA City, North Coast, Northern, Oakland, Sacramento-San Joaquin, San Diego, San Francisco and Southern.

San Francisco Bay Area schools may participate in the Alameda Contra Costa Athletic League (ACCAL), Bay County League (BCL), Bay Football League (BFL), Marin County Athletic League (MCAL), Western Catholic Athletic League (WCAL), North Central Athletic League (NCAL), West Bay Athletic League (WBAL), Bay Shore Athletic League (BSAL), Private School Athletic League (PSAL), Hayward Area Athletic League (HAAHL), Peninsula Athletic League (PAL), or the Small School Bridge League (SSBL).

Student Body
The student body information provided in this Guide is intended to give applicant families the geographic, ethnic, and middle school backgrounds of each school's student body. Student ethnicity is determined by the student (students self-identify), and the terminology used is that which the particular school has reported. Schools to which many families commute normally share carpool lists.

The Admission Process
Although the admission process for Bay Area private high schools officially begins the fall of a student's eighth grade year, many families and schools begin preparations in the seventh grade year. Some eighth grade counselors present general overviews of the application process to parents and/or students in the spring of seventh grade. Some even meet with individual families and students in the spring and summer to explore possible high school options. A number of schools invite families of students in grades six through eight to their open houses. Throughout the Bay Area, high school fairs provide students and parents the opportunity to meet with admission directors and current students and obtain information on schools. The dates and locations of the fairs for local as well as boarding schools can be obtained from any independent K-8 school or high school. They are usually held in September and October.

Tours of schools and open houses begin as early as August. Open houses are usually held evenings and weekends and are open to prospective students and their families. Some schools invite both students and parents to tour, while others invite only students. Applicants often "shadow" a current student throughout the day and may be interviewed and/or asked to do a writing sample during their visit. It is absolutely essential that parents or applicants call early for an appointment to visit a school as some schools have limited appointments available and offer visits on a first come first served basis.

Application forms are available directly from schools and/or on their websites in early fall. Many application forms require applicant and parent essays as well as teacher recommendations; therefore, it is a good idea to begin the process early. Most schools have a December or early January due date for applications. Parents may be asked to write short commentaries addressing topics such as why the school is a match for the child, a parent's perspective on the student's strengths and challenges, and special circumstances or other pertinent information the family is interested in sharing with the school. The student portion of the application usually asks students to describe their interests or hobbies, challenges and strengths, and co-curricular activities. A typical essay requires students to write about a special challenge or event that impacted their life, the importance and significance of a special possession, or about an individual whose life interests them.

The application also includes recommendation forms. The BAIHS share recommendation forms to be completed by the applicant's current school principal or counselor and current math and English teachers. The forms normally ask teachers to evaluate various aspects of the student's academic and personal qualities and rate them on a scale from "poor" to "one of the best ever."

Catholic schools within an archdiocese or diocese may choose to use the standard recommendation form of the archdiocese or diocese for principals/teachers that asks the principal, eighth grade teacher, or counselor to report the student's grades as well as conduct and effort, and rate the student in terms of academic achievement, leadership ability, work/study habits, and involvement in activities. Catholic schools may also require a clergy recommendation form. If a school does not require a clergy recommendation form, it is advisable to submit one if applicable to your family. Some forms ask parents to describe the family's spirituality in the event that the family is not of a particular faith and does not attend a church.

Catholic high schools are becoming increasingly competitive. In some counties, they are unable to accommodate all of the Catholic students graduating from Catholic elementary schools. Most Catholic high schools give preference to Catholic students attending a Catholic elementary school and Catholic students attending non-denominational schools. It is not mandatory to be a member of the Catholic Church for admission.

Jewish high school students are generally members of congregations or Jewish community centers who have or have not attended Jewish day schools. Jewish high schools use different requirements of Judaic backgrounds and practices in identifying potential candidates for admission. Applicants may be required to provide a Jewish professional recommendation from a rabbi, Jewish Studies teacher, cantor, or Jewish youth group leader.

Christian schools usually require references from a clergy member and/or an educator as well as standardized academic assessments for admission consideration.

Some schools seek additional letters of recommendation. However, families should be very selective about the kind and type of additional information they submit. One admission director said, "The thicker the file, the thicker the student." Another admission director gave this rule of thumb, "If you are tempted to send 'extras' ask this: 'Does it demonstrate specific talents or abilities that won't come through in the application packet or process, and are those talents or abilities pertinent to the school's programs?'"

In addition to the application forms, recommendations, transcripts, and school interviews and/or visits, most high schools require some form of standardized test. The most commonly accepted standardized tests include: the Secondary School Admission Test (SSAT), the Independent School Entrance Examination (ISEE), and the High School Placement Test (HSPT). Recently some schools are also accepting scores from standardized tests administered during the school year as part of a middle school's regular testing program. These include but are not limited to: the Educational Records Bureau Test (ERB), the California Achievement Test (CAT), and the California Test of Basic Skills (CTBS). Transfer applicants may be required to take the Preliminary Scholastic Aptitude Test (PSAT) or the Scholastic Aptitude Test (SAT).

The SSAT and ISEE are offered at numerous Bay Area locations. These tests require pre-registration as well as a registration fee. They are usually scheduled on Saturday mornings and are approximately three hours long. The tests include a writing portion and a multiple-choice aptitude test. The SSAT aptitude portion contains two sections of math, a section of synonyms and analogies, and a section of reading comprehension as well as a writing sample that is not scored. The ISEE has verbal and quantitative reasoning, including reading comprehension and mathematics achievement as well as a timed essay. On the test registration form, students can indicate which schools should receive the scores by filling in the appropriate school codes. Information about location and dates of the SSAT can be found at www.ssat.org; those for the ISEE at www.erbtest.org.

Catholic schools administer the HSPT on site usually in January. It has five timed aptitude portions, totaling two and a half hours. The multiple choice sections include verbal, quantitative, reading, mathematics, and language. Registration for this test is available directly through the Catholic schools. More information can be found at www.stststesting.com.

Since individual schools vary in their test requirements, it is very important that applicants check the specific details and take the appropriate exams. It is also important to check the rules that apply to each of the different tests. For instance, the SSAT can be taken numerous times, while the ISEE has a minimum six month interim between test administrations; the HSPT can be taken only once. Various publishers offer test preparation and review books specific to individual tests. In addition, there are test preparation courses available through educational professionals and corporate organizations.

Grades are automatically submitted to the high school after the parents sign a Transcript Release Form contained in the admissions packet. This form gives the student's present school permission to send grade reports and standardized assessment results to the selected high schools. High schools are generally interested in the sixth, seventh and eighth grade achievement records. If a middle school does not give letter grades, the high school will use whatever assessments the middle school provides. High school applicants are considered on the basis of standardized test scores, recommendations, grades/assessments, school visit/interviews, applicant essays, and sometimes parent essays. Application fees vary and are not refundable and may be waived for a family applying for financial aid.

The application process generally ends in December or January. Interviews may be held as late as February, and the majority of schools mail acceptance letters or post admission results on their website in mid-March. Each year, the BAIHS share the same notification date; Catholic schools also share a common date. Most Catholic school notifications are sent the week before the BAIHS notification. Schools expect parents and students to make a commitment within a week of the notification date. Schools will ask for a nonrefundable deposit to secure the student's space for the fall. Deposits generally range from $500 - $2,500 and are required to secure a student's place until another payment is due in June or July.

Give careful consideration to school information in the Admission Section of this Guide. Take note of the following: **Minimum admission requirements, Preferences, We are looking for..., What kind of student do you best serve? What sets the school apart from others?** This will help parents and students begin to narrow the school options.

Parents and students do not have to attend every open house and every event the school offers. It generally does not pay to take any review courses or attend summer camps at a particular high school as it does not impact the admission decisions. Students who have interests and talents in a specific area should seek schools that value these talents and should emphasize their interests during the admission process. It may behoove an applicant with special talents in areas such as arts or athletics to contact the respective department heads directly at a school's open house, as this could be an "extra" voice or "tipping factor" for the candidate in the admissions process.

Admission Directors' Advice to Parents: " We urge parents to set aside their own desires — such as those based upon social status, family expectations, or legacies — and to focus on what is best for their student. We recommend families talk first about realistic choices in terms of finances, geography, type of school (boarding or day school, coed or single sex, religiously affiliated, etc.) and begin the search with these parameters in mind. Let your teen know that competition is keen for admission to Bay Area high schools, as we clearly do not have enough spaces for all the qualified students that apply. Keep in mind that it is best to have an open mind and not put your hopes into just one school."

"Start early! The biggest mistake families make is not being organized; call in time to schedule a school visit and check online for application instructions and materials. Adhere to all application deadlines. Never suggest anything that could be interpreted as a bribe. Schools are looking to work in partnership with families and want to accept students that will be successful within their school environment."

Admission Directors' Advice to Students: "Do you feel that you would fit in at this school? It's important to pay attention to your instincts after spending a morning or afternoon at the school. Can you see yourself doing well and enjoying the school? Think about priorities and decide what things you must have and what things you could do without. Never choose a school because your friends are going there. It is the wrong reason and is detrimental to the process. Keep an open mind, explore options. What is a good fit for one of your friends might not be a good fit for you."

"Relax. You will go to high school. Be yourself. It is only natural to be nervous. If you see something about the school that interests you and it lends itself to a conversation, bring it up in the interview. Most importantly, read the information about the school prior to your appointment so you can ask questions or receive clarification of information provided. It pays to prep yourself about the school prior to your interview. You should appear an 'informed consumer.' Remember that you are interviewing a school just as much as they are interviewing you."

What to Look for in a High School
There are many factors to consider when choosing a high school. School size is one consideration. Schools can range in size from fewer than 100 to more than 1,600 students. Large schools are usually thought of as schools with more than 1,000 students. Large schools offer a larger pool of peers from which to choose friends, and often offer more choices of co-curricular activities and sports. However, they are also likely to have more cliques and subcultures. A large school may appeal to more independent, self-directed students. Small schools often offer more individual attention. They may also offer more opportunities for a student to sample co-curricular activities as a beginner—in large schools, activities may be populated by students who have already reached a level of achievement in a specific area such as sports, orchestra, etc.

Additional considerations include class size and teaching styles. Some schools have mostly large classes with teacher-directed instruction, while other schools emphasize smaller, more seminar-like classes. Parents and students need to take learning styles and instruction preferences into consideration.

It is important to assess the course offerings at a given school since these will be the choices available. High schools vary in the number of honors and Advanced Placement courses offered as well as in the variety within specific disciplines. Each school listed in this Guide has been asked to include a complete list of its course offerings.

Students and families should explore co-curricular activities available. They should ask questions about the percentage of students involved in various activities and the opportunities for participation at different grade levels. Co-curricular activities can run the gamut from foreign exchange programs to working internships to debate teams, special interest clubs and competitive sports.

Educational consultants, school advisors, and teachers can be very helpful in recommending high schools that would be a good match for students considering their individual interests, abilities, learning styles, and motivation.

Single Sex or Coed?

There are advocates for both single sex and coed school environments. Both groups have research to support their positions. The pros and cons of single sex or coed schools should be investigated and considered by families and students. It is important to be aware of the choices available and remain open to exploring both options. Most single sex schools in this Guide have arrangements with other schools to provide coed classes and activities.

Religious Affiliation or Not?

Religious requirements are a very personal decision. Religiously affiliated schools require varying levels of religious participation. Some programs are designed to embrace a specific religious venue and mandate that students be affiliated with their sect or identify themselves as so. Non-religious schools make no claims to be of one belief.

Cost

The high schools included in this Guide charge tuition ranging from approximately $8,000 to more than $31,000 annually. Parents should expect tuition increases annually regardless of the overall state of the economy. (The percentages given for tuition increases refer to annual increases.) In addition to tuition, there are activity fees, field trip costs, textbook costs, and expected but optional, tax deductible contributions. Schools were asked to identify approximate projected costs for family budgeting purposes. Most schools require parents to make an initial nonrefundable deposit applicable to tuition upon acceptance to their school. Payment options for the remainder of tuition vary from school to school. Some schools allow parents to pay monthly, while other schools have one or multiple installment payment plans. Many schools offer tuition refund plans for an additional cost that provide insurance for tuition payment(s) should a student need to leave during the school term. This guide asks schools what tuition increases parents can expect. The percentages listed are for annual increases.

Indexed Tuition/Flexible Tuition/Financial Aid

Paying for private high school tuition presents a challenge to many families. Middle income families are feeling the pinch, and schools are concerned about being able to serve an economic cross section of students. In order to broaden economic diversity, more and more schools are offering indexed tuition, flexible tuition, or financial aid. Indexed tuition, flexible tuition, and financial aid decisions are based on a family's assets, family size, discretionary expenses, current and other educational expenses, as well as any extraordinary circumstances. This money is not a loan; consequently, it is not expected to be repaid.

Unless a school is using its own criteria, most schools participate in the School Scholarship Service (SSS). Aid using this service is based on a family's ability to pay as demonstrated by the information provided by parents on the Personal Financial Statement (PFS) form from SSS. Both custodial as well as non-custodial parents need to provide the necessary financial information. If one parent does not comply, an explanation will be required by the school. All parents will be asked to include their most recent tax return and applicable attachments, W-2's or a Business/Farm statement if they are self-employed. This information is necessary whether parents/guardians are separated, divorced, or not married.

While each family is expected to contribute to tuition to the maximum extent that is economically feasible, the schools do not expect tuition levels to be the same for all. Financial aid, indexed, or flexible tuition funding is distributed out of a school's operating budget and unrestricted endowment income, as well as from targeted funds put aside for student opportunities. Schools encourage families to apply if they have any concerns regarding their ability to pay for full tuition. A financial aid administrator notes, "You know what the answer is if you do not apply for aid." Financial aid does not have to be repaid. It is NOT a loan. Aid forms are available with application materials and are expected to be submitted by a deadline date. Schools do not guarantee funding, nor are they able to fund all requests as their funding is limited. Consequently, they cannot fund all the deserving families and students that apply for aid. The schools try to be as equitable as possible and give first priority to their current families. Most of the time, parents receive the aid offer or denial of aid with the acceptance notification letters. Families may be placed on a financial aid wait list should additional funding be made available. Usually the school will continue the financial aid award for the term of the student's enrollment assuming family circumstances remain unchanged. Generally, tax returns and relevant attachments, W-2's, Business/Farm Statements, as well as the form for divorced or separated parents are required each year. Because of limited funding, schools want to make sure that need is demonstrated annually.

Private scholarship funds are increasingly available for students. The Independent Scholarship Fund (ISF) offers both need and merit-based scholarships for students in parochial or independent schools located in Alameda or Contra Costa counties (www.independent.org/students/isf/). The Guardsmen Scholarship Program provides tuition assistance to students through Grade 12 who have already received a Guardsmen Scholarship in their prior school. Eligibility requirements are based on need. (www.guardsmen.org) Other scholarship organizations can be found on the National Association of Independent School's website at: www.nais.org/files/pdfs/schcholarship.pdf. None of these private funding sources need to be repaid.

Conventional loans may also be available. Other sources might include home equity loans, 401 K borrowings, personal loans, low interest credit card loans, and gifts. Currently, monetary gifts are not subject to gift tax if the tuition is paid directly to the school based on a school invoice. Always check with tax professionals for current regulations.

Academic Programs

Basic criteria for evaluating academic programs include curriculum (including number of honors and Advanced Placement courses offered), graduation requirements, SAT I and II scores, number of National Merit Scholars, percentage of graduates enrolling in colleges and universities, college and university placements, faculty credentials, instruction formats, and teacher/student ratio. Results in some of these categories reflect the profile of the students admitted to the high school. If a high school admits only above average students, then it would follow that these students remain highly motivated and matriculate to some of the most selective colleges and universities. Schools included in this Guide were asked what percentage of the most recent graduates enrolled in colleges and universities and the names of the schools attended. Although it would be helpful to know what percentage of their students graduate from said colleges and universities, most high schools do not track this information. Parents should keep in mind that some students begin their college education at a two-year junior college and transfer to a four-year institution. This approach can save families considerable money and can work well for a student who can enjoy smaller classes at a junior college and possibly the opportunity to develop study skills in a less pressured environment.

Curriculum

Most Bay Area private high schools design their curriculum and graduation requirements around the University of California (UC) subject requirements for admissions, sometimes called the "A-G

requirements." Be aware that state high school graduation requirements do not meet UC or California State University (CSU) admission
standards. Under the A-G requirements, students must take 16 units
of high school courses in specific subject areas with at least 7 of the
16 units taken in the last two years of high school. The A-G subjects
and their current requirements are: A. History/Social Science—2
years required; B. English—4 years required; C. Mathematics—3 years
required, 4 recommended; D. Laboratory Science—2 years required, 3
recommended; E. Language other than English—2 years of the same
language required, 3 recommended; F. Visual and Performing Arts
requirements— 1 year required; G. College Preparatory Electives—2
additional semesters from courses fulfilling requirements A-F.

Advanced Placement (AP) courses are college-level courses offered to qualified students in various subject areas. Upon completion,
students may take a special Advanced Placement test for that specific
subject area. Depending upon the score earned, some colleges will accept the course for college credit or place a student in a more advanced
course. Generally a score of 3 or above will be recognized. There are
currently 22 subject areas covered by Advanced Placement exams offered by the College Board Testing Service. This might enable qualified
students to accelerate their matriculation through college.

The most important factors in college admission are grades in
college prep courses, standardized admission tests, overall grade point
average, and class rank. Colleges and universities are interested in the
extent to which students have challenged themselves academically.
The most highly selective institutions are likely to attribute more
importance to these factors than less selective schools. Most colleges
and universities include the academic core courses and eligible college
preparatory elective courses in calculating the overall grade point average of a student; however, some independent colleges only consider
grades in the academic core subjects.

Students at international high schools can also receive extensive
college credit through one of two all-honors programs called the International Baccalaureate (IB) and French Baccalaureate (FB or Bac)
degree programs. The IB program is internationally recognized as one
of the most comprehensive honors programs available in the United
States and abroad. Schools must apply to the International Baccalaureate Organization (IBO) to become members, and the school's teachers
must complete a rigorous training program. The IB is designed to
emphasize critical thinking, intercultural understanding and exposure
to a variety of points of view. The IB is a very challenging international
two-year curriculum offered during the junior and senior years and is
available in French, English and Spanish. Students can move globally
from one IB program to another. A student must take courses in six
different subject areas and pass a comprehensive exam in each area. A
majority of the courses must be considered college level, and students
must score a grade of 5 or more on a scale of 1-7 to earn college credit.
Similar to AP credit, each college or university determines whether

or not to accept the credit. Currently, colleges and universities in over 100 countries accept the IB diploma.

The French Baccalaureate is divided into different specialized tracks depending on what course of study a student wants to pursue or the student's scholastic aptitude. Certain courses are harder than others and are "weighted" equivalent to American "honors" courses. The Bac diploma is awarded at the successful completion of externally assessed examinations and is the essential credential needed for admission to a French national university.

Faculty

Public school teachers are required by law to hold a California teaching credential, which requires a bachelor's degree, one year of specialized teacher training, student teaching, a passing score on the CBEST exam and a criminal background check. However, due to teacher shortages, thousands of teachers in California are teaching on "emergency credentials," which allow candidates who have not yet obtained a credential to teach.

Private school teachers are not required by law to have a California teaching credential. Many private school teachers are credentialed for the state of California, while others hold credentials from other states. Private schools may use their discretion about teaching qualifications. For instance, schools may choose to hire a Ph.D. in biology to teach biology without regard to a specific credential.

Most private schools require teachers to have earned at least a bachelor's degree. Faculty qualifications are often described in available school literature. Many schools list brief biographies about individual teachers and administrators on their websites, as well as in their admissions packets.

Private schools set their own policies concerning continuing teacher education. Teachers may be required to attend teacher in-service days and participate in various professional activities, such as conferences and graduate level college courses. Some schools offer salary incentives that reward continuing teacher training.

All employees of schools must have criminal record summaries from the Department of Justice and the Federal Bureau of Investigation submitted to a school before they can be hired.

Standardized Tests and College Entrance

More than 1.3 million students annually enter the National Merit Scholarship Program of the National Merit Scholarship Corporation (NMSC) by taking The Preliminary Scholarship Assessment Test/National Merit Scholarship Qualifying Test (PSAT/NMSQT) in the fall of 11th grade. The test is administered by the Educational Testing Service for the College Board, and students must meet published program entry/participation requirements if they choose to be considered for the National Merit Scholarship Program. Highest-scoring participants in each state are notified if they qualify as "Commended Scholars" or

"Semifinalists." Of the 50,000 highest scorers, more than two-thirds will be recognized as Commended Scholars and approximately 16,000 will qualify as Semifinalists. In order to qualify as a Commended Scholar, a student must score in approximately the top 5% in his or her state; to qualify as a Semifinalist, a student needs to score close to the top 1% of students in his or her state. The NMSC then uses selection criteria to determine Finalists, including the student's academic record, information about the school's curricula and grading system, two sets of test scores, school recommendation, information about the student's activities and leadership, and the Finalist's self-descriptive essay. (Source: http://www.nationalmerit.org/nasp.html)

Many colleges and universities will accept either the SAT or the ACT scores to fulfill admission requirements. The Scholastic Assessment Test (SAT) is the most common test taken by high school seniors seeking college admission. It is administered by the Educational Testing Service sponsored by the College Board and measures math problem solving, critical reading and writing. Each section is scored on 200 to 800 point basis. The math section includes topics such as exponential growth, absolute value, functional notation with emphasis onlinear functions, manipulations with exponents, and properties of tangent lines. Students have a total of 70 minutes to answer multiple choice questions and write responses. The critical reading section allows 70 minutes to answer multiple choice questions about facts and implications from 100 to 800 word reading passages. These questions are designed to test reading comprehension, sentence completion, and critical reading skills. The 60 minute writing section has multiple choice questions in grammar and usage as well as a student-written essay. This Guide requested mean SAT scores for critical reading, math and writing sections. These are included in each school's profile in the academic program section as well as listed in the Appendix. A composite score of the math, critical reading and writing sections is also provided in the Appendix.

In 2006, over 2.1 million high school seniors took the American College Test (ACT). The ACT is an achievement test developed to measure what a student has learned in classes taken. There are four sections which include English, math, reading, and science. The English section contains 75 multiple choice questions answered in 45 minutes covering usage/mechanics questions as well as rhetorical skills. The math section has 60 questions about algebra, geometry, and trigonometry that are answered over sixty minutes. The ACT reading test is a 35 minute, 40 question section covering various selections from social studies, natural sciences, prose, fiction, and humanities. The science section has 40 questions timed in 35 minutes and measures interpretation, analysis, evaluation, reasoning and problem-solving skills. There is also an optional 30 minute writing test. Scores on each section range from 1 to 36. A composite score is an average of the section scores. The composite average for students in 2007 was 21.2. (Source: www.act.org)

In addition to taking the SAT or the ACT, many schools require students to take at least two or three SAT II subject tests. The SAT is the name for the College Board Achievement Test also referred to as the Scholastic Achievement Test, formerly the Scholastic Aptitude Test. The SAT II tests are specific to a particular discipline and are designed to measure achievement in over 30 subject areas. As with the SAT, these are graded from 200 to 800. SAT II scores may be used by colleges for entrance, to direct a student's course of study in college, or to determine whether a student is exempt from taking certain college courses. Some colleges and universities, including the University of California, require applicants to submit both SAT or ACT scores and SAT II test scores. SAT II scores were not requested of the schools in this Guide, though some schools provided them.

The 2007 national mean for college-bound seniors taking the SAT was 515 in Math, 502 in Critical Reading, and 494 in Writing. The national mean for the SAT II varies by subject area and can be found at www.collegeboard.com. Recent mean scores for entering freshmen at several colleges and universities are the following: UC Berkeley-SAT Math 671, Critical Reading 629, Writing 620-700, ACT 28; UCLA-SAT Math 660, Critical Reading 629, Writing 610-690, ACT 27; UC Davis-SAT Math 608, Critical Reading 562, Writing 550-650, ACT 24; California State Polytechnic U San Luis Obispo-SAT Math 639, Critical Reading 594, Writing 590-660, ACT 28; Sonoma State University-SAT Math 450-560, Critical Reading 450-550, Writing N/P, ACT 18-23; Duke-SAT Math 690-790, Critical Reading 690-770, Writing 680-780; Pepperdine U-SAT Math 628, Critical Reading 612, Writing 600-670, ACT 26; Arizona State University-SAT Math 559, Critical Reading 547, Writing 550-630, ACT 23; USC-SAT Math 685, Critical Reading 665, Writing 650-700, ACT 29. (Source: www.princetonreview.com).

High school grade point average (GPA) has always been an important factor in college admission. Evaluation of GPAs has become more difficult because of grade inflation, the practice of weighting GPAs, and the different grading practices in high schools. Weighting of GPAs refers to a practice of giving an extra point credit in calculating a student's GPA for grades achieved in specific classes such as AP classes. Thus, an A in a regular class would result in a 4.0 grade point for the class, whereas an A in an AP class would result in a 5.0 grade point. Schools included in this Guide were asked to give the unweighted GPA. Means in test scores and GPAs do not reflect the whole picture. A mean can be affected by extreme scores at either end of the range because it is based on the total scores divided by the number of students. Therefore, parents should consider SAT mean scores and GPAs keeping in mind their statistical limitations.

Learning Differences/Disabilities

A learning difference or disability affects the way students of average to above average intelligence process, receive, or express information. It is said the only thing disabling about a learning disability or difference is not knowing about it. With intervention and support, a student can learn compensatory strategies. If a student has learning differences, it is important to choose a school that makes accommodations and provides the necessary support. The extent of services offered varies among the schools. Each school in this Guide was asked what special programs or resources it has for students with learning disabilities or differences. Some have special programs that require separate applications. Other schools set aside a certain number of places in each freshmen class for students with learning disabilities and give them additional study guides, untimed tests, and tutorial assistance. If no programs or resources are provided by the school, students may be referred to outside tutors. Additional charges for many of these programs may be assessed, and parents should inquire about the costs.

Entering high school students need to be self-advocates and comfortable with discussing their educational strengths and challenges. It is advisable to discuss any specific learning issues with the respective admission director in order to ascertain if the school is an appropriate fit. Some of the schools in this Guide do an excellent job accommodating a broad range of student abilities.

If a teen has needs that cannot be accommodated by the schools represented in this Guide, it is advisable to consult a school placement specialist for help finding an appropriate placement. Excellent sources for information on learning disabilities are the Schwab Foundation for Learning in San Mateo, (650) 655-2410 (now a part of www.greatschools. net) and Learning Disabilities Online (www.ldonline.com).

Uniforms/Dress Code

Advocates say uniforms help students focus on learning rather than clothes, reduce expensive clothes competition, deter gang issues, and increase school pride and identity. "Dress does affect behavior," says a principal at a boys school with a uniform policy that allows a wide range of choices but is strictly enforced. Opponents see uniform policies as totalitarian and interfering with students' rights of expression. Most schools requiring uniforms have a wide range of "wardrobe options." Uniforms today often consist of khaki pants and shorts, polo shirts, corduroys, gabardine slacks, and sweatshirts. It is interesting to note that even in private schools without uniforms or dress codes, students tend to "self-uniform," typically wearing jeans and t-shirts or sweatshirts. Besides dress, schools often restrict other personal ornamentation. Some private schools prohibit unnatural hair colors, spikes, body piercings, etc.

Student Conduct and Health

Adolescence is a time when teenagers naturally transform from being dependent upon their parents and families to becoming their own individual. As a result, the parent roles begin to move from manager to consultants. Teens need consultants instead of managers. Each family needs to develop limits and discuss realistic expectations. It is a time of self discovery, testing limits, and risk-taking. Healthy risk-taking is exhibited in academically rigorous classes, in sports, clubs, on stage, and sticking one's neck out in running for a school office. Unhealthy risk-taking involves drug use (including inhalants), drinking, smoking, sexual promiscuity, reckless driving, cheating, and eating disorders. Ask how the individual schools handle peer pressure and what support networks are built in. Teenagers suffer considerable angst from internal as well as external pressures. It would be naïve not to think that teenagers are going to be exposed to these sorts of pressures.

No school can guarantee that its students will not be exposed to drugs, alcohol, and other temptations. All schools must abide by the laws prohibiting illegal drug, tobacco and alcohol possession, use, and distribution by minors. Thus, schools' standard codes of conduct prohibit such activities on campus as well as at school-sponsored events. In this Guide, schools were asked about any additional relevant aspects of their rules of conduct, and more importantly, how they handle students' violation of these rules. One school may have zero tolerance and immediately expel a student who brings alcohol onto campus; another school may send the students and parents to a counseling program. Schools were asked if they provide education on drug/alcohol use and AIDS awareness. Most of them do, but some do not.

Be informed and find out what sort of counseling network exists for teens. Counseling is like insurance, "You don't need it until you need it, then you are glad you have it." A school that responds with hesitation when parents ask how they handle these issues should be looked upon with suspicion. All high schools should be prepared to deal with such issues as drug, alcohol, and tobacco use; sexual activity; harassment based on sex, sexual orientation, race, ethnicity, or religion; and other issues that arise in our society.

Fundraising and Parent Participation

All schools would like parents to participate in their fundraising efforts. Indeed, for schools to be attractive for grant and foundation support, the schools must show a high level of parent, faculty, and alumni participation. Pledges or donations are encouraged because schools often depend on these funds to bridge the gap between tuition and actual educational costs. Schools count on families donating funds at appropriate giving levels. Many schools allow parents to make monthly payments toward their pledges or donations. If schools have required parent participation, it is noted in the individual school profile under the Parent Involvement section.

After-School Activities

Most high schools have an open campus after dismissal time and do not account for students' whereabouts after normal school hours. Most private high schools have plenty of after-school activities to keep interested students busy—all on the honor system. In addition, some schools are "open" or "closed" all day or "open" only during lunch.

Editor's Notes

1. "N/P" for "Not provided" indicates that the school gave no direct response to the question asked. If the school provided alternative or explanatory information, such information is included, usually in quotations. N/A indicates the school's response to be either "Not Available" or "Not Applicable."

2. Schools appear in this Guide at the Editor's discretion. Schools that would like to be considered for future editions may contact Pince-Nez Press at (415) 267-5978 or susan@pince-nez.com.

3. Information regarding the school's standing with federal, state, or city/county agencies; allegations of misconduct, lawsuits and other such information is beyond the scope of this Guide.

4. Indexed tuition, flexible tuition, and financial aid information relates to financial support options provided by or through the school, not aid from other sources. These financial support options do not have to be repaid. Additional outside funding sources are provided.

5. Much of the information in this Guide reflects a compilation, condensation, or edited version of information provided by the schools. Quotes indicate that either a verbatim response or a statement of opinion of the school is used. All information provided by the school is subject to editing.

6. Schools' data change regularly; thus, families should rely on the individual school's most up-to-date information for the facts upon which they base their decision. Schools' websites have been provided, but their accuracy depends on how often they are updated. If a certain fact is crucial to your decision, please ask the school about it directly.

Abbreviations & Shortcuts

ABC: A Better Chance
ACCAL: Alameda Contra Costa Athletic League
ACS: Accrediting Commission for Schools
ACSI: Association of Christian Schools International
ACT: American College Test
ADD: Attention Deficit Disorder
ASCD: Association for Supervision and Curriculum Development
AWSNA: Association of Waldorf Schools, North America
BAAD: Bay Area Admissions Directors
BAC: Bay Area Conference
BAIHS: Bay Area Independent High Schools
BAISSC: Bay Area Independent Secondary School Counselors
BALD: Bay Area Learning Directors
BART: Bay Area Rapid Transit (subway system)
BATDC: Bay Area Teacher Development Collaborative
BCL: Bay County League
BFL: Bay Football League
BJE: Bureau of Jewish Education
BSAL: Bay Shore Athletic League

C: College
CAIS: California Association of Independent Schools
Cal: California
CASE: Council for Advancement and Support of Education
CAT: California Achievement Test
CBEST: California Basic Educational Skills Test
CC: Community College
CIF: California Interscholastic Federation
CMC: Coastal Mountain Conference
CTBS: California Test of Basic Skills
EBISA: East Bay Independent School Association
ECIS: European Council of International Schools
ERB: Educational Record Bureau
ESL: English as a Second Language
ETC: Educational Testing Service
FB: French Baccalaureate
F/T: Full-time
G: Grade
Govt.: Government
HAAL: Hayward Area Athletic League
HS: High School
HSPT: High School Placement Test
IB: International Baccalaureate
IBO: International Baccalaureate Organization
IEP: Individual Educational Plan
ISBOA: Independent School Business Officers Association
ISEE: Independent School Entrance Exam
ISF: Independent Scholarship Fund
ISM: Independent School Management
JC: Junior College
JV: Junior Varsity
K-8: Kindergarten through eighth grade
K-12: Kindergarten through twelfth grade
LA: Los Angeles
MA: Master's degree
MCAL: Marin County Athletic League
M.Ed.: Master of Education
MFT: Master of Family Therapy
Muni: SF's public system of buses, cablecars, and streetcars
N/A: Not Available or Not Applicable
NAAJHS: North American Association of Jewish High Schools
NACAC: National Association of College Admission Counseling
NAIS: National Association of Independent Schools
NAPSG: National Association of Principals of Schools for Girls
NASS: National Association of Street Schools
NASSP: National Association of Secondary School Principals
NCAL: North Central Athletic League
NCEA: National Catholic Educational Association

NCGS: National Coalition of Girls' Schools
NCS: North Coast Section
NMSC: National Merit Scholarship Corporation
NMSQT: National Merit Scholarship Qualifying Test
N/P: Not Provided
OIB: L'option internationale du baccalaureat, option of the French Baccalaureate not to be confused with the International Baccalaureate.
PAAD: Peninsula Association of Admissions Directors
PAL: Peninsula Athletic League
PEJE: Partnership for Excellence in Jewish Education
PFS: Personal Financial Statement
POCIS: Bay Area People of Color in Independent Schools
PSAL: Private School Athletic League
PSAT: Preliminary Scholarship Assessment Test
PSSP: Parent Support Services Program
P/T: Part-time
RAVSAK: is a transliterated Hebrew acronym that stands for "The Community Jewish Day School Network."
SAT or SAT I: Scholastic Achievement Test; formerly the Scholastic Aptitude Test
SAT II: Scholastic Achievement Test-Subject Test; formerly the Scholastic Aptitude Test-Subject Test
SAT 9: Stanford Achievement Test
SF: San Francisco
SSAT: Secondary School Admission Test
SSATB: Secondary School Admission Test Board
SSBL: Small School Bridge League
SSS: School Scholarship Service
TABS: The Association of Boarding Schools
TBA: To be announced
U: University
V: Varsity
WACAC: Western Association of College Admissions Counselors
WASC: Western Association of Schools and Colleges
WBAL: West Bay Athletic League
WBSA: Western Boarding School Association
WCAL: Western Catholic Athletic League
WCEA: Western Catholic Educational Association

Abbreviations/shortcuts for colleges and universities:

BYU: Brigham Young University (Provo, Utah)
CalArts: California Institute of the Arts (Valencia, CA)
Cal Poly: California Polytechnic State University
CC: Community College (various locations)
CCA: California College of the Arts (San Francisco/Oakland)
FIDM: Fashion Institute of Design and Merchandising (SF/LA)
LA: Los Angeles

MIT: Massachusetts Institute of Technology
NYU: New York University (New York)
Parsons: Parsons/ The New School for Design (NYC)
Penn: University of Pennsylvania
RISD: Rhode Island School of Design
RPI: RPI Institute (Troy, NY)
SC: State College
SD: San Diego
SF: San Francisco
SFAI: San Francisco Art Institute
SFCC: City College of San Francisco
SJ: San Jose
SJSU: San Jose State University
SLO: San Luis Obispo
SMU: Southern Methodist University (Texas)
SU: State University
U-: University of
UC: University of California
UOP: University of the Pacific (California)
USC: University of Southern California
USD: University of San Diego
USF: University of San Francisco
UVA: University of Virginia

PART TWO: Bay Area Private High Schools

Archbishop Mitty High School
5000 Mitty Avenue
San Jose, CA 95129
(408) 252-6610 *fax (408) 252-0518*
www.mitty.com

Timothy Brosnan, Principal
Greg Walker, Director of Admissions, gwalker@mitty.com

General
Coed Catholic day high school. (70% Catholic). Founded in 1964. San Jose Diocesan high school. Nonprofit. **Enrollment:** Approx. 1,650. **Average class size:** 27. **Accreditation:** WASC. **School year:** Sept.-June. **School day:** 7:50 a.m.-2:35 p.m. **Location:** Off Lawrence Expressway, near Hwy. 280.

Student Body
Geographic breakdown (counties): 100% from Santa Clara County. **Ethnicity:** 58.8% Caucasian (non-Latino); 17.8% Asian; 12.4% Latino; 3.7% African-American; 0.3% Native American; 0.1% other non-White; 3.7% multi-ethnic; 3.2% "no response." **International students (I-20 status):** 0. **Middle schools (freshman):** N/P.

Admission
Applications due: January (call for date). **Application fee:** $65. **Application process:** September through February; 8th graders are invited to spend a day shadowing. Visits should be scheduled early because spaces are limited. An open house for families is held in November. **No. of freshman applications:** More than 1,200 for 425 places. **Minimum admission requirements:** N/P. **Test required:** HSPT (given at school in January). **Preferences:** Catholic. "We are looking for college-bound students who seek a value-centered education." **What kind of student do you best serve?** "Students who respond to their world with competence, insight, understanding, courage, and compassion based on a tradition of faith and moral values."

Costs
Latest tuition: $12,900 (includes $825 registration) payable in 1, 2, or 10 payments. **Sibling discount:** None. **Tuition increases:** N/P. **Other costs:** Approx. $650 for books. **Percentage of students receiving financial aid:** 16%. **Financial aid deadline:** February (call for date). **Average grant:** Approx. $5,725. **Percentage of grants of half-tuition or more:** 38%.

School's Mission Statement/Goals

"Archbishop Mitty is the Catholic, coeducational, college preparatory school of the Diocese of San Jose. We embrace the Catholic educational mission of developing community, teaching the message of the Gospels, and promoting service, peace, and justice. Through our rigorous academic program, we seek to prepare our students for college and for responsible leadership in the global society of the 21st century. At the same time, we work diligently with parents to foster the development of each student. Recognizing that each individual is created in the image and likeness of God, we celebrate and affirm our diverse cultural community and encourage students to respond to their world with competence, insight, understanding, courage, and compassion based on a tradition of faith and moral values."

Academic Program

Courses offered (AP=Advanced Placement, H=Honors, (AP)=AP option, (H)=Honors option): **English:** English I, English I Accelerated, World Literature, English II H, American Literature, English III AP, English IV AP, Oral Composition, Written Composition, African-American Literature, British Literature, Contemporary Authors, Cultures in Conflict, Literature of Rebellion, Shakespeare; **Math:** Algebra I, Algebra I Accelerated, Geometry (H), Algebra II (H), Algebra II/Trigonometry H, Trigonometry, Statistics (AP), Pre-Calculus (H), Calculus, Calculus AB AP, Calculus BC AP, Computer Science AP; **Languages:** French I, French II-III (H), French IV (AP), Spanish I, Spanish II-III (H), Spanish IV (AP), Spanish V, Mandarin I-III; **P.E.:** P.E. 9, Body in Motion, Personal Fitness, Cross Training, Softball/Basketball, Strength and Conditioning for Competition, Football Conditioning, Pilates, Nets, Resistive Exercise, Team Sports, Volleyball/Badminton, Volleyball/Tennis, Water Sports; **Religious Studies:** Intro to Catholic Christianity; Personal and Social Ethics; Ethics, Culture, and Justice–El Salvador; Ethics, Culture, and Justice–India; Ethics, Culture, and Justice–California; Ethics, Culture, and Justice–Native American Experience; Ethics, Culture, and Justice–South Africa Spirituality; Liturgical Ministry, Intro to Philosophy; **Science:** General Science, General Science Accelerated, Biology (H/AP), Chemistry (H/AP), Chemistry in the Community, Environmental Science (AP), Physics (H/AP); **Social Studies:** American Government and Civics, World History (AP), U.S. History (AP), American Govt. (AP), Contemporary American Issues, Ethnic Studies, European History AP, Psychology; **Arts:** Visual Art I/Studio, Visual Art I/ Computer Based Design, Visual Art II/The Book as Art, Visual Art II/Digital Photography, Visual Art II/Drawing, Visual Art II/Graphic Design, Visual Art II/Painting, Visual Art II/2D-3D Design, Visual Art II/20th Century Art, Visual Art II/Western Art; Concert Band, Wind Ensemble, Symphonic Band, Jazz Band, Vocal Ensemble, Concert Choir, Jazz Choir, Drama and Performance I, Drama and Performance II/Acting, Drama and Performance II/Film and Film Production, Drama and Performance II/Production and Performance,

Dance Performance I-II, Music Theory AP. **Computer lab/training:** More than 200 computers for student use in the technology center, library, and counseling center. **Grading:** A-F. **Graduation requirements:** 240 units including 8 semesters of English; 6 semesters of math; 4 semesters of modern language (in the same language); 1 semester of Intro to Philosophy; 2 semesters of P.E. and visual and performing arts (in single area of study); 7 semesters of religious and social studies; 5 semesters of science; 6 semesters of electives. **Average nightly homework (M-Th):** N/P. **Faculty:** 103 (N/P gender, degrees). **Faculty ethnicity:** N/P. **Faculty selection/training:** N/P. **Teacher/student ratio:** 1:16. **Percentage of students enrolled in AP:** N/P. **Most recent senior class profile (mean):** SAT Math 570, SAT Critical Reading 561, SAT Writing 575. **GPA:** N/P. **National Merit Scholarship Program:** Last year, the school had 9 Semifinalists and 31 Commended Scholars. **College enrollment:** 99.7%. (N/P 4-yr, 2-yr). **Recent (last 2 yrs) colleges:** "... accepted to more than 180 4-year institutions including all of the [UC and CSU] campuses, Stanford, Santa Clara, Ivy League schools, and a wide variety of other public and private universities throughout the United States."

Other Indicators the School is Accomplishing its Goals

"Each year, Archbishop Mitty generates a Mission Effectiveness Report to its alumni, parents, and students to measure the achievement of school-wide learning results, the fulfillment of its mission, and success in academics and co-curricular activities. This report consistently receives excellent reviews and positive feedback."

Campus/Campus Life

Campus description: The school has a 25-acre campus which includes classrooms/administration, outdoor fields, aquatic center, two gyms and a performing arts center. **Library:** Open to students from 7:30 a.m.–4:30 p.m. (N/P volumes, etc.) **Sports facilities:** Two gymnasiums, aquatic center, football field, baseball field, soccer field, softball field. **Theater/arts facilities:** "State-of-the-art center for the performing arts opened in spring 2003." **Open/closed campus:** Closed. **Lunches:** Food service available on campus. **Bus service:** N/P. **Uniforms/dress code:** N/P. **Co-curricular activities/clubs:** More than 25 clubs and organizations including African American Student Union, Creative Student Association, Latino American Student Union, National Honor Society, Scrapbooking Club, Anime, French Club, Math Club, Portuguese Club, Self Defense Club, Asian Pacific Islander Student Union, Guitar Club, Math Team, Robotics, Ski and Snowboarding Club, Contemporary Health Issues, Irish American Club, Mock Trial, South Asian Student Association, Ultimate Frisbee Club, California Scholastic Federation, Peer Counseling, Performing Arts (Beginning Choir, Concert Choir, Jazz Choir, Chamber Choir, Concert Band, Symphonic Band, Wind Ensemble, Jazz Band, Exodus, Drama and Performance, Improvisation Team, Instrumental Concert, Fall Musical, Winter Play, Spring

Musical, Pep Band, Fine Arts Festival, Jazz on the Green), Retreats, LIFE/Emmaus (Campus Ministry Leadership Team), Student Government, Yearbook. **Foreign exchange program/internships:** The Board of Regents and the school sponsor a corporate internship program each year, which assists students in obtaining paid internships with partner Silicon Valley companies. **Community service:** The Christian Service program is administered through each student's religious studies class with students performing a minimum of 25 hours per year. Students also have the opportunity to go on immersion trips to Appalachia, El Salvador, Fort Apache, San Jose Emergency Housing Consortium, St. Anthony's Foundation San Francisco, Habitat for Humanity (Louisiana), Mexico, India, and South Africa. **Typical freshman schedule:** 2 semesters of each: English I, math, modern language, and religious studies; 1 semester of each: Contemporary American Cultures, P.E., arts elective, and general science.

Student Support Services
Counselor/student ratio (not including college counselors): 1:275. **Counseling:** "The school has 6 full-time counselors (all of whom have graduate degrees in counseling psychology) and 11 advisors. At the beginning of the freshman year, each student is assigned an individual counselor for personal counseling and academic and college guidance counseling. The school holds workshops to assist with PSAT and SAT preparation and assists students with college applications. The school also has science and math tutorial centers where students can receive help with areas of difficulty and can make up missed work due to absence." **Learning differences/disabilities:** N/P.

Student Conduct and Health: N/P.

Summer Programs
Academic summer school and numerous sports camps for students in G3-9.

Parent Involvement
Parent participation: Voluntary participation through the Archbishop Mitty Parents' Association. **Parent/teacher communication:** N/P. **Parent education:** N/P. **Donations:** N/P.

Sports
The school has 65 teams in 24 sports competing in the WCAL. Boys compete in football, cross-country, water polo, basketball, soccer, wrestling, track and field, baseball, swimming and diving, volleyball, badminton, tennis, and golf. Girls compete in field hockey, tennis, volleyball, cross-country, water polo, golf, basketball, soccer, track and field, softball, swimming and diving, and badminton.

What Sets School Apart From Others

"Archbishop Mitty High School is the Catholic, coeducational, college preparatory school of the Diocese of San Jose. The school embraces the Catholic educational mission of developing community, teaching the message of the Gospels, and promoting service, peace, and justice. Through its rigorous academic program, it seeks to prepare its students for college and for responsible leadership in the global society of the 21st century. Recognizing that each individual is created in the image and likeness of God, the school celebrates and affirms its diverse cultural community and encourages students to respond to their world with competence, insight, understanding, courage, and compassion based on the tradition of faith and moral values."

How Parents/Students Characterize School

Parent response(s): "As a Mitty Alumni, I continue to look back over the years at what Mitty provided me as a student. I believe the learning environment and the school atmosphere have not only guided me, but my two siblings to become successful/honorable adults and citizens. From a very small age, we have always imagined our children attending Mitty, so they too would reap the rewards that my siblings and I did."
Student response(s): "I want to be a lawyer and Mitty has prepared me by giving me the opportunity to take classes that pushed me to work hard and challenged me academically." "Mitty's academic program challenged me to write eloquent essays, solve complex calculus problems, and convoluted physics equations. At the same time, I was always able to ask teachers for help and develop a solid understanding of the class material." "I had an amazing time at Mitty. It was the perfect environment for me. I learned so much—about education, about life—and met so many great people. It was like home." "I am leaving for New York in two days. Although I am in a frantic rush to get everything packed, I wanted to tell you there isn't a day, let alone an hour, where I do not find myself thinking about a lesson learned, a friend made or an experience had at Mitty. Mitty has been the best four years of my life by hiring the best teachers and giving the students so much to participate in. Although I will soon be 3,000 miles away, Mitty will always be close to my heart."

Archbishop Riordan High School

175 Phelan Avenue
San Francisco, CA 94112
(415) 586-8200 *fax (415) 587-1310*
www.riordanhs.org

Father Thomas J. French, S.M., President
Mr. Kevin R. Asbra, Principal
Mr. Dion Sabalvaro, Director of Admission, dsabalvaro@riordanhs.org

General

Boys Catholic day high school. (72.5% Catholic; 13.2% Christian; 6.1% non-Christian, 8.2% other/unknown). Operated by the Archdiocese of San Francisco. Founded in 1949, administered by the Society of Mary. **Enrollment:** 650. **Average class size:** 25. **Accreditation:** WASC. **School year:** Approx. Aug. 15-May 30. **School day:** Approx. 7:45 a.m.-2:45 p.m. **Location:** Off Ocean Avenue near Hwy. 280 (southwestern part of the city), across the street from City College of San Francisco. Accessible by BART (Balboa Station), Muni Metro, and five Muni bus lines.

Student Body

Geographic breakdown (counties): Approx. 78% from San Francisco; 15% from San Mateo; 5% from Alameda; 2% other. **Ethnicity:** 23.3% Caucasian; 22.6% Hispanic; 17.5% Filipino; 11.3% multi-ethnic; 9.8% Chinese; 7.2% African-American; 4.8% Asian: 1.3% Pacific Islander; 2.2% other. **International students (I-20 status):** N/P. **Middle schools (freshman):** 73% came from 37 parochial schools; 18% from 21 public middle schools; 9% from 12 private, non-parochial schools.

Admission

Applications due: Mid-December (call for date). **Application fee:** $75 for freshman, $100 for late applications and transfer students, and $100 for international students. **Application process:** Tours of the school for parents and students are given throughout the year. An annual open house is held on the first Sunday in November. During fall semester, interested students may spend a day at the school shadowing a current student. Applications are due in mid-December, and a placement examination is administered in January. Decisions are mailed mid-March. **No. of freshman applications:** 450 for 180 places. Six new students were admitted to G10, 3 to G11. **Minimum admission requirements:** "We provide a Catholic college preparatory education to young men with varying academic abilities." **Test required:** HSPT. **Preferences:** None. "**We are looking for** well-rounded young men who will get involved and contribute to our school community." **What kind of student do you best serve?** "We excel in educating young men. Specializing in single gender education, we recognize and account for the cognitive development of young men. Our college prep curriculum focuses on boys and provides them with a values-based education. Therefore, the young man who comes to Archbishop Riordan finds our environment conducive to learning and is able to strive for his full potential. Archbishop Riordan High School is a Catholic school of 650 students that engages young men in the process of educating the 'whole person,' promoting individual growth and development in the intellectual, spiritual, social, and physical aspects of life."

Costs

Latest tuition: $12,960 payable in 1, 4, or 10 payments. **Sibling discount:** N/P. **Tuition increases:** Approx. 5%. **Other costs:** $600 registration fee, uniforms approx. $250. **Percentage of students receiving**

financial aid: 32%. **Financial aid deadline:** January 31. **Average grant:** Approx. $2,000. **Percentage of grants of half-tuition or more:** Less than 1% (max. grant of $4,000).

School's Mission Statement/Goals

"Archbishop Riordan High School, an Archdiocesan Catholic high school in the Marianist tradition, prepares young men of the Bay Area for leadership through its inclusive college preparatory curriculum. Archbishop Riordan emphasizes formation in faith and dedicates itself to community service and justice. In a diverse family environment, the school encourages its students to develop their individuality through academics, athletics, and the arts."

Academic Program

"Archbishop Riordan's minimum graduation requirements meet or exceed the University of California's A-G requirements. Archbishop Riordan utilizes a 4x4 block schedule. The school year is split into two semesters, and students take four courses per semester. Each class lasts 80 minutes, thus providing sufficient time for students and teachers to delve more deeply and actively into topics and activities. The 4x4 block allows students to take eight courses per year rather than the traditional six. Over their four high school years, Archbishop Riordan students take up to eight more classes than students in schools with traditional schedules. This college preparatory curriculum is designed to fulfill the UC and Cal State systems' entrance requirements 'with ample room to spare to sample the expanded elective opportunities.'" Fourteen AP courses are offered to juniors and seniors. **Courses offered** (AP=Advanced Placement, H=Honors, (AP)=AP option, (H)=Honors option, *= must qualify to take): **Computers:** Computer Applications, Desktop Publishing, Computer Programming, Web Design; **English:** Intro to Composition, Intro to Literature, World Literature (H*), AP English Language/Comp, American Literature, Journalism; **Math:** Algebra I (H*), Algebra I a-b, Plane Algebra, Modern Geometry (H*), Algebra II, Advanced Algebra (H), Math Analysis, Trigonometry/Statistics, Functions, Statistics (AP), Calculus AB (AP); Calculus BC (AP); **P.E.** P.E. 9-12; **Religious Studies:** Christian Character and Faith, Scriptures and Sacraments, Life Issues, Christian Lifestyles; **Science:** Physical Science, Ecology, Biology (H*), Chemistry (AP), Earth Science, Anatomy-Physiology, Physics (AP), Environmental Science (AP); **Foreign language:** Spanish I-III (AP), Italian I-III, American Sign Language I-II; **Social Science:** Geography & World History I (H*), World History II 1450-present (AP*), AP European History*, Economics, U.S. History (AP), AP U.S. Government & Politics*; **Arts:** Intro to Theater Arts, Intro to Video Production, Instrumental Music, Intro to Acting, Intermediate Band I-II, Forensics (Speech & Debate), Art I-IV, Concert Band, 20th Century American Music, Jazz Band, Advanced Video Production. **Computer lab/training:** "State-of-the-art." **Grading:** A-F. Conduct grades ("satisfactory," "warning," and "unacceptable conduct") are also given for each class and homeroom. **Graduation requirements:** 5 years English; 4 years religious studies and college preparatory electives; 3 years math and social science; 2 years foreign language; 1 year visual and performing arts; 1 semester P.E.; 100 hours community service. **Average nightly homework (M-Th):** 2-3 hours. ARHS utilizes PowerSchool, a web-based program by which parents may track their son's academic progress. **Faculty:** 45; 71% male, 29% female; "45% have earned one or more master's degrees; and 64% possess teaching credentials. Four are Marianist Priests or Brothers." **Faculty ethnicity:** 90% Caucasian; 6% Latino; 4% Asian. **Faculty selection/training:** "Faculty members are selected through a rigorous screening process which includes a series of interviews, reference checks, and teaching demonstrations before the school's students. The administration places the highest priority on applicants who possess graduate teaching credentials or master's degrees and who have classroom teaching experience. The faculty continuously refines its knowledge of educational research through scheduled in-service days—featuring outside speakers as well as presentations by faculty members themselves. In addition, teachers and administrators regularly attend professional seminars to continue their education in graduate programs. The school awards grants to its teachers to further their formal education." **Teacher/student ratio:** 1:25. **Percentage of students enrolled in AP:** 25%; pass rate 60%. Seniors may participate in the XL program (Accelerated Program for High School Students) and take advanced course work at City College (across the street from the school). Classes may be integrated directly into the day program, and students may opt to receive either high school or college credit. **Senior class profile (mean):** SAT Math 497, SAT Critical Reading 502, SAT Writing 508. **GPA** (average, non-weighted): 2.78. **National Merit Scholarship Program:** N/P. **College enrollment (last class):** 99% (169 students); 61% in 4-year, 38% in 2-year, 1% in technical schools. **Recent (last 3 yrs) colleges:** UC (Berkeley, Davis, Irvine, LA, Riverside, SD, Santa Barbara, Santa Cruz), CSU (Chico, Fresno, Fullerton, Hayward, Humboldt, Long Beach, Monterey, Pomona, SLO, Sacramento, SD, SF, SJ, Sonoma), Columbia, Dartmouth, NYU, Colgate, UOP, Dillard, American, Clark, USC, Beloit, Bard, Stanford, Syracuse, Emerson, George Washington, Oberlin, Chaminade, Georgetown, USF, Santa Clara, USD, Portland, Xavier, Boston C, Fordham, Regis, St. Mary's, Arizona, Oregon, Washington, Arizona SU, Nebraska, Illinois, SFCC, Skyline, Canada, Diablo Valley, and C of Marin.

Other Indicators the School is Accomplishing its Goals
"67% of our graduates are first generation college students (parents did not earn a college degree in the U.S.)."

Campus/Campus Life
Campus description: Since its founding in 1949, the school has occupied a 400,000 sq. ft. campus in the southwestern part of the city.

The building has two classroom wings, a courtyard, a large caféteria, 41 classrooms, a library, science and computer labs, gym and a chapel. The school's immediate plans include upgrading the science labs with computers. **Library:** Open 7:30 a.m.-6 p.m.; online catalog, 14,000 print volumes, 80 periodical subscriptions, study space for 80 students and 20 computers with Internet access. **Sports facilities:** A full-size gym, weight room, wrestling room, full-size football field, track, and a baseball diamond. **Theater/arts facilities:** 1,200-seat theater. The school has a musical instrument program and school band with approximately 50% of students taking instrument lessons. (Students may fulfill their one-year fine/performing arts requirement by studying a band instrument as a part of the school curriculum.) Ninety percent of the students are beginners at musical instruments. Students who continue with study may try out for the school's marching band, concert band, jazz band, or wind ensemble. **Open/closed campus:** Closed. **Lunches:** "The caféteria is open from 7 a.m.-1:15 p.m. and provides a hot breakfast and lunch daily for approximately $4/day for breakfast and $5 for lunch." **Bus service:** City bus and BART service only. **Uniform/dress code:** "Students wear khaki slacks or shorts, four colors of polo shirts (long or short sleeved), and school athletic shirts, sweaters, and school sweatshirts. Students may wear casual, dress, or athletic shoes. On dress days, students wear a white dress shirt, tie, white V-neck sweater, khaki slacks, and dress shoes. No hats, dyed hair, pony-tail/braids, or visible tattoos are allowed. Students may wear one stud or post earring." **Co-curricular activities/clubs:** Clubs vary with student interest. Currently, African American Student Union, Arab Student Coalition, Art Club, Asian Student Coalition, Block Club, Bowling Club, California Scholarship Federation, Campus Ministry, Yell Leaders, Chess Club, Choral Group, Close-Up Program (trip to Washington, D.C.), Computer and Games Club, Crusader Brothers, Crusader Newspaper, Drama, Dance Committee, Euro Club, Philippine American Coalition, Interact, Jazz Band, Lance (Yearbook), Lancers Service Club, Math Club, National Honor Society, Photography Club, Pep Band, Science Club, Ski Activities, Speech & Debate, Stage Crew, Student Government. **Foreign exchange program/internships:** None. **Community service:** "Hundreds. Please see website." **Typical freshman schedule:** Math, English, physical science or biology, religion, a visual or performing art class and P.E.

Student Support Services

Counselor/student ratio (not including college counselors): 1:175. **Counseling:** Each grade has a counselor who engages in academic and personal counseling. The school has a peer counseling program to assist students in the lower division with conflict resolution and to provide peer support programs. College and career counseling is provided through the four years and includes assemblies, individual counseling, and evening programs (including presentations to parents to discuss college financial aid). The school has a full-time college counselor. **Learning differences/disabilities:** "The school has a Resource Specialist Program with 62 students currently enrolled. The Resource Specialist works with classroom teachers to help the teachers understand the student's special need and make the necessary accommodations to maximize the success of each student. To qualify, students must have current psycho-educational assessments and/or an IEP (Individual Educational Plan). Students in the program include individuals with specific learning exceptionalities, ADD and English as a Second Language needs. Students receive specific individual instruction in a variety of areas, study groups, assistance in arranging for extra time for exams, opportunities to study in groups, and other services. The purpose of the program is to provide students with learning exceptionalities additional support in the mainstream ... to help each student achieve his maximum potential in each class, while developing the necessary compensation and coping skills to succeed independently."

Student Conduct and Health

Code of conduct: "The school has behavior rules relating to classroom conduct, insubordination and disrespect, alteration or falsification of documents, inappropriate language, smoking (not allowed on or within 1/4 mile of campus), trespassing, vandalism and graffiti, hazing, theft, fighting, weapons, gang-related activity, harassment, and drugs and alcohol." **How school handles drugs/alcohol:** "Students found using, selling, possessing, soliciting, or under the influence of alcohol, illegal narcotics, or controlled substances at any time are liable for dismissal. Students caught selling, providing, or transmitting alcohol or drugs will be expelled. Students who seek help with a substance abuse problem will be referred confidentially to the Guidance Department for assessment, which may lead to professional counseling and drug-testing." **Prevention and awareness programs:** The required P.E./Health curriculum begins in 9th grade with instruction that includes human sexuality, drug and alcohol abuse education, and sexually transmitted diseases. This instruction continues in the elective P.E. courses for G11-12.

Parent Involvement

Parent participation: Parents are required to attend three evening parent meetings during the year and are invited to join or attend meetings of the Parent Board and the Parent Guild. Three mandatory parent meetings are held during the year. **Parent/teacher communication:** Each semester consists of two quarters. The school mails parents report cards quarterly. Only semester grades appear on the students' transcripts. Teachers send academic deficiency reports mid-quarter for students whose average is less than a "C." Parent/teacher conferences are held at the end of the first and third grading periods. Parent education: "[In its fifth year], the school's Parent Support Services (PSS) program is a specially-designed program for the parents and guardians of the students. ... The PSS program consists of a variety of experiences including Freshman Parents Cluster meetings; two nationally-acclaimed video-based series on the parenting of teens; various college and career evenings for parents and sons; occasional book-based series on teen and parent issues; special needs groups (such as single parents, Spanish-speaking parents, parents of African-American students, PAAC parents, parents of divorce, families with grief and loss issues, etc.); an interdepartmental Father-Son day for upper classmen; and special presentations (such as study skills and teen health and risk issues). These activities are generally held during weekday evenings unless otherwise specified. Parents and guardians are free to give their suggestions and concerns to the coordinator of the PSS program so that other topics and experiences may be developed." **Donations:** "Each family is required to actively participate in school-wide fundraisers."

Sports
The school has 9 sports and 24 teams including football, basketball, baseball, wrestling, track, cross-country, golf, and tennis. Half the student body participates in team sports, competing in the WCAL. Intramural sports are played during the lunch period.

What Sets School Apart From Others
"Archbishop Riordan is an all-boys, Catholic high school that blends the traditional strengths of a structured, supportive Catholic education with research-supported innovations in curriculum, teaching methodology, and assessment. Its expansive Advanced Placement offerings and its Research Specialist Program serve the specialized needs of all its students. The Marianists emphasis on developing academic, spiritual, social, and athletic excellence — manifested in its excellent music and drama programs as well as its athletic teams — forms the foundation for success in college and post-secondary careers. Archbishop Riordan proudly offers its resources to all young men of the San Francisco Bay Area who seek an education rooted in Christian values."

How Parents/Students Characterize School
Parent response(s): "I believe that Riordan fosters the academic, social, and spiritual development of young men in a family environment. The faculty and staff know all of the students. Students are not lost in the shuffle. The campus provides activities, athletics and support services from 7 a.m. until sometimes 10 p.m. The campus is often open and busy seven days a week. The staff are dedicated and involved, and the students benefit from the extra support. It is a safe environment that parents can feel a part of." **Student response(s):** "I came to Riordan with a big head, full of myself. Today, I am more humble and positive. When I look at the big picture, I have a better perspective."

The Athenian School

2100 Mt. Diablo Scenic Boulevard
Danville, CA 94526
(925) 362-7223 *fax (925) 855-9342*
www.athenian.org

Eleanor Dase, Head of School
Christopher Beeson, Director of Admission and Financial Aid,
  chris.beeson@athenian.org
Nina Wang, Assistant Director of Admission and Financial Aid,
  nina.wang@athenian.org

General

Coed day and boarding high school with day-only middle school. Non-sectarian. Independent. Founded in 1965. Nonprofit, member, NAIS, TABS, CAIS, BAIHS, CASE, ERB, SSATB, WBSA, BAAD, EBISA. **Enrollment:** 450 (300 in G9-12 incl. 42 boarding students). **Average class size:** 15. **Accreditation:** WASC/CAIS. **School year:** Sept.-June. **School day:** 8:10 a.m.-3:40 p.m. **Location:** In Danville, 32 miles east of San Francisco. Accessible from the school's buses, which serve communities from Oakland and Berkeley to Pleasanton and Livermore twice daily. The buses connect with BART at five different BART stations, allowing students from throughout the East Bay to attend. A late bus leaves Athenian at 5:45 p.m. (6:30 during basketball season) and takes students to the Walnut Creek BART station.

Student Body

Geographic breakdown (counties): Of day students, 61% are from Contra Costa; 37% from Alameda; 2% from other Bay Area counties; of boarding students, 14% are from 10 foreign countries, California, and Washington, D.C. **Ethnicity:** 59% Caucasian (non-Latino); 23% Asian; 2% Latino; 8% African-American; 4% Middle Eastern or East Indian; 4% multi-ethnic. **International students (I-20 status):** 10%. **Middle schools (freshman):** 38% came from 14 public middle schools; 45% from 12 private, non-parochial schools; 11% from 4 parochial schools; 6% international students from 3 schools abroad.

Admission

Applications due: Approx. January 15 (call for date). **Application fee:** $75. **Application process:** Open houses for parents and students are held each fall and in early January. Applicants must visit Athenian; observe two classes; take a student-led tour; and meet students, faculty, and admission staff. The application consists of an information form, parent and student essays, academic transcripts for the past two years, recommendations, and admission test scores. **No. of freshman applications:** 230 for 72 places. **Minimum admission requirements:** Individual consideration of each candidate's multiple facets, though the typical student has a very strong academic record, teacher recommendations, writing, and test scores. **Test required:** ISEE or SSAT. **Preferences:** "Athenian seeks students with 1) the demonstrated ability to succeed in our challenging, interdisciplinary, and international college preparatory program; 2) an enthusiasm for learning and personal development beyond the classroom; 3) an interest in taking part in a diverse community of students and teachers, as well as a respect for individuality and differences; and 4) an understanding and appreciation for Athenian's mission, philosophy, and culture." "**We are looking for** students who demonstrate that they are ready for an academic challenge through strong recent grades, essays, recommendations, and test scores, as well as students who want to grow as individuals and world citizens." **What kind of student do you best serve?** "Students who want 1) to achieve and learn because it broadens their perspective of themselves and the world, 2) to develop a sense of compassion to contribute to a better future for us all, and 3) to prepare for lives of purpose and personal fulfillment."

Costs
Latest tuition: $27,520 payable in 2 or 10 payments. **Sibling discount:** None. **Tuition increases:** Approx. 6-8%. **Other costs:** $1,000 for books, field trips, and incidental expenses. **Percentage of students receiving financial aid:** 20%. **Financial aid deadline:** Approx. January 15 (call for date). **Average grant:** $19,055. **Percentage of grants half-tuition or more:** 79%.

School's Mission Statement/Goals
"The Athenian School prepares students for the rigorous expectations of college and for a life of purpose and personal fulfillment. We offer a challenging academic program with a difference: intellectual inquiry is active, learning is interactive, the disciplines are interrelated, and analysis and creativity thrive simultaneously. The acquisition of knowledge becomes authentic and joyous. We cultivate the personal qualities of each student to become an integrated human being with integrity, strong moral character, aesthetic sensitivity, and physical well being. The Athenian community requires students to face life directly through open communication, while developing their inner strength to exceed their perceived potential and emerge compassionate, responsible adults. We instill an appreciation of the reciprocal relationship between the individual and cultures, society and the natural world. We value the power and beauty of multiculturalism within our diverse community. We embrace the principles of democratic governance, stewardship of the environment, respect for human dignity, and service as a way of life. By providing an atmosphere of intellectual, artistic, and physical challenge within the warmth of a nurturing community, we develop in our students the confidence and skills required to meet the complexities of their future."

Academic Program

Courses offered (AP=Advanced Placement, H=Honors, (AP)=AP option, (H)=Honors option): **Humanities:** Core Courses: G9: Humanities I: World Literature, Humanities I: World Cultures, Humanities I: Art; G10: American Studies: Literature and American Studies: U.S. History; Literature seminars: Writer's Workshop, Journalism, Crime and Punishment (H/AP), Early Classics of English Literature (H/AP), Native American Literature (H/AP), Plato (H/AP), Gender Studies (H/AP), Shakespeare (H/AP), Creative Writing (H), The Political Novel (H/AP), Salinger, Conrad, and Melville (H/AP), Poetry (H/AP), Humanitas (H/AP), African American Literature (H/AP), The Bible as Literature (H/AP), Good and Evil in Literature (H/AP), Bay Area Literature (H/AP), Russian and Japanese Literature (H/AP), Buddhist Philosophy (H/AP), Latino Studies (H/AP), and The Vietnam Conflict (H/AP). "Each year a designated sequence of appropriate literature seminars prepares students for the AP exam in literature." **History seminars:** AP European History, AP World History, Humanitas (H), Ancient Civilizations (H), Latin American History (H), Gender Studies (H), Modern Chinese History (H), Global Politics (H), African History (H), Classical Worlds (H), Latino Studies (H), The Vietnam Conflict (H); Middle East History (H). **Math:** Algebra I, Geometry, Algebra II (H), Pre-Calculus (H), Calculus AB (AP), and Calculus BC (AP), Statistics, Statistics (AP). **Languages:** Spanish I-II, Spanish III (H), Spanish IV-V (AP), French I-II, French III (H), French IV (AP); Mandarin Chinese I-IV, Mandarin Chinese III (H) in 2009, Mandarin Chinese IV (AP) in 2010. **Sciences:** Conceptual Physics, Calculus-based Physics (H), Chemistry, Advanced Chemistry H, Biology (Honors option), Advanced Biology (H), Environmental Science, Applied Sciences (H), Robotics. **Fine Arts:** Humanities I: Art (a core course: two and three dimensional, drama, and music), Art of Architecture, Media and Society, Humanitas, 2-Dimensional Art I & II (drawing, collage, painting), 3-Dimensional Art I & II (sculpture, ceramics, and metal arts), Visual Design I & II (2-D, 3-D, and computer media), Digital Arts I & II (still images, moving, sound collage, video and animation), Studio Art (AP), 2-D Art: Photography I & II, Ceramics, Stained Glass, Fashion Design, Yearbook Arts. Drama: Dramatic Arts I & II (theater and performance), Voices in Theater, Cinema Studies (film, screenwriting, directing, and production), Rehearsal and Performance: Drama. Music: Instrumental Musical Ensembles, Advanced Combo, Choir I-II, Advanced Choir. Dance: Dance I, Musical Theater Dance Production and Choreography. **P.E.:** Basketball Conditioning (coed), Wrestling Conditioning (coed), Dance, Dance Team, Fencing, Sailing, Ultimate Frisbee, Yoga, Hiking, Weight Training, AWE Conditioning, Rock Climbing, Swim Conditioning, Women's Soccer Conditioning, Independent P.E. **Other:** The Athenian Wilderness Experience (G11), Interim program (faculty-led educational and community service trips), Internships, Independent Study, Round Square international exchange, Network of Complementary Schools exchange, Outdoor Education programs, Speech and Debate, Robotics Program, Airplane

Construction Program, Community Service, Town Meeting. **Computer lab/training:** Computers available for student use in lab (80), library, and classrooms. All 9th grade students receive training on computer use as part of the Humanities curriculum; many other courses throughout the curriculum utilize computers. **Grading:** A-F; grades and written evaluations for each course. **Graduation requirements:** 4 years English; 3 years history, foreign language, laboratory science; 2 1/2 years fine arts; and P.E. or athletic participation during each year of enrollment. In addition, students must complete community service each year and the Athenian Wilderness Experience before the beginning of senior year. **Average nightly homework (M-Th):** G9: 2-3 hours; for other grades, dependent on courses student selects. **Faculty:** 40 (28 f/t, 12 p/t); 50% male, 50% female; 71% hold master's degrees; 5% hold doctorates. **Faculty ethnicity:** 77% Caucasian (non-Latino); 7% Asian; 9% African-American; 7% Latino. **Faculty selection/training:** "The department chairs perform the initial screening. Select candidates may be asked back to teach a class in their discipline. The entire department is invited to interview the candidate. Faculty and students make evaluations. Recommendations are made to the Department Chair and Academic Dean." **Teacher/student ratio:** 1:10. **Percentage of students enrolled in AP:** "In the last academic year, 73 students (NP % students) took 102 exams: pass rate 84%." **Senior class profile (mean):** SAT Math 651, SAT Critical Reading 620, SAT Writing 629. **GPA:** 3.6. **National Merit Scholarship Program:** Two Finalists, 16 Commended. **College enrollment (last class):** 90-100% in 4-year, 0-10% in 2-year. **Recent (last 3 yrs) colleges:** UC (Berkeley, LA, Davis, SD, Santa Cruz, Santa Barbara, Irvine), Williams, Wellesley, Dartmouth, Yale, Princeton, Columbia, Penn, Johns Hopkins, Emory, Michigan, U-Chicago, USC, Occidental, Pomona, and "many others."

Other Indicators the School is Accomplishing its Goals
"Athenian graduates are indeed prepared for 'the rigors of college and lives of purpose and personal fulfillment,' as our Mission Statement describes. Alumni have achieved distinction in many endeavors, including law, medicine, business, the arts, communication, education, science, and community leadership. Athenian fosters in its graduates an understanding of themselves as contributing citizens in an international community who continue to learn and develop throughout their lives. See the quotes below from students and parents in 'Student/Parent Statements.'"

Campus/Campus Life
Campus description: Athenian's campus is spread over 75 acres of rolling, oak-covered hills at the base of Mount Diablo. Its academic buildings include 24 classrooms, the Fuller Brawner Science Center with laboratories, Kate and Dyke Brown Hall (student-services offices and assembly, and caféteria), a new library, the new Center for the Arts,

four computer laboratories, two faculty/administrative buildings, two dormitories and a boarding activities center, music classrooms, and the Fuller Commons building (a student lounge and meeting space). In 2009, Athenian will open the Eleanor Dase Center, a new music and multipurpose building. In addition, the campus includes a large gymnasium, locker rooms, competition swimming pool, three athletic fields, tennis courts, 15 faculty residences, and ten buildings housing grades 6-8. **Library:** 15,000 print volumes; 43 periodical subscriptions and many electronic subscriptions; over 30 computers with Internet access; study and meeting rooms; online catalog; research and study space for 50-75 students. Open to students 8 a.m.-4 p.m. and 7 p.m.-10 p.m. Mon.-Wed. **Sports facilities:** Gymnasium, new all-weather sports field, swimming pool, baseball field, softball field, rock climbing wall, and weight room. **Theater/arts facilities:** A new theater and fine arts center with an art gallery, black-box performance space, studio art classrooms, and a dance studio. Photography and dark room facilities, chorus rooms, and music practice rooms are also available. **Open/closed campus:** Closed until second semester of 10th grade; open thereafter with parent permission. **Lunches:** Athenian's cafeteria serves hot entrees, soups, and salad. **Bus service:** Two bus lines serve 1) Berkeley, Oakland, Orinda, Lafayette, and Walnut Creek/Alamo; and 2) Pleasanton, Dublin and San Ramon. Many of these pickup points are at BART stations, allowing students to travel from most of the East Bay to Athenian's bus stops. **Uniforms/dress code:** "Students are to dress in good taste and wear clothes that are clean and in good repair." **Co-curricular activities/clubs:** Activities and organizations include newspaper, Chess Club, International Student Organization, literary magazine, orchestra, Community Action Board, debate, admission hosts, theater tech. group, Interweave, Multicultural Alliance, Round Square International Exchange and Service, yearbook, and more. **Foreign exchange program/internships:** Athenian is a member of the Round Square Conference of International Schools, which provides international exchange opportunities at the more than 40 Round Square schools in more than ten countries on five continents. In addition, Athenian hosts exchange students each year from Round Square schools. Internships can be arranged on an independent study basis. **Community service:** More than 200 organizations and activities. In G9, students participate in organized events on and off campus. Juniors and seniors arrange and complete a project in their individual areas of interest. **Typical freshman schedule:** Humanities I: Literature, Humanities I: Cultures, Humanities I: Fine Arts (studio, music, and drama), math (typically Algebra I, Geometry, or Algebra II), Conceptual Physics, and foreign language (Spanish or French I, II, or III). P.E., performing arts, community service, morning meetings, and advisory meeting periods are also part of the 9th grade weekly schedule.

Student Support Services

Counselor/student ratio (not including college counselors): 1:225. **Counseling:** "Students meet every other week with a faculty member who serves as their academic advisor. That teacher also serves as the primary contact for parents for academic and extracurricular affairs. The counseling program includes peer education, health education, advising, and support programs for students, staff, and families. Two full-time co-directors of college counseling provide individual and group guidance regarding college and university selection, application, and admission. The college counseling program brings college representatives and speakers to campus every year. The College Counseling Office also provides a library of publications, videos, and computer databases for exploring colleges and financial aid. The office also facilitates test preparation programs." **Learning differences/disabilities:** Teachers can provide some basic "reasonable" accommodations. Limited tutoring is available.

Student Conduct and Health

Code of conduct: In addition to prohibiting illegal activities, the school states, "We hold all members responsible for dealing with each other in a humane and gentle way. We prize the display of responsibility and good taste. Integrity, respect, and trust are treasured standards." **How school handles drugs/alcohol:** A student Discipline Committee makes recommendations to the Dean of Students regarding the consequences of rule infractions (which range from community service and privilege reductions to expulsion from the school). **Prevention and awareness programs:** Each year, the health program brings speakers and seminars to campus to educate Upper School students about drugs, alcohol, and sexually transmitted diseases. In addition, the sophomore health class addresses each of these issues.

Summer Programs

Programs include Devil Mountain Summer Camp, Summer School, Athenian Sports Camp, the Summer ESL for international students, and programs run by outside groups who use the school's facility. Prices vary.

Parent Involvement

Parent participation: "Parents are strongly encouraged to participate in the Athenian Parent Association, which coordinates parents' volunteer and fundraising activities, provides informational and social programs, and serves as a conduit for parent input to the school. Parent volunteering includes work days and organizing events such as the annual auction." **Parent/teacher communication:** Parents and students receive grades with comments at least twice a year; in some cases, midterm grades and comments can increase the reports to four times per year. **Parent education:** The school psychologist provides workshops, seminars, and information sessions for all parents. **Dona-**

tions: "Because tuition does not cover the entire expense of educating students at Athenian, parents are strongly encouraged to contribute to the extent they are able."

Sports

Interscholastic sports teams include soccer, volleyball, tennis, cross-country, basketball, baseball, golf, softball, swimming, track and field, and wrestling. P.E. classes include martial arts, yoga, weight training, ultimate frisbee, and rock climbing, among others.

What Sets the School Apart from Others

"With distinctive meaningful programs, The Athenian School goes far beyond preparing talented and diverse students for outstanding colleges. Athenian empowers its graduates to become world citizens with lives of purpose and personal fulfillment. Athenian's distinguishing features include: an exciting and challenging academic curriculum, nationally award-winning service learning, an amazing required wilderness course, and extraordinary international experiences unmatched by any Bay Area school. Athenian encourages students to find the colleges or universities that best fit them, and most students gain admission to their first-choice school. Most importantly, Athenian students develop a deep understanding of themselves, extraordinary skills for achievement, an appreciation for differences and change, and the compassion to make a positive difference in the world." Several distinctive features further distinguish the school: • The required Athenian Wilderness Experience; • Vital international programs: As a founding member and the only Bay Area school in the prestigious Round Square Conference of International Schools, Athenian fosters international understanding and a commitment to diversity through international exchanges, annual conferences, and community service projects around the world. • Town Meeting provides a forum for any member of the community (student, faculty or staff) to make a proposal regarding the school for debate and discussion. Through this forum, students have a voice in the running of Athenian; • An excellent and well-developed service learning program won a national award in 2007; • Our residential community faculty (over 20) and students (nearly 42) make Athenian the Bay Area's only nonsectarian boarding program. Residential faculty is particularly available to both day and boarding students. The residential population at Athenian fosters a strong sense of international community, which supports students and faculty alike; • Diversity (international and domestic): The Athenian student body represents a wide variety of communities from the Bay Area, the United States, and around the world — which come together in an educational environment which places the greatest emphasis upon education and mutual respect among its members. We value individuality and differences; • Engaging interim experiences — faculty-led educational and community service trips; • Nationally successful robotics program and airplane construction project; • Engaging seminar courses on a wide variety of topics in literature and history; • Strength in the fine and performing arts; • An extraordinary campus supports the school's programs by providing a beautiful and inspiring setting; • Bus service bringing together students from throughout the East Bay."

How Parents/Students Characterize School

Parent response(s): "A true community, Athenian is an incredibly human and humane learning environment. The teaching connects academic material to the surrounding world. Athenian is a microcosm of what the world should be: diverse (relatively), based on mutual respect, and challenging each person to be and do his or her best." "I've written books about the best education but despaired of finding such a high school. To my delight, Athenian is that ideal environment. Students are challenged to think, argue, explore, and try out new skills. Athenian helps teenagers find their place in the world. My son has become, literally, a better person, citizen, and a better sort of grownup." "After our oldest Athenian graduate son's resounding success at UCLA, we know that our younger children will graduate not only strong academically but as compassionate human beings. Athenian encourages students to evolve above and beyond academic excellence." "At Athenian, we expected that not only our children's intellect would be developed but their individuality, personal morality, creativity, and senses of humor and fun. Athenian promised us all this. We have stayed at Athenian because that is exactly what we have found." **Student response(s):** "At Athenian, I learned how to use my mind to the fullest; I was well ahead of my peers in college. The school fosters early independence and discipline." "Being part of Athenian is being part of a comprehensive community. It is a way to learn, to teach, to find mentors and friends. Athenian is a place where no one is forgotten, where everyone matters. Athenian provides a platform from which to explore the outside world and gain an unshakable respect for other cultures and our natural environment. Athenian stimulates our thirst for knowledge, supplies our hearts with deep human connection, challenges our core values, and strengthens our highest aspirations for who we can be as human beings." The Athenian School creates well-rounded individuals ready for the real world. Athenian did just that for my classmates and for me. Athenian brought together a diverse, intelligent, and respectful student body of unmatched caliber. Athenian's excellent faculty is always ready to mediate instead of dictate. The extensive array of activities educates students about diversity and encourages communication. Athenian is an ideal place for a respectful student who is ready to learn being surrounded by academic and personal intelligence. For me, Athenian has been the ideal school." "Athenian contributed to my growth as an intellectual and an individual. The Athenian community helped me understand my role as a citizen of the world. I will be able to contribute to the greater society thanks to Athenian's rich ideals and supportive atmosphere. I will always cherish and stay connected to this amazing place."

The Bay School of San Francisco

35 Keyes Avenue
San Francisco, CA 94129-0610
(415) 561-5800 fax (415) 561-5808
www.bayschoolsf.org

Malcolm H. Manson, Founding Head of School
Annie Tsang, Director of Admission, atsang@bayschoolsf.org

General

Coed day high school. Nonsectarian. Independent. Founded in 2004. Nonprofit, member CAIS, NAIS, CASE, BAAD, BAIHS. **Enrollment:** Approx. 300. **Average class size:** 13. **Accreditation:** In progress; WASC/CAIS. **School year:** 9-mo. calendar. **School day:** 8:10 a.m.-3:30 p.m. (sports or physical activities until 5 p.m.). **Location:** In the Presidio of San Francisco. Accessible by the 28, 29, and 43 MUNI bus lines, Golden Gate Transit, free PresidiGo Shuttle.

Student Body

Geographic breakdown (counties): 61% from San Francisco; 29% from Marin; 5% from the Peninsula; 4% from the East Bay, 1% other. **Ethnicity:** 72% Caucasian; 8% Asian/Pacific Islander; 8% Latino; 3% African-American; 1% Middle Eastern, 8% identify themselves as multi-ethnic. **International students (I-20 status):** 0. **Middle schools (freshman):** 22% from 12 public middle schools; 69% from 25 private, non-parochial schools; 9% from 3 parochial schools.

Admission

Applications due: Early January (check website). **Application fee:** $80. **Application process:** Students/parents interested in the school are encouraged to visit the website and complete the online inquiry form to request information and sign up for an open house. Open houses for families of prospective 8th graders are scheduled throughout the fall. Campus visits are strongly recommended and run from September through the application deadline. Interviews are required and can be scheduled by calling the admission office. Part I of the application must be received prior to scheduling an interview. **No. of freshman applications:** 480 for 75 places. **Minimum admission requirements:** N/P. **Test required:** SSAT. **Preferences:** N/P. **We are looking for:** "Active and engaged students possessing a wide spectrum of backgrounds, interests, and abilities, who are committed to a challenging college preparatory program." **What kind of student do you best serve?** N/P.

Costs

Latest tuition: $29,500 payable in 1, 2 or 10 payments. **Sibling discount:** None. **Tuition increases:** Approx. 3-5%. **Other costs:** Comprehensive materials and service fee of $2,900, including all books and

materials, food service, laptop computer rental, athletic uniforms/
equipment, and required school trips and programs. **Percentage of
students receiving financial aid: 38%. Financial aid deadline:** Second
week of February (please check website). **Average grant:** $20,000 based
upon combined total of tuition and materials/service fee. **Percentage
of grants of half-tuition or more: N/P.**

School's Mission Statement/Goals

"The Bay School was created by an experienced and visionary group
of educators and founding partners. Our mission is to offer to our
students the skills and knowledge they will need to be thoughtful
citizens and capable leaders in the year 2040. This will be the year our
first class turns fifty and will be at the height of their leadership in
an increasingly complex world. Fueled by observing the discoveries
of today's world as well as predicting the shape of our future world,
our mission focuses on three pillars: science and technology; world
religions and cultures; and ethics. We are an imaginative, engaging,
and demanding college preparatory school, emphasizing science,
technology, world religions and ethics in a diverse, compassionate
and trusting community."

Academic Program

"The Bay School curriculum challenges students to become skilled and
versatile problem solvers in an increasingly complex world. Emphasizing depth, our courses promote critical thinking and draw meaningful
connections between traditional academic disciplines, and between
students' course work and their lives. The freshman and sophomore
years address a broad foundation of basic skills, structured in an integrated approach that emphasizes the interrelationships between topics
and subjects. As students advance to their junior and senior years, the
program is increasingly driven by their individual interests and talents.
Because students take the equivalent of four semester-long courses
each trimester, they are able to take what amounts to six year-long major
courses each year in our program. Thus, they are able to do challenging
and timely extra course work in their areas of greatest interest while
continuing studies across all disciplines. Classes meet for 80 minutes,
four times per week, on a rotating block schedule. Each trimester is
twelve weeks in length." **Courses offered:** (AP=Advanced Placement,
(AP)=AP option, (H)=Honors or Honors option): **English:** Humanities
I-II, Writing Workshop, American Literature, Dramatic Literature,
Fiction, Poetry, Shakespeare, Advanced Composition, Literature of
Forgiveness, other advanced electives; **Math:** Math 1-3, Analysis of
Functions, Statistics, Game Theory, Analytic Geometry, Calculus (H).
Science: Conceptual Physics, Astrophysics (H), Calculus-based Physics
(H), Chemistry I-II (H), Organic Chemistry, Biology I-II (H), Bioethics,
Biotechnology, Environmental Science, Field Biology, Marine Science,
Geology, Hydrology; **History:** Research in the Community, U.S. His-
tory, Comparative Govt., Political Economy, Modern Genocide, U.S.

Foreign Policy, Western Civilization; **Foreign Languages:** Spanish I-IV (H) and advanced electives, Mandarin Chinese I-IV (H) and advanced electives, French II-IV (H) and advanced electives; **P.E.:** Martial Arts, Yoga, Health and Human Sexuality, Dance, Cross-training; **Arts:** Studio Arts: Drawing, Painting, 3-Dimensional Design; Music: Jazz, Music Composition, Electronic Music Studio, Chamber Music; Dance: Dance in a Cultural Context, Social Dance, Choreography; Drama: Drama, Intensive Performance Workshop; Digital **Arts:** Digital Imaging, Video Production, Yearbook Design. **Other:** Religion and Philosophy courses: African American Spirituality and Philosophy, The Bible, Faith and Religion in America, Hinduism, Comparative Philosophy, The Problem of Evil. **Computer lab/training:** Laptop Essentials, Computer Science I, II, and III. The digital media lab is equipped with Mac and Windows desktops and video editing workstations. All students and faculty are provided laptops for use at school and at home. **Grading:** A-F and written comments at the end of each trimester. **Graduation requirements:** 23 credits required (each trimester course earns .5 credit). **Average nightly homework (M-Th):** Varies by grade; averages 45 min.-1 hr per subject. **Faculty:** 32 f/t and 3 p/t faculty; 46% male, 54% female; 51% hold advanced degrees; 6% hold doctorates. **Faculty ethnicity:** "30% faculty of color." (N/P ethnicities). **Faculty selection/ training:** "The school is very selective in its hiring, and the faculty is comprised of master teachers having extensive knowledge and skills related to their disciplines — educators who are inspired by our mission and deeply invested in the school beyond the school day. They have a deep understanding and interest in individual learning styles and are committed to adapting their teaching methods to engage all students." **Teacher/student ratio:** 1: 8. **Percentage of students enrolled in AP:** N/P. "Because the AP program generally promotes breadth over depth, we have designed our own advanced courses in each discipline, better suited to our mission. Students are still encouraged to take the AP exams, and often prepare for them with the help of faculty and score well." **Senior class profile (mean):** Sat Math 594, SAT Critical Reading 614, SAT Writing 624. **GPA:** N/P. **National Merit Scholarship Program:** "Eight of the Bay School's 52 founding senior class members earned National Merit Commendations and 4 earned Semifinalist status in 2007." **College enrollment (last class):** 100%; 95% in 4-year, 5% in 2-year. **Recent (first graduating class) colleges:** "Our 52 seniors were admitted to 130 different colleges and earned well over $500,000 in merit scholarships. ... Acceptances include: MIT, Stanford, Wellesley, UC Berkeley, Amherst, Bowdoin, Reed, Tufts, Duke, Carleton and the U.S. Naval Academy."

Campus/Campus Life

Campus description: "The Bay School is located in the heart of San Francisco's Presidio National Park. The school opened its doors in the fall of 2004 following the completion of a $15 million renovation of a 66,000 square foot historic building. The campus features three state-of-the-art science laboratories, 30 classrooms, drawing and painting studios, and digital media lab, as well as spacious student commons and dining areas. The Bay School campus is surrounded by expansive open space providing magnificent views overlooking San Francisco Bay and the Golden Gate Bridge." **Library:** The 3,000 square foot library has a "capacity of 12,000 volumes" and features an online library catalog linked to more than 30 databases and electronic reference sources. The library collection also includes a parent resource section, an educators' collection and Spanish, French, and Mandarin titles. **Sports facilities:** "The majority of Bay's indoor sports practices take place at the YMCA Letterman Gymnasium and Main Post Gymnasium complexes, both within walking distance of campus. Bay's outdoor sports teams hold practices primarily at Paul Goode and Fort Scott Fields in the Presidio. Bay also uses Rec and Park facilities throughout the city, the miles of dirt trails that wind through the Presidio, and open space areas such as Crissy Field." **Theater/arts facilities:** An art studio, digital media lab, drama/dance studio, and several practice rooms for both individual and group musical study. **Open/closed campus:** Closed. Seniors can be granted off campus privileges. **Lunches:** "Included in comprehensive fee and on campus. All meals are organic, local whenever possible, and prepared by an on-site caterer. Meals are shared by Bay School students, faculty, and staff in our 4,500 square foot dining hall/commons area." **Bus service:** Campus accessible by MUNI, Golden Gate Transit, PresidiGo. **Uniforms/dress code:** "The school's dress code emphasizes the business-like nature of the school operation. While informality is encouraged, neatness and appropriateness is required." **Co-curricular activities/clubs:** Over 20 student clubs including: a 40+ person engineering club, yearbook, chess, student council, hip-hop, community service, literary magazine, outing, fantasy gaming, salsa, a cappella, and Model U.N. **Foreign exchange programs/internships:** N/P. **Community service:** Community service opportunities are offered throughout the year. Students can participate in the Community Service Club as members or on a drop-in basis. Service opportunities are often student-driven and have included a wide range of events from volunteering at food pantries to planting trees. Each year the Community Service Club organizes fundraisers for charities close to the hearts of the club members. Additionally, all Bay School sophomores are required to take a one-trimester course titled Research in the Community. As part of this course, students must complete fieldwork centered on a community issue and design a research project that either raises awareness of or directly addresses an issue in depth. **Typical freshman schedule:** Humanities I (3 trimesters), Conceptual Physics (2 trimesters), Chemistry (1 trimester), foreign language (2 trimesters), math (2 trimesters), laptop essentials, research skills, study skills (once per week, 2 trimesters), Writing Workshop (1 trimester), art elective (1 trimester). Freshmen also have 3 monitored study hall periods per week.

Student Support Services

Counselor/student ratio (not including college counselors): 1:260.
Counseling: "Student counseling services are provided by one (65%
time) licensed psychotherapist as school counselor and an interfaith
chaplain. The school counselor is available for counseling services
including crisis intervention, individual counseling, group counseling, and parent consultation. The Bay School chaplain supports students with tools of ethical reflection and also serves as a confidential
counselor with whom life situations may be shared." **Learning dif-
ferences/disabilities:** "A part-time clinical psychologist provides the
following services: consultation, education, creation and implementation of Individual Learning Plans, self-advocacy, and implementation
of accommodations both at Bay and on standardized testing. Students
with identified learning and attention differences at Bay are: bright,
understand how they learn, consult with teachers, and work hard in
an academically rigorous program."

Student Conduct and Health

Code of conduct: "The Bay School emphasizes ethical thinking in
both its mission and its practice. Students meet together every morning for 25 minutes to engage with the school's precepts which are
stated goals for conduct. Bay's Conduct Review Council is an elected
body comprised of both students and faculty that meets to review
any violations of student behavior codes and to determine appropriate consequences consistent with the stated policies of the school.
The Student Council meets in conjunction with the Conduct Review
Council to create the Ethics Committee which discusses the ethical
health of the school on a regular basis." **How school handles drugs/
alcohol:** "There will be no possession, use, distribution, or display of
alcoholic beverages, cigarettes, drug paraphernalia, marijuana, and/or
other illegal or dangerous drugs of any kind on campus, at school
sponsored events and functions, or while in transit to/from a school
sponsored event. Violations of this expectation result in a meeting with
the Conduct Review Council and serious consequences." **Prevention
and awareness programs:** "The school hires a drug and alcohol abuse
prevention program which works carefully and thoroughly with 9th
graders and then follows up with upper level grades. Students take a
trimester long course entitled 'Choices in Relationships' which covers
a myriad of teenage health and relationship topics. The course meets
once a week for an hour during the sophomore year."

Summer Programs

The Bay School hosts several summer programs, including: Bay Area
Shakespeare Camp, First Graduate Summer Session, and the YMCA
Community Program.

Parent Involvement

Parent participation: Parents are encouraged to participate in the many events and activities organized by the Parents' Association. Parents are actively involved as mentors and community liaisons for students' Senior Projects. **Parent/teacher communication:** Written comments from teachers are sent to parents twice during each trimester, including a letter grade at the end. Parents are encouraged to contact students' advisors at any time, preferably by e-mail. Teachers will let the advisor know of any change in performance between reporting periods. **Parent education:** "The Parents Education Resource Group focuses on programs dealing with adolescent development, communication and college admission." **Donations:** N/P.

Sports

The Bay School is a member of the BAC in the BCL – Central Division. The school fields varsity boys and girls teams in soccer, basketball, baseball, softball, volleyball, golf, cross-country, track, tennis, and sailing. All students are required to participate in some form of physical activity each trimester, either as part of an athletic team, physical activity class, or an approved off-campus program. Physical activity class offerings include yoga, hip-hop dance, martial arts and physical conditioning, as well as a recreational swimming program. All activity classes are scheduled before and after the academic day.

What Sets School Apart From Others

Intersession: "Each year at the Bay School a highlight of the spring program is the week-long project period called 'Intersession' during which students and teachers focus on the exploration of one specific area or topic of interest. The program is a direct expression of the school's academic philosophy valuing 'depth over breadth,' and an appreciation of the importance of linking academic study to real world experience and practice. Intersession course offerings include a wide variety of activities and topics that vary from year to year, and have included wilderness adventures, cultural exploration through dance and art, in-depth courses in programming and digital media, fashion design and filmmaking." • "The Senior Projects and Field-based Learning Program is a required culminating experience of the 12th grade year. Seniors work with a mentor (often from outside school), to broaden their skills and knowledge in an area of personal intellectual interest. Planning begins during the winter of junior year. Projects must involve a minimum of 65 hours of field work, and students earn full academic credit for a two trimester elective course. Sample projects from the class of 2008 included a student who designed focus groups and research studies to help Kashi Co. understand their teenage market; a student who developed methodologies for studies of conduction systems in the heart in a UCSF lab; and a group of students who constructed an electric car for competition. The Bay School employs a full-time senior project coordinator both to help the seniors look within, and to guide them to exceptional mentors in order to make the most of their opportunities in the program." • Morning Meeting: "Each morning, our entire community of students, faculty, and staff gathers together for a twenty-minute period from 8:10 to 8:30 a.m. Our morning meeting is designed to bring our community together each day, and to set aside a special time for sharing with peers, colleagues, and friends. Listening to live student musical performances, faculty speakers, or watching a short documentary alerting us to current events are a few examples of ways we spend this time. In addition, we take five minutes of Morning Meeting to close our eyes and position ourselves mentally for the day ahead. We believe that this practice calms us before the busyness of the academic day."• "A Bay School education is based upon the foundation of a broad and challenging college preparatory curriculum. In addition, it offers an innovative science program in which all students complete three core sciences (physics, chemistry, and biology) in their first two years. The curriculum is intentionally structured to meld the intellectual aesthetic and spiritual domains through cross-over academic offerings. Students are encouraged to make the important connections between classroom learning and its applications to life in the world surrounding them. The Bay School culture honors human qualities equally with academic competence in the selection of students, faculty, and staff."

How Parents/Students Characterize School

Parent response(s): "When my daughters remarked to me, 'There are no cliques, Mom,' I thought, 'What a uniquely healthy culture in which young people can grow.' And, because Bay developed its curricula based on the most current educational theory, the academics are stellar. Close personal relationships with teachers encourage student achievement in this academically rigorous environment. Our two sports-minded daughters are thriving in an exciting athletic program, while the music program has awakened a new found love of jazz in one of our girls. It's a great school." **Student response(s):** "There's something about The Bay School that is hard to describe. Something that makes it easy to talk to people. Something that makes you grin spontaneously while walking down the hallways. Something that makes you want to be a better person. The Bay School is not a brand new school anymore, but it maintains the openness, the warm-hearted friendliness, and the boundless opportunities that make a new school special. Coming into The Bay School, each person (students and teachers alike) brings every part of themselves—be it intense academic focus, an artistic passion or a unique sense of humor—and the resulting mix is as refreshing as it is educational."

Bellarmine College Preparatory

960 West Hedding Street
San Jose, CA 95126
(408) 294-9224 *fax (408) 294-4086*
www.bcp.org

Mark Pierotti, Principal
Bill Colucci, Director of Admissions, bcolucci@bcp.org

General

Boys Catholic day high school. (Jesuit) (75% Catholic). Founded in 1851 at Santa Clara University. Nonprofit. **Enrollment:** Approx. 1,550. **Average class size:** 25. **Accreditation:** WASC/WCEA. **School year:** Aug.-June. **School day:** 8:15 a.m.-2:40 p.m. **Location:** Near downtown San Jose. The College Park CalTrain station is on campus; the Light Rail stops nearby. Close to Hwys. 880, 280 and 101.

Student Body

Geographic breakdown (counties): Approx. 75% from Santa Clara; 15% from San Mateo; 5% from Alameda; 5% from Santa Cruz. **Ethnicity:** Approx. 56% Caucasian (non-Latino); 13% Latino; 9% Filipino; 5% African-American; 5% Chinese; 2% Japanese; 2% Vietnamese; 1% Korean; 1% American Indian; 6% multi-ethnic. **International students (I-20 status):** N/P. **Middle schools (freshman):** 55% came from 40 parochial schools; 10% from private, non-parochial schools (N/P # schools).

Admission

Applications due: Approx. December 30 for applicants to G9, April 30 for other grades (call for exact dates). Decisions are mailed in March for G9, early June for other grades. **Application fee:** $70. **Application process:** In November, Bellarmine hosts an open house for seventh and eighth grade students and families. Eighth graders may make an appointment to shadow a current student for a day. The school shares teacher recommendation forms with other Diocese high schools and requires an entrance test. A clergy recommendation is not required. **No. of freshman applications:** 900 for 380 places. Ten new students were admitted to G10, 4 to G11, and 2 to G12. **Minimum admission requirements:** "Above-average grades and passionate involvement in two or more co-curricular activities." **Test required:** HSPT, administered in January; results may be sent to other schools. **Preferences:** Catholics. **"We are looking for** grades, test scores, recommendations, results of entrance exam, active involvement in parish, and ability to maintain academic excellence while demonstrating a high level of involvement in co-curricular activities." **What kind of student do you best serve?** "We serve the college-bound student who wishes to become involved in a variety of co-curricular activities, while also experiencing the benefits of Jesuit education. There is a family atmosphere here, and we hope that students will seek to give something back to the school."

Costs
Latest tuition: $13,800 payable in 10 payments. **Sibling discount:** None. **Tuition increases:** "Vary." **Other costs:** Books, approx. $350-$450/year. **Percentage of students receiving financial aid:** 20%. **Financial aid deadline:** Approx. February 1 (call for date). **Average grant:** $3,500. **Percentage of grants half-tuition or more:** 42%.

School's Mission Statement/Goals
"Bellarmine College Preparatory is a community of men and women gathered together by God for the purpose of educating the student to seek justice and truth throughout his life. We are a Catholic school in the tradition of St. Ignatius of Loyola, the Founder of the Society of Jesus. As such, our entire school program is dedicated to forming 'men for others' — persons whose lives will be dedicated to bringing all their God-given talents to fullness and to living according to the pattern of service inaugurated by Jesus Christ."

Academic Program
Courses offered (H=Honors, AP=Advanced Placement, (H)=Honors option, (AP)=AP option): **English:** English 1, English 2 (H), Rhetoric, American Literature 1-2, English Language AP, Holocaust Literature, Modern American Authors, Mythology of Wilderness, Literature of War, Comedy and Tragedy, Creative Writing 1 — Exploring Modern Literary Genres, English Literature AP, Science Fiction, British Literature 1-2, Faulkner Seminar H, Joyce Seminar H, Shakespeare 1-2, Poetry and Prayer, Literature of the Counterculture 1-2, Gender Roles in Literature, Film Composition and Literature, Creative Writing 2 — Exploring Poetry and Short Fiction, African-American Literature, Screenwriting, Modern Media Literature; **Social Science:** World Cultures, World History (AP), U.S. History (AP), U.S. History Seminar H, Intro to Psychology, Psychology AP, American Government AP, Conflict in the Modern World, Economics, African-American Experience 1-2, American Law, Philosophy of the Believing Person, AP Human Geography, AP European History; **Math:** Algebra 1 & 1 Accelerated, Geometry (H), Algebra 2 (H), Intro to Finite Math, Trigonometry, Pre-Calculus (H), Integrated Pre-Calculus/Physics H, Calculus, AP Calculus AB & BC, Probability and Statistics (AP), Computer Science (AP), Multi-Variable Calculus; **Languages:** Mandarin Chinese 1-2, 3-4 (H); French 1-3, 4 (AP); Spanish 1-2, 3 (H), 4-5 (AP); Latin 1-2, 3 (H), 4 AP; **Science:** Earth Science, Biology (H/AP), Chemistry (H/AP), Integrated Physics/Pre-Calculus H, Physics (H/AP), Anatomy and Physiology, Geology, Environmental Science AP, Marine Biology; **Religious Studies:** Intro to Catholic Christianity, Christian Scriptures, Christian Ethics, Social Justice/College Guidance, Comparative Religions, Christian Prayer and Meditation,

Marriage and Family, Ethics and Service Learning, Confirmation, Philosophy for the Believing Person; **Arts:** Fine Arts 1-3, Drawing 1-2, Ceramics 1-2, Mixed Media Sculpture, Intermediate Wheel Throwing, Photography, Digital Video Production, Graphic Design 1-2, Acting 1-2, Symphonic Band, Jazz Ensemble, Percussion Ensemble 1-3; **Computer Science:** Computer Science A AP, Computer Science AB AP, Intro to Java Programming, Web Design, Advanced Web Design, Multimedia Authoring, Advanced Topics in Computer Science; **P.E.:** P.E. 1, Advanced P.E. **Computer lab/training:** The school is PC based; school computers are networked; wireless connections are available. **Grading:** A-F. **Graduation requirements:** UC admission requirements + 6 semesters of religious studies and 85 hours of community service. **Average nightly homework (M-Th):** G9: 1.5-2.5 hours; G10-12: 2-3 hours. **Faculty:** 120 (including 10 Jesuits); 75% male, 25% female; 60% hold master's degrees; 5% hold doctorates. **Faculty ethnicity:** 88% Caucasian (non-Latino); 8% Latino; 2% Asian; 2% African-American. **Faculty selection/training:** "Faculty is selected from a large, highly competitive pool of applicants. Teachers are awarded enrichment grants during the summer. Teachers participate in in-services during the year." **Teacher/student ratio:** 1:17. **Percentage of students enrolled in AP:** N/P; pass rate 86%. **Senior class profile (mean):** N/P SAT or GPA. **National Merit Scholarship Program:** 20 National Merit Finalists. **College enrollment (last class):** 95.2% enrolled in 4-year, 4.8% in 2-year. **Recent (last 2 yrs) colleges:** UC (Berkeley, Davis, Irvine, LA, Santa Barbara, Riverside, SD, Santa Cruz), CSU (Cal Poly-SLO, Chico, Humboldt, Monterey Bay, Sacramento, SD, SF, SJ, Stanislaus), Boston C, Creighton U, Loyola U-Chicago, Saint Joseph's U, C of the Holy Cross, Fordham, Georgetown, Gonzaga, Loyola Marymount, Santa Clara, Seattle U, USF, U.S. Air Force Academy, U.S. Military Academy West Point, U.S. Naval Academy, community colleges, Azusa Pacific U, CCA, Cal Lutheran U, Cal Tech, Harvey Mudd, Menlo C, Pomona, St. Mary's, Stanford, Thomas Aquinas C, USD, UOP, USC, Westmont C, Boston U, Brandeis, Brown, Clark Atlanta, Colorado State-Fort Collins, Columbia, Cornell, Duke, Florida A&M, Harvard, Howard, Johns Hopkins, Lewis & Clark, Morehouse, NYU, Northern Arizona, Northwestern, Princeton, RPI, St. Mary's (MD), Salve Regina U, Tulane, U-Arizona, U-Colorado-Boulder, U-Miami, U-Nevada-Reno, U-Oregon, U-Portland, U-Washington, Wesleyan, Whitman, and Yale.

Other Indicators the School is Accomplishing its Goals

"Bellarmine is an exemplary Jesuit school, outstanding both in its academic and co-curricular programs. Ninety-five percent or more of every senior class attends a four-year university. The athletic program is arguably the most successful in the area. Moreover, Bellarmine is the California State Champion in Speech & Debate, a national champion in robotics, and boasts superb programs in theater, music, and fine arts."

Campus/Campus Life

Campus description: The campus consists of 19 acres in a residential area of San Jose near The Alameda and 880. It includes classrooms and administration buildings, a Science Center, theater, pool, sports fields and a Jesuit residence. A new chapel was completed in 1999. **Library:** 37,000 print volumes; 35 computers; open to students 8 a.m.-5 p.m. **Sports facilities:** Gymnasium, 40-meter pool; soccer (turf), baseball, and football (turf) fields; and an all-weather track. **Theater/arts facilities:** 225-seat theater. **Open/closed campus:** Closed. **Lunches:** "Available on campus." **Bus service:** None. **Uniform/dress code:** "Relaxed dress code." **Co-curricular activities/clubs:** Faith: Campus Ministry, Christian Life Community, Christian Service; Service-Oriented Clubs: Block B Club, Christian Service Core Group, Environmental Action Society, Immersion Program, Service Club; Scholastic: Bellarmine Tutorial Society, California Scholarship Federation, Chess Club, Computer Programming Club, Junior Classical League/Latin, French Club, Library Club, Literary Seminar, Math Club, National Forensic League/Speech & Debate, Science Fiction Club, Strategic Games Club; Leadership: Amnesty International, Democrats Club, Republican Club, Student Government/ASB, Yell Leaders; Ethnic Clubs: African-American Student Union, Asian Society, Filipino Student Association, Indian Student Coalition, Irish Club, Italian Brotherhood, Jewish Life Community, Latino Students Union, Vietnamese Brotherhood; Arts: Anime/Japanimation Club, Band (Pep/Concert/Jazz), Cardinal Newspaper, Choir, Club Mud/Ceramics/Arts, Film Watchers Association, Music & Music Appreciation, Photography Club, Writer's Guild, Sanguine Humours/Improv, Theatre Arts, Theatre Tech Crew; Athletics/Hobbies: Auto Club, Billiards Club, Bowling Club, Fishing Club, Golf Club, Ice Hockey Club, Intramurals, International Soccer Club, Magicians Club, Mountain Bike Club, Robotics, Ski Club, Student Athletic Trainers, Triathalon Club, Ultimate Frisbee Club. **Foreign exchange programs/internships:** None. **Community service:** "Opportunities include immersion trips to Mexico and El Salvador." **Typical freshman schedule:** 7 periods of 50-minute classes, with 6 classes per day: English I, math, foreign language, 1 semester social studies, 1 semester fine arts, religious studies, science.

Student Support Services

Counselor/student ratio (not including college counselors): 1:130. **Counseling:** The school offers personal and academic counseling and has four full-time college and career counselors. **Learning disabilities/differences:** "A learning specialist focuses specifically on working with students who have learning differences."

Student Conduct and Health

Code of conduct: "Standard." **How school handles drugs/alcohol:"** Varies, with proactive involvement by the counseling department." **Prevention and awareness programs:** Included in curriculum.

Summer Programs: Six-week summer school (for G6-12).

Parent Involvement
Parent participation: Mothers' Guild and Dads' Club. **Parent/teacher communication:** Homeroom, parent-teacher conferences. Quarterly grades, progress reports, ParentConnect Internet communication. **Parent education:** "Regular programs throughout the year focusing on drug and alcohol education, human sexuality, the college application process, and parenting are provided by the school's counseling department." **Donations:** "Parent Pledge Program (optional)."

Sports
Boys compete through the WCAL in football, baseball, water polo, swimming, tennis, golf, track, cross-country, basketball, soccer, volleyball, wrestling, and lacrosse.

What Sets School Apart From Others
"College prep environment on a Catholic, Jesuit campus. We emphasize educating the whole person: mind, heart, spirit, body, imagination."

How Parents/Students Characterize School
Parent response(s): "Great, supportive community." "All the teachers care about my son." **Student response(s):** "I like all of my teachers." "Bellarmine offered me an incredible number of opportunities, including retreats and immersion programs." "I know every person in my senior class."

Bentley School
1000 Upper Happy Valley Road
Lafayette, CA 94549
(510) 843-2512 *fax (925) 299-0469*
www.bentleyschool.net

Rick Fitzgerald, Head of School
Arlene Hogan, Dir. of K-12 Admission, ahogan@bentleyschool.net
Robert Gleeson, Dir. of HS Admission, rgleeson@bentleyschool.net

General
Coed day high school. Nonsectarian. Independent. The K-8 school was founded in 1920. The high school was established in 1998 with G9-10. As of 2007, seven classes have graduated. Nonprofit, member CAIS, NAIS, BAIHS, EBISA, CASE, POCIS, SSATB, ERB, BAAD, ABC, the College Board. **Enrollment:** Currently 225 to grow to 290. The school has capacity for entering freshmen classes of 90 students. **Average class size:** 12. **Accreditation:** NAIS, WASC. **School year:** Sept.-June. **School day:** 8 a.m.-3:15 p.m. **Location:** Just off Hwy. 24 in Lafayette, a suburb

5 miles east of Oakland, 10 miles east of San Francisco. Shuttles pick up students at various locations.

Student Body
Geographic breakdown (counties): 52% from Alameda; 48% from Contra Costa. **Ethnicity:** 55% Caucasian (non-Latino); 32% Asian; 6% Latino; 7% African-American. **International students (I-20 status):** 1. **Middle schools (freshman):** 60% came from the school's own lower school; 20% from public middle schools; 20% from private non-parochial schools. (N/P # schools).

Admission
Applications due: Late January (call for date). **Application fee:** $75. **Application process:** The school hosts open houses October through November. Applicants are interviewed by a member of the admissions committee and submit transcripts, past test scores, and teacher recommendations. Applicants must write an essay and submit a self-portrait. Decisions are mailed mid-March. **No. of freshman applications:** 385 for 90 places; 24 new students were admitted to G10; 10 to G11. **Minimum admission requirements:** N/P. **Test required:** ISEE or SSAT. **Preferences:** None. "We are looking for individuals who want to challenge themselves academically, creatively, and personally." **What kind of student do you best serve?** "We best serve students with a variety of gifts and talents who are committed, intellectually curious, creative risk-takers and who will be generous, supportive, respectful members of our community and the world at large."

Costs
Latest tuition: $24,865 payable in 1 or 2 payments. **Sibling discount:** None. **Tuition increases:** Approx. 5%. **Other costs:** $500-$800. **Percentage of students receiving financial aid:** 28%. **Financial aid deadline:** January (call for date.) **Average grant:** $9,500. **Percentage of grants half-tuition or more:** 55%.

School's Mission Statement/Goals
"Scire Desidero: I Desire to Know—Bentley School inspires inquiry, academic excellence, personal achievement, and character by engaging students' intellect and creativity, and by encouraging them to embrace values that enrich their community and the world." "Core Values: As we pursue our mission, we are guided by the values at the heart of a Bentley education. These core values define and sustain our traditions and illuminate our future endeavors: Integrity — Honor, character, dignity, compassion, and ethical responsibility is a fundamental ideal in our community and in our approach to teaching and learning. Excellence — Our comprehensive and academically rigorous curriculum promotes a lifelong pursuit and love of learning; provides a range of challenging opportunities in academics, athletics and the arts; encourages balance in students' individual interests and goals.

Ingenuity—the support of intellectual inquiry is developed by encouraging students to explore their individual skills and talents and by provoking a willingness to articulate ideas and to engage critical thought. Courage—we provide an environment that allows students to take risks and to confront challenges in creative and individual ways. This environment allows students to develop a capacity to overcome and to be strengthened by experiences of adversity. Inclusion—we are a community with multiple perspectives, representing diverse backgrounds and experiences. We welcome unfamiliar and dissenting ideas, always promoting respectful and compassionate relationships among students, teachers, and parents."

Academic Program

"Bentley's mission is to prepare students for success in the global community of the 21st century. Inherent in this mission is the school's commitment to a rigorous, traditional college preparatory curriculum. During the first two years in the upper school, all students generally take a predetermined set of core courses. Those courses are designed to prepare students for the more demanding junior and senior years when students have the opportunity to undertake Advanced Placement work in a variety of areas. Students graduate with a regular college preparatory diploma, or with an honors or high honors diploma." **Courses offered** (AP=Advanced Placement, H=Honors, (AP)=AP option, (H)=Honors option): **English:** American Literature, British Literature, Public Speaking, Classical Literature, World Literature, AP Literature & Composition, AP Language and Composition, Creative Writing, African-American Literature, Shakespeare, Poetry; **Math:** Algebra I, Geometry, Algebra II (H), Pre-Calculus (H), AP Calculus (AB & BC), Applied Statistics; **History:** Modern European History, U.S. History (AP), 20th Century World History, Ancient & Medieval History, AP European History, Theory of Knowledge, Asian Studies, AP U.S. Government, AP Comparative Government, AP Economics; **Computer Science:** Computer Literacy I-II, Advanced Computer Literacy, AP Computer Science; **Science:** Biology (AP), Chemistry (AP), Physics (AP), (B or C), Conceptual Physics, Marine Biology, Environmental Science; **Social Science:** Intro to Psychology, Leadership; **Foreign language:** Spanish and French through AP Spanish and French Language, AP Spanish and French Literature, Latin I through AP Latin; **Arts:** Intro to Visual Art, Art II, Art History (AP), Drawing and Painting, Music Theory (AP), Acting, Intro to Theater Arts, Intro to Musical Arts, Chorus, Jazz Ensemble, Chamber Music Ensemble, Ceramics, Sculpture, Dance. **Special programs:** A Mini-Semester Week, held each winter, allows students to take courses outside the traditional curriculum. Examples are Life with Picasso, A History of 20th Century Sport, Greek Comedy Central, and Web Page Design. **Other:** "All entering students participate in a retreat just prior to the beginning of classes in September [so they can] become familiar with high school culture and rules, socialize, meet teachers, and participate in outdoor activities, including river rafting, a ropes course, swimming, and hiking." **Computer lab/training:** Two computer labs with 80 PCs and 15 Macintosh computers. Computer literacy is required for graduation. **Grading:** A-F. **Graduation requirements:** 22 credits and a GPA of 2.5 minimum, including 4.5 years English (public speaking, American and British literature required); 4 years history (U.S. and 20th Century World History required); 3 years science (chemistry, biology, and physics required) and language; 2 years art; 6 seasons physical activity; 60 hours community service; senior essay; and computer literacy. **Average nightly homework (Mon-Th):** G9-10: 30-40 min. per class; G11-12: 40-50 min. per class. **Faculty:** 43 f/t faculty; 52% male, 48% female; 65% hold master's degrees, 25% hold doctoral degrees. **Faculty ethnicity:** 90% Caucasian (non-Latino); 10% Latino or African-American. **Faculty selection/training:** "Faculty is selected based upon experience (primarily in independent schools), educational preparation (degree must be held in subject area taught), ability to contribute to extra-curricular program, and ability to fulfill responsibilities as an advisor to 7-9 students. The school has in-services, continuing education and summer workshops for teachers." **Teacher/student ratio:** 1:7. **Percentage of students enrolled in AP:** N/P. **Most recent senior class profile (mean):** N/P. **National Merit Scholarship Program:** 50% of present 11th grade are Commended Scholars or above. **College enrollment (last class):** 100% in 4-year. **Recent (last 3 yrs) colleges:** UC (Berkeley, LA, Santa Cruz, Davis, SD), Stanford, Penn, Brown, Amherst, Swarthmore, U-the Redlands, Pomona, and Reed.

Other Indicators the School is Accomplishing its Goals
"The Upper School division has received recognition from students and parents for its strong academic program, diverse extra-curricular activities, exceptional music and drama programs and exemplary advisee program. The school is further recognized for its strong sense of community and supportive teachers."

Campus/Campus Life
Campus description: The school is located in the community of Lafayette on a 19-acre campus abutting the north side of Highway 24. The campus has 7 buildings, which house classrooms, science labs, an art studio, library, computer lab, and offices. The school has landscaped grounds with a central courtyard that provides informal seating for socializing and study. **Library:** 2,000 sq. ft.; 5,000 print volumes; 30 periodical subscriptions; 25 computers (all with Internet access); 8 CD-ROMs; online catalog; study space for 36 students. Open to students from 7:30 a.m.- 5 p.m.; full-time librarian. **Sports facilities:** The campus has an athletic center, and the outdoor area includes a soccer field, basketball facilities, and five tennis courts. **Theater/arts facilities:** A student and performing arts center was completed in early 2004. The facilities also include an art studio and a music building. **Open/closed campus:** Closed. **Lunches:** Hot lunches are available daily. **Bus**

service: Private van service from Rockridge BART station and other locations in Berkeley and Oakland. **Uniforms/dress code:** The dress code requires that clothing be "whole, clean and appropriate for the classroom." Jeans are permitted. **Co-curricular activities/clubs:** Sports, drama, music, literary magazine, yearbook and student council, swing dance, Diversity Club, Amnesty International, Bentley Fights AIDS, Chess Club, Ecology Club. **Foreign exchange programs/internships:** None. **Community service:** Students work with the community service Coordinator to identify appropriate projects. (Examples N/P) **Typical freshman schedule:** Seven periods of approx. 50 minutes each: Classical Literature, Ancient & Medieval History, Geometry, Physics, foreign language and a class in theater, art, and/or music.

Student Support Services
Counselor/student ratio (not including college counselor): 1:225. **Counseling:** Each student is assigned a faculty advisor who acts as a personal counselor as well as an academic advisor. The school has a full-time college counselor and social counselor. **Learning disabilities/differences:** "No special programs."

Student Conduct and Health
Code of conduct: "Standard." **How school handles drug/alcohol usage:** Zero tolerance. **Prevention and awareness programs:** Outside speakers.

Summer Programs: None.

Parent Involvement
Parent participation: No required hours. "Parents are invited to participate in the Bentley Parent Association." **Parent/teacher communication:** "Through the dean of students and direct e-mail and phone contact with teacher." Parent/teacher conferences are held three times per year, and grades are given three times per year. **Parent education:** Lecture series. **Donations:** "Families are requested to contribute to the school's Annual Giving Fund and Capital Campaign."

Sports
Students participate in the BCL. Currently the school offers, for girls, tennis, basketball, soccer, crew, volleyball, softball and cross-country, and for boys, tennis, basketball, soccer, crew, and cross-country.

What Sets School Apart From Others
"1) Traditional, core-centered/focused approach to the academic curriculum; 2) Strong emphasis on the development of the students' nonacademic talents; 3) Strong emphasis on the importance of integrity (student 'directed' Honor Code) and a sense of community."

How Parents/Students Characterize School

Parent response(s): "The school is a warm and caring environment that embraces a sense of community and encourages creativity. It is a place that encourages not only a student's academic endeavors, but places equal value on the arts and athletics. The students are very well-rounded." **Student response(s):** "I came to Bentley as a shy, unmotivated student. I am now leaving as a confident and mature student. Bentley's teachers were supportive of me and my interests, and I look forward to going to college on the east coast in the fall." "I've been here for 12 years, and if I could stay here for the rest of my life, I would. Bentley has prepared me to go off and contribute to the world; so I guess I have to leave, but Bentley will always be in my heart and in my soul."

Berean Christian High School

245 El Divisadero Avenue
Walnut Creek, CA 94598
(925) 945-6464 *fax (925) 945-7473*
www.berean-eagles.org

Nelson Noriega, Principal
Mrs. Seana Shafer, Registrar, sshafer@berean-eagles.org

General

Coed Christian day high school. Independent. Founded in 1968. Nonprofit. **Accreditation:** ACSI, WASC. **Enrollment:** Approx. 400. **Average class size:** 22. **School year:** August-May. **School day:** 8:30 a.m.-3 p.m. **Location:** In a residential neighborhood, 25 miles east of San Francisco. Two private buses transport students from the Benicia and Brentwood areas.

Student Body: N/P.

Admission

Applications due: End of February (call for exact date). Applications are available the end of January. **Application fee:** $370. **Application process:** N/P. **No. of freshman applications:** Over 150 for approx. 100 places. **Minimum admission requirements:** Grades, test scores, and references. Each applicant is interviewed by a member of the admission committee. **Test required:** N/P. **Preferences:** N/P. **"We are looking for..."** N/P. **What kind of student do you best serve?** N/P.

Costs

Latest tuition: $8,000. **Sibling discount:** N/P. **Tuition increases:** Approx. 5%. **Other costs:** Approx. $175 for consumables which is included in the registration fees; other fees throughout the year include activity fees, P.E. uniforms and supplies. **Percentage of students receiving financial aid:** 10%. **Financial aid deadline:** May (call for exact date). **Average grant:** N/P. **Percentage of grants of half-tuition or more:** N/P.

School's Mission Statement/Goals
"Berean Christian High School is dedicated to providing a quality, Bible-centered education to develop lifetime followers of Christ."

Academic Program
"Berean Christian High School is a college preparatory and general education high school where the Christian faith is fully integrated into all courses."

Other Indicators the School is Accomplishing its Goals: N/P.

Campus/Campus Life
Campus description: The school has owned its own campus since 1985. The 6.3 acre campus, adjacent to a three acre city park, has five major buildings including 19 classrooms, a library, a practical arts/learning center, a "state-of-the-art" gymnasium, and a student center. **Library:** "Yes." **Sports facilities:** In 2007, the school installed an athletic field that is used for football, soccer and lacrosse games and is surrounded by a practice track. "**Theater/arts facilities:** N/P. **Open/closed campus:** N/P. **Lunches:** N/P. **Bus service:** N/P. **Uniforms/dress code:** N/P. **Co-curricular activities/clubs:** N/P. **Foreign exchange programs/internships:** N/P. **Community service:** N/P. **Typical freshman schedule:** N/P.

Student Support Services/Student Conduct and Health/Summer Programs/Parent Involvement
N/P.

Sports
"Over two-thirds of students participate in at least one season of after-school sports. Students compete in the Diablo Valley Athletic League. Boys compete in soccer, cross-country, basketball, baseball, volleyball, tennis, lacrosse, track, golf and swimming; girls compete in volleyball, cross-country, tennis, basketball, soccer, swimming, track, and softball. The football team participates in the Bay Football League."

What Sets School Apart From Others /How Parents/Students Characterize School: N/P.

Bishop O'Dowd High School

9500 Stearns Avenue
Oakland, CA 94605
(510) 577-9100 *fax (510) 638-3259*
www.bishopodowd.org

Joseph G. Salamack III, M.A., M.S., Principal
Tyler Kreitz, Admissions Director, tkreitz@bishopodowd.org

General

Coed day high school. Catholic (approx. 60% Catholic). Founded in
1951. Nonprofit. **Enrollment:** 1,180. **Average class size:** 25. **Accreditation:** WASC, WCEA, Blue Ribbon School. **School year:** Aug.-June.
School day: 8:30 a.m.-3 p.m. **Location:** In the Oakland hills off I-580,
near Golf Links/98th Ave. exits. Accessible by BART and AC Transit.

Student Body

Geographic breakdown (counties): Alameda, Contra Costa, San
Francisco. **Ethnicity:** 45% Euro-American; 18% African American; 7%
Asian; 10% Latino; 5% Pacific Islander and 15% multi-ethnic. **International students: (I-20 status):** N/P. **Middle schools (freshman):** Approx.
46% from Catholic schools, 33% from private/independent schools and
23% from public/charter schools. Eighty public and private elementary
and middle schools represented.

Admission

Applications due: December (call for date) **Application fee:** $90.
Application process: Applicants and parent/guardian submit an online application and recommendations from the applicant's previous
school. Applicant provides an essay, demonstrates commitment to the
goals and objectives of faith-based education, and provides recommendation of minister of religion. Tours of the school for students
are available in October and November. An open house for students
and parents is held in November. **No. of freshman applications:** 600+
(N/P # places). **Minimum admission requirements:** A combination of
strong grades, HSPT scores, recommendations and personal essays.
Entering freshmen's mean score on the entrance exam was in the 80th
percentile, with nearly 55% in the top quartile. **Test required:** HSPT.
Preferences: "Students are selected on the basis of academic potential
with preference given to students continuing their Catholic education." "**We are looking for** students with high academic and moral
standards." **What kind of student do you best serve?** "Consistent with
our mission statement, we promote honesty and integrity in scholarship while maintaining high standards. The school community fosters
an environment in which students are expected to take responsibility
for their learning."

Costs

Latest tuition: $12,700. **Sibling discount:** N/P. **Tuition increases:** N/P. **Other costs:** $900 registration fee plus wardrobe and books ($ N/P). $2,100 laptop fee (one time). **Percentage of students receiving financial aid:** 20%. **Financial aid deadline:** Call for date. **Average grant:** N/P. **Percentage of grants half-tuition or more:** N/P.

School's Mission Statement/Goals

"Bishop O'Dowd High School is a Catholic, coeducational, college preparatory high school administered by the Diocese of Oakland. The school affirms the teachings, moral values, and ethical standards of the Catholic Church. It is a unique and diverse community. The faculty and administration strive to develop young men and women of competence, conscience, and compassion through an integrated academic, spiritual, and extra-curricular program. Bishop O'Dowd High School seeks to develop persons of influence who are loving, open to growth, religious, intellectually competent, and skilled leaders committed to justice and peace."

Academic Program

"Bishop O'Dowd utilizes a two-semester per year, seven courses per semester block schedule, in which students attend three classes on a Black Day and four on a Gold Day. Each class is 85 minutes in length. Students have a study hall option in the Black schedule's 55-minute Meeting Period (MP). MPs are used for club meetings, counseling sessions, tutoring, make-up work, and study halls. Graduates meet the California state requirements for successful completion of secondary schools. The standards of curriculum are the product of the University of California's recommendation for enrollment in its programs and the school's ESLRs (Expected Schoolwide Learning Results). (See website for further explanation of ESLR)." **Courses offered** (AP= Advanced Placement, H= Honors, (AP)=AP option, (H)=Honors option): The core requirements include religion, English, social studies, science, math, computer science, world language, fine arts, health and P.E. Students are encouraged to broaden their educational program through electives. AP courses are offered in art, English literature, U.S. history, American and comparative government, French, Spanish, biology, environmental science, calculus, computer science, statistics and psychology. Art offerings include drawing, design, and ceramics. Music includes beginning music, symphonic, jazz and concert band, and string orchestra. Drama classes are offered, and three stage productions are performed a year. **Computer/lab training:** N/P. **Grading:** N/P. **Graduation requirements:** "UC admission requirements." **Average nightly homework (M-Th):** N/P. **Faculty:** N/P #, gender; 54% have master's degrees, 3% have doctorates. **Faculty ethnicity:** "65% are Catholic; 81% European-American; 8% Hispanic; 6% African-American; and 5% Asian/Pacific Islander." **Faculty selection/training:** N/P. **Teacher/student ratio:** N/P. **Percentage of students enrolled in AP:**

N/P; pass rate 67%; **Senior class profile (mean):** N/P. **National Merit Scholarship Program:** 7 Finalists, 15 Commended Students, National Achievement Program (for Outstanding African-American Students). **College enrollment (last class):** 98%; 93% in 4-year; 5% in 2-year. "Typically about 33% choose a UC school; 40% attend Catholic, private, or other religious universities; 22% enroll in the CSU system and 5% take advantage of our excellent junior college system." **Recent (last 3 yrs) colleges:** Academy of Art U, American U, Arizona SU, Barnard, Bennington, Boston C, Boston U, Bowdoin, Brown, Bucknell, Cal Lutheran, CCA, all CSU campuses, all UC campuses, Carleton, Columbia, Cornell C, Cornell U, Dartmouth, DePaul, Dickenson, Dillard, Dominican U. Emerson, Emory, Evergreen SC, Fordham U, Franklin Marshall, George Washington, Georgetown, Gonzaga, Goucher, Grambling, Grinnell, Hamilton, Harvard, Hawaii Pacific, Hofstra, Holy Cross, Holy Names, Howard, Ithaca C, John Carroll U, Johns Hopkins, Kalamazoo C, Langston U, Middlebury, Mills, MIT, Montana SU, Mount Holyoke, New Mexico SU, New Mexico Tech, Northeastern U, Notre Dame de Namur, Northwestern, NYU, Oberlin, Occidental, Oregon SU, Pacific U, Pepperdine, Pitzer, Pomona, Portland SU, Purdue, Rutgers, St. Andrew's, St. John's, St. Martin's U, St. Mary's (CA), Santa Clara, Sarah Lawrence, Scripps, Seattle U, Skidmore, Smith, SMU, Stanford, Syracuse, Trinity, Tufts, U-Colorado at Boulder, U-Hawaii, UNC, U-Notre Dame, U-Oregon, U-Pittsburgh, U-Redlands, USD, USF, USC, U-Chicago, U-the Pacific, U-Utah, U-Vermont, U-Washington, Utah SU, Vanderbilt, Vassar, Villanova, Wheaton, Whitman, Whittier C, Willamette U, Wooster, and Xavier.

Other Indicators the School is Accomplishing its Goals
"The 1,175 students at Bishop O'Dowd are expected to extend themselves to reach their academic, social, and spiritual potential while contributing to a just, peaceful, and spiritually-wise society. For some this challenge is met in our Advanced, Honor's and AP classes. Our Honors Level Curriculum is designed to stimulate highly motivated students to go beyond the traditional college preparatory curriculum. Students who need help in one or more subjects receive tutorial assistance from our teachers in our highly touted 'Dragon Success' program. The school prides itself in its advanced technology, wireless campus and integrated use of laptops within the curricula."

Campus/Campus Life
Campus description: The campus is located on a hillside overlooking the San Francisco Bay. In 1991, the science labs were updated as the school was made accessible to the physically challenged with the addition of an elevator. A two-story, 10-classroom addition was built in 1993. A performing arts center has opened recently. The school's academic facilities include a science lab, Apple and IBM computer labs, wireless foreign language lab and a counseling center. **Library:** The school's library has online access and computer workroom. (N/P

hours, etc.) **Sports facilities:** Two gymnasiums and related sports facilities with new synthetic playing field and track. **Theater/arts facilities:** Drama, music and art rooms; "state-of-the-art" performing arts theater. **Open/closed campus:** Closed. **Lunches:** Caféteria on campus. **Bus service:** A/C transit specific line running from Rockridge through Montclair. Private bus running from Alameda to campus via San Leandro BART station. **Uniforms/dress code:** Students wear the Bishop O'Dowd polo shirt; they may wear jeans, khakis or dress slacks. **Co-curricular activities/clubs:** Over 50 clubs that recognize and encourage diversity, service, activity, scholarship and varied interests. Service clubs include California Scholarship Federation, Campus Ministry Leadership, Crozier (newspaper), Junior Statesmen of America (debate), Mitre (yearbook), and Student Government clubs. **Foreign exchange programs/internships:** N/P. **Community service:** "Four year service learning program." **Typical freshman schedule:** 2 semesters of math, English, geo-history, foreign language or freshmen reading, fine arts (art, music, drama); 1 semester of Hebrew scriptures, Christian sexuality, P.E. and 1 semester computer lab, keyboarding, and directed study.

Student Support Services
Counselor/student ratio (including college counselors): 1:233. **Counseling:** The counseling department is staffed by six counselors to assist students in academic, college and personal counseling in addition to the pivotal academic support programs, test prep workshops, free tutoring and extended library hours on campus. **Learning differences/disabilities:** A Director of Learning Needs works with students, teachers, and parents to assist those with learning differences and cognitive and emotional problems.

Student Conduct and Health
Code of conduct: "A basic goal of Bishop O'Dowd High School is that students learn to base human relations on Christian principles of justice, service and love. The highest priority is given to the students' spiritual, moral, intellectual and physical development. They are expected to accept responsibility to grow in character, to respond to advice and suggestions, and to learn to accept school rules as expressions of mutual freedoms and responsibilities. It is the duty of the students, parents/guardians and school to create a climate characterized by mutual respect, personal integrity, pride in one's work and achievement. Through regulatory action and disciplinary policies, students are educated to appreciate the importance of developing responsibility and self control." **How school handles drugs/alcohol:** N/P. **Prevention and awareness programs:** N/P.

Summer Programs
Summer school, sports camps, AIM High Youth Mentoring.

Parent Involvement
Parent participation: Active parent body and Parents' Association that helps the school in fundraising and other volunteerism. **Parent/teacher communication:** N/P. **Parent education:** N/P. **Donations:** N/P.

Sports
Sixteen sports with over 700 athletes participating on 55 teams. Member of Hayward Area Athletic League (See website for most recent titles won).

What Sets School Apart From Others
"O'Dowd High School is a Christian community. The community is composed of students, parents/guardians, faculty, staff, alumni and friends. The school seeks to assist parents/guardians in their education responsibility by offering a challenging college preparatory curriculum in a Christian environment. Through the curriculum, 100 hours of volunteer work and a well-rounded program of activities, Bishop O'Dowd strives to promote the discovery of the historical past and encourage critical interpretation of real world experience while fostering the awareness of individual responsibility as a God-centered citizen. Bishop O'Dowd High School strives to strengthen and develop in each student a sense of responsibility by encouraging self-discipline, respect for the rights of others, and service to the larger community. The vision is for its students to each accept the challenge of the future and live a meaningful life."

How Parents/Students Characterize School
Parent response(s): "O'Dowd does an outstanding job of ensuring that its students take responsibility for their own actions. My son has grown in many ways and is leaving this school well-prepared for college and for being a contributing member of society." **Student response(s):** "Sports at O'Dowd are important. The school spirit is uncanny." "I will miss O'Dowd. I have enjoyed many friendships both with my teachers and classmates. What I have learned the most is who I am and who I have become. I will always be grateful."

The Branson School
P.O. Box 887
Ross, CA 94957
(415) 454-3612 *fax (415) 454-4669*
www.branson.org

Thomas "Woody" Price, Head of School
Phil Gutierrez, Director of Admission, phil_gutierrez@branson.org
Lisa Neumaier, Assoc. Dir. of Admission, lisa_neumaier@branson.org

General

Coed day high school. Independent. Founded in 1916. Nonprofit, member CAIS, NAIS, NACAC, NASSP, POCIS, ERB, SSATB, ABC, BAAD, CASE, Making Waves, and the College Board. **Enrollment:** 320. **Average class size:** 16. **Accreditation:** WASC/CAIS. **School year:** Aug.-June. **School day:** 8 a.m-3 p.m. **Location:** In the town of Ross, 15 miles north of San Francisco. Accessible by public transportation.

Student Body

Geographic breakdown (counties): 11% from San Francisco; 82% from Marin; 2% from Alameda; 4% from Contra Costa; .03% from Sonoma County; .03% from Solano County. **Ethnicity:** 79% Caucasian (non-Latino); 7% Asian; 3% Latino; 7% African-American; .02% Middle-Eastern; .009% Native-American; .006% East Indian. **International students (I-20 status):** 0. **Middle schools (freshman):** 39% (29 students) came from 6 public middle schools; 61% (46 students) from 16 private or parochial schools.

Admission

Applications due: January (call for exact date). **Application fee:** $100. **Application process:** Inquiries should be made when the student is in the 8th grade and includes scheduling a mandatory campus tour. The school hosts open houses in October and December and invites prospective students to a number of other admission-related events during the admission season, including Fine Arts Night, fall and spring dramatic performances, athletic events, Winter Concert, etc. Notifications are mailed mid-March. **No. of freshman applications:** Approx. 400 (N/P # places). **Minimum admission requirements:** "The school considers each candidate individually and fairly. There are no specific high or low test scores or grades that automatically assure or deny entrance; there are no automatic cutoff points." **Test required:** SSAT or ISEE from an applicant's 8th grade year or STAR results from an applicant's 7th grade year. **Preferences:** "We are looking for students who are highly academically motivated, who can benefit from The Branson School program and can contribute to the community, who can be successful in academic and extracurricular activities, and who have a serious desire to attend the school." **What kind of student do you best serve?** "Students who are passionate about learning; solid academic students who are bright and ready for a rigorous academic program; students who have pursued outside interests (i.e., sports, fine arts, community service, etc.)."

Costs

Latest tuition: $31,315 payable in 1 or 2 payments (June and January or through a 10-month payment plan available through outside agency). Credit cards are also accepted. **Sibling discount:** None. **Tuition increases:** Approx. 5%. **Other costs:** Approx. $1,000 for books and incidental expenses; $1,000 fee for lunch program. **Percentage of**

students receiving financial aid: 17%. **Financial aid deadline:** January (call for exact date). **Average grant:** $21,000. **Percentage of grants of half-tuition or more:** 82%.

School's Mission Statement/Goals

"The Branson School inspires excellence in a nurturing, vibrant educational community based on personal and intellectual integrity. At the heart of Branson is a trusting, dynamic relationship between dedicated teachers and students. Through the vitality, breadth, and rigor of its programs, Branson encourages students to think critically, communicate clearly, develop their individual talents and interests, and pursue a lifelong passion for learning. Branson believes that diversity of people and thought enriches us all and promotes responsible leadership in the global community."

Academic Program

Courses offered (AP=Advanced Placement, H=Honors (AP)=AP option, (H)=Honors option): **English:** English I-II, American Literature I-IV H, American Literature V: The Composing Process, African American Literature I-III H, British Literature I-V H, World Literature I-III H, Language & Composition AP; **Arts:** Beginning Acting, Intermediate Acting, Advanced Acting, Acting Performance Honors, Dance I-IV, Dance Performance Ensemble, Chorus, Chamber Singers, Music And Performance, Performance Seminar: Jazz, Performance Seminar: Classical, Photography: Beginning, Intermediate, Advanced, Drawing & Painting: Beginning, Intermediate, Advanced, Ceramics: Beginning, Intermediate, Advanced, Art History (AP), Digital Media I & II; **Math:** Algebra I, Algebra/Geometry, Geometry, Geometry/Algebra II, Algebra II, Pre-Calculus (H), Statistics AP, Calculus AB AP, Calculus BC AP, Economics; **History:** Roots of Civilization, U.S. History (AP), Modern World History (AP), Senior Seminar: Issues in American Govt., Senior Seminar: The Modern Middle East, Senior Seminar: Pre-Modern China, Senior Seminar: Renaissance/Reformation, Senior Seminar: Cuban History, Senior Seminar: The Good Life: An Introduction to Ethics, Senior Seminar: Modern Africa, Senior Seminar: History of Modern China, Senior Seminar: The History of American Labor, Senior Seminar: Comparative Eastern Religions, Senior Seminar: Golden Ages, Senior Seminar: The History of the Balkans, Senior Seminar: Screening Modern China, Senior Seminar: Survey of African-American Studies; **Science:** Environmental Science, Biology, Marine Biology, Chemistry (H/AP), Physics, Physics C AP, Biotechnology, Comparative Anatomy & Physiology, Advanced Environmental Studies; **Languages:** French I-III Honors, French IV (AP), French V Honors (French Literature), Spanish I-III Honors, Spanish IV (AP), Spanish VI, Italian I-III, Italian IV AP, Latin I-III, Latin IV AP, Mandarin. **Non-departmental courses:** Health & Wellness for all freshmen and Choices & Challenges for all sophomores. **Other:** Branson offers a senior internship, which allows seniors to pursue intensive work in an area of their own personal interest during the last month of school. **Computer lab/training:** The school has a computer lab with 20 Mac computers, as well as a number of computers in the library and in the writing center. Wireless access is also available. **Grading:** A-F. Teachers write progress reports twice a year, or more often for students experiencing difficulty. **Graduation requirements:** 4 years English, 3 years math, 3 years lab science, 3 years of one foreign language or 2 years of two different foreign languages, 3 years history, 2 years fine arts, yearly community service. Each student must be enrolled in at least 5 academic solids each trimester, including fine arts. **Average nightly homework (M-Th):** G9: 1.5 hours; G10: 2.5 hours; G11-12: 2.5 to 3-4. **Faculty:** 41 f/t, 11 p/t; 50% men, 50% women; 44% master's degrees, 1% doctorates. **Faculty ethnicity:** "13.5% are teachers of color." (N/P ethnicities) **Faculty selection/training:** "The Academic Dean begins the process with a telephone interview. Promising candidates visit the campus, preferably teach a class and are interviewed by faculty and administrators." **Teacher/student ratio:** 1:8. **Percentage of students enrolled in AP:** 97%; pass rate 76%. **Senior class profile (mean):** SAT Math 664, SAT Critical Reading 646, SAT Writing 671; GPA: "Branson does not publish class rankings or GPA's." **National Merit Scholarship Program:** "Out of 75 students, 2 students in the [last class] were National Merit Semi-Finalists, and 1 student was awarded as a Finalist. One student was awarded as a National Achievement Scholar, and one student was awarded as a National Hispanic Achievement Scholar." **College enrollment (last class):** 100% in 4-year. **Recent (last 3 yrs) colleges:** Amherst, Barnard, Bates, Bentley, Boston C, Boston U, Bowdoin, Brown, Bucknell, Cal Poly-SLO, Carleton, Chapman, Claremont McKenna, Colgate, Colorado C, Cornell, Dartmouth, Davidson, Duke, Emory, Georgetown, Grinnell, Harvard, Haverford, Hobart William Smith (NY), Johns Hopkins, Kalamazoo, Kenyon, Lafayette, Lehigh, Lewis & Clark, Loyola Marymount, Middlebury, NYU, Northwestern, Notre Dame, Oberlin, Occidental, Penn, Pepperdine, Princeton, U-Redlands, Reed, RISD, St. Andrew's (Scotland), Santa Clara, Scripps, Skidmore, SMU, Stanford, Swarthmore, Trinity C, Tufts, UC (Berkeley, Davis, LA, SD, Santa Barbara, Santa Cruz), U-Chicago, U-Colorado-Boulder, U-Denver, U-Edinburgh, U-Miami, U-Michigan (Ann Arbor), U-Oregon, U-Puget Sound, U-Richmond, USC, USD, USF, UVA, Vanderbilt, Vassar, Villanova, U-Washington, Washington & Lee, Washington U (St. Louis), Wesleyan, Whitman, William & Mary, and Yale.

Other Indicators the School is Accomplishing its Goals

"Students remain in contact with Branson teachers long after they have graduated. They continue to be competitive and excel in colleges and universities, and in their chosen professions across the globe. "

Campus/Campus Life

Campus description: The school is located on the site of a former dairy farm in Ross, a town 15 miles north of San Francisco. The 17-acre campus includes 31 classrooms, a gymnasium complex, a playing field, art gallery, tennis courts, and an auditorium and theater. **Library:** 12,000-volume collection and "state-of-the-art research facilities." **Sports facilities:** Athletic Center with fitness room and two gymnasiums. Teams use the College of Marin's athletic facilities for most sports programs, including its swimming pools and athletic fields. **Theater/arts facilities:** Art gallery, music studios, dance studio, auditorium/theater, outside amphitheater, Little Theater, digital photography lab, ceramics studio. **Open/closed campus:** Closed. **Lunches:** All students participate in the student lunch program. **Bus service:** Available from the East Bay and San Francisco. **Uniforms/dress code:** All students are expected to be well dressed and well groomed whenever they are at school. Students should also not have any torn or ragged clothing or clothing with inappropriate slogans. **Co-curricular activities/clubs:** "See school website for the most updated clubs list as they change as often as a student has an idea for a new club." **Foreign exchange programs/internships:** "There are no specific organized programs. However, students have been supported and encouraged to pursue such options. Students in the past have studied in Mexico, China, England, and at the Oxbow Program in Napa, CA." **Community service:** "See school website for current opportunities." **Typical freshman schedule:** Introduction to Western Tradition and British Literature, Roots of Civilization, Algebra I or Algebra/Geometry, Environmental Science or Biology, foreign language (French, Spanish, or Latin), Fine Arts, Health & Wellness.

Student Support Services

Counselor/student ratio (not including college counselors): 1:320. **Counseling:** A part-time licensed therapist is available to counsel students. College counseling begins the sophomore year with students taking the PSAT and SAT II; in junior year, students take the PSAT in October, and meet with the college counselor in groups and individually. The College Counseling office consists of a full-time Director of College Counseling, full-time College Counselor, and a College Counseling Assistant. College representatives visit the school in the fall, and families attend informational meetings and meet with the college counselor. Seniors meet with college representatives, and take the SATs; families and/or students meet the counselor to prepare applications. **Learning differences/disabilities:** The Allen Rand Center was established by a Branson family to serve as an on-campus resource for students. Staffed by a trained learning specialist, the Rand Center is a quiet study area, a place for small group study sessions, and one-on-one tutorials and extended time testing.

Student Conduct and Health

Code of conduct: "The Branson School places a high value on ethical standards and outlines its expectations in the Student Handbook. Matters of academic integrity are governed by the Honor Code. All students, upon admission to Branson, are required to sign a written pledge to abide by this code. Infractions of the Honor Code are heard before the Honor Council – an elected panel of eight students and two faculty members. The Honor Council suggests effective disciplinary measures to the Head of School." **How school handles drugs/alcohol:** "The school enforces a drugs and alcohol policy which states that dealing, use, possession, being under the influence of drugs and alcohol, and possession of drug paraphernalia shall result in immediate removal from The Branson School. The policy applies when the offense occurs while a student is on school grounds, going to or coming from school, during the lunch periods whether on or off campus, and during or while going to or coming from a school activity. This policy also applies during the hours of the regular school day if a student has cut class and is off campus." **Prevention and awareness programs:** "Awareness Committee on Drugs and Alcohol (ACODA) sponsors speakers, provides a discussion forum, and promotes the drug and alcohol policy of the school. Branson is a member of the Northern California Community of Concern. The school's Parent Education Committee responds to topical interests with workshops and speakers in these areas as well."

Summer Programs

The school has a four-week summer session for students aged 8-15, which includes classes and sports camps.

Parent Involvement

Parent participation: All parents are members of the school's Parent Association and are invited to attend monthly PA meetings. **Parent/teacher communication:** Grade reports are sent home six times a year. Two of these reports contain extensive narrative comments by individual teachers. In addition, parents are encouraged to communicate with teachers, class deans and/or faculty mentor advisors with any concerns. **Parent education:** The freshmen and sophomore class deans invite parents to an evening conversation at the beginning of the school year to address issues and concerns specific to those grade levels. All parents are also invited to school arranged speaker series evenings. Finally, the Parents' Association invites faculty, administration and outside speakers to present information on topics of interest to the school community. **Donations:** "Parents contribute both financially and through their volunteer efforts."

Sports

The school is a member of the MCAL, and more than 80% of the student body participates in one or more sports. The school has more than 25 interscholastic teams in 18 sports for boys and girls including: soccer, tennis, cross-country, swimming, golf, sailing, track, and basketball; for girls, softball and volleyball; and for boys, baseball and lacrosse. Fencing and mountain biking are offered as club sports.

What Sets School Apart From Others:

"The Branson School dedicates itself to the full development of the individual student in preparation for the challenges of higher education and life. The school promotes enduring habits of intellectual curiosity, appreciation of the arts, physical fitness, and respect for self and others. Integrity, honesty, and the development of moral and ethical principles are emphasized as a framework for responsible behavior at Branson and beyond. Habits of inquiry, independent thinking, and imagination are fostered through a rich and rigorous curriculum. The essence of Branson is a deep respect for every individual, regardless of cultural, racial, and philosophical differences. The goal is for students to leave Branson strong in character, well prepared for further education, determined to fully develop their own gifts, and ready to share those gifts generously with the wider community. • At Branson, we feel it is essential not merely to prepare students for college but to encourage them to become responsible, active citizens. Hence, students are required to participate in both school and community service programs. The lessons our students learn through their community service work complement those learned in the classroom and allow students to feel they can make a meaningful, positive difference in the larger world. Through community service, students learn to exercise leadership, work cooperatively, broaden their own understanding, and deepen their respect for others, regardless of their circumstances.• At the core of the Branson experience is the Honor Code. In joining the Branson intellectual community, each student agrees to live by clear ethical rules of conduct. The Honor Council, an elected group of students and faculty members, promotes and maintains the school's commitment to the Honor Code. The Code values hard work and accomplishment, respect for others' ideas and belongings, and ethical behavior on campus. The social contract undertaken by the student body not only creates a sense of pride and safety but an underlying key to effective learning and growth."

How Parents/Students Characterize School:

Parent(s) responses: "I think Branson prepares students for not only college, which is obviously part of the objective, but they prepare them for life. I think our children came out of here much, much better people than when they came in." "I think because the student has an incredibly personal experience with the teachers – and I don't think you can find it anywhere else – that student/teacher relationship is the best." **Student response(s):** " . . . it lets you become your own person. I am who I am partly because I've come through Branson." "The campus is gorgeous. Walking around campus in the mornings when no one else is here or at night when I come back to pick up my backpack—it's just beautiful. It makes me smile every time I see it."

Cardinal Newman High School

50 Ursuline Road
Santa Rosa, CA 95403
(707) 546-6470 *fax (707) 544-8502*
www.cardinalnewman.org

Michael Truesdell, President
Janie Orthey Rockett, Admissions Dir., rockett@cardinalnewman.org.

General

Boys Catholic day high school. (N/P % Catholic) Archdiocese of Santa Rosa. Founded in 1964. Nonprofit (N/P memberships). **Enrollment:** Approx. 430. **Average class size:** 24. **Accreditation:** WCEA/WASC. **School year:** 9-mo. calendar. **School day:** 7:55 a.m.-2:25 p.m. **Location:** In Santa Rosa off of Old Redwood Highway on Ursuline Road.

Student Body

Geographic breakdown (counties): Approx. 98% from Sonoma; 2% Napa. **Ethnicity:** N/P. **International students (I-20 status):** N/P. **Middle schools (freshman):** N/P.

Admission

Applications due: First week in January. **Application fee:** $100 for G9 and $120 after deadline. **Application process:** Tours of the school for parents and students are given throughout the year. A Student Visitation Day is held in October for 8th graders and two annual open houses are held on a Sunday in October and in February. During the school year, interested students may spend a day at the school shadowing a current student. Applications are due the first week in January, and placement examinations are administered beginning in December and held once a month through May. Decisions are mailed the first week in March. **No. of freshman applications:** N/P. **Minimum admission requirements:** N/P. **Test required:** HSPT. **Preferences:** None. "**We are looking for** students seeking college and university entrance. The comprehensive curriculum is tailored to meet the diverse needs and educational objectives of all students. The overall development of the student is balanced through his involvement in diverse cultural and physical extracurricular activities, student government, and the provision of comprehensive counseling and disciplinary programs." "**What kind of student do you best serve?**" (See prior statement).

Costs

Latest tuition: $11,100. **Sibling discount:** N/P. **Tuition increases:** Approx. 3%. **Other costs:** $425 registration; approx. $350 for books;other fees include athletic fees and miscellaneous class fees. **Percentage of students receiving financial aid:** N/P. **Financial aid deadline:** First week in January. **Average grant:** N/P. **Percentage of grants of half-tuition or more:** N/P.

School's Mission Statement/Goals

"Cardinal Newman is a Catholic, college preparatory high school for young men. Our mission is to educate our students in the wholeness of mind, body, and spirit through the teachings of Jesus Christ. Our students learn to apply leadership skills and talents in service to others. We challenge each student to work to his highest potential in the lifelong pursuit of learning and excellence." "God shall call on me and I will hear the Lord." — John Henry Cardinal Newman 1801-1890

Academic Program

"The college-prep curriculum is designed to fulfill the UC and CSU systems' entrance requirements." **Courses offered**: (AP=Advanced Placement, (AP)=AP option, (H)=Honors or Honors option): Seven AP courses and 6 Honors courses are offered to Juniors and Seniors. AP **Courses offered**: Biology, Calculus, English, Latin, Physics, Spanish, U.S. History. Honors courses offered: Algebra II, Chemistry, English 11, Spanish III, Trigonometry/Pre-Calculus. **Grading:** N/P. **Graduation requirements:** N/P. **Average nightly homework (M-Th):** N/P. **Faculty:** 35 faculty; (N/P gender); 20 master's degrees. **Faculty ethnicity:** N/P. **Faculty selection/training:** N/P. **Teacher/student ratio:** 1:12. **Percentage of students enrolled in AP:** N/P. **Senior class profile (mean):** N/P. **National Merit Scholarship Program:** N/P. **College enrollment (last class):** 90% in 4-year, 3% in 2-year. **Recent (last 3 yrs) colleges:** Northwestern, Yale, UC (Berkeley, LA, SD, Santa Cruz, Merced), Santa Clara, Miami U-Ohio, Pepperdine, U-Illinois, U-Washington, CSU (Fullerton, Cal Poly-SLO, Chico, Bakersfield, Humboldt, Sacramento, SD, SF, SJ, Sonoma), Santa Rosa JC, U-Oregon, Linfield C, Loyola U-Chicago, U-Colorado, Mesa CC, Ft. Lewis C, U-Maryland, UOP, Hartnell C, USD, USF, Montana SU, Loyola Marymount U, Diablo Valley C, Simpson U, Cal Lutheran U, SD City C, and Dominican U.

Campus/Campus Life

Campus description: N/P. **Library:** "Yes." **Sports facilities:** Football field, tennis courts, soccer fields, baseball field, and track. **Theater/arts facilities:** N/P. **Open/closed campus:** N/P. **Bus service:** N/P. **Uniforms/dress code:** Dress code. **Co-curricular activities/clubs:** N/P. **Foreign exchange programs/internships:** N/P. **Community service:** "It is the goal of Cardinal Newman to challenge our students to create and support positive social change in the communities where they live and work. This can best be accomplished by meaningful service in the community, tied to the skills and interests that the students have to offer. Students are required to complete a total of 25 community service hours per year, culminating in a senior service project." **Typical freshman schedule:** English 9, math, theology, foreign language, P.E. 9, Biology or Computers/Health, elective (art, music, Public Speaking).

Student Support Services

Counselor/student ratio: N/P. **Counseling:** "To help achieve Cardinal Newman's goal of educating the whole person, a counseling program is provided for all students. Information on such topics as academic progress and potential (including performance in classes), appropriate career options in keeping with a student's goals and talents, process of making college application and obtaining financial aid for college, is available. Students and parents are encouraged to discuss any of these areas with a member of the counseling department. Substance abuse information is provided, and different support groups are organized as need arises. Cardinal Newman has three types of counseling available for students: 1) Spiritual guidance and counseling; 2) Academic/College counseling; 3) Personal counseling and services for students with special needs. In addition, the school offers academic support services. Cardinal Newman takes great pride in the academic success of our students. To achieve the optimum performance from each, and every, student requires personal motivation, parental involvement, and ongoing support and direction from the school." **Learning differences/disabilities:** "If need should surface, a licensed personal counselor is available to make evaluation and or referral to an outside agency. The academic support system at CNHS begins at the Admissions Placement Interview and continues through graduation and college enrollment. Academic support includes the following programs: Admissions Placement Interview; Frosh Summer School; Frosh Counseling Program; Class Level Student Review Meetings; Teacher Tutorial Meetings & Appointments; Academic Probation Progress Reports; Sophomore Planning Meetings; Summer Academic Review & Counseling; and Junior/Senior Graduation Status review."

Student Conduct and Health

Code of conduct: "Students are expected to act in a way that will show consideration and respect for fellow students, faculty, staff and visitors. They should strive to create a positive and harmonious atmosphere within the school community, and be a favorable reflection on Cardinal Newman High School. This may be accomplished when students recognize their responsibilities and obligations in the school's life." **How school handles drugs/alcohol:** "Substance abuse — the use, possession, or sale of tobacco, alcohol, or illegal drugs, or paraphernalia associated with their use on or near the school campus or at any school-sponsored activities will be treated with zero tolerance. Students who are in the company of students who are in possession or who are using tobacco, alcohol or drugs will also be subject to disciplinary action. Drug testing may be required for any student violating the Substance Abuse Policy." **Prevention and awareness programs:** "Schools are partners with parents and students in prevention of student alcohol, drug and tobacco use. Cardinal Newman High School shall undertake: 1) Prevention curriculum at each grade level; 2) Annual in-service training on substance abuse prevention; 3) Annual parent education program(s); 4) Dissemination of the Policy and related procedures to students, parents and staff; 5) Individual, small group and peer helping programs, and/or referral to community; 6) Development of alternatives to alcohol and other drug use by supporting extracurricular programs and activities."

Summer Programs: Summer school and summer athletic camps.

Parent Involvement

Parent participation: Parent participation is not required, but most parents choose to volunteer for one or more events throughout the year. **Parent/teacher communication:** Formal report cards throughout the year and ongoing communication among parents, teachers and counselors during the school year. Faculty web pages are available for tracking of grades and assignments. **Parent education:** N/P. **Donations:** N/P.

Sports

Football, cross-country, water polo, swimming, wrestling, basketball, golf, tennis, track and field, rugby, lacrosse and baseball.

What Sets School Apart From Others

"The Cardinal Newman High School community has committed itself to the principles of Christian education and the pursuit of educational excellence. In emphasizing the teachings of Christ, the faculty, staff, students and parents strive to work together to establish a living Christian community. • Cardinal Newman recognizes that the primary responsibility for the spiritual, moral, intellectual, physical and social development of the student belongs to the family. We serve to facilitate and supplement the family in this vital task. • It is the firm belief of the Cardinal Newman community that quality education is best realized, and future leaders nurtured, in a caring, Christian environment. We encourage students to develop and enhance their creative and critical thinking abilities. Our results include an increased embrace of moral values and social responsibility. • As a Catholic school, Cardinal Newman strives to imbue Christian values through the study of the Bible and the teachings of the Church. In our effort to help students understand Christ's teachings and form similar values, our campus ministry program provides experiences in prayer, liturgy, retreats, and community service. Our students, parents, and faculty have opportunities to share in worship and to develop Christian awareness. • Cardinal Newman offers a college preparatory curriculum for those students seeking college and university entrance. The comprehensive curriculum is also tailored to meet the diverse needs and educational objectives of all students. The overall development of the student is balanced through his involvement in diverse cultural and physical extracurricular activities, student government, and the provision of comprehensive counseling and disciplinary programs."

How Parents/Students Characterize the School: N/P.

Castilleja School

1310 Bryant Street
Palo Alto, CA 94301
(650) 328-3160 *fax (650) 326-8036*
www.castilleja.org

Joan Lonergan, Head of School
Jill Lee, Director of Admission and Financial Aid

admission@castilleja.org

General

Girls day high school and middle school. Nonsectarian. Independent. Founded in 1907. Nonprofit, member CAIS, NAIS, NCGS, BAIHS, CASE, BAAD, ERB, SSATB, NAPSG. **Enrollment:** 415. **Average class size:** 14. **Accreditation:** WASC/CAIS. **School year:** Sept.-June. **School day:** 8 a.m.-3:15 p.m. **Location:** In Palo Alto, near Stanford University. A public van service transports students between the school and the Palo Alto University Ave. CalTrain station.

Student Body

Geographic breakdown (counties): 2% from San Francisco; majority from San Mateo and Santa Clara. **Ethnicity:** 61% Caucasian (non-Latina); 23% Asian; 8% Latina; 5% African-American; 3% multi-ethnic. **International students (I-20 status):** 1%. **Middle schools (freshman):** 69% from Castilleja middle school. Of new middle school students, 70% were from public schools and 30% from private, non-parochial schools; of new freshmen, 38% were from public schools and 62% from private, non-parochial schools.

Admission

Applications due: January (call for date). **Application fee:** $75. **Application process:** Student and parent questionnaires, teacher recommendations, standardized testing, transcripts, on-campus interviews. Details are provided in the admission packet. **No. of freshman applications:** Four for every place (N/P # places). Castilleja does not admit new students to G12. **Minimum admission requirements:** No absolute cut-off. "Typically admitted students are stellar students, have earned A's and high B's." **Test required:** ISEE or SSAT for high school. **Preferences:** "We value the relationships we have developed with current families, and, to that end, siblings are given special consideration in the admission process. As with all applicants, the sibling candidate must be a strong student and good citizen in order to gain admission to Castilleja." **"We are looking for** self-motivated, enthusiastic learners who will both contribute to and benefit from our community." **What sort of students do you best serve?** "Castilleja students are curious, motivated students who possess a sincere eagerness to learn and an understanding of the advantages of a single-sex educational environment."

Costs
Latest tuition: $29,900 payable in 2 or 10 payments. **Sibling discount:** None. **Tuition increases:** Approx. 6-10%. **Other costs:** Approx. $400-$500 for books, $200 for uniforms. **Percentage of students receiving financial aid:** 16%. **Financial aid deadline:** Call for date. **Average grant:** $21,500. **Percentage of grants of half-tuition or more:** 88%.

School's Mission Statement/Goals
"Castilleja School inspires a quest for knowledge and learning that lasts a lifetime. To prepare our students for the wider world, we infuse our challenging college preparatory curriculum with a global program that fosters awareness, compassion, and engagement with issues beyond Castilleja. Our comprehensive academic program and extensive co-curricular offerings develop in each student the self-confidence to reach her full potential. Above all, our faculty and staff dedicate themselves to excellence in educating young women and in cultivating young leaders."

Academic Program
Courses offered (AP=Advanced Placement, H=Honors, (AP)=AP option, (H)=Honors option): **English:** English I-II, English III Honors, English AP Electives: American Literature since 1900, Asian Literature, British Literature - the Nineteenth Century, British Literature since 1900, Colonialism and Post-Colonialism, Coming of Age, Contemporary World Literature, The Family in Literature, Friends and Lovers, The Literature of Rebellion, Modern European Literature, Poetry, Shakespeare, Tragic Mode, Non-AP Elective: Creative Writing. **Fitness and Wellness:** Fitness and Wellness I-II. **History:** Cultures and Civilizations, The American Political System, The Individual and Society, U. S. History H/AP, African Studies, Economics, European History AP, International Relations, Latin American and Caribbean History, Modern East Asia, Music History (see Arts), Russian History, Women's Rights and the Politics of Gender. **Math:** Algebra I-II, Algebra I H, Coordinate Geometry and Matrices (H), Trigonometry, and Modeling (H), Algebra II, Precalculus with Applications, Introductory Calculus AB H, Introductory Calculus BC H, Calculus AB AP, Calculus BC AP, Statistics AP, Advanced Topics: Mathematical Modeling, Advanced Topics: Probability, Introduction to Engineering. **Languages:** Chinese I-III, French I – Lit/Lang AP and Advanced Seminar, Latin I – Vergil/Lit AP, Spanish I - Lit/Lang AP and Advanced Seminar, Italian Culture and Language. **Science:** Physics (H), Chemistry (H/AP), Biology (H/AP),

Biotechnology and Bioethics, Human Physiology, Introduction to Organic Chemistry and Biochemistry, Physics C AP. **Arts:** Core Arts, Introduction to the Arts, Dance Production Workshop I-II, Chorus I-II, H Choir, Music History, Advanced Theater Arts, Drama I-II, Public Speaking, Advanced Drawing and Painting, Design and Sculpture I-II, Drawing and Painting I-II, Film I-II, Photography I-II, Studio Art AP. **Interdisciplinary:** Contemporary American Culture, Global Issues: Public Health, the Environment, and Economic Data and Policy, Introduction to Philosophy. **Computer lab/training:** Introduction to Computer Programming; Intermediate Programming. **Grading:** N/P. **Graduation requirements:** 4 years English; 3 years math, history and one foreign language; 2 years lab science, and Fitness and Wellness; 3 semesters fine/performing arts; Senior Talk. **Average nightly homework (M-Th):** 3+ hours. **Faculty:** 63; 24% men, 76% women; 82% hold advanced degrees. (N/P degrees). **Faculty selection/training:** "Prospective faculty members are solicited through national search organizations and other school contacts. The interview process involves teaching a sample lesson, campus tour, observing a class, and interviewing with the Academic Dean, Head of School, and the Department Head. All faculty members undergo formal reviews on a regular basis. Castilleja encourages professional growth by making available funding for national conferences, advanced courses, summer stipends, etc. The school also sponsors bi-annual in-service days which consist of a nationally regarded educational expert working with all faculty for a day or attending several seminars at the CAIS conference." **Teacher/ student ratio:** 1:7. **Percentage of students enrolled in AP:** 50%; pass rate 96%. **Senior class profile (mean):** SAT Math 673, SAT Critical Reading 701, SAT Writing 706; GPA: "First 5th 4.24-3.95, Second 5th 3.94-3.72, Third 5th 3.69-3.38, Fourth 5th 3.35-2.97, Fifth 5th 2.94-2.28." **National Merit Scholarship Program:** 13 Commended students, 13 Semifinalists, 1 National Hispanic Scholar. **College enrollment (last class):** [Last 5 years] 100% in 4-year colleges. **Recent (last 3 yrs) colleges:** Amherst, Bennington, Boston U, Bowdoin, Brown, Bucknell, Cal Poly-Pomona, Carleton, Carnegie Mellon, Chapman, Claremont McKenna, Colby, Columbia, Cornell, Dartmouth, DePauw, Duke, Embry Riddle-Daytona Beach, Emory, George Washington, Georgetown, Gonzaga, Goucher, Harvard, Johns Hopkins, Juniata C, McGill, Mercer, Middlebury, Mills, MIT, Northwestern, Notre Dame de Namur, NYU, Oberlin, Penn, Pomona, Princeton, Santa Clara, Scripps, Seattle Pacific, SMU, St. Andrews, Stanford, Swarthmore, Temple, Tufts, UC (Berkeley, Irvine, LA, Merced, SD), UNC-Chapel Hill, U-Chicago, U-Michigan, U-Notre Dame, U-Oregon, U-Rochester, USC, USD, Vanderbilt, Vassar, Villanova, Wellesley, Willamette, and Yale.

Other Indicators the School is Accomplishing its Goals

"Our commitment to providing opportunities for students to do their best work and be their best selves manifests itself not only through our course offerings but also in this environment of small classes and close teacher-student relations. Ours is a real community, where teachers come to know their students as individuals both in the classroom and out. It is an atmosphere that fosters respect for learning and encourages challenges, where students know they will find the support and resources they need for both academic and extracurricular risk-taking."

Campus/Campus Life

Campus description: The Joan Z. Lonergan Fitness and Athletic Center was completed in 2008. The Gunn Family Administration Center and theater renovations were completed in 2002. The campus includes five buildings surrounding a circular courtyard. A former residence hall has been renovated and houses a student center, library, dining facilities, foreign language classrooms, language lab, senior lounge, multimedia and training labs, faculty center, and offices. **Library:** The Library/Media Center includes a 12,000-volume library, electronic databases and study space for students. **Sports facilities:** Deep-water 8-lane pool; gymnasium; regulation size softball field; general field space. **Theater/arts facilities:** The campus has a large theater, dance studio, art gallery, choral room, private music practice rooms, as well as two art studios. **Open/closed campus:** Closed except for senior privileges. **Lunches:** A full lunch and snack program is mandatory and was developed with a nutritionist. **Bus service:** Van service between the school and the Palo Alto University Ave. CalTrain station. **Uniforms/dress code:** White or navy blue collared shirts or Castilleja sweatshirt with uniform light blue skirt or navy blue pants (no jeans or sweat pant material); uniform shorts. Dress white uniform for traditional or formal occasions. **Co-curricular activities/clubs:** AIDS Awareness, American Red Cross Club, Amnesty International, Anime and Manga Club, Arts & Crafts, Asian Student Union, AWA Crafting, Bell Choir, Bead Club, Beechwood Tutors, Black Student Union, Castilleja Arts Project, Castilleja Free Press, Chess Club, Comparative Religions Club, Counterpoint (newspaper), Dance Club, Debate, Elizabeth Seton Tutoring Club, Emergency Medical Response, Environmental Club, Film Club, Feminism Club, Interact International Politics Club, Jazz Club, JSA, Junior Classical League, Kickboxing Club, Kids for Christ, Knitting Club, Latina Student Union, Liberal Activists, Math Club, Millard Fillmore, Mochuelo (literary magazine), Model UN, Paintbrush (yearbook), Passport to the Globe, Peer Advising, Peer Tutoring, Prisms, Physics Club, Puzzle Club, Puppet Club, Rainbow Alliance, Red Key (Admissions), Robotics, Running for a Reason, Scrapbooking, Seton Science, Sirens (Chorus), Ski and Snowboard Club, Society of Competent People (life skills), South Asian Student Union, Snapshot (photo), Speech & Debate, Students Taking Action Now: Darfur, Tech Club, Triathlon Club, Ultimate Frisbee, Yoga, Youth Philanthropy Worldwide. **Foreign exchange programs/internships:** The Global Programs at Castilleja has as its aim to promote global education as a part of every student and faculty member's educational experience. "Global

Investigator" trips to India and China were launched in 2008, allowing every student the opportunity to travel to a developing nation during her junior year. The school has organized exchanges with the Junshin School in Tokyo and is working on expanding such opportunities. The school sponsors trips to various countries, such as Mexico, France, and Canada, for short-term study. A summer internship program is available to sophomores, juniors, and seniors in professional fields such as medicine, technology, small business, journalism, and politics. A workshop is also offered on finding summer jobs and internships and research help. Internship opportunities are also available during the school year. Career speaker events and brown bag lunches with science professionals are held throughout the year. **Community service:** Castilleja does not have hour requirements, though all students, with guidance from advisors and the community service coordinator, involve themselves in community service activities. Castilleja students set personal community service goals, work toward reaching those goals, and each semester, every student writes a reflection about her service goals and activities. Examples of community service opportunities are: Ecumenical Hunger Club, Palo Alto Nursing Home Club, Beechwood Tutoring Club, overseas programs including Amigos de las Americas and Los Niños. **Typical freshman schedule:** Most students take English, physics, history, math, and foreign language (Human Development and P.E. for one semester). Some students take a fine arts class as well as or instead of one of the core academic classes mentioned above. Classes meet for an average of four periods a week for 45-75 minutes each class.

Student Support Services

Counselor/student ratio (not including college counselors): 1:46 (One full-time licensed counselor, a counseling intern, and individual class deans.) **Counseling:** "The school has a part-time licensed clinical social worker available to students for group and individual sessions as well as a part-time counseling intern. All students meet weekly with a faculty advisor in groups of 8-10. Advisors monitor the social and academic progress of their advisees, explain school policies, discuss community issues, assist in course selection, serve as a resource, and provide support. Freshmen have a 12th grade peer advisor who co-facilitates the group. Every grade participates in annual retreats focusing on themes and skills which foster growth and group strength. Castilleja offers an academic counseling program to assist students in the planning of their academic programs—the goal of the entire process is to ensure that the student has a course load that will best meet her needs and the school's demands. Castilleja offers peer tutoring to assist students in academic need as well as to provide leadership opportunities for the student body. Castilleja has a full-time college counselor who maintains a close relationship with each student beginning in her junior year." **Learning differences/disabilities:** "No formal program but will make accommodations for students who need extra time on exams and standardized tests."

Student Conduct and Health

Code of conduct: "Students who commit serious infractions risk 'severe consequences, including the possibility of suspension or expulsion.' Serious infractions include, in addition to illegal activities, dishonesty of any kind, behavior that causes significant physical or emotional harm to others in the school community (e.g., harassment), and 'behavior at or away from school that seriously violates the school's philosophy or negatively reflects upon the character of the school.' Most disciplinary offenses are heard by a Student-Faculty Judicial Council made up of five students and three faculty members." **How school handles drugs/alcohol:** "If a student is concerned about her own drug or alcohol use, or the drug or alcohol use of a peer, the response will not be punitive. Students may seek help from either the Counselor or the Dean of Students. At a minimum, any student who commits a serious infraction will be out on one year probation." **Prevention and awareness programs:** "These issues are addressed within the Human Development Department as part of the broader concept of health and wellness. The department's goal is to offer courses which contribute to the development of emotional literacy and resiliency in Castilleja students. Resources are also available through the school counselor."

Summer Programs

Summer camp program for girls completing G1-6. Incoming freshmen are encouraged to participate in "Fast Start," which is a program designed to introduce freshmen to high school academics. The subject areas include math, science, and English.

Parent Involvement

Parent participation: "The school encourages all parents to become involved and values the high percentage of parents who volunteer their time and financial support." **Parent/teacher communication:** The school sends grades on a quarterly basis. First and third quarter grades are accompanied by comment cards for every student from every teacher, which the school considers the most essential means of evaluating students. Progress reports are used to inform parents of dramatic shifts in a student's academic performance. Faculty advisors are also an important contact person for parents. **Parent education:** Parent seminars, as well as a Speaker Series, are sponsored by the Parent Association and the administration to focus on adolescent issues, including healthy communication, decision making, and boundaries; sexuality and body image; drugs and alcohol; and negotiating transitions into high school and college. **Donations:** "Expected to the extent possible both in terms of time and fundraising."

Sports

"About 70% of students participate in interscholastic athletics. Castilleja offers 11 varsity and junior varsity sports in the Upper School:

basketball, cross-country, golf, lacrosse, soccer, softball, swimming, track and field, tennis, volleyball, and water polo. In the past two years, three athletes signed national letters of intent to compete at the Division I level at Santa Clara, UCLA, and Stanford. Other scholar athletes are competing at the college level around the country."

What Sets School Apart From Others

"Academic excellence and a focus on leadership development, both in and out of the classroom, are all within the context of an all-girls educational environment, an essential distinction from other schools in Northern California. Our Global Program (and Global Investigator curriculum during which all 11th grade girls travel to a developing country such as India or China) and our Fitness and Wellness curriculum set us apart. Prior to graduation, 12th grade students prepare and deliver a speech to the entire Upper School. In addition, our seniors meet and introduce eminent guests who visit the school and our classrooms. In recent years, these visitors have included Former Vice President Al Gore, Her Majesty Queen Noor of Jordan, former Secretaries of State Madeleine Albright, George Schultz, and Condoleezza Rice. Our guiding philosophy, 'Women Learning, Women Leading,' defines our expectations that our students participate as citizens of a small school and a larger world."

How Parents/Students Characterize School

Parent response(s): "We realize that it is no small undertaking to evaluate the progress of many students; the faculty does so with obvious care and a concern for the wholeness of the student. This just confirms our belief that education at Castilleja extends beyond the dynamism of the classroom into those many other formal and informal opportunities when students interact with faculty and staff members. The girls are very fortunate, and we, as parents, remain grateful." **Student response(s):** "It is a friendly environment where students are able to express their thoughts and feelings freely without having to worry about whether they are right or wrong. I feel Castilleja is unique in the fact that we are all able to share our ideas no matter how different they are, and that we are free to be ourselves, and not what others want us to be." "The teachers are amazing; they aren't only your teachers, they are your friends." "Castilleja is a school where individuality is encouraged and accepted." "Castilleja always instilled in me a desire to make a difference in the world. I left high school without a clear idea of HOW exactly I wanted to do that, but I did leave knowing that with the many blessings I'd been given and the top notch education I received comes an opportunity, or some would say an obligation, to use those tools to make a positive impact."

Chinese Christian High School
750 Fargo Avenue
San Leandro, California 94579
(510) 351-4957 *fax (510) 351-1789*
www.ccs-rams.org

Mr. Robin Hom, Superintendent
Mrs. Mary Chan, Admissions Director, Mary_Chan@ccs-rams.org

General
Coed Christian day secondary and elementary school (K-12). An educational ministry of Bay Area Chinese Bible Church. Founded in 1979. Nonprofit. **Enrollment:** 225. **Average class size:** 20. **Accreditation:** WASC/ACSI. **School year:** August - June. **School day:** 8:25 a.m.-3:15 p.m. **Location:** Near the Greenhouse Shopping Center at the junction of Hwys. 880 and 238. Accessible by BART, AC Transit, and school's bus system.

Student Body
Geographic breakdown (counties): 92% from Alameda; 7% from Contra Costa; 1% other. **Ethnicity:** 3% Caucasian (non-Latino); 88% Asian; 1% Latino; 1% African-American; 7% multi-ethnic. **International students (I-20 status):** 10%. **Middle schools (freshman):** 10% are from 5 public middle schools; 90% from 3 parochial schools.

Admission
Applications due: Rolling admissions process, "the earlier the better." **Application fee:** None. **Application process:** Application submitted along with report cards and references, student and parent interview, placement test. **No. of freshman applications:** "Approx. 20 from new students." (N/P # places) **Minimum admission requirements:** Grades, test scores, references, interview. **Test required:** Any nationally-normed standardized tests, e.g. SAT-10, CAT-6. **Preferences:** "We are looking for students who want to pursue excellence in every area of life: academic, physical, emotional, and spiritual." **What kind of student do you best serve?** "We best serve students who are willing to learn, willing to work, and willing to love others as themselves."

Costs
Latest tuition: $8,350. **Sibling discount:** $950 for 2nd child; $2,050 3rd child. **Tuition increases:** Approx. 5%. **Other costs:** Approx. $150-$250 for books; $700-$1,000 other fees, depending on program. **Percentage of students receiving financial aid:** 10%. **Financial aid deadline:** Rolling. **Average grant:** $3,500. **Percentage of grants of half tuition or more:** 8%.

School's Mission Statement/Goals

"The mission of Chinese Christian Schools is to transform students' lives through a saving knowledge of Jesus Christ and Bible-based, Christ-centered education so they may be thoroughly equipped to fulfill God's perfect plan for their lives."

Academic Program

Courses offered (AP=Advanced Placement, H=Honors, (AP)=AP option, (H)=Honors option): **English:** English I, World Lit, American Lit, British Lit, Advanced Literature and Composition, AP Language, AP Lit.; **Math:** Algebra I, Geometry, Algebra II & III (H), Pre-Calculus (H), AP Calculus AB & BC; **Science:** Science 9, Physics (AP), Biology (AP), Chemistry (AP), Psychology (AP); **History:** World History, U.S. History (AP), AP European History, Government, AP U.S. Govt., Economics (AP); **Foreign language:** Mandarin I-111 (H), AP Chinese; Spanish I- III; **Arts:** Art I, II, III (AP); Music I, Drama. **Computer lab/training:** C++ Programming, AP Computer Science. **Grading:** A+ - F. **Graduation requirements:** "Varies by type: California, CCS, or Honors." **Average nightly homework (M-Th):** 2-4 hours. **Faculty:** 40 (N/P gender); 25% master's degrees, 10% doctorate degrees. **Faculty ethnicity:** 90% Asian; 10% Caucasian. **Faculty selection/training:** "Faculty are chosen for their Christian character and calling, love for their subject matter, and love for their students." **Teacher/student ratio:** 1:12. **Percentage of students enrolled in AP:** 80%; pass rate 75%. **Senior class profile (mean score):** SAT Math 621, SAT Critical Reading 574, SAT Writing 566; GPA: 3.6. **National Merit Scholarship Program:** Since 1997, CCS has graduated 8 National Merit Scholars, 2 National Merit Finalists, 3 current Semi-Finalists still in the 2008 competition, and 29 National Merit commended students. **College enrollment (last class):** 100%; 90% accepted at 4-year colleges, 75% at UC schools. **Recent (last 3 yrs) College enrollment (last class):** Boston U, BYU, Cal Poly (Pomona, SLO), Chabot C, C of San Mateo, CSU (East Bay, SD, SF, SJ), Contra Costa CC, Diablo Valley C, Georgetown, Harvey Mudd, Mt. San Antonio C, Ohlone C, Pensacola Christian C, UC (Berkeley, Davis, Irvine, LA, Merced, SD, Riverside, Santa Cruz), U-Guam, UOP, U-Washington, and Westpoint.

Other Indicators the School is Accomplishing its Goals

"2003 U.S. Department of Education National Blue Ribbon School of Excellence. ACSI Exemplary School Program Award 2002-3, 2006-7. CIF Scholastic Championship Team Award (17 times – 3 years). BCL Sportsmanship Award (2005-7). 64% of graduates are CIF Scholar Athletes. 42% of graduates are AP Scholars."

Campus/Campus Life

Campus description: The 10.2 acre facility, leased from the San Lorenzo Unified School District, has a multipurpose room, 38 classrooms, 4 dedicated science labs, computer lab with 30 stations, and 2 mobile computer labs with 8 laptops each. **Library:** "Approx. 25,000 volumes." (N/P hours etc) **Sports facilities:** Sports field, play areas with basketball and volleyball courts. **Theater/arts facilities:** 300-seat multipurpose room with stage. **Open/closed campus:** Closed campus with video surveillance. **Lunches:** Hot lunches prepared on-site or catered. **Bus service:** CCS provides school bus service to Fremont/Union City, Oakland, and Alameda. **Uniforms/dress code:** "Coordinated dress uniform policy." **Co-curricular activities/clubs:** "Numerous academic, artistic, service, special interest, athletic, and co-curricular clubs and organizations (check website)." **Foreign exchange programs/internships:** Sister school relationship with five schools in China; foreign student and student exchange programs conducted annually. **Community service:** Regular service opportunities provided for all students, as well as service projects by various clubs and organizations. **Typical freshman schedule:** Homeroom, English I, Geometry, Physics, World History, Mandarin II, P.E. and Bible.

Student Support Services

Counselor/student ratio (not including college counselors): 1:30 Pastoral counseling through on-site pastor staff. **Counseling:** College and academic advising through regularly scheduled meetings and appointments, plus by-appointment for students and families. **Learning differences/disabilities:** "Teachers will accommodate learning difference/disabilities as much as resources permit."

Student Conduct and Health

Code of conduct: "High standards of conduct and attitude are expected and enforced." **How school handles drugs/alcohol:** The school practices "redemptive discipline" and handles each case individually, depending on the circumstances and context of the situation. **Prevention and awareness programs:** Programs and assemblies addressing good academic, moral, physical, and spiritual habits and disciplines are conducted throughout the year.

Summer Programs

"Summer school classes are offered to allow students to make up work or get ahead. Sports camps are provided for those who wish to develop their athletic skills. Students are made aware of a number of summer internships, jobs, and student programs from which they might benefit."

Parent Involvement

Parent participation: "The school has an active Parent-Teacher Fellowship as well as parent support for specific programs such as sports, robotics, and student travel/exchange." **Parent/teacher communication:** Parents can access student's grades 24/7 through PowerSchool. All school staff has e-mail and voice-mail capabilities, and regular newsletters and announcements are sent home in hardcopy and electronically. **Parent education:** Seminars and classes held regularly, sponsored by the school, the church, and Christian ministries. **Donations:** "General and specific donations are always welcome. We do not have a lot of fundraisers."

Sports
Member BCL, CIF. Sports include boys and girls volleyball, basketball, soccer, track, cross-country, and tennis.

What Sets School Apart From Others
"Chinese Christian Schools is Christian in philosophy, Chinese in culture, college-preparatory in academics. We have developed an international reputation for superior academics, innovative programs, and a supportive, loving staff."

How Parents/Students Characterize School
Parent response(s): N/P. **Student response(s):** N/P. "The most common phrase used by students and families is that CCS is like a 'second family.' Students compete with, not against, each other, challenging them to do their best and celebrating each other's achievements."

The College Preparatory School
6100 Broadway
Oakland, CA 94618
(510) 652-0111 *fax (510) 652-7467*
www.college-prep.org

Murray Cohen, Head of School
Jonathan Zucker, Director of Admissions and Financial Aid,
jonathan@college-prep.org

General
Coed day high school. Nonsectarian. Founded in 1960. Nonprofit, member CAIS, NAIS, BAIHS. **Enrollment:** 350. **Average class size:** 14. **Accreditation:** WASC/CAIS. **School year:** Sept.-June. **School day:** 8 a.m.-3:15 p.m. **Location:** Near Lake Berkeley/Oakland border near Lake Temescal. Accessible from the Rockridge BART station and by AC transit.

Student Body
Geographic breakdown (counties): 73.9% from Alameda; 25.8% from Contra Costa; .3% from San Francisco. **Ethnicity:** 60% Caucasian (non-Latino); 21% Asian-American; 6% African-American; 6% multiracial; 5% Latino; 1% Middle Eastern American; 1% Native American. **International students (I-20 status):** 1. **Middle schools (freshman):**

29% came from public middle schools; 57% from private, non-parochial schools; 13% from parochial schools; 1% home-schooled. (N/P # schools) Applications were received from 87 schools; matriculates from 42 schools.

Admission

Applications due: Mid-January (call for date). **Application fee:** $75. **Application process:** Families contact the Admissions Office in the fall of the student's 8th grade year. The school considers personal statements, grades, teacher recommendations, an interview, and the results of an entrance examination. Three open houses, one each in October, November, and December are held for prospective applicants and parents. A member of the Admissions Committee interviews each applicant in December or January. Half-day student classroom visits are optional but encouraged. Entrance exams are given at the school in January, but may be taken at any testing site. Acceptances are sent mid-March. **No. of freshman applications:** 325 for 90 places. Two new students enrolled in G10, 2 in G11. **Minimum admission requirements:** None. **Test required:** ISEE or SSAT. **Preferences:** "Students of color are encouraged to apply." **"We are looking for** intellectual risk-takers who want to pursue a serious, purposeful education with others who feel the same way. We also pay special attention to each applicant's willingness to share in and contribute to the lives of others." **What kind of student do you best serve?** "Intellectually curious and academically talented students of promising character. Students who can thrive in and contribute to the school in any number of co-curricular areas such as athletics, arts, and debate."

Costs

Latest tuition: $28,600 payable in 1-3 payments. **Sibling discount:** None. **Tuition increases:** Approx. 5-7%. **Other costs:** Approx. $600 for books, $400 for other fees. Need-based financial aid is available. **Percentage of students receiving financial aid:** Over 23%. **Financial aid deadline:** January (call for date). **Average grant:** $19,150. **Percentage of grants of half-tuition or more:** 72%.

School's Mission Statement/Goals

"College Prep, a community of students, teachers and staff, prepares our students for productive, ethical lives in college and beyond through a challenging and stimulating education in an atmosphere of consideration, trust, and mutual responsibility."

Academic Program

"Our four-year curriculum meets or exceeds the entrance requirements of all major colleges and universities. We encourage students who have satisfied our graduation requirements to enroll in Advanced Placement classes or independent study projects. Our curriculum emphasizes: clear expression in writing and speaking – in English and in at least one other language (Chinese, French, Japanese, Latin, and Spanish), broad historical and cultural perspectives, strong foundations in mathematics and science, art and aesthetic development as an integral part of the curriculum, health and P.E. for all students, and 21st-century technological literacy." **Courses offered** (AP=Advanced Placement, H=Honors, (AP)=AP option, (H)=Honors option): **Arts:** Drawing and Design, Two- and Three-Dimensional Studios, Photography, Advanced Projects, Acting, Digital Video and Performance, Drama, Stagecraft, Theater Production, Chorus, Advanced Vocal Ensemble, Beginning Instruments, Orchestra, Chamber Music, Jazz Band, AP Music Theory, Beginning, Intermediate, and Advanced Dance; **English:** English I-II, English Seminars (e.g., Classic Modern Fiction; Nineteenth-century American Literature; Reading Women; From Sappho to Tupac: Poetry Past and Present, East and West; and Telling Stories: The Art of Fiction Writing); **History:** World Civilizations, Western Civilization, U.S. History, History Seminars (e.g., American Sports History; Art History; Economics; Introduction to Linguistic Science; and International Law, Human Rights, and Genocide); **Foreign Languages:** Chinese, French, Japanese, Latin, Spanish, Language Seminars (e.g., Language and Film from the Francophone World; Advanced Spanish Conversation with Genre Survey of Prose, Poetry, and Film); **Math:** Mathematics I-IV, AP Calculus, AP Multivariable Calculus, AP Statistics; **Science:** Physical Science, Chemistry (AP), Biology (AP), Physics (AP), AP Environmental Science, Science Electives (e.g., Animal Behavior, Astronomy, and Issues in Science); **Wellness Curriculum:** P.E., Health Education. **Other offerings:** Audio Engineering, Computer Science, Forensics, Freshman Foundations, Independent Study, Philosophy, Psychology, Women's Studies. **Computer lab/training:** The school has three computer labs; there is a mobile laptop cart; the campus is completely networked and wireless. Computer literacy is part of the required Freshman Foundations course. The school has a full-time technology director and two full-time technology integrators. **Grading:** A-F and teacher evaluations 4 times a year. **Graduation requirements:** 4 years English; 3 years history, science and P.E.; completion of level III math; completion of level III foreign language; 4 semesters fine arts; one semester Freshman Foundations and Sophomore Health. **Average nightly homework (M-Th):** G9-10: 30-40 min. per class; G11-12: 40-50 min. per class. **Faculty:** 51; 84% hold advanced degrees (N/P gender, degrees). **Faculty ethnicity:** 69% Caucasian (non-Latino); 8% African-American; 5% Hispanic/Latino; 14% Asian American; 4% multi-ethnic. **Faculty selection/training:** "Faculty is selected for thorough knowledge of their subjects and strong teaching skills. Prospective teachers are required to make a related presentation and have interviews with several members of the administration and faculty. The school has a generous professional development fund that both encourages and permits continuing education." **Teacher/student ratio:** 1:8. **Percentage of students enrolled in AP:** 37%; pass rate 98%. **Senior class profile (mean):** SAT Math 715, SAT Critical Reading 716, SAT Writing 719;

GPA: 3.58 (academic courses only). **National Merit Scholarship Program:** 65% of the students in the latest class were either Semifinalists (23 students) or Commended (33 students). **College enrollment (last class):** 100% in 4-year. **Recent (last 2 yrs) colleges:** American, Amherst, Barnard, Bates, Boston C, Boston U (4), Bowdoin, Brown (5), Bucknell, UC (Berkeley (10), Davis (5), LA (3), SD (4), Santa Barbara (8), Santa Cruz (7)), CCA, California Institute of Technology (3), Carleton (6), Carnegie Melon, U-Chicago (5), Claremont McKenna (2), Colgate, U-Colorado at Boulder (3), Colorado C (2), Columbia (12), Cornell (5), Dartmouth (6), Duke, Emory (2), George Washington, Georgetown (5), Grinnell, Hampshire, Harvard (13), Indiana U, Kenyon, Lake Forest, Lehigh, Macalester (3), MIT (6), McGill (5), Middlebury (5), U-Minnesota, NYU (7), Northwestern (3), Oberlin (7), Occidental (4), Pacific, Penn (7), Pitzer (2), Pomona (2), Princeton (7), U-Puget Sound (4), RPI, U-Rochester, Santa Clara, Sarah Lawrence, Scripps, Smith (2), USC, Stanford (12), Swarthmore, Tufts (4), Vanderbilt, Vassar (2), Washington U-St. Louis (4), U-Washington (2), Wesleyan (7), Williams (4), Worcester Polytechnic Institute, and Yale (5).

Other Indicators the School is Accomplishing its Goals

"College Prep alumni go on to extraordinary collegiate experiences, become conscientious local and global citizens, and pursue lives of generosity and self-discovery."

Campus/Campus Life

Campus description: "Our 14 buildings are nestled into a green urban valley on Broadway, near the Oakland-Berkeley line. Two rows of wood shingle-sided buildings face each other on either side of a wooded canyon; classrooms and offices open onto the common walkways and courtyards between the buildings. Several classrooms have round tables for a discussion format. A native plant garden and landscaped walkways provide students with outdoor spaces for socializing, studying, and engaging in informal activities such as games of chess and juggling. An amphitheater is tucked away on the hillside." **Library:** 3,200 sq. ft.; 2 librarians; study space for 54 students plus additional seating areas; over 15,000 titles, 874 reference volumes, 561 videocassettes and DVDs, 54 print periodicals, 21 subscription databases, a growing collection of e-books; video/DVD viewing area; private study room and reference/teaching room (both multimedia equipped); 17 PCs available for student use, 2 for staff; T1 network connection, laptop connectivity, photocopier, and scanner. **Sports facilities:** Gymnasium and one casual-play field on-site; pool, tennis courts, and other playing fields contracted off-site. **Theater/arts facilities:** Auditorium, large art classroom, prep room, dance studio, dark room. **Open/closed campus:** Open. **Lunches:** None served on campus. **Bus service:** Public transportation to Rockridge BART; school shuttle between BART and campus. **Uniforms/dress code:** "Common sense and good taste." **Co-curricular activities/clubs:** Over 40 clubs, including Math Club, Pride-in-Diversity Club, Eco Club, school publications, and the school's nationally prominent debate team. **Foreign exchange programs/internships:** None. **Community service:** Shelters, soup kitchens, tutoring at Oakland schools, Partners Program (see Summer Programs, below), Rebuilding Together, Habitat for Humanity, Adopt-a-Family, Oxfam. **Typical freshman schedule:** English I, Math I or II, Physical Science, foreign language (Chinese, French, Latin, Japanese, Spanish), World Civilizations, arts (visual, dance, drama, music) or Debate, P.E. or team sports, Freshman Foundations.

Student Support Services

Counselor/student ratio (not including college counselors): 1:350. **Counseling:** "The school has one full-time counselor/health educator whose assistance ranges from study skills to short-term crisis counseling. He provides drug, alcohol, AIDS, etc., education for freshmen and sophomores as part of the curriculum, participates in retreats for all classes, and helps the Dean of Students coordinate the advisor program (selected seniors act as advisors to small groups of incoming freshmen). Each student, in addition, has an academic advisor. The school has two full-time college counselors." **Learning differences/disabilities:** "The school does not test students but, when needed, recommends outside sources for assessment and then makes suitable accommodations on an individual basis in line with professional recommendations. The Learning Center is administered by a Learning Services Coordinator."

Student Conduct/Health

Code of conduct: "The rules are based on fundamental principles of honesty and respect and are an outline to aid us in learning to abide by and to apply our guiding principles. College Prep will not tolerate harassment of students, faculty, staff or others in our midst, either on or off school grounds, by anyone, including their peers, superiors or subordinates, parents of students, visitors or guests." **How school handles drugs/alcohol:** Possessing, distributing, or otherwise facilitating the use of drugs or alcohol on campus or at a school event will lead to immediate suspension with the possibility of expulsion. This rule also applies to the use or abuse of controlled substances. Students should not ingest medication that is not prescribed for them or distribute prescription medication to other students. **Prevention and awareness programs:** "These issues are discussed in Freshman Foundations and Sophomore Health—required courses that inform students about issues faced by adolescents, including stress, peer pressure, relationships with parents, drugs and alcohol, and sexuality, and that help students develop decision-making skills. In addition, each grade level attends a yearly retreat designed to achieve particular goals of the school. The 9th grade retreat focuses on integrating new 9th graders into the school; the 10th grade retreat deals with issues surrounding adolescence; the 11th grade retreat is intended to encourage leadership among students; and the senior retreat is about the transition from high school to college."

Summer Programs

"The school offers a tuition-free Partners Program during the summer for middle-school students from Oakland public schools who are bright, able, and motivated. The program leads students toward an academic high school experience. College Prep students serve as teaching assistants."

Parent Involvement

Parent participation: Parents voluntarily serve the school through the Parents' Association as well as by gardening on campus, judging debates, participating in open houses, etc. No required hours. **Parent/teacher communication:** Report cards four times a year; conferences with advisors, teachers, and the assistant head as well. **Parent education:** Informational and/or support events are organized by the school and by the Parents' Association as needed, occasionally in response to issues as they arise. **Donations:** "Parents are solicited for the Annual Fund and occasionally for a capital campaign. The Parents' Association sponsors a fundraising auction annually."

Sports

Students compete in the BCL in coed cross-country, golf, swimming, and track; girls compete in volleyball, tennis, softball, basketball, and soccer; boys in soccer, basketball, volleyball, tennis, and baseball.

What Sets School Apart From Others

"At College Prep, we meet each day to do what we love – ask hard questions, delve into the possibilities, and expand our capacities. Our classes, filled with bright students and energetic teachers, demand our best efforts and grant us chances to expand our thinking and develop our personalities in interesting ways. If you are like most students at College Prep, you'll come to realize that acquiring knowledge isn't an end in itself. It's what we do with our intelligence that matters. We acknowledge the value of work while understanding it's also necessary to reserve plenty of time to play, to rest, to volunteer, to develop our entire selves – and have fun doing it."

How Parents/Students Characterize School

Parent response(s): "The accomplishment of College Prep is the extraordinary warmth among its students. Adolescence is usually not marked by its tolerance, but the students of College Prep cherish diversity. ... As a group, they lend moral and affectionate support to each of their number. There is a palpable embracing of the individual by the student body. ... As a consequence, each child at College Prep realizes his talents about as close to the fullest as is humanly conceivable." **Student response(s):** "I love this school. I love this school because

I'm only 17 years old, and I have learned already to be a man—who is depended on and respected. I've learned to trust and be trusted, to share my feelings, my thoughts, and my opinions. I've learned to love people in different ways. I love this place because I came in cynical and vain, and I'm leaving with a sense of hope and with a feeling of peace."

Contra Costa Christian School

2721 Larkey Lane
Walnut Creek, CA 94597
(925)934-4964 *fax (925)934-4966*
www.contracostachristian.org

B.J. Huizenga, Head of School
Lisa Asher, Admissions Director, lasher@cccss.org

General
Coed Christian day high school. Independent. Founded in 1978. Nonprofit, member ACSI, CSI. **Enrollment:** Approx. 400. **Average class size:** 15. **Accreditation:** WASC. **School year:** 10-mo. calendar. **School day:** 8 a.m.-3:05 p.m. **Location:** In Walnut Creek accessible by BART.

Student Body
Geographic breakdown (counties): Approx. 98% from Contra Costa. **Ethnicity:** Approx. 68% Caucasian (non-Latino); 9% Asian; 9% Latino; 5% African-American; 9% multi-ethnic. **International students (I-20 status):** N/P. **Middle schools (freshman):** N/P.

Admission
Applications due: February (call for date). **Application fee:** $300; $1,000 for foreign students. **Application process:** Recommendations from teacher and pastor, testing, interviews. **No. of freshman applications:** N/P. **Minimum admission requirements:** N/P. **Test required:** N/P. **Preferences:** N/P. "We are looking for students of Christian families." What kind of student do you best serve? N/P.

Costs
Latest tuition: $8,730. **Sibling discount:** "Yes." **Tuition increases:** Approx. 3%. **Other costs:** Fees for sports (N/P amount). **Percentage of students receiving financial aid:** 5%. **Financial aid deadline:** April (call for exact date). **Average grant:** "15% off." **Percentage of grants of half-tuition or more:** N/P.

School's Mission Statement/Goals

"CCCS is a distinctively Christian learning community, committed to academic excellence, preparing children of Christian families to live out their purpose as builders of God's Kingdom."

Academic Program

Courses offered: "Honors courses offered." (N/P description) **Computer lab/training:** "Yes." **Grading:** N/P. **Graduation requirements:** N/P. **Average nightly homework (M-Th):** "Varies by grade." **Faculty:** Approx. 50 (N/P gender, degrees). **Faculty ethnicity:** N/P. **Faculty selection/training:** N/P. **Teacher/student ratio:** 1:15. **Percentage of students enrolled in AP:** N/P. **Senior class profile (mean score):** SAT Math 548, SAT Critical Reading 544, SAT Writing 576; **GPA:** N/P. **National Merit Scholarship Program:** N/P. **College enrollment (last class):** Approx. 93% (N/P 4-yr, 2-yr). **Recent colleges:** N/P.

Other Indicators the School is Accomplishing its Goals: "WASC accredited."

Campus/Campus Life

Campus description: N/P. **Library:** "Yes." **Sports facilities:** "Sports fields, pool and gym nearby." **Theater/arts facilities:** N/P. **Open/closed campus:** Closed. **Lunches:** "Yes." **Bus service:** None. **Uniforms/dress code:** "Dress code." (Description N/P) **Co-curricular activities/clubs:** "Yes." **Foreign exchange programs/internships:** N/P. **Community service:** "Yes." **Typical freshman schedule:** Biology, math, English, Spanish, P.E., Bible, health, elective.

Student Support Services

Counselor/student ratio: N/P. **Counseling:** N/P. **Learning differences/disabilities:** "Resource director."

Student Conduct and Health

Code of conduct: "Yes." (Description N/P) **How school handles drugs/alcohol:** Zero tolerance. **Prevention/awareness programs:** "Yes."

Summer Programs: N/P.

Parent Involvement

Parent participation: "Required 30 hours." **Parent/teacher communication:** "Ren Web." **Parent education:** N/P. **Donations:** "Yes."

Sports

Swimming, basketball, baseball, volleyball, soccer, cross-country.

What Sets School Apart From Others

"Academic excellence. A Christian school for Christian families."

How Parents/Students Characterize School

"We believe that education works best for the child when the home, the church and the school work as partners. Students are taught to think through every subject area from a Christian world and life view. Our goal is to prepare and equip students to serve God excellently in whatever work he is calling them to do."

Convent of the Sacred Heart High School

2222 Broadway
San Francisco, CA 94115
(415) 563-2900 *fax (415) 929-0553*
www.sacredsf.org

Andrea Shurley, Head of School
Caitlin Curran, Admissions Director, ccurran@sacredsf.org

General

Girls day high school. Independent Catholic (49% Catholic). Founded in 1887. Nonprofit, member NAIS, CAIS, BAAD, BAIHS, SSATB, National Blue Ribbon School, NACAC, NCGS, ABC, and NCEA. **Enrollment:** Approx. 200. **Average class size:** 14. **Accreditation:** WASC/CAIS. **School year:** Sept.-June. **School day:** 8:15 a.m.-3:15 p.m. **Location:** In the Pacific Heights area of San Francisco accessible by the 1, 22, 24, 41, and 45 Muni bus lines.

Student Body

Geographic breakdown (counties): 79% from San Francisco; 7% from Marin; 9% from San Mateo; 4% from Alameda; 1% from Contra Costa. **Ethnicity:** 62% Caucasian (non-Latino); 20% Asian; 7% Latino; 7% African-American; 4% multi-ethnic. **Middle schools (freshman):** 26% came from Convent of the Sacred Heart Elementary School; 4% from 2 public middle schools; 40% from 8 private, non-parochial schools; 30% from 7 parochial schools.

Admission

Applications due: Approx. January 3 (call for date). **Application fee:** $75. **Application process:** Tours are conducted September through February. In November, applicants and their families may attend an open house and see classes in session. **No. of freshman applications:** "Four applications for every available spot." (N/P # places) **Minimum admission requirements:** N/P. **Test required:** HSPT (preferred test) or SSAT. **Preferences:** Siblings and legacies. **"We are looking for** young women who want to be engaged in their education and are willing to take on a strong academic program and leadership roles within the school community." **What sort of student do you best serve?** (See "Other Indicators the School is Accomplishing its Goals.")

Costs

Latest tuition: $29,200 payable in 2 or 10 payments. **Sibling discount:** None. **Tuition increases:** Approx. 5%. **Other costs:** Approx. $400 for books, $150 for uniforms. **Percentage of students receiving financial aid:** 30%. **Financial aid deadline:** February (call for date). **Average grant:** $14,000. **Percentage of grants of half-tuition or more:** N/P.

School's Mission Statement/Goals

"The Schools of the Sacred Heart in the United States, members of a world-wide network, offer an education that is marked by a distinctive spirit. Sacred Heart schools are committed to the individual student's total development: spiritual, intellectual, emotional, and physical. Sacred Heart Schools emphasize serious study, social responsibility, and growth in faith. Sacred Heart schools commit themselves to educate to a personal and active faith in God; a deep respect for intellectual values; a social awareness which impels to action; the building of a community as a Christian value; and personal growth in an atmosphere of wise freedom."

Academic Program

"Every student is enrolled in a challenging and enriching academic program. The program emphasizes serious study and teaches to each student's total spiritual, intellectual, emotional and physical development. The administration, faculty, and student body are committed to intellectual honesty and leadership development. Students are treated seriously as scholars and leaders. Each student is required to take a minimum of six courses for credit each semester. Every student graduates with a program which satisfies the UC course requirements for admission." **Courses offered** (AP=Advanced Placement, H=Honors, (AP)=AP option, (H)=Honors option): **English:** English I-II (H), American Literature (H), English IV, Film As Literature, Creative Writing, Writer's Workshop, Intro to Journalism, Journalism I-III, AP English Language and Composition, AP English Literature and Composition; **Math:** Integrated Math I-II, Integrated Math III (H), Pre-Calculus (H), Calculus, Statistics, AP Calculus AB, Quantitative Analysis, AP Calculus BC; **Science:** Biology (H/AP), Chemistry (H/AP), Physiology, Physics (H), Anthropology, Marine Biology, AP Environmental Science, AP Human Geography, AP Physics C: Mechanics; **History:** History I-II, U.S. History (AP), International Relations, Economics, The American Century, Women's Studies, AP Psychology, AP Comparative Govt., AP European History, AP U.S. Government & Politics; **Foreign Languages:** French I-III, IV (H), Spanish I-III, IV (H), Japanese I-IV, Mandarin I-IV, Latin I-IV, AP French Language, AP French Literature, AP Spanish Language, AP Spanish Literature; **Arts:** Ceramics, Choir, Chamber Choir, Coed Choir, Drama, Drawing, Instrumental Chamber Group, Intro to Cinema, Intro to Music Theory, Musical Theater, Music Appreciation, Open Studio/Independent Study, Painting, Photography, Printmaking Sculpture, Yearbook Design and Production, AP Art

History, AP Music Theory, AP Studio Art: Drawing Portfolio. **Other:**
Humanities, Intro to Religion, World Religions, Moral Philosophy and
Theology, Philosophical Theology and Mysticism; P.E. I- II. **Computer
lab/training:** Computer I-II (H) (each a semester), AP Computer Science A, AP Computer Science AB. "Each student has access to the
Internet, an e-mail address and Palm technology to facilitate communication, organization and learning. Students have access to over
100 computers on campus, all with Internet access. Technology is
integrated throughout the curriculum. Students have access to equipment, including scanners and digital cameras, and are required to take
a year of computer science." **Grading:** A-F. **Graduation requirements:**
4 years English, history, math and theology; 3 years lab science and
foreign language; 2 years P.E.; 1 year fine arts and computer science;
100 hours community service. **Average nightly homework (M-Th):**
3-3.5 hours **Faculty:** 36; 28% male, 72% female. (N/P degrees). **Faculty
ethnicity:** N/P. **Faculty selection/training:** "We look for teachers who
are knowledgeable in their subject areas; who have a strong commitment to education; who desire small classes for interactive learning;
who want to support students outside of the classroom through athletics, service, or club activities; who will accept and embrace the goals
of Sacred Heart education; who understand the benefits of teaching
in a single sex environment; and who have the desire and ability to
engage students in the classroom. Teachers take advantage of CSH's
full support for professional development by attending conferences
and workshops." **Teacher/student ratio: 1:7. Percentage of students
enrolled in AP:** 90%; pass rate N/P. **Most recent senior class profile
(mean)** SAT Math 567, SAT Critical Reading 606, SAT Writing 632;
GPA: N/P. **National Merit Scholarship Program:** 1 National Merit
Finalist, 3 Commended. **College enrollment (last class):** 100% in 4-
year. **Recent (3 yr) colleges:** Barnard C, Bates C, Boston C, Boston U,
Bucknell U, Brown, UC (Berkeley, Davis, LA, Santa Barbara, SD, Santa
Cruz), Cal Poly-SLO, Carleton C, C of the Holy Cross, Colorado C,
Cornell U, Harvard, Lehigh, Loyola Marymount U, NYU, Northwestern,
Oberlin, Occidental, U-Oregon, Penn, Princeton, USD, USF, Santa
Clara, Sarah Lawrence, Skidmore, Vassar, and Yale.

Other Indicators the School is Accomplishing its Goals

"Due to our small student body and class size, we are able to concentrate on individual students at every level. One of our strongest programs is our AP program, with 24 different class offerings providing
an AP opportunity for every student. Of the last 4 graduating classes,
98% of the students enrolled in at least one AP course during their
4 years. The average number of AP courses taken by students is 3.
The College Board recognized 40 students as Advanced Placement
Scholars. Nineteen students were recognized for having received a
grade of 3 or higher on 3 or more AP exams. Seven were named AP
Scholars with Honor, granted to students with a 3 or higher on 5
AP exams. Thirteen students were AP Scholars with Distinction, an

award granted to students who received a grade of 3 or higher on 6 or more AP exams on full-year courses. One student was recognized as a National Scholar, granted to students who receive an average grade of at least 4 on all AP exams taken, and grades of 4 or higher on eight or more of these exams." "CSH's reputation as an outstanding program for young women in San Francisco reaches beyond Bay Area communities to the college community as well. Over 70 college representatives come to our campus each fall to speak with students. Our graduates attend some of the most competitive colleges in the U.S. and abroad. CSH has been recognized by the U.S. Department of Education as a Blue Ribbon School."

Campus/Campus Life
Campus description: The school is housed in the three-story Flood Mansion at the crest of the Pacific Heights neighborhood, overlooking the San Francisco Bay and the Golden Gate Bridge. The building has ground floor meeting rooms, classrooms, and a chapel; second floor student center, computer lab, classrooms and offices; and a third floor library, art studio, and classrooms. Downstairs is a theater and cafeteria. In 2004, the new 42,000 sq. ft. Siboni Arts and Science Center opened. The new building houses biology, physics and chemistry labs; 2 math classrooms; an art studio and a student center. In addition, there is a 355-seat theater/lecture hall. **Library:** Open 7 a.m.-6 p.m. Approx. 8,000 print volumes; online catalog; 40 periodical subscriptions; study seating for 35 students. **Sports facilities:** The campus includes a full-size gymnasium and indoor track. **Theater/arts facilities:** The new Siboni Arts and Science Center includes an art center with kilns and ceramics studio, outdoor art terraces and a 355-seat theater with raked seating and backstage space, including room for proposed dance studios and music practice rooms. **Open/closed campus:** Open for juniors and seniors; sophomores may sign out. **Lunches:** Students bring their lunches or eat in the cafeteria; juniors and seniors may eat off campus. **Bus service:** Public. **Uniforms/dress code:** Uniforms consist of a gray skirt, white shirt, and burgundy sweater. Seniors wear blue sweaters. Beginning second quarter, students may wear khaki pants. No unnatural hair colors or facial piercing. Occasional free dress days. **Co-curricular activities/clubs:** Clubs include Art, Black History Celebration, College Hostess, Network Homelessness Project, Debate, Environmental, Girls' Athletic Association, International Students, Harvard Model Congress, Junior Statesmen of America, Newspaper, Outdoors, Publicity, Simple Gifts, Social, Spirit, Student Admissions, Students Against Drunk Driving (SADD), Yearbook. Activities include Student Council, Clubs Council, Guest Speakers Program, National Honor Society, and California Scholarship Federation. In 2000, Stuart Hall High School opened several blocks away. Girls from CSH and boys from SHHS participate together in extra-curricular programs, service projects and social activities, allowing "a serious focus on academics for young women and young men along with the

benefits of a co-educational campus experience." **Foreign exchange programs/internships:** Students may participate in an exchange program among 19 Sacred Heart schools in the U.S., living with a host family or boarding at a Sacred Heart school with boarding facilities. (Sophomores and juniors with a B+ average are eligible to apply.) **Community service:** 100 hours required for graduation. The school offers a variety of activities relating to the elderly, the environment, the handicapped, the sick, the economically disadvantaged, and the newly immigrated. **Typical freshman schedule:** English I (H); Theology I; History I; French, Spanish, Japanese or Mandarin; Integrated Math I (H); Biology (H); Computer Studies I (1 semester); Intro to Art (1 semester); and P.E. I.

Student Support Services

Counselor-student ratio (not including college counselors): 1:200. **Counseling:** The school has a part-time counselor in the Office of Student Services and a Community Service Director. The Head of School provides academic counseling and advising to students. The college counseling office consists of the College Counselor and an Assistant College Counselor. During the freshman year, students take the National Education Development Test. Freshman and sophomores have one group presentation each year by the College Counselor and meet individually with the College Counselor as well. Sophomores take the PSAT in the spring. During the junior year, students take the PSAT in the fall; have weekly group meetings and individual sessions with the College Counselor; and take the ACT, SAT I, and SAT II in the spring. Seniors continue to meet with the College Counselor, both individually and in group sessions, and take the SAT I and SAT II again in the fall. **Learning differences/disabilities:** "No special programs or resources."

Student Conduct and Health

Code of conduct: "The Code of Ethics, discussed in the Student Handbook, focuses on respect for others, respect for others' property and school property, respect for education, and school spirit." **How school handles drugs/alcohol:** "Drug and alcohol usage or possession will not be tolerated and will result in serious punishment of either expulsion or suspension. This policy is in effect whether a student is on campus, in uniform, or attending a school-sponsored function." **Prevention and awareness programs:** "Drug/alcohol abuse prevention is part of the freshman/sophomore community program and is often the subject of guest speakers on campus. These subjects are also discussed in classes. Sexually transmitted diseases are discussed as part of the human sexuality curriculum, which includes topics of body image and self-acceptance, building healthy relationships, and family planning. The program includes guest speakers, lecturers, and in-class discussion."

Summer Programs
"Summer programs offered in partnership with Stuart Hall High School. See website for details."

Parent Involvement
Parent participation: No required hours. "Parents have a very active opportunity to participate through the Parents' Association as Room Parents and as volunteers for various events and activities." **Parent/teacher communication:** Formal reports are sent to parents 4 times a year. Other evaluations are given as needed. Each teacher maintains a website. **Parent education:** Speaker series; evening presentations for parents on college admission and financial aid/scholarships. **Donations:** "Parents are encouraged to lend their financial as well as volunteer support for the fundraising activities of the school."

Sports
CSH students compete in the BCL in volleyball, cross-country, tennis, golf, basketball, swimming, track and soccer. In 2003, fencing and badminton were introduced as coed sports. They are offered to CSH and SHHS. Students may also participate in crew.

What Sets School Apart From Others
"CHS offers a strong academic program which utilizes all the resources the city has to offer. The school actively provides leadership opportunities for young women and a values-based education."

How Parents/Students Characterize School
Parent response(s): N/P. **Student response(s):** "My four years at CSH have been important because I have learned a lot about myself as a person. CSH has helped academically, but more importantly, it has given me the chance to look deeply at who I am and the person I wish to become. CSH has given me a foundation in everything I would like to see in myself throughout life. It has given me a strong faith and strong sense of self, in addition to a well-rounded education."

Cornerstone Academy
501 Cambridge Street
San Francisco, CA 94134
(415) 585-5183 *fax (415) 469-9600*
www.cornerstone-academy.net

Mr. Derrick Wong, Principal
Mr. Carl L. Kahae, Registrar, carl.kahae@cornerstone-academy.net

General
Coed Baptist high school. Independent. Founded in 1975. Nonprofit. **Enrollment:** Approx. 100. **Average class size:** 25. **Accreditation:** WASC. **School year:** 9-mo. calendar. **School day:** 8 a.m.-3 p.m. (campus

is open 7 a.m.-6 p.m.) **Location:** In Portola Heights, off Silver Ave. and Cambridge Street. Near Hwys. 280 and 101.

Student Body
Geographic breakdown (counties): 85% from San Francisco; 13% from San Mateo; 1% from Alameda; 1% from Contra Costa. **Ethnicity:** 94% Asian; 1% Latino; 5% multi-ethnic. **Foreign students (I-20 status):** N/P #. **Middle schools (freshman):** 60% came from 4 public schools; 30% from 2 parochial schools; 10% other.

Admissions
Applications due: Open enrollment. **Application fee:** $20 domestic; $200 international. **Application process:** N/P. **No. of freshman applications:** "Varies." (N/P #). **Minimum admission requirements:** "Grades, test scores, math and English teacher recommendations are very critical to admissions; GPA: 2.5-3.0." **Preferences:** N/P. **"We are looking for** students who love serving Our Lord Jesus Christ and want to strive for educational excellence." **What kind of student do you best serve?** "Students who are willing to work, study and play hard. A student who never gives up. A student who loves serving each other and Our Lord Jesus Christ."

Cost
Latest tuition: $7,550/domestic; $10,550/international. **Sibling discount:** None. **Tuition increases:** Approx. 5%. **Other costs:** Annual re-registration $450; annual Snow Retreat $150. **Percentage of students receiving financial aid:** N/P. **Financial aid deadline:** N/P. **Average grant:** N/P. **Percentage grants of half-tuition or more:** N/P.

School's Mission Statement/Goals
"To guide students toward excellence in academic, social, physical, and spiritual development based on Christian principles. To prepare students for productive lives as responsible citizens in a competitive society. To create and develop a community of mutual support comprised of the school, students' families, and Cornerstone Evangelical Baptist Church."

Academic Program
Courses offered: Courses offered (AP=Advanced Placement, H=Honors (AP)=AP option, (H)=Honors option): "AP Calculus, Honors Classes – Math, English, and Science at all grade levels." **Computer lab/training:** N/P. **Grading:** A-F. **Graduation requirements:** Minimum 250 units. **Average nightly homework (M-Th):** 2-3 hours. **Faculty:** 18 f/t (N/P gender, degrees). **Faculty ethnicity:** "Asian and Caucasian." (N/P%) **Faculty selection/training:** N/P. **Teacher/student ratio:** 1:25. **Percentage of students enrolled in AP:** "N/A". **Senior class profile (mean score):** N/P. **College enrollment (last class):** 99%. (N/P 4-yr, 2-yr) **Recent colleges:** "100%." (N/P names).

Other indicators the School is Accomplishing its Goals: N/P.

Campus/Campus Life
Campus description: "The school has six major buildings on 4.5 acres. The science building has the chemistry lab and a science resource room. The foreign language building consists of several classrooms, a listening lab and the ESL program. High school students have access to our 60+ workstation computer lab with Internet connectivity. There are hardware and software security measures to ensure the students are as safe as possible in the lab. A modern kitchen and café." **Library:** "2." (N/P hours, etc.) **Sports facilities:** The school has two gyms, boys and girls locker rooms, tennis court, and outside basketball courts. **Theater/arts facilities:** Theater, with 200 person capacity. **Open/closed campus:** Closed campus. **Lunches:** Hot lunches made daily. **Bus Service:** SF Muni bus stop a block away. **Uniform/dress code:** Uniform. **Co-curricular activities/clubs:** Journalism, yearbook, debate, science, drama, dance, golf. **Foreign exchange programs/internships:** "Approved F1 Visa school." **Community service:** N/P. **Typical freshman schedule:** N/P.

Student Support Services
Counselor/student ratio (not including college counselors): 1:100. **Counseling:** Three part-time counselors. **Learning differences/disabilities:** "Not available."

Student Conduct and Health
Code of conduct: "Male students are to conduct themselves as gentlemen at all times and females, likewise. Students normally police themselves for the most part." **How school handles drugs/alcohol:** "Not tolerated. Referred immediately to Dean of Students and Principal for attention; outcome either suspension or expulsion." **Prevention and awareness programs:** Health class instructed by P.E. department.

Summer Program: None.

Parent Involvement
Parent participation: N/P. **Parent/Teacher communication:** Via e-mail; conference upon request. **Parent education:** N/P. **Donations:** N/P.

Sports: None.

What Sets School Apart From Others
"38% of graduates admitted to UC system."

How Parents/Students Characterize School
Parent response(s): "Safe environment for our student with a loving and caring faculty." **Student response(s):** N/P.

Crystal Springs Uplands School
400 Uplands Drive
Hillsborough, CA 94010
(650) 342-4175 *fax (650) 342-7611*
www.csus.org

Amy C. Richards, Head of School
Andrew P. Davis, Director of Admission, admission@csus.org

General
Coed day high school and middle school (G6-12). Nonsectarian. Founded in 1952. Nonprofit, member NAIS, CAIS, CASE, ERB, SSATB, BAAD, BAIHS, SSATB. **Enrollment:** 350. **Average class size:** 14. **Accreditation:** WASC/CAIS. **School year:** August-June. **School day:** 8:05 a.m.-3 p.m. (2:20 p.m. on Fridays). Late start (9:05), first Wednesday of every month. **Location:** Hillsborough, mid-way between San Francisco and Palo Alto (accessible by CalTrain and the school's shuttle).

Student Body
Geographic breakdown (counties): 90% from San Mateo; 6% from Santa Clara; 3% from San Francisco, 1% East Bay. **Ethnicity:** 55% Caucasian; 23% Asian-American; 3% Latino; 2% African-American; 17% multi-ethnic. **International students (I-20 status):** None. **Middle schools (freshman):** 17 (27%) came from 9 public middle schools; 11 (17%) from 6 independent, non-parochial schools; 6 (9%) from 3 parochial schools and 30 (47%) from the school's middle school.

Admission
Applications due: Mid-January (see website or call for date). **Application fee:** $75. **Application process:** Informational open houses are held three times a year, in October, November and December. Families should call to reserve places. The Admissions Office can be contacted after September 1st to request an application. Part I of the application (basic biographical information and some parent comments) needs to be submitted, along with the application fee, before a visit can be scheduled. Once Part I is received, the Admission Office will contact the family with a date for the student's half-day visit (which will include visiting classes with a student host, an interview and lunch). The rest of the application is due by the January deadline. Three academic recommendations are required along with the results of a standardized test. CSUS uses the BAAD common application forms, deadlines, and response dates. **No. of freshman applications:** Approx. 180 applications for 30-35 places. CSUS occasionally, but rarely, accept students into G10-12. **Minimum admission requirements:** "There are no 'cut-offs' in terms of grades or scores." **Test required:** ISEE or SSAT must be taken after January 1st of the year the student is submitting the application. The ISEE is administered on campus in December

and January (students must register for the test directly with ISEE at www.iseetest.org). **Preferences:** "CSUS is an academically challenging school, and we therefore seek students who are enthusiastic learners whose application form, interview, recommendations and transcript illustrate the likelihood of their success and happiness in an academically enriched environment such as ours. We do not have a guaranteed sibling or legacy admission policy, but we do value those relationships and will consider them in the admission process." **"We are looking for** motivated and engaged students who will contribute to our community in a variety of ways — academically, athletically, in the fine arts or as leaders. Having a mix of diverse students with diverse interests serves the school community well, for students learn as much from one another in the Commons as they do inside the classroom." **What kind of student do you best serve?** (See prior statement).

Costs
Latest tuition: $30,075 payable in 1 payment or in 2 if tuition insurance is purchased at a cost of approx. $155. A 10-payment plan is available through an outside agency (tuition insurance required). **Sibling discount:** None. **Tuition increases:** "Annual increases are to be expected." **Other costs:** Books cost approx. $700 per year. **Percentage of students receiving financial aid:** Approx. 19%. **Average grant:** $21,082. **Percentage of grants of half tuition or more:** 53%.

School's Mission Statement/Goals
"CSUS believes that students learn best in an environment that promotes learning in diverse ways about a complex world and nurtures the individual within a community of mutual trust, caring and respect."

Academic Program
"CSUS is committed to offering a challenging academic program in a supportive environment. We encourage students to take risks in their thinking, whether that occurs in class discussion or in writing. We hope to graduate students who are fascinated by ideas, who have their own points of view, and who are interested in sharing their ideas with others." **Courses offered** (AP=Advanced Placement, H=Honors, (H)=Honors option): **English:** English I-III, IV (AP) and second semester electives in G10-12; **History:** Comparative Cultures; Modern Europe; The Second World War; Judaism, Christianity and Islam; U.S. History and Government (more than 80% AP); AP European History; AP American Government and Politics; History of Art (AP); **Foreign Languages:** French I-II, French III (H), French Language (AP), French Literature (AP), French Culture, Spanish I-II, Spanish III (H), Spanish Literature (AP), Spanish Language (AP); **Math:** Math I-II, Math II (Advanced) Math III, Math III (Advanced), Advanced Pre-Calculus, Pre-Calculus/Calculus (H), AB Calculus (AP), BC Calculus (AP), Advanced Topics in Mathematics, Statistics; **Science:** Biology (AP), Chemistry (H), Astronomy, Physics (H/AP); **Arts:** Art (H/AP), Ceramics, Photography

(H), Video Production, Graphic Design, Dance (H), Dance Production, Advanced Dance Performance, Acting I-III, Production and Design, Mixed Chorus, Crystal Chorus, Madrigals, Mann's Men, Vick's Chicks, Orchestra, Jazz Band, AP Music Theory. **Computer lab/training:** Every classroom has network accessibility for every student with the option of an Ethernet line or a wireless connection. There are three electronic classrooms (with desktop computers for each student) located throughout the school. In addition, there is a student computer lab with Macs and PCs. The school's full-time technology staff services more than 250 personal computers, printers and network servers. Technology classes include Beginning Skills and Graphic Design, and the school's integration specialist assists faculty members with new and innovative technology instruction to enhance the learning process. **Grading:** A-F; given at quarters and semesters. **Graduation requirements:** 4 years English; 3 years history, foreign language, math, and laboratory science; 2 years fine arts; and 3 years of courses in the Mind/Body Program. P.E. or athletics are required through junior year. **Average nightly homework (M-Th):** Generally, G9: 2.5-3 hours; G10-12: 3 hours. **Faculty:** 34 f/t, 14 p/t; 50% hold master's degrees, 6% hold doctorates, and 2% hold JDs. (N/P gender) **Faculty ethnicity:** "15% of color." (N/P ethnicities) **Faculty selection/training:** "Faculty are interviewed by the relevant department and the administration, and give on-site teaching demonstrations. Faculty remains current and qualified with professional development assistance (workshops, school visits, classes) and in-service programs as well as peer assessment." **Teacher/student ratio:** 1:9. **Percentage of students enrolled in AP:** 95%; pass rate 99%. Two AP scholars with distinction, 6 AP scholars with honors, and 16 AP scholars. **Senior class profile** (mid 50%): SAT Math 650-740, SAT Critical Reading 610-750, SAT Writing 620-750; GPA: 3.63. **National Merit Scholarship Program:** 11 Semifinalists, 21 Commended students and 1 National Achievement Scholar in the last class. **College enrollment (last class):** [Last 4 years] 100% in 4-year. **Recent (last 3 yrs) colleges:** Alfred, Allegheny, Amherst, Arizona SU, Bard, Barnard, Bates, Berklee C of Music, Boston C, Boston U, Bowdoin, Brandeis, Brown, Bryn Mawr, Bucknell, UC (Berkeley, Davis, LA, Merced, SD, Santa Barbara, Santa Cruz), Cal Poly-SLO, Carleton, Carnegie Mellon, U-Chicago, Claremont-McKenna, Clark, Colby, Colgate, U-Colorado (Boulder), Columbia, Connecticut C, Cornell, U-Dallas, Dartmouth, Deep Springs, U-Denver, Duke, U-Edinburgh, Evergreen SC, George Washington, Georgetown, Hamilton, Hampton, Harvard, Harvey-Mudd, Hawaii Pacific Howard, Johns Hopkins, Lake Forest, Lehigh, London School of Economics, McGill, MIT, Middlebury, Mount Holyoke, NYU, UNC (Chapel Hill), Northeastern, Northwestern, Notre Dame de Namur, Occidental, U-Oregon, UOP, Parsons, Penn, Pepperdine, Pomona, Princeton, U-Puget Sound, Purdue, Reed, RPI, RISD, Rochester Institute of Technology, USF, SFSU, Santa Clara, Skidmore, Smith, Soka U-America, USC, SMU, St. John's C, St. John's U, St. Olaf, Stanford, Suffolk, Swarthmore, Tufts, Tulane, U-Utah, Vanderbilt, Vassar, Washington U, U-Washington, Wellesley, Wesleyan, Westminster, Whitman, Williams, Worcester Polytechnic Institute, and Yale.

Other Indicators the School is Accomplishing its Goals

"The vitality in the classroom, the strong interest in learning and the mutual respect of teachers and students are indicators that CSUS is a good place for students. Another measure of our success is the high level of community involvement. Parents, siblings, and current students come to the plays, the performances, the games, and other school events in large numbers, supporting one another. Finally, when our graduates go on to college, they are forceful in seeking similar relationships with their professors as they had with their CSUS teachers. Graduates recognize the importance of their one-on-one relationships with teachers and coaches."

Campus/Campus Life

Campus description: The school has a ten-acre suburban campus located on the San Francisco Peninsula midway between San Francisco and Palo Alto. The main building is the Crocker Mansion, an 85-year-old building now housing the library, administrative offices, and classrooms. Two newer buildings house the theater, student center, cafeteria, interactive classrooms, 5 science laboratories (completely renovated in 2006), and a computer laboratory. **Library:** The school's library, in a wing of the Uplands Mansion, includes 3 separate rooms for study, providing seating space for 86 students; an online card catalog; 7 computers with Internet access; 23 databases; 12,000 print volumes; 36 periodicals and 4 daily newspapers. **Sports facilities:** The Gryphon Center, a new fitness center and gymnasium, was completed in January 2003. It contains 2 full-size basketball/volleyball courts, fully equipped fitness room, locker rooms, training facility, dance studio, coaches' offices and classrooms. The outdoor campus includes 3 tennis courts, a large field (to be turfed in 2009) for soccer and other outdoor sports, and a smaller practice field. Open to students 8 a.m.-5 p.m. **Theater/arts facilities:** 400-seat theater. Yearly performances include a fall dramatic production, spring musical, Evening of Dance, Fine Arts Night and holiday performances. **Open/closed campus:** Closed. **Lunches:** Hot lunches and cold snacks are provided daily; the cost is included in the tuition. **Bus service:** The school's bus runs between the school and the CalTrain San Mateo station. (Cal train serves communities from San Francisco to San Jose). Late afternoon and evening shuttles are available. **Uniform/dress code:** "No formal dress code although students are expected to use their discretion and dress respectfully." **Co-curricular activities/clubs:** Activities include Crystal Visions (literary magazine), Crystal Ball (yearbook), Asian Awareness Club, French Club, Spanish Club, Cardinal Club (community service), Bay Area Music Makers, Rainbow Alliance, Fuzzy Green Environmentalists, Key Club (admissions), Junior Statesmen of America, Art for Recovery, Math Team, Outdoor Club, Botball, and Ultimate Frisbee.

Foreign exchange programs/internships: The school has had summer travel programs to France, Spain, China, England and Guatemala. Affiliated with Maine Coast Semester. **Community service:** Though not required, students volunteer with a wide variety of charities including working in soup kitchens, elderly homes, homeless shelters, Rebuilding Together and the American Red Cross. **Typical freshman schedule:** Six to 8 periods of 45-65 minutes each plus one 80-minute science lab each week; 35 minutes for lunch; and, Tuesday-Thursday, a 40-minute consultation/snack period. Advisory, Biology, French II, Comparative Cultures, English 9, Geometry, P.E./Fitness, study hall.

Student Support Services
Counselor/student ratio (not including college counselors): 1:350. **Counseling:** "Each student has an advisor. A health counselor is available for personal counseling. Students approach the counselor for help, or students are referred to counseling if the school notices changes in the student's behavior or attitude. There are two college counselors. College counseling begins in earnest during the junior year, as students are encouraged to explore colleges during spring break or summer before the senior year. During the 1st semester of the senior year, all students take 'College Quest' to meet with the college counselor and manage the college application process." **Learning differences/disabilities:** "Students with documented learning disabilities are given accommodations (i.e., extra time, use of laptops for essay tests). Please request a copy of our brochure addressing the school's program for students with learning differences."

Student Conduct and Health
Code of conduct: "The school has three major rules: remaining on campus; abstaining from drugs, alcohol, and/or tobacco at school events or on campus; and being honest (including academic honesty)." **How school handles drugs/alcohol:** "The customary penalty for use of drugs in connection with school life is immediate expulsion, if a student is 'caught.' However, if we hear a student is struggling with a potential addiction, or we suspect one, we will refer the student to counseling." **Prevention and awareness programs:** "Middle school students learn about sexuality, HIV/AIDS, and related issues in G7, and about tobacco, alcohol, and other drugs and addictions in G8. Ninth graders are presented with topics ranging from depression and suicide to eating disorders, sexuality and violence."

Summer Programs
For students entering GK-9 the following fall, the school offers a variety of programs in academic subjects, athletics and fine arts.

Parent Involvement
Parent participation: "Welcomed, but not required. The CSUS Parent Association seeks to promote cooperation among the parents, the

school, the community, and alumni, to encourage the members to participate in school activities and to further the aims and objectives of the school. All parents are members. Other volunteering, including driving students to away games or serving as a class parent, is encouraged." **Parent/teacher communication:** Quarter and semester grades are sent home; twice a year, parents, the student, and the advisor meet to discuss the student's progress. Teachers or advisors call parents if a student is experiencing academic difficulty. Dean's notices (usually behavior and discipline) and progress reports (mid-quarter academic notices for students doing particularly well or having difficulty) are also sent to parents. **Parent education:** The CSUS Parent Association offers programs to the entire parent body and to grade-level parents where an expert might speak to specific issues (adjusting to high school, driving, and social issues). CSUS is part of the "Common Ground" group of schools that together host a number of speakers and other educational activities throughout the year. **Donations:** "The CSUS Fund supports school programs annually. Over 90% of parents participate each year. The Parent Association hosts one major fundraiser each year, Mansion Madcap, to raise funds to support the faculty."

Sports
Students participate on a variety of competitive interscholastic athletic teams as a member of the WBAL (Central Coast Section), including, for boys and girls, soccer, basketball, baseball, 8-man football, volleyball, swimming, track and field, cross-country, and tennis; and coed golf and badminton. Normally more than 80% of the students participate in team sports.

What Sets School Apart From Others
"What sets CSUS apart from other good independent schools is the contrast between the way we look and the way we act. We look like a traditional college preparatory school, but we act like a small college. Again and again, CSUS students rave about the relationships they develop with their teachers. We ask a great deal of our students in extracurricular activities, academics and athletics; students respond well to these challenges and then challenge us! Our students are unafraid to be different and are encouraged to take academic risks. Our students thrive in the world 'after CSUS,' and we think that is in part because they learn so much from the CSUS community during their four to seven years here."

How Parents/Students Characterize School
Parent response(s): "My son and daughter both graduated from CSUS and what has amazed me is how central the school has remained in their lives. They credit CSUS with teaching them how to write and how to think for themselves; I cannot imagine a better place for them to have gone to school!" **Student response(s):** "Aside from having played a total of thirteen sports seasons in my past six and a half years

at CSUS, I've been amazed by the other 349 people that I go to school with. Whether their strength is in math or the sciences, or English and history and language, or just ... everything, every student here is a student first. But we are also musicians, actors and actresses, athletes, computer wizards, and student leaders." "Participating in student government has given me the opportunity to experience the amazing support system here. There is a mutual respect between the faculty/administration and the students. What isn't a given is how committed these teachers are to helping us understand and make connections. The commitment to academic excellence isn't just about getting good grades and taking the hardest classes. Teachers here at CSUS meet with their students during free periods, study halls, before and after school, and even at lunch, if necessary, to help us out. It's amazing how supportive they are of our activities and interests, even outside the classroom. I see my teachers at games, plays, and other events that we participate in. I have grown during my time at CSUS in ways that I never thought possible."

De La Salle High School
1130 Winton Drive
Concord, CA 94518
(925) 686-3310 *fax (925) 686-3474*
www.dlshs.org

Br. Christopher Brady, F.S.C., Principal
Mark DeMarco (Class of '78), President
Joseph Grantham, Admissions Director, granthamj@dlshs.org

General
Boys Catholic day high school. (80% Catholic). Founded in 1965. Non-profit. **Enrollment:** Approx. 1,000. **Average class size:** 30. **Accreditation:** WASC. **School year:** Aug.-June. **School day:** "Block Schedule" (N/P hours). **Location:** In East Bay accessible by BART and bus.

Student Body
Geographic breakdown (counties): N/P. **Ethnicity:** 63% Caucasian (non-Latino); 4% Asian; 10% Hispanic; 4% African-American; 7% Filipino; 1% Native American; 11% multi-ethnic. **Middle schools (freshman):** 60% came from local parochial schools. (N/P # schools)

Admission
Applications due: Early December (call for date or visit website). Applications completed and submitted online. **Application fee:** $75. **Application process:** Transcripts, grade school test scores, teacher recommendations, interview (if requested by DLS), entrance exam. **No. of freshman applications:** 450 (N/P # places). **Minimum admis-

sion requirements: N/P. Test required: HSPT. Preferences: N/P. "We are looking for young men of Faith, Integrity, and Scholarship." What kind of student do you best serve? (See prior statement.)

Costs

Latest tuition: $13,200. Sibling discount: None. Tuition increases: N/P. Other costs: Book rental fee $300. Percentage of students receiving financial aid: 24%. Financial aid deadline: Mid-February (call for date or visit website). Average grant: $6,850. Percentage of grants of half tuition or more: 10%.

School's Mission Statement/Goals

"De La Salle High School is a Roman Catholic educational community where students are loved, instructed, and guided according to the traditions of the Brothers of the Christian Schools and the charism of St. John Baptist de La Salle, founder of the Brothers and Patron of Teachers. • De La Salle High School provides a Catholic, Lasallian education rooted in a liberal arts tradition which prepares young people for life and college. The school seeks to educate students spiritually, academically, physically, and socially through the promotion of a vital faith life, sponsorship of strong academic programs, a wide range of student activities, and the witness of a concerned and dedicated faculty, administration, and staff. • De La Salle High School recognizes and promotes the dignity and respect of each student by providing an environment that is moral, caring, and joyful. Within such a setting, the school seeks to challenge its students to serve others, especially the poor, and to deepen a sense of responsibility for humanity's future. • De La Salle High School seeks to serve qualified students with varied academic needs and diverse social, cultural, and economic backgrounds and does so in partnership with parents and all those who are committed to living the Lasallian heritage."

Academic Program

Courses offered: N/P. "Mathematics, Music, Art, Science, Social Studies, and Foreign Languages." "De La Salle cooperates with neighboring Carondelet High School, a Catholic high school for girls, in offering both schools a vast list of coeducational academic courses and activities." Computer lab/training: N/P. Grading: A-F. Graduation requirements: 240 credits. (N/P courses, # credits each). Average nightly homework (M-Th): N/P. Faculty: N/P. Faculty ethnicity: N/P. Faculty selection/training: N/P. Teacher/student ratio: 1:30. Percentage of students enrolled AP/pass rate: 25%; pass rate 70%. Senior class profile (mean): SAT Math 588, Critical Reading 575, Writing 563; GPA: N/P. National Merit Scholarship Program: N/P. College enrollment (last class): 98% to "major colleges and universities"; 87% to 4-year, 11% to 2-year, 2% other." Recent colleges: N/P.

Other Indicators the School is Accomplishing its Goals: N/P.

Campus/Campus Life
Campus description: N/P. Library: N/P. Sports facilities: N/P. Theater/arts facilities: N/P. Open/closed campus: N/P. Lunches: N/P. Bus service: N/P. Uniforms/dress code: N/P. Co-curricular activities/clubs: N/P. Foreign exchange programs/internships: N/P. Community service: N/P. Typical freshman schedule: English, math, Religious Studies, World History, foreign language, First Aid/Health and Physical Science.

Student Support Services
Counselor/student ratio (not including college counselors): 1:200. Counseling: N/P. Learning differences/disabilities: The school's Spartan Success Program is a specialized remedial program designed to help incoming 9th graders in the area of math and study skills; limited to 30 students.

Student Conduct and Health: N/P.

Summer Programs
Required for all conditionally accepted incoming 9th graders.

Parent Involvement: N/P.

Sports
Fall: Cross-country, football, water polo; Winter: basketball, soccer, wrestling; Spring: baseball, golf, lacrosse, rugby (club only), swimming and diving, tennis, track and field, and volleyball.

What Sets School Apart From Others
"A Catholic Lasallian education, where students 'Enter to Learn, and Leave to Serve.' A De La Salle graduate is a man of: Faith, Integrity, and Scholarship."

How Parents/Students Characterize School: N/P.

Drew School
2901 California Street
San Francisco, CA 94115
(415) 409-3739 fax (415) 346-0720
www.drewschool.org

Sam Cuddeback, Head of School
Elizabeth Tilden, Director of Marketing and Enrollment
et@drewschool.org

General

Coed day high school. Independent. Founded in 1908. Nonprofit, member CAIS, NAIS, BAIHS, BCL, SSATB, BAAD. **Enrollment:** Approx. 250. **Average class size:** 14. **Accreditation:** WASC/CAIS. **School year:** Sept.-June. **School day:** 8:15 a.m.-3 p.m. Mon-Thurs. and until 2:30 p.m. Friday. **Location:** In a residential neighborhood between Pacific Heights and Presidio Heights, accessible by the 1 and 24 Muni bus lines.

Student Body

Geographic breakdown (counties): "We enroll students from San Francisco, the Peninsula, Marin County, and the East Bay." (N/P %). **Ethnicity:** "Students of color make up 20% of our student body." (N/P % ethnicities). **International students (I-20 status):** 5%. **Middle schools (freshman):** 20% came from public middle schools; 75% from private, non-parochial schools; 5% from parochial schools (N/P # schools).

Admission

Applications due: Early January (call for date). **Application fee:** $75. **Application process:** "Parents should try to attend one of our open houses, and students should plan on spending a half day with us during the fall. We evaluate each student individually and give equal consideration to transcripts, standardized test scores, teacher recommendations, the writing sample and the interview." **No. of freshman applications:** Approx. 375 (N/P # places). **Minimum admission requirements:** None. **Test required:** SSAT, ISEE, or ERB. **Preferences:** None. **"We are looking for** students who have a positive attitude and the commitment and motivation to achieve academic success. Drew students also have an interest in participating in a wide range of extra-curricular programs, including athletics, the arts, music, and community service." **What kind of student do you best serve?** "We are committed to enrolling students of diverse backgrounds from the Bay Area and around the world. All Drew students have the desire and the motivation to meet their individual potential."

Costs

Latest tuition: $28,500. **Sibling discount:** None. **Tuition increases:** Approx. 5%. **Other costs:** None. **Percentage of students receiving financial aid:** 38%. **Financial aid deadline:** Early January (call for date). **Average grant:** $15,675. **Percentage of grants of half-tuition or more:** N/P.

School's Mission Statement/Goals

"Our mission is to enhance the academic talents and self-esteem of our students and better enable them to meet the challenges and opportunities of being international students."

Academic Program

Courses offered (AP=Advanced Placement, H=Honors, (AP)=AP option, (H)=Honors option): **Arts:** (AP/Advanced) Studio Art, Animation, Dance, Drama, (Advanced) Drawing and Design, Filmmaking/Digital Video, Painting, Photography, Printmaking, Sculpture; **English:** English I-II, Writing for College, American Voices in Modern Drama, Love, SciFi Literature, Explorations of Identity, Modernism, Cinema, Survey of American Literature & Thought, The Harlem Renaissance, Literature of Our Place, Fact & Fiction: Unique Voices in Modern Fiction, Contemporary World Poets, Shakespeare, Environmental Literature, The Memoir, Form & Function (Creative Writing), Cinema: Theory & Practice; **Foreign language:** American Sign Language, French I-III (Conversation and Composition), French IV (H), AP French, Spanish I-II, Spanish Conversation, Spanish III H, Spanish IV, AP Spanish, Mandarin (2-4), American Sign Language (1-3); **Math:** Integrated Math (1-3), Statistics, Pre-Calculus, Calculus (AP), Advanced Math Topics; **Music:** Music Fundamentals, Music and Culture, History of Jazz, Digital Music Recording I-II, Digital Music Composition; **Science:** Integrated Science, Biology, Advanced Biology (Cell and Molecular, Anatomy and Physiology), Genetics, Evolution and Ecology, Marine Science, Chemistry (H/AP), Physics (H/AP); **Social Science:** World History (Africa/Islamic World), Renaissance/Revolutions (French/Russian), U.S. History (H), Anthropology, Sociology, Civics/Humanities, Economics, Psychology. **Computer lab/training:** Two computer labs work off the school's server with Mac and PC/Windows capabilities. **Grading:** A-F with written comments given at 3 marking periods each semester. **Graduation requirements:** 4 years English; 3 years math and social science; 2 years science, foreign language and P.E.; 1 year fine arts. **Average nightly homework (M-Th):** Approx. 2 hours (1/2 hour per subject). **Faculty:** 35 f/t and p/t. (N/P gender, degrees). **Faculty ethnicity:** "15% faculty of color." (N/P ethnicities) **Faculty selection/training:** N/P. **Teacher/student ratio:** 1:11. **Percentage of students enrolled in AP:** 25%; pass rate 92%. **Senior class profile (mean):** SAT N/P; GPA: 3.33 **National Merit Scholarship Program:** N/P. **College enrollment (last class):** 98% to 4-year (N/P rest). **Recent (last 4 yrs) colleges:** American U, Bennington, CalArts, CSU (Chico, Humboldt, SD, SF), Carnegie Mellon, SFCC, Clark, Colgate, C of Marin, Concordia, Cornell, Emerson, George Washington, Humboldt SU, Lewis & Clark, Loyola Marymount, Morehouse, Mount Holyoke, Northeastern, Parsons, Pitzer, Simmons, Skidmore, Smith, UC (Berkeley, Davis, Irvine, LA, Riverside, Santa Barbara, SD, Santa Cruz), U-Colorado (Boulder), U-Denver, U-Puget Sound, U-Redlands, USD, USF, and USC.

Other Indicators the School is Accomplishing its Goals: N/P.

Campus/Campus Life

Campus description: Completed in the fall of 2001, the campus includes 12 large classrooms, 2 new science labs, 2 seminar rooms, a library, 2 computer labs, a learning resource center, music rehearsal space, and an outdoor courtyard. **Library:** The library is open before, during, and after school until 4:30 p.m. "The continually evolving collection consists of up-to-date reference material and circulating books in non-fiction, fiction, and biography; print magazines and periodical databases; a College Resources collection; and videos and DVD's on a variety of subjects that support the curriculum. Computers with Internet access, including the Drew Library's online catalog, are available in the library and adjoining computer lab." **Sports facilities:** The school uses off-site gym and city fields. **Theater/arts facilities:** Theater space and an art studio designed for natural light. Drew students produce one play each semester in which they have the opportunity to act, design, and produce. **Open/closed campus:** Open. **Lunches:** Students bring lunches or visit nearby cafés/food stores. **Bus service:** North Bay students have the option of daily bus service. **Uniforms/dress code:** "Although Drew does not have a formal dress code, students' clothing must be reasonably clean and in good repair, not excessively revealing or distracting, and not showing emblems or slogans that are offensive or profane." **Co-curricular activities/clubs:** Student Council, International Club, Adventure Society, Amnesty International, Chess and Games Club, Community Service, Drama Group, Thai Club, Spanish Club, Yearbook, UNITY (multi-cultural awareness), Gay-Straight Alliance, Dragon Ambassadors, Bowling Club, WERD (school's literary magazine). **Foreign exchange programs/internships:** Exchange programs, Senior Project Internships, DEALL Internships. **Community service:** Cobb Middle School After-school Helpers, Blood Drive, Penny Drive for Breast Cancer, SF Food Bank, Glide Memorial. **Typical freshman schedule:** English, math, science, history, foreign language, and art or music.

Student Support Services

Counselor/student ratio (not including college counselors): 1:250. **Counseling:** "In addition to offering supportive counseling services for anxiety/stress, depression/hopelessness, sleeplessness, boredom, peer relationships, drug and eating issues, our school counselor views his role as an advocate for students and their families. There are many situations, both inside and outside of school, that affect the lives of students. A conversation with our counselor can help someone at school be informed of what challenges he or she is facing. He will offer support, as well as appropriate communication to the teachers, to accommodate the student's needs. The counselor is available for confidential meetings with students and families from 9 a.m. to 3:30 p.m. (M, W, TH) and Fridays from 9 a.m. to 2:30 p.m." **Learning differences/disabilities:** "Drew is committed to supporting students with various learning profiles including those with documented learning differences. Drew offers supplemental assistance through its Learning Support Program and offers several assistive technology applications to help students succeed."

Student Conduct and Health

Code of conduct: "The rules are based on fundamental principles of honesty, responsibility, concern for others, self-respect, and reverence for life. Drew espouses certain values that are consistent with its educational objectives. In addition to minimal compliance with the rules, students who choose to attend Drew are expected to give allegiance to these values. Students are expected to show basic courtesy to all members of the community and to visitors. Students should treat the school seriously and refrain from conduct that detracts from that environment." **How school handles drugs/alcohol:** "Students will not possess or use illegal drugs or alcoholic beverages during school, or sell or distribute drugs or alcohol at any time. Students found to be selling or distributing drugs or alcohol will be dismissed from Drew. Students who are using drugs or alcohol will receive counseling and helpful intervention to the extent that the school is able to provide it." **Prevention and awareness programs:** Covered in a health and wellness class required of all freshmen and new students.

Summer Programs

Drew's Summer Program offers for-credit courses in a broad range of disciplines in 1-, 4-, or 6-week session. Students have the choice of taking one or two courses. The program is open to all middle school and high school students. Drew also offers a "Drew in Africa" program in the summer. Students spend approximately 3 weeks in Senegal as part of a cultural exchange and global community service project.

Parent Involvement

Parent participation: "The Drew School Parent/Guardian Association is an integral part of the Drew community. Its mission is two-fold: to offer vigorous, impassioned support of the academic and philosophical goals of the school and to nurture a community of fellowship for the parents and guardians of Drew, which allows all of us to honor our diversity yet be united by the commonality of our parenthood." **Parent/teacher communication:** "Drew recommends that parents and teachers exchange e-mail addresses as an efficient method of communication, although private messages may be left on a teacher's voice-mail." Parent/teacher conferences are on two days in early November. Meetings with parents, guardians, teachers, administrators and students can be set up at the family's request. **Parent education:** N/P. **Donations:** "The school engages in fundraising to cover a portion of its annual operating budget."

Sports

"Drew participates in the Bay Area Conference of the BCL West Division and fields teams in the following areas: for boys, soccer, basketball, baseball, volleyball and tennis; for girls, volleyball, basketball, soccer and tennis; coed cross-country. The emphasis is on participation. Wherever possible, a 'no cut' policy is employed, and all students who are willing to make a serious commitment to the team are encouraged to get involved, regardless of their age or skill level."

What Sets School Apart From Others
"We seek to provide our students with the skills and confidence to be truly independent thinkers and responsible decision makers. Drew provides an environment that is safe and nurturing for students in the process of growing into adulthood. Our faculty is talented and come to us with a variety of teaching and life experiences. Small classes and a close-knit community characterize the Drew experience. The value we place on experiential learning is manifested in our Drew Education for Active Lifelong Learning program. For a week each spring, students can choose from a variety of experiences ranging from participating in an exchange program with students from Quebec or seeing the wildlife in the Galapagos to learning how to sail or dance."

How Parents/Students Characterize School
Parent response(s): "My oldest son graduated from Drew two years ago, and we did not think twice about sending our youngest, who is a freshman this year. The two boys could not be more different, but Drew is a school that embraces all kinds of kids. The teachers continue to make learning fun and really know how to connect with their students."
Student response(s): "Drew is a school where teachers learn as much from the students as students learn from the teachers. The classroom experience is such a collaborative effort. I always feel that I can openly express my thoughts without being unfairly judged."

East Bay Waldorf School
3800 Clark Road
El Sobrante, CA 94803
(510) 223-3570 *fax (510) 222-3141*
www.eastbaywaldorf.org

Sabine Kully, Chair, College of Teachers
Morgan Cleveland, Administrator, morgan@eastbaywaldorf.org
Audrey Lee, HS Admissions Director, audrey@eastbaywaldorf.org

General
Coed day high school and lower school (K-8) based on Waldorf principles. Nonsectarian. Independent. Founded in 2000, lower school founded in 1980. Nonprofit, member AWSNA, BAIHS, BAAD, EBISA. **Enrollment:** 43 (high school). **Average class size:** 12-15. **Accreditation:** WASC, AWSNA. **School year:** Aug.-June. **School day:** 8:15 a.m.-3:25 p.m. **Location:** In El Sobrante, on Clark Road off San Pablo Dam Road at the trailhead of Wildcat Canyon Regional Park; accessible by school bus and AC Transit.

Student Body

Geographic breakdown (counties): 54.6% from Alameda; 41.8% from Contra Costa; 1.8% from San Francisco; 1.8% from Solano. **Ethnicity:** 72.9% Caucasian; 3.6% African-America; 3.6% Asian; 10.9% Hispanic; 7.2% Pan-Pacific; 1.8% Middle Eastern. **International students (I-20 status):** None. Three to 5 students visit for 3 months from Spanish- or German-speaking countries. **Middle schools (freshman):** 84% are from Waldorf elementary schools; 16% from private, non-parochial, or public schools (N/P # schools).

Admission

Applications due: January (call for date). **Application fee:** $75. **Application process:** "Request an information/application packet from the school office. Attend a high school open house (call for dates); schedule a student visit to the high school. Once you have submitted your completed application, recommendation forms (BAIHS), and the application fee, an admissions interview for the parents and student will be arranged. Written, academic, and artistic work samples are requested from the student." **No. of freshman applications:** N/P. **Minimum admission requirements:** None. **Test required:** ISEE. **Preferences:** Siblings and Waldorf lower school students. "**We are looking for** students who love learning and who want to develop their capacities in a school environment that values academic learning, artistic discipline, and student initiative." **What kind of student do you best serve?** "Our program serves students of diverse backgrounds who enjoy learning through active inquiry, artistic expression, and experiential education."

Costs

Latest tuition: $18,800 payable in 10 payments. **Sibling discount:** 10% for 1, 15% for 2, and 25% for 3 or more. **Tuition increases:** Approx. 5%. **Other costs:** Approx. $1,000 for books and supplies. **Percentage of students receiving financial aid:** 47%. **Financial aid deadline:** February (call for date). **Average grant:** Approx. $5,000. **Percentage of grants of half-tuition or more:** 0.

School's Mission Statement/Goals

"The high school at the East Bay Waldorf School strives to enable adolescents to become inspired, purposeful, and effective in the world, with a lifelong love of learning. The Waldorf high school curriculum meets the unique needs of adolescents with rigorous academics, artistic discipline, and practical challenge, preparing students to face the future with confidence, competence, and initiative. The high school both contributes to and benefits from the rich natural and cultural resources of the San Francisco Bay Area."

Academic Program

"The high school offers a comprehensive curriculum, including academic and artistic offerings, which exceeds college entrance requirements and prepares students for a full range of career goals. The curriculum is carefully designed to address the developmental stages of adolescence. Each of the core subjects is visited each year with a different emphasis through the main lesson blocks which focus on one subject for 1.5 hours per morning for a period of three or four weeks. These morning lessons rotate subject areas (history, chemistry, literature, etc.) throughout the year, and they supplement the year-long classes in English, mathematics, social studies, foreign language, art, music, P.E., and movement. Thus, for example, different aspects of the field of biology are brought in G9-12. The culmination of the high school education is the ability of students to think for themselves with the confidence that they can make a positive contribution in life. ... The make-up of the student body and curriculum offered is similar to that of Waldorf schools throughout the country." **Courses offered** (AP=Advanced Placement, H=Honors, (AP)=AP option, (H)=Honors option): **English:** English 1-2, English 3-4 (H), Comedy and Tragedy: Dramatic Literature, World Mythology, Poetry, Evolution of Language, Archetypes in the Bible, Shakespeare, The Quest, Russian Literature, Modern World Literature, The Transcendentalists; **History/Social Studies:** Foundations of U.S. History, American Government, Economics, Civil War-World War II, World War II-Present, Revolutions, Ancient Civilizations, Greek Thought, World History: Rome through the Renaissance, World Religions, Modern World History, Symptomotology; **Foreign language:** Spanish 1-4, German 1-4; **Science:** Anatomy, Human Physiology, Cellular Biology, Botany, Zoology, Evolution and Genetics, Environmental Science and Ecology, Geology and Physical Geography, Water Systems and Climatology, Astronomy, Organic Chemistry, Inorganic Chemistry, Chemistry of Elements, Biochemistry and Chemical Technology, Thermodynamics, Kinetics, Electricity and Magnetism, Optics and Acoustics; **Math:** Geometry (H), Math Analysis and Trigonometry (H), Pre-Calculus, Calculus (H), Combinatorics, Conic Sections, Logarithms and Exponents, Trigonometry, Surveying, Projective Geometry, Analytic Geometry; **Arts:** History of Art, History of Music, History of Architecture, Choir, Orchestra, Instrumental Ensemble, World Music, Drama I-IV, Play Production, Eurhythmy I-IV, Art Survey, Dark and Light, Block Printing, Modeling, Painting, Veil Painting, Sculpture, The Figure in Drawing and Painting, Portraiture, Stone Carving, Basketry, Pottery, Weaving, Papermaking, Iron Forging, Woodworking, Carpentry, Stained Glass, Jewelry/Metalwork, Bookbinding, Photography, Elective Media, Art Elective; **P.E.:** P.E./Movement I-IV, Outdoor Education; **Other:** Health and Addictions, Relationships and Sexuality, Communication Skills, Child Development; **Work Program:** On-Site Building Project, Off-Site Service Project, Individual Vocational Internships, Serving the World, Community Service. Special Programs: Independent Study,

Junior Projects, Senior Projects, Gardening. **Computer lab/training:** "We offer courses on computer technology and integrate technology use when appropriate into our coursework. High school computer resources include computer workstations (over 12), including Internet access." **Grading:** A-F and individual written evaluations. **Graduation requirements:** Requirements are designed to exceed UC/CSU and private university entrance requirements for admission and include 40 credits each in English and visual and performing arts, including music; 30 credits each in history, social science, math, lab science and foreign language; 20 credits in P.E. and movement; and 45 additional credits of high school coursework. **Average nightly homework (M-Th):** Varies, 2-3 hours. **Faculty:** 21; 38% male, 62% female; 67% "have completed a post-graduate course of study." (N/P degrees) **Faculty ethnicity:** N/P. **Faculty selection/training:** "The faculty is selected from teachers trained in the Waldorf method (2-3 years post-baccalaureate training resulting in teacher certification), and who have at least a bachelor's degree or the equivalent in their fields of specialization." **Teacher/student ratio:** 1:5. **Percentage of students enrolled in AP:** Not offered. **Most recent senior class profile (mean)** SAT Math 565, SAT Critical Reading 568, SAT Writing 570; GPA: 3.36. **National Merit Scholarship Program:** N/P. **College enrollment (last class):** 92%; 77% to 4-year, 15% to 2-year. **Recent (last 3 yrs) colleges:** Art Institute of Chicago, Bates, CSU (SF, Cal Poly-SLO, Chico, Sacramento, Sonoma), Colorado C, Cornell U, Eugene Lang C of the New School for Social Research, Lewis & Clark, NYU, Occidental, Smith, St. John's C, St. Mary's C of California, Soka U, Tulane, UC (Davis, Santa Barbara and Santa Cruz), U-Puget Sound, and Whitman C.

Other Indicators the School is Accomplishing its Goals

"Waldorf education addresses the child as no other education does. ... By the time they reach us at the college and university level, these students are grounded broadly and deeply and have a remarkable enthusiasm for learning. Such students possess the eye of discoverers and the compassionate heart of the reformer, which, when joined to a task, can change the planet." (A. Zajonc, Ph.D., Amherst College.) • "Waldorf graduates stand out from the crowd in numerous ways. They are mature, creative, intelligent, multi-dimensional and profoundly self-motivated. In an age of conformity and materialism, Waldorf students are profoundly compassionate and free-thinking. They are engaged with the most vital issues of our time and in ways which utilize and evoke the deepest dimensions of human consciousness. In this sense, they are luminaries and world redeemers, cultural physicians, at a time when the world needs them most." (D. Richards, Berkeley High School) • "Being personally acquainted with a number of Waldorf students, I can say that they come closer to realizing their own potentials than practically anyone I know." (J. Weizenbaum, MIT)

Campus/Campus Life

Campus description: The campus, nestled against the East Bay hills, is located on 11 acres adjacent to the trailhead of Wildcat Canyon Regional Park. Students have been involved with building projects on the grounds, including construction of biology ponds, Japanese garden, high school amphitheater, carved granite sculptures, and a solar-powered straw bale craft studio near the school's biodynamic garden. **Library:** "A growing library plus Internet computer research resources." (N/P hours etc.) **Sports facilities:** N/P. **Theater/arts facilities:** N/P. **Open/closed campus:** Closed campus (seniors have off-campus lunch weekly). **Lunches:** Students bring their own snacks and lunches. **Bus service:** Two school bus routes from central East Bay and Contra Costa locations, including BART stations, plus AC Transit. **Uniforms/dress code:** "The dress code emphasizes appropriate dress where individual expression is balanced by support for the atmosphere needed for learning." **Co-curricular activities/clubs:** Drama club, instrumental ensembles, environmental/ecology, eurythmy troupe, Model U.N., social club, student government, yearbook, student activism, performing arts events, and sports. **Foreign exchange programs/internships:** A three-month international exchange program is offered in G10. "The Waldorf movement worldwide enables us to offer a unique program where a student can visit a school and family environment that share basic values and education goals, with no exchange of tuition." G11 students choose a vocational or professional field that they would like to explore. The students spend two weeks in internships, followed by written reports and presentations on their experiences. Seniors complete Senior Projects, in which they focus on an area of particular interest; these projects may include an internship experience. All seniors also participate in a service program called "Serving the World," in which they engage in service work in nonprofit organizations away from home for several weeks. Some of these organizations include Camphill Communities for developmentally disabled adults and children located in the U.S. and abroad, public school kindergartens in disadvantaged neighborhoods, an orphanage in Rio de Janeiro, and the Wildlife Institute in Moscow. **Community service:** "Students in G10 visit a village in Mexico to help with building projects for an orphanage or medical clinic. High school students volunteer their services for local environmental clean up. Our hope is to offer a real enrichment to the student's experience and to help our local community as well." **Typical freshman schedule:** Mornings begin with a 1.5 hour main lesson period; subjects rotate in 3-4 week intensive blocks. After a short break, students have 45-minute classes in math, English, history, foreign language, art, music, P.E. and movement.

Student Support Services

Counselor/student ratio (not including college counselors): 1:43. "Each high school grade is guided by a sponsor or sponsors, who both teach and serve as mentors to the students during their high school careers." **Counseling:** "The counseling program includes personal and group counseling. The school has a college and career counselor on staff who meets extensively with juniors and seniors and their families, as well as provides parents of all high school students with college and career guidance. The school offers guidance for test taking and some test preparation classes." **Learning differences/disabilities:** "The school has several resource teachers on the K-12 staff who are available to support students with mild learning differences. These services include consultation with students and parents on learning challenges; referral for assessment, tutoring, and therapeutic programs; and consultation with teachers on classroom and assessment practices to meet the needs of students with diverse learning styles."

Student Conduct and Health
Code of conduct: "Violation of school rules results in disciplinary action and may result in suspension or dismissal." **How school handles drugs/alcohol:** The campus is tobacco, alcohol, and drug-free. Students are referred to counseling for substance abuse. **Prevention and awareness programs:** "Educational programs for all students on health, addiction, sexuality, and communication, including visiting speakers."

Summer Programs: "None. Community service is encouraged."

Parent Involvement
Parent participation: "Voluntary, though the school believes the support of parents is critical to the success of the high school experience. The school hopes that parents will be involved in as many ways as their schedules allow, as drivers, chaperones, organizers, and in fundraising." **Parent/teacher communication:** Parents are encouraged to attend parent meetings and to communicate closely with their child's class sponsor. Parents and teachers communicate through semi-annual parent/teacher conferences, progress reports, evaluations, and report cards. **Parent education:** Parents have a suggested reading list, a parent library, and informational lectures and events. **Donations:** "Parents are asked to contribute to the school through volunteerism and the annual fund."

Sports
The school, a member of the NCS and CIF, offers seasonal games and competitions with other schools. Sports include basketball, volleyball, soccer, track and field, and baseball. The P.E. program may include hiking, biking, sea kayaking, fitness training, swimming, yoga, gardening, archery, African dance, basketball, soccer, wind surfing, ultimate frisbee, and rock climbing.

What Sets School Apart From Others
"The teachers are committed to and united in their philosophy of educating the whole human being. The wisdom of an integrated cur-

riculum teaches young people to become independent thinkers who approach life with scientific observation and artistic sensibility, and who take initiative in life."

How Parents/Students Characterize School

Parent response(s): "The high school is the crown of the Waldorf curriculum. Students are able to go deeply into each subject and to follow up their individual interests with special projects and internships. The teachers are very enthusiastic and inspiring. I am amazed at how deeply the curriculum meets the development of students at each age. My daughter loves learning and loves school. She is challenged and maintains a curiosity about the world, while some of her friends from other schools have become jaded and bored. She is nourished and appreciated by her teachers and fellow classmates. I am incredibly grateful that such a school exists, and that the teachers are so dedicated to nurturing my daughter's whole being." "The qualities of the education have been: steadfastness, depth, integrity, wholeness. The students have been encouraged to see things from different perspectives. These young people have the capacity to fully engage in what they are doing in a cooperative and caring way, with purpose, responsibility, joy, and humor." "My son has been taught in a way that allows him to see ideas and concepts from many different perspectives. He is currently taking double majors at his university in music and engineering." **Student response(s):** "I love this school! I am so happy to be here!" "Our small school community feels like my family." "I love the teachers. I feel like they know what I am capable of and who I am."

Fremont Christian School

4760 Thornton Avenue
Fremont, CA 94536
(510) 744-2242 *fax (510) 791-7672*
www.fremontchristian.com

C.K. Rankin, Superintendent
Tricia Meyer Principal, tmeyer@fremontchristian.com
Laura Johnson, Admissions Dir., ljohnson@fremontchristian.com

General

Coed Christian day high school. "FCS is the largest department of Harbor Light Church." Non-denominational. Founded in 1968. Nonprofit, (memberships N/P). **Enrollment:** 218 (high school). **Average class size:** 17. **Accreditation:** WASC/ACSI. **School year:** 10-mo. calendar. **School day:** 8 a.m.-2:30 p.m.; optional period at 7 a.m. **Location:** In Fremont, one mile off Hwy. 880 at Thornton Avenue.

Student Body

Geographic breakdown (counties): 100% from Alameda County; **Ethnicity:** 41% Caucasian (non-Latino); 32% Asian; 7% Asian Indian; 12% Latino; 7% African-American; 1% multi-ethnic. **International students (I-20 status):** 4%. **Middle schools (freshman):** 80% are from school's own junior high program; 20% from public middle schools. (N/P # schools).

Admission

Applications due: May-July. **Application fee:** $60. **Application process:** Recommendations, test scores, transcript, personal interview, math placement test, and writing assessment. **No. of freshman applications:** N/P. **Minimum admission requirements:** "2.0 GPA with no Fs; no suspensions/expulsions. For foreign students, a 61 on TOEFL for admission after 9th grade. Prior to 9th grade, each situation is evaluated individually." **Test required:** TOEFL." **Preferences:** N/P. "**We are looking for** students who will thrive within our nurturing family environment that offers students the opportunity to build quality relationships within the learning context of specialty programs like biotechnology, fine arts and athletics. **What kind of student do you best serve?** "The middle 50% of college-bound students."

Costs

Latest tuition: $10,260 (4% discount if paid in advance). **Sibling discount:** "Yes. Varies by number of siblings. **Tuition increases:** 5-8%. **Other costs:** $280 tech fee and registration. Academic field trips, overnight trips, novels and optional activities may incur fees. **Percentage of students receiving financial aid:** 10%. **Financial aid deadline:** June (call for exact date). **Average grant:** $2,000. **Percentage of grants of half-tuition or more:** 10%.

School's Mission Statement/Goals

"Fremont Christian School's mission is to partner with the family to build tomorrow today by providing a learning environment in which students will be equipped to grow continually in mind, body, spirit and community following Christ's example in Luke 2:52: A Sound Mind—developing intelligence, wisdom and understanding. A Sound Body—developing the habit of a physically healthy lifestyle. A Sound Spirit—developing the habit of a Biblically-based Christian lifestyle. A Sense of Community - developing the habits of giving time, money, and talent."

Academic Program

Courses offered (AP=Advanced Placement, H=Honors, (AP)=AP option, (H)=Honors option): **English:** English 9-10 (H), English 11: American Literature, AP English Language & Composition, English 12: English (British) Literature, AP English Literature & Composition, Advanced Composition and Rhetoric. **Social studies:** World

Geography, World History, U.S. History (AP), Civics, Economics, AP U.S. Govt. & Politics; **Math:** Algebra I-II, Geometry, Analytic Geometry/Trigonometry, (PreCalculus), AP Calculus AB; **Science:** Introduction to Physical Science, Biology I, AP Biology, Chemistry, Physics, Biotechnology I;**Languages:** American Sign Language I-II, Spanish I-III, AP Spanish Language. **Arts:** Art Drawing, Art Design, AP Studio Art, Concert Choir, Vocal Ensemble, Symphonic Band, Intermediate Handbells, Advanced Handbells. Theatre Arts; **Bible:** Old Testament Survey, Life of Christ/Gospels, Early Church History & Pauline Epistles, Senior Seminar; **Other:** P.E., Computer Applications, Adobe Photoshop, Web Page Design++ Programming; United Study Body (USB) Council, Yearbook. **Computer lab/training:** Computer Applications and computer elective required for graduation. **Grading:** A-F. **Graduation requirements:** English (50 credits); Bible (40 credits); social studies (30 credits); math (20-40 credits, contingent upon level of rigor); science (20 credits); P.E. (20 credits); computer education (15 credits); fine arts (10 credits) electives (55 credits) - Total of 260 credits (10 credits is equivalent to one year). **Average nightly homework (M-Th):** 2-3 hours. **Faculty:** 24 f/t, 3 p/t; 41% male, 59% female; 11% hold master's degrees, less than 1% hold doctorates. **Faculty ethnicity:** 73% Caucasian; 4% African-American; 8% Hispanic; 15% Asian. **Faculty selection/training:** "All faculty must be Evangelical Christians, hold a bachelor's degree and a CA credential in the subject they are teaching, or be enrolled in a credentialing program." **Teacher/student ratio:** 1:15. **Percentage of students enrolled in AP:** Approx. 29%; pass rate N/P. **Senior class profile (mean):** SAT N/P; GPA: N/P. **National Merit Scholarship Program:** 2 Commended Scholars per year for last 3 years. **College enrollment (last class):** [Last 3 years] 70% in 4-year, 25% in 2-year; remaining 5% pursued technical training, entered the work force or began serving in the military. **Recent (last 3 yrs) colleges:** Alabama A&M U, American U-London/Paris, American U-Washington, D.C, Arizona SU, Azusa Pacific U, Babson C, Bethany U, Biola U, Boston C, Brandeis U, CSU (Cal Poly-Pomona, Cal Poly -SLO, Chico, Fresno, Fullerton, Hayward, Humboldt, Long Beach, LA, Monterey Bay, Northridge, Sacramento, San Bernadino, San Diego SF, SJ, San Marco, Sonoma, Stanislaus),CCA, Calvin C, Chapman U-LA, The Citadel Military C, Cornell, DeVry Institute of Technology, Dominican U, Duke, Evangel U, FIDM, Fresno Pacific U, Gonzaga, Gordon C, LeTourneau U, Loyola Marymount U, NYU, Northwest U, Northwest Nazarene U, Northwestern U, Notre Dame de Namur U, Otis College of Art and Design, Parsons, Point Loma Nazarene, RPI, USF Conservatory of Music, Santa Clara, Seattle Pacific U, Simpson U, St. Mary's C of Cal, Syracuse, Texas Christian U, The Master's C, U-Arizona, UC (Berkeley, Davis, Irvine, LA, Merced, Riverside, SD, Santa Barbara, Santa Cruz), U-Hawaii-Hilo, U-Hawaii-Manoa, U-Maryland-College Park, U-Michigan-Ann Arbor, U-Oregon, UOP, U-Redlands, USF, USC, U-Tulsa, U-Washington, Vanguard U, Virginia SU, Washington U-St. Louis, Westmont C, Wheaton, Willamette, and William Jessup U.

Other Indicators the School is Accomplishing its Goals

"The performance of the mid-50 college bound seniors shows FCS is going beyond merely strong performance by the top 10% of a class and helping average students grow."

Campus/Campus Life

Campus description: "We are located on a 16-acre facility that houses our Preschool-12 program as well as Harbor Light Church. We are presently engaged in a building project to include a new secondary campus office, artificial turf fields, boys locker room, fine arts practice building, biotech laboratory, physical science lab, new 20 classroom building, and new faculty housing all to be completed on or before Fall 2010. Our plans extend to a new gymnasium, more classroom buildings, a new library, and more through 2016." **Library:** Offers study location and Internet access at lunch and after school. Online access to 15 EBSCO databases available to all students to research from home. (N/P hours, etc.) **Sports facilities:** Gymnasium, 2 fields. **Theater/arts facilities:** 1,800+ seat auditorium with full lighting and sound systems. A 200+ seat room for smaller performances equipped with a kitchen. **Open/closed campus:** Closed. **Lunches:** Traditional cafeteria and box lunches, and snack bar. **Bus service:** School owned buses for athletic events and field trips only. **Uniforms/dress code:** Uniforms. **Co-curricular activities/clubs:** Advanced Handbells, Badminton Club, California Scholastic Federation (CSF), Chapel Worship Band, Chess Club, Concert Choir, Drama, Creative Expressions (Art), Interact (Service Club), Math Tutoring, Peer Tutoring (CSF), Prayer Warriors, Scrivenery (publication), Theatre Arts, Vocal Ensemble, Warrior Band, United Student Body, Yearbook. **Foreign exchange programs/internships:** N/P. **Community service:** List provided each year; school service opportunities available. 15-20 service hours required of every student every year. Typical freshman schedule: "We consider many scheduling variables to help students fulfill their desire to take fine arts courses and meet their college goals. Many students will take Bible, English, and a language other than English, Biology, Geometry, World Geography, P.E. or Computer Applications, Concert Choir."

Student Support Services

Counselor/student ratio: N/P. **Counseling:** Guidance done by individual teachers; referrals are made to area counselors. Pastoral staff of Harbor Light church is also available. FCS also contracts with area counselors for time management and self-care seminars. **Learning differences/disabilities:** "We make 504 accommodations for students who can perform at grade level."

Student Conduct and Health

Code of conduct: "Students and parents must adhere to policies and procedures indicated in the Student-Parent Handbook that addresses many behaviors including bullying and plagiarism." **How school han-**

dles drugs/alcohol: Dismissal. **Prevention and awareness programs:** Informal through science, P.E. and Bible courses.

Summer Programs: None.

Parent Involvement
Parent participation: Parent Fundraising Ministry. **Parent/teacher communication:** PowerSchool is used for the daily posting of homework as well as the posting of grades for completed assignments. Teachers are available by e-mail, and in-person meetings are available upon request. **Parent education:** N/P. **Donations:** None required.

Sports
The school is a member of the North Coast Section, BCL, Division V. Fall: Girls varsity tennis; boys soccer (JV,V), girls volleyball (JV,V) cross-country. Winter: boys basketball (JV,V), girls basketball (JV,V). Spring: boys baseball (V), girls softball (V), golf (V), track & field (V)."

What Sets School Apart From Others
"Our fine arts department is the jewel in the crown at FCS. With bi-annual trips to New York City for invitational choir festivals, frequent community performances, regular partnerships with civic and church music organizations, and bi-annual musicals, we have 100 high school students in the award-winning Concert Choir. Additionally, we have smaller instrumental (i.e. Jazz Band, hand bells) and vocal performance (i.e. Women's Ensemble, Co-ed Ensemble, Girls Chorale groups). • Advanced Composition & Rhetoric: This one-year course provides a scholastic approach for non-remedial sophomores to effectively prepare them for the rigorous demands of upper-level high school and, ultimately, college-level coursework. The course centers on five key elements: (1) composition accuracy in the building of grammar, (2) composition efficiency in the development of vocabulary, (3) communication efficacy in the extensive study of the art and science of rhetoric and literary reasoning, (4) communication fluency via effective means of oral presentation, and (5) a brief unit on SAT readiness for the writing component. This is a fifth required English course."

How Parents/Students Characterize School
Parent response: N/P. **Student response(s):** N/P. "Our students and parents particularly appreciate the friendly, warm, nurturing environment provided by the faculty of FCS. They also enjoy our attention to minimizing scheduling conflicts so that students can be actively involved in performing arts groups, athletics and leadership. Parents often remark on how much they like their children's school friends. Positive relationships at school speak highly to our parents."

The Harker School, Upper School

500 Saratoga Avenue
San Jose, CA 95129
(408) 249-2510 fax (408) 984-2325
www.harker.org

Chris Nikoloff, Head of School
Nan Nielsen, Admissions Director, nann@harker.org

General

Coed day high school. Nonsectarian. Independent. Founded in 1893.
Nonprofit, member CAIS, NAIS, BAIHS, ERB, SSATB, CASE, CIF.
Enrollment: 563. **Average class size:** 18. **Accreditation:** WASC/CAIS.
School year: Sept.-June. **School day:** Varies – 8 a.m. to between 2:40
p.m. and 3:30 p.m. **Location:** In San Jose, via Saratoga exit off Hwy.
280.

Student Body: N/P.

Admission

Applications due: Mid-January (call for date). **Application fee:** $75.
Application process: Open houses are held in November and early
January. Applicants submit an application and schedule an interview.
The application includes applicant statements and parent statements.
The school uses the BAIHS forms for math and English teacher recommendations. The school also seeks a letter of personal recommendation. Decisions are sent mid-March. Admission forms are available
on the school's website. **No. of freshman applications:** N/P. **Minimum
admission requirements:** "Primarily A's and B's; minimum 80th national percentile in reading comprehension and math; good teacher
recommendations." **Test required:** Applicants take the ERB CTP III
admission test on two dates in January. SSAT and ISEE scores are also
accepted. **Preferences:** N/P. "We are looking for students who seek a
strong academic program with opportunities for sports, drama, debate,
music, art and technology." **What sort of student do you best serve?**
"Students with a keen interest in learning, a commitment to preparing
for a university education, and interest in active participation in an
area beyond academics. Sports, debate, drama, music, and technology
are areas in which our students find their passion."

Costs

Latest tuition: $20,674-$29,894. **Sibling discount:** None. **Tuition
increases:** Approx. 8%. **Other costs:** Approx. $750 for books, $25-
$100 other fees. **Percentage of students receiving financial aid:** 10%.
Financial aid deadline: N/P. **Average grant:** $12,000. **Percentage of
grants of half-tuition or more:** N/P.

School's Mission Statement/Goals

"Our mission is to prepare students for a successful college experience. We achieve academic excellence through the development of intellectual curiosity, personal accountability, and a love of learning. Our comprehensive program and dedicated staff help students discover, develop, and enjoy their unique talents. We instill kindness, respect, and integrity within a safe and nurturing environment. Our dynamic community honors individuality, embraces diversity, and prepares students to take their places as global citizens."

Academic Program

"The academic year is divided into two semesters. Classes meet 4 times a week and include three 50-minute periods and one 75-minute period." **Courses offered** (AP=Advanced Placement, H=Honors, (AP)=AP option, (H)=Honors option): **English:** The Myth and the Journey (H), A Survey of British Literature (H), A Survey of American Literature (H), AP English, Literature into Film, Asian Masterpieces, Great Novels, 20th-Century Women Writers, Literature of the Holocaust, Madness in Literature, Satire and Comedy, Shakespeare's Tragedies & Comedies; **Math:** Algebra I (H), Algebra II/Trigonometry (H), Geometry (H), Pre-Calculus (H), Advanced Mathematics with Calculus, Advanced Geometry, AP Calculus (AB & BC), Statistics (AP), Multivariate Calculus H, Linear Algebra H, Differential Equations H, Discrete Mathematics; **Science:** Physics (H), Chemistry (H/AP), Biology (H/AP), AP Physics (B & C), Seminar in Modern Physics, AP Environmental Science, The Human Genome Project, Astronomy, Evolution, Electronics, Ecology, Human Anatomy and Physiology, Study of Organic Chemistry, Engineering; **History and Social Sciences:** World History I-II; Economics; U.S. History (AP); AP European History; AP U.S. Government and Politic; AP Psychology; Asia: China, Japan, India; Business Internship; Western Political Thought & Philosophy, International Issues & Public Policy; **Languages:** French I-II, III (H), IV; AP French Language; AP French Literature; French Prose; French Literature and Film; Japanese I-II, III-IV (H), V H; Latin I-II, III (H), IV; AP Latin: Virgil; AP Latin Literature; Spanish I-II, III (H), IV; AP Spanish Language; AP Spanish Literature; Contemporary Issues in the Spanish Speaking World; The Latin American Short Story; Literature, Film and Art of the Spanish Speaking World; **Communications:** Public Speaking, Debate, Advanced Argumentation & Debate; **Computer Science:** Computer Science I, Graphic Arts, Video & Motion Graphics, Scripting Languages, Programming, AP Computer Science (A & AB), Advanced Topics in Computer Science: Advanced Algorithms and Data Structures, Computer Graphics; **Arts:** Study of Theater Arts, Study of Music, Study of Visual Art, Acting, Advanced Acting, Advanced Scene Study, Student-Directed Showcase, Technical Theater, Dance, Dance Troupe, Choirs (Down Beat!, Bel Canto, Cantilena), Drawing, Advanced Drawing, AP Art History, Painting, Ceramics, Sculpture, Architecture, Stone Carving, Graphic Arts, Orchestra, Jazz Band. **Computer** lab/training: The school has 7 computer labs. Computer Science is a required class freshman year. **Grading:** A-F. **Graduation requirements:** 4 years English; 3 years math (including Algebra I, Algebra II/Trig and Geometry) and science (including Physics, Chemistry, and Biology); 2 years history; third year proficiency in a foreign language; 1 year fine arts and computer science; 1 semester public speaking; 1 semester ethics. **Average nightly homework (M-Th):** 3-4 hours. **Faculty:** 80 (N/P gender, degrees). **Faculty ethnicity:** 10% Asian; 85% Caucasian; 2.5% Indian; 2.5% Hispanic. **Faculty selection/training:** "Faculty is selected through a rigorous screening program involving interviews and on-site teaching demonstrations. Each faculty member has either a valid teaching credential or a master's degree with previous teaching experience. Various on-site workshops are provided throughout the year. Additionally, the entire faculty is required to attend at least one off-site continuing education workshop/seminar per school year." **Teacher/student ratio:** 1:8. **Percentage of students enrolled in AP:** N/P; pass rate 100%. **Senior class profile (mean):** SAT Math 712, SAT Critical Reading 688, SAT Writing 702; GPA: 3.8. **National Merit Scholarship Program:** 43 National Merit Semifinalists, 51 Commended students; 62% received National Merit Recognition. **College enrollment (last class):** [Last 2 years] 100% in 4-year colleges. **Recent (last 3 yrs) colleges:** American, Antioch, Babson, Bennington, Boston C, Boston U, Brandeis, Brown, CSU (Long Beach, Sacramento, SLO, SJ), Carnegie Mellon, Claremont McKenna, Columbia, Cornell, Dartmouth, DePaul, Emory, George Washington, Georgetown, Hampshire, Harvard, Johns Hopkins, Kansas SU, Kasturba Medical C, Manipal, Lake Forest C, Lehigh, Loyola Marymount, MIT, Montana SU, NYU, Northwestern, Occidental, Penn, Pitzer, Pomona, Princeton, Principia, RPI, Rice, Ripon, Royal C of Surgeons, Santa Clara, Scripps, Smith, SMU, Stanford, Trinity U, Tulane, U.S. Air Force Academy, U-Arizona, UC (Berkeley, Davis, Irvine, LA, Riverside, SD, Santa Barbara, Santa Cruz), U-St. Andrew's (Scotland), U-Chicago, U-Michigan, UOP, U-Portland, USF, USC, Vassar, Wellesley, Wheaton, Whittier, and Yale.

Other Indicators the School is Accomplishing its Goals
"College admissions (100% of Harker graduates receive multiple college offers each year), test scores, campus spirit, and alumni and parent feedback."

Campus/Campus Life
Campus description: The 16-acre campus, with lawns and gardens, has 7 buildings, housing classrooms and offices. There are 12 science labs, 5 computer labs, a gymnasium, dance room, art studios, and student lounge ("The Edge"). **Library:** 11,000 print volumes, 55 periodical subscriptions, 15 computers, online database subscriptions, CD-ROMS, videos, online catalog (N/P hours). **Sports facilities:** Gymnasium, pool, 2 playing fields and tennis courts. **Theater/arts facilities:** Three art studios. The performing arts department has full

light and sound board, utilizes gymnasium space for performances. **Open/closed campus:** Closed. **Lunches:** Included in tuition. "Two gourmet chefs oversee an extensive menu, which includes a variety of vegetarian and vegan offerings daily." **Bus service:** Inter-campus only. **Uniforms/dress code:** "Dress code." (N/P description) **Co-curricular activities/clubs:** Ambassadors, Amnesty International, Art, Biology, Book Club, Computer Science, Dance, Drama, Future Business Leaders of America, Film, Games, Gay-Straight Alliance, HEART (environmental), Junior Classical League, Junior States of America, Key, International, Literary Magazine, Newspaper, Robotics, Science Olympiad, Spirit, Web Team, Yearbook. **Foreign exchange programs/internships:** "All juniors participate in a mentoring program. They are paired with someone from the business community in an area in which the student has strong interests. Students may receive credit for summer internship employment experiences." **Community service:** Ten hours per year for 3 years are required. "Extensive opportunities offered." (N/P examples). **Typical freshman schedule:** English, math, Physics, World History, foreign language, 1 semester Public Speaking, 1 semester Computer Science.

Student Support Services

Counselor/student ratio (not including college counselors): 1:250. **Counseling:** "A full-time counselor does academic tracking and follow-up and is available for social and emotional issue support. Our staff of 3 college counselors provides informational events for freshman and sophomores, and, in the junior year, begins meeting 1:1 with students." **Learning differences/disabilities:** "We are not a school for students with significant learning problems. Faculty and administration work with students and families to enhance the learning environment of all students."

Student Conduct and Health

Code of conduct: "Standard." **How school handles drugs/alcohol:** "On first alcohol/tobacco violation (on campus/campus event), the student is suspended and required to obtain counseling; on second violation, the student is dismissed. For other controlled substances (on campus) the student is dismissed; for off campus, the student is required to obtain counseling." **Prevention and awareness programs:** Part of a required health course.

Summer Programs

Harker offers an academic summer institute and sports camp, as well as debate, robotics and a performing arts conservatory.

Parent Involvement

Parent participation: "Not required, but highly appreciated. Opportunities are numerous, including library volunteers, parent leadership and an annual fashion show fundraising event run by parent volunteers." **Parent/teacher communication:** Parent/teacher conferences are held each fall. Report cards are issued 4 times per year. In addition, teachers communicate with parents on an as-needed basis by phone and e-mail. All teachers post their assignments on their website. **Parent education:** Occasional speakers address various issues relating to education, teenagers, college admission, and financing a college education; monthly K-12 newsletter, regular e-mail announcements and a parent intranet. **Donations:** "Parents provide fundraising support for the 'margin of excellence' at Harker through the Annual Fund and the Capital Campaign. Annual Fund donations range from $50 to $20,000."

Sports
Aerobics, baseball, basketball, cross-country, football, golf, self-defense, soccer, softball, swimming, tennis, track and field, volleyball, wrestling, and weight-lifting.

What Sets School Apart From Others
"Our small class size and academic rigor create an atmosphere where strong individual effort and personal responsibility are expected. The faculty — and entire Harker community — has created a caring and supportive environment with enough structure to provide guidance and enough freedom to support the development of individual accountability and a positive self-image. Incorporation of technology in the curriculum is well developed and ever increasing. Clubs, sports, community service and activities provide opportunities for all students to explore a wide range of interest. In short, Harker provides its students an exemplary college-prep education, a supportive and lively social experience and a lifelong sense of community."

How Parents/Students Characterize School
Parent response(s): "Our son is incredibly well-prepared at UC Berkeley due to his education at Harker. Not only is he prepared academically, but his time-management skills are so well developed that he's finding he has a lot of free time and that other students are coming to him for help." "Our daughter recently made the Dean's List for her outstanding academic record at the Medill School of Journalism at Northwestern U. We want to thank Harker for giving her a wonderful education that prepared her so well for college. Thank you very much again for having so many wonderful and caring teachers for our daughter, and for our son who is currently a Harker student." **Student response(s):** "I can't express how much I loved being a part of the Performing Arts Department ... a show choir, a jazz band, an orchestra, a girls' choir, a guys' gig group, a dance team, and the list goes on. Not to mention we won best musical the first year we entered the competition. This only shows that our school excels whether it is mathematics, science, or the arts." "A large portion of why I have decided to continue my study of biological sciences stems from my experience with teachers

that are motivated and passionate about the subject they teach." "I am eternally grateful to this school for helping me grow, find my talents, and giving me mediums and the opportunities to explore whatever I wanted and loved to do."

Head-Royce School
4315 Lincoln Avenue
Oakland, CA 94602
(510) 531-1300 *fax (510) 530-8329*
www.headroyce.org

Paul D. Chapman, Head of School
Catherine Epstein, Director of Admissions, cepstein@headroyce.org

General
Coed day high school with K-5 lower school and G6-8 middle school. Nonsectarian. Independent. Founded in 1887 as the Anna Head School, a girls school. It merged with the Josiah Royce School, its "sibling" boys school, in 1971. Nonprofit, member CAIS, NAIS, BAIHS, POCIS, EBISA, CIF, CASE, BCL, SSATB, BAAD, ERB. **Enrollment:** Approx. 340 in the high school. **Average class size:** 15. **Accreditation:** WASC/CAIS. **School year:** Aug.-June. **School day:** 8:25 a.m.-3:20 p.m. **Location:** In a residential neighborhood in the Oakland Hills between Hwys. 13 and 580. Students can take BART to the Fruitvale station and take the #53 AC Transit bus to campus. Three AC buses provide supplemental transit from Berkeley and Oakland to the campus. Two private bus services transport students from Contra Costa County and North Berkeley.

Student Body
Geographic breakdown (counties): 80% from Alameda; 15% from Contra Costa; 5% from other counties. "67 zip codes, 33 communities." **Ethnicity:** 54% Caucasian (non-Latino); 11% African-American; 16% Asian; 5% Latino; 14% multi-ethnic. **International students (I-20 status):** 2. **Middle schools (freshman):** Approximately 2/3 of the freshman class move up from the Head-Royce middle school. The remainder typically come from "up to 20 independent, parochial and public middle schools." (N/P %).

Admission
Applications due: Mid-January (call for date). **Application fee:** $75. **Application process:** Parents should complete an application in early December and schedule their child for the ISEE in December or January. Applicants spend a half day on campus between October and February for class visits. Interviews are on Saturdays in late January or early February. Transcripts and recommendations from current math

and English teachers are required as well as a student essay. **No. of freshman applications:** Over 150 for 30 places. (50-60 slots of the 80-90 available are taken by the school's middle school students.) **Minimum admission requirements:** "Most of our students have an A/B average or above and score 70% and above on the ISEE." **Test required:** ISEE and SSAT accepted. **Preferences:** Siblings; underrepresented students of color; and children of faculty, alumni, and trustees. "**We are looking for** intellectually curious, academically motivated, community-minded students who will contribute to the school community and profit from small class instruction with talented and engaging faculty." **What kind of student do you best serve?** (See prior statements).

Costs
Latest tuition: $27,000 (upper school) payable in 2 payments. (Other payment plans available through outside agency.) **Sibling discount:** None. **Tuition increases:** Approx. 5%. **Other costs:** Books, activity fee, P.E. uniforms, calculators and supplies are approx. $1,000. Transportation is extra. **Percentage of students receiving financial aid:** 25%. **Financial aid deadline:** Mid-January (call for date). **Average grant:** $14,000. **Percentage of grants of half-tuition or more:** 50%.

School's Mission Statement/Goals
"The mission of Head-Royce is to inspire in our students a lifelong love of learning and exuberance for academic excellence, to promote understanding of and respect for diversity that makes our society strong, and to encourage constructive and responsible citizenship. The school nurtures the development of the whole child through a program that seeks to develop intellectual abilities such as scholarship and disciplined critical thinking; to foster in each student integrity, ethical behavior, self-esteem, compassion, and a sense of humor; to nurture aesthetic abilities such as creativity, imagination, musical and visual talent; to promote leadership and social responsibility, an appreciation of individual and cultural differences, and a respect for the opinions of others; and to encourage joyful, healthy living and physical fitness. All members of the Head-Royce community—students, alumni, faculty, staff, administrators, parents, and trustees—are dedicated to a balanced educational environment within which each student can thrive."

Academic Program
Courses offered (AP=Advanced Placement, H=Honors, (AP)=AP option, (H)=Honors option): **Computer Science:** Keyboarding and Word Processing, AP Computer Science, Advanced Program Design Seminar; **English:** English 9: Composition and Literature, English 10: Composition and American Literature, English 11: Western Classical Literature, English 12: Contemporary Women's Literature, Creative Writing, Japanese Literature and Culture, Latin American Literature, Literature and Film, Literature of the American West, Modern

Drama and Playwriting, Science Fiction, Shakespeare, or Southern Writers. Electives include: Expository Writing, Speech and Debate I, Speech and Debate II, Public Speaking; **Arts:** Intro to 2-dimensional Art/Advanced 2-dimensional Art, AP Art Studio, Intro to Film and Video/Advanced Film and Video, Graphic Design, Drama I-II, Intro to Theater, Intro to 3-dimensional Art/Advanced 3-dimensional Art, Photography/Advanced Photography, Photojournalism, Head-Royce Wind Ensemble, Head-Royce Orchestra, Caravan, Jazz Band, The Head-Royce Chorus, Colla Voce (vocal ensemble), AP Music Theory; **Foreign Languages:** French I-IV, Advanced French Seminar, AP French Language, AP French Literature, Latin I-V, AP Latin: Vergil, Spanish I-V, Advanced Spanish Seminar, AP Spanish Language, AP Spanish Literature; **History:** History 9: History of the Emerging World, History 10: U.S. History, AP U.S. History Seminar, History 11: Western Culture and Civilization, AP European History Seminar, History 12: AP Art History, Intro to Economics, Intro to Political Philosophy and Ethics, Intro to Psychology, Issues in Latin America, The Legacy of Vietnam, Understanding the Middle East, The U.S. from 1945 to 1975, Comparative World Religions; **Math:** Algebra II (H), Geometry (H), Pre-Calculus (H), AP Statistics, AP Calculus; **Science:** Conceptual Physics, Chemistry, Biology (AP), AP Physics, Science 12: Astronomy, Genetics and Biotechnology, Ecology and Natural History of the Bay Area, Electronics, Biotechnology: Applications and Ethics, Marine Biology, Neurobiology. **Computer lab/training:** The high school uses laptop carts with Mac computers. Students are required to be computer proficient to graduate. **Grading:** A-F. **Graduation requirements:** The graduation requirements are designed to exceed the UC requirements for admission. 4 years English, history and P.E.; 3 years math, science and foreign language; 1.5 years electives; .5 year fine arts; computer keyboarding proficiency; health and safety; and 60 hours community service. **Average nightly homework (M-Th):** G9-10: 30 min. per subject; G11-12: 40 min. or more per subject. **Faculty:** 115; 42% male, 58% female; 63% have master's degrees; 7% have doctorates. **Faculty ethnicity:** 70% Caucasian (non-Latino); 15% Asian; 8% African-American; 5% Latino; 2% Middle Eastern. **Faculty selection/training:** "Faculty is selected through administrative screening, including placement agencies, resumes, interviews, etc. Professional development funding helps keep faculty professionally up-to-date. We have in-services twice a year." **Teacher/student ratio:** 1:9. **Percentage of students enrolled in AP:** 100%; pass rate 85%. **Senior class profile (mean):** SAT Math 668, SAT Critical Reading 651, SAT Writing 661; GPA: N/P. **National Merit Scholarship Program:** Last year's graduating class included 10 Semifinalists, 10 Finalists, and 3 Winners. **College enrollment (last class):** 100% in 4-year colleges. **Recent (last 3 yrs) colleges:** UC (Berkeley, LA, Davis, Santa Barbara, Santa Cruz and SD), Oberlin, Brown, USC, Boston U, Carnegie Mellon, Colby C, Emory, Harvey Mudd, Northwestern, Princeton, Stanford, Cal Poly-SLO, Occidental, Yale, NYU, Duke, Penn, Spelman, Scripps, U-Colorado, Barnard, Harvard, Boston U, and Santa Clara.

Other Indicators the School is Accomplishing its Goals
"Alumni and parent feedback, college admissions, test scores."

Campus/Campus Life
Campus description: The campus, in a residential neighborhood, consists of 14 acres in a canyon in the Oakland Hills with a view of the San Francisco Bay. "Each of the three schools (lower, middle and upper) has its own modern facilities." **Library:** The library, new in 2008, includes silent study room and main research area with tech center; 64 periodical subscriptions, electronic databases; 18,000 print volumes; 14 computers (with Internet access); laptop cart and an online catalog. Open to students from 7:45 a.m.-5 p.m. **Sports facilities:** An 8-acre athletic complex with an outdoor swimming pool, 3 tennis courts, a regulation soccer field, baseball/softball diamond, 2 basketball courts, and a large gymnasium. **Theater/arts facilities:** Auditorium with a capacity of 320 and a Creative Arts Center. New World Languages building opened in 2007. A new high school classroom building with a café opened August 2008. **Open/closed campus:** Juniors and seniors only have off-campus privileges. **Lunches:** Most students purchase organic, home-cooked lunches or bring bag lunches. **Bus service:** A private bus service is available to students commuting from Orinda, Lafayette, Danville, and Walnut Creek. Another private bus service is available from North Berkeley. Current cost is $1,700/year. (AC Transit provides supplementary service from Berkeley and Oakland.) **Uniforms/dress code:** "No specific requirements other than clean and neat and not distracting or offensive to others." **Co-curricular activities/clubs:** Activities include community service, outdoor education (sea kayaking, high ropes courses, river rafting), debate, student newspaper, yearbook, drama, instrumental and vocal groups, Latin Club, Kaleidoscope Club (Multicultural), Martial Arts Club, Mountain Biking Club, Improv Club, Afro-American Student Club, Creative Writing Club, A.S.I.A. Club, Chess Club, The Earth Society, French Club, Gay Lesbian Awareness Group, Italian Club, Junior Statesmen, Reading & Poetry, Spanish Club, Thespian Society, Video/Film. Other: Recent Senior Projects include students working at internships at crisis intervention centers, the French Consulate, the San Francisco Museum of Modern Art, and KTVU; volunteering at the elementary schools and for AIDS services; creating photo essays; working as stagehands, park rangers, and athletic trainers; and painting murals. **Foreign exchange programs/internships:** The school has recently taken groups of students to China, Europe and Latin America. The school is a member of School Year Abroad, offering junior year in Italy, Spain, France, India, and China. **Community service:** Project Open Hand, SPCA, coaching Little League, tutoring, outdoor cleanup, etc. **Typical freshman schedule:** Geometry, 3D Art, homeroom, Physics, history, English, 9, Spanish II, and Drama.

Student Support Services

Counselor/student ratio (not including college counselors): 1:320. **Counseling:** "The school has a full-time school counselor who also advises the student community service board. Academic advising is done by faculty, deans, and the head of the upper school. Peer counseling also takes place. A full-time Director of College Counseling works actively with students and parents to coordinate college planning and help with the college admissions process. Meetings, workshops, and individual family meetings occur during the sophomore, junior, and senior years." **Learning differences/disabilities:** "We have a learning specialist to help us diagnose and support LD kids."

Student Conduct and Health

Code of conduct: "Students are expected to act responsibly and to actively support the goals of Head-Royce. In addition to abiding by the major school rules, all members of the Head-Royce community are expected to treat each other with courtesy and respect. The administration and faculty reserve the right to remove a student from Head-Royce whose behavior has been disruptive to the learning environment of the school, damaging to the school community, or to the school's reputation within the greater community." **How school handles drugs/alcohol:** "The school's 'likely response' to a first alcohol/drug use offense is, after due process, substance abuse counseling, 5-10 day suspension or expulsion, and on the second offense, expulsion. Students who use tobacco on or in the vicinity of the school grounds receive substance abuse counseling and may be suspended with repeated infractions." **Prevention and awareness programs:** "These issues are addressed in a freshman course called Health and Safety. The course teaches skills to prevent, identify, and treat health problems and increase students' knowledge of safe and unsafe behavior. The course is team taught by the school counselor and a P.E. teacher. CPR and First Aid are included in the Health and Safety curriculum."

Summer Programs

The school has extensive summer programs for K-12; a few credit courses are offered for high school math.

Parent Involvement

Parent participation: Parents are encouraged to contribute 16 hours per family per year. **Parent/teacher communication:** "Report cards, comments, and conferences as needed. Regular mailings about high school events." **Parent education:** "We offer in-services, coffees and ongoing programs for parents. **Donations:** "Donations are 'voluntary but strongly encouraged.' Each year parents are requested to participate in annual giving. The school seeks 100% participation from parents."

Sports
Approximately 80-85% of students participate in at least one season of after-school sports. Students compete in BCL in boys soccer, cross-country, basketball, baseball, volleyball, tennis, lacrosse, track, golf and swimming, and in girls volleyball, cross-country, tennis, basketball, soccer, swimming, track, golf and softball.

What Sets School Apart From Others
"Outstanding faculty, great facilities (gym, fields, pool, performing arts center, fine arts studios, technology labs, library), international programs (School Year Abroad), community service (required), Advanced Placement high school program, integrated technology curriculum including digital video, and senior projects."

How Parents/Students Characterize School
Parent response(s): "The academic level is very high. People really respect each other and are open to new ideas. There is a good emphasis on community service, and this is a very diverse community of lifelong learners." **Student response(s):** "I love the community atmosphere. Where else would I consider some of my teachers as better friends than some of my peers?"

Holy Names High School
4660 Harbord Drive
Oakland, CA 94618
(510) 450-1110 *fax (510) 547-3111*
www.hnhsoakland.org

Sr. Sally Slyngstad, SNJM, Principal
Sandra Carrillo, Admissions Director, scarrillo@hnhsoakland.org

General
Girls Catholic day high school. (N/P % Catholic) Founded in 1868 as the first secondary school in Oakland. Nonprofit. Diocese of Oakland school. **Enrollment:** Approx. 275. **Average class size:** 25. **Accreditation:** WASC/CAIS, member NCEA, NCGS. Blue Ribbon School. **School year:** Aug.-June. **School day:** 8 a.m.-3 p.m. **Location:** In the Oakland Hills, accessible by bus/BART.

Student Body
Geographic breakdown (counties): 82% Alameda, 15% Contra Costa; 3% Solano. **Ethnicity:** 35% African American; 27% Caucasian; 20% Hispanic/Latina; 10% multi-ethnic; 6% Asian/Pacific Islander; 2% other. **International students (I-20 status):** None. **Middle schools (freshman):** 30% are from 13 public middle schools; 16% from 24 private, non-parochial schools; 54% from 44 parochial schools.

Admission

Applications due: January (visit website for date). **Application fee:** $75. **Application process:** The school holds an open house in October and an information night is in November. To apply, parents submit an online application. Eighth grade applicants must meet the following qualifications: "Performance on the HSPT entrance exam indicating ability to succeed at Holy Names; grades received in the 7th and 8th grade should demonstrate that she is working to potential; a favorable recommendation from the principal, math and English teachers, or counselor at her present school; and an admission interview giving us insights into her interests, personality, motivation, and assessing student's capabilities in a college-prep curriculum." **No. of freshman applications:** 200 (N/P # places). **Minimum admission requirements:** See above. **Preferences:** N/P. **Test required:** HSPT, which is given at the school in early January. **"We are looking for** demonstrated academic ability to benefit from the school curriculum, responsible citizenship, and reasons for enrolling which are compatible with the school's philosophy. Though we look at a lot more than test scores, students admitted generally score in the 50th percentile or above on the HSPT." **What kind of student do you best serve?** (See prior statement).

Costs

Latest tuition: $10,800 payable in 1, 2, or monthly payments. **Sibling discount:** None. **Tuition increases:** Approx. 4-5%. **Other costs:** $650 registration fee; $300-$700 for books, extracurricular activity fees, and uniforms. **Percentage of students receiving financial aid:** 35%. **Financial aid deadline:** April (call for date). **Average grant:** $2,500. **Percentage of grants of half-tuition or more:** 18%.

School's Mission Statement/Goals

"Holy Names High School, a small Catholic school for young women, provides an academically challenging college preparatory education in a vibrant learning environment. Our diverse community nurtures spirituality, encourages artistic expression, and promotes justice, preparing the next generation for leadership and service."

Academic Program

Students take 7 courses a semester. **Courses offered** (AP= Advanced Placement, H=Honors, (AP) =AP option, (H)=Honors option): Courses N/P. AP courses are offered in calculus, chemistry, English Lit. and Composition, French, French Lit., Spanish, studio art and U.S. History. Honors classes are offered in geometry, advanced algebra/trig., pre-calculus, English 9-11, government and economics, and chemistry. Students may also participate in a four-year program in art, drama, choral and instrumental music. **Computer lab/training:** N/P. **Grading:** A-F, weighted grades for honors and AP courses. **Graduation requirements:** All students are expected to meet the core requirements for UC with 260 credits for graduation; 4 years English, religion, social studies; 3 years math; 2 years foreign language, science, visual and/or performing arts; 1 year P.E.; 1 semester health, technology; 80 hours community service. **Average nightly homework (M-Th):** 2 hrs. **Faculty:** 28 (21 f/t, 7 p/t); 16% male, 84% female; 62% master's degrees; 3% doctorates. **Faculty ethnicity:** 85% Euro-American; 14% Latino; 1% African-American. **Faculty selection/training:** Teaching candidates must have a bachelor's degree with a credential or master's degree. **Teacher/student ratio:** 1:11. **Percentage of students enrolled in AP:** 34%; (57 students took 80 Advanced Placement Exams in 9 subject areas); pass rate 100%. **Senior class profile (mean):** SAT N/P; GPA. N/P. **National Merit Scholarship Program:** N/P. **College enrollment (last class):** 100%; 83% in 4-year, 17% in 2-year. **Recent (last 3 yrs) colleges:** American C, Amherst C, Arizona SU, Babson C, Benedict C, Berkeley City C, Boston U, Brown, CSU (Chico, East Bay, Fresno, Fullerton, Humboldt, Long Beach, LA, Monterey Bay, Northridge, Sacramento, SLO, Polytechnic, San Bernardino, SF, Sonoma, Stanislaus), Cal Lutheran U, Cheyney C, Clark Atlanta U Contra Costa CC, Diablo Valley C, Dominican U, Evansville U, Evergreen SC, Florida A&M U, Fordham U, George Washington U, Gonzaga U, Hampton U, Hawaii Pacific U, Holy Names U, Howard U, Kansas U, Lewis and Clark U, Linfield C, Long Beach SU, Loyola Marymount U, Loyola U, Chicago, Macalester C,, Metropolitan SU at Denver, North Carolina SU, Northeastern U, Randolph C, Regis U, Santa Clara, Savannah C of Art and Design, Scripps C, Seattle U, Smith C, Spelman C, St. Mary's C, Stillman U, and Sweet Briar C.

Other Indicators the School is Accomplishing its Goals

"Holy Names has twice received a Blue Ribbon Exemplary Award from the U.S Department of Education. Schools awarded this mark of excellence are evaluated primarily on evidence of superiority of their leadership, teaching, environment, curriculum, instruction, parent and community support, student achievement, and organizational vitality."

Campus/Campus Life

Campus description: Holy Names was established on the shores of Lake Merritt in 1868 by the Sisters of the Holy Names. When it outgrew the original campus in 1931, it moved to its present site on Harbord Drive. The school is situated on 5.78 acres in a wooded, residential area of the Upper Rockridge section of Oakland. The stately, three-story building completed in 1931 includes classrooms, offices, gym, cafeteria and a Gothic-style auditorium that seats 500. **Library:** 8,000 print volumes; 14 computers with Internet access; 30 paper periodical subscriptions augmented by a generous number provided by Gale Databases; open 7:45 a.m.–4:30 p.m. **Sports facilities:** Gymnasium. **Theater/arts facilities:** Full auditorium/theater with seating for 500; 8 music practice rooms. **Open/closed campus:** Closed. **Lunches:** Food may be purchased in the cafeteria. **Bus service:** AC Transit supplementary. **Uniforms/Dress code:** The school uniform includes a pleated plaid skirt, navy blue twill pants or walking shorts with collared polo shirts in white, red or navy. **Co-curricular activities/clubs:** Activities include Student Council, Class Councils, dances, Mother-Daughter Luncheon, Father-Daughter Dance, blood drive, school barbecues, Frosh Family Picnic, Spirit Week, 13 interscholastic athletic teams, drama productions, and yearbook. Clubs: Ambassadors, Art and Film, Campus Ministry, Diversity, Mock Trial, Model UN, Multicultural, Thespians, Student Newspaper. Students are welcome to start new clubs. Honor Societies: Block Society, California Scholarship Federation, National Honor Society. **Foreign exchange programs/internships:** N/P. **Community service:** 20 hours required each year. Students volunteer at social service agencies, churches, hospitals and schools including Elizabeth House, Alameda County Food Bank, Piedmont Gardens Retirement Center, Alta Bates, Children's Hospital, St. Anthony Foundation, St. Vincent's Dining Room, and Girls Inc. **Typical freshman schedule:** Intro to Catholic Christianity/Hebrew Scriptures, World Cultures I, foreign language, math, P.E./Health, science, visual and performing arts and English 9.

Student Support Services
Counselor/student ratio (not including college counselors): 1:135. **Counseling:** N/P. **Learning differences/disabilities:** "Students with learning differences/disabilities are provided support and accommodations in the regular curriculum."

Student Conduct and Health
Code of conduct: "High standards of conduct expected." No pagers or cell phones during the school day. **How school handles drugs/alcohol:** "The school has a no tolerance policy for alcohol/illegal drug use on campus." **Prevention and awareness programs:** Included in 9th grade Health/Science class.

Summer Programs: Summer Bridge program for incoming 9th graders.

Parent Involvement
Parent participation: "Parent volunteers are asked to serve on a Principal's Advisory Council and others help with various events throughout the year." **Parent/teacher communication:** "Progress reports are mailed 4 weeks after the beginning of each quarter, and report cards are mailed at the end of each 8-week quarter. Parents can e-mail teachers and/or look at their daughter's current grades on the HNHS website. Additionally, parents receive a monthly parent newsletter." **Parent education:** The counseling department provides a grade-level event each year. **Donations:** "Parents are expected to make contributions to the school."

Sports

Students compete in eight sports in the Bayshore Athletic League. "In the last five years, every one of the HNHS teams has earned NCS recognition for a GPA of 3.0 or higher and more than half the athletes have been recognized by NCS for GPAs of 3.5 or higher."

What Sets School Apart from Others

"Only single sex Catholic high school in West Contra Costa and Alameda counties." • "HNHS has a tradition of dedication to the fine arts. We have an outstanding performing and visual arts department." • "We provide a safe and secure environment." • "We offer a two-week period between first and second semesters which allows students to select from a wide-range of on-campus, off-campus classes, community service and internships."

How Parents/Students Characterize School

Parent response(s): "My daughter had a wonderful four years at Holy Names during which she has gained immense knowledge." "Thanks to all at HNHS for the gifts shared with our daughter." "Excellent education, creative and challenging!" "There is much appreciation for teaching, guiding, and nurturing our young women. Holy Names has been the best for my daughter. It helped her grow in confidence and be the best she can be." "Holy Names provided a nurturing environment for our daughter. She is prepared for college and will have many lasting memories of HNHS." "Holy Names provides a safe environment, a college prep education, an emphasis on community involvement and social justice. It promotes women as future leaders and encourages students to respect and embrace diversity." **Student response(s):** "I love Holy Names! It is the best school in the world!" "Holy Names offered me a remarkably wonderful high school experience. Its diversity, intellectual challenges, and amazing community have made me an even better person." "Holy Names has provided me with an outlet to express myself, teachers to support me, and a loving community of friends. I love it!" "Holy Names is the safest, warmest environment you can be in." "Holy Names is a small community of talented young ladies. We work hard day in and day out and still find time to have fun with all of our great friends."

Immaculate Conception Academy

3625 – 24th Street
San Francisco, CA 94110
(415) 824-2052 *fax (415) 821-4677*
www.icacademy.org

Sister Janice Therese Wellington, O.P., Principal
Gina Espinal, Admissions Director, gespinal@icacademy.org

General

Girls Catholic day high school (85% Catholic). Founded in 1883. Nonprofit. Sponsored by the Dominican Sisters of Mission San Jose. **Enrollment:** Approx. 265. **Average class size:** 17. **Accreditation:** WASC. **School year:** Mid Aug.-early June. **School day:** 8:15 a.m.-3:05 p.m. **Location:** At 24th and Guerrero Street, 4 blocks from the 24th St. BART station. Also accessible by several Muni bus lines.

Student Body

Geographic breakdown (counties): 79% from San Francisco; 10% from San Mateo; 11% from other Bay Area counties. **Ethnicity:** 12% Caucasian (non-Latino); 15% Asian-American; 43% Latino; 9% African-American; 21% multi-ethnic. **International students (I-20 status):** 3. **Middle schools (freshman):** 8% from 6 public middle schools; 5% from 3 private, non-parochial schools; 87% from 21 parochial schools.

Admission

Applications due: December (call for date). **Application fee:** $75. **Application process:** Students can shadow in October and November (call to schedule an appt.) and visit during the open house held late October. Students should complete an application and submit it on interview day held late November (call for date). Applicants take the HSPT admission test in mid-January. Applicants submit the completed application, student and parent essays, certificates of Baptism and Communion, and report cards. **No. of freshman applications:** More than 190 for 80 places. **Minimum admission requirements:** "Admission to ICA is based on the desire to receive a Catholic education, admissions interview, performance on the HSPT test, academic record and personal recommendations from teachers/principal, and satisfactory conduct, effort and attendance." **Test required:** HSPT. **Preferences:** N/P. "**We are looking for** motivated young women who will embrace a Catholic education and have a desire to learn." **What kind of student do you best serve?** (See prior statement).

Costs

Latest tuition: $9,900 payable in 10 payments. **Sibling discount:** None. **Tuition increases:** N/P. **Other costs:** $560 registration fee, $400-$800 for books and fees. **Percentage of students receiving financial aid:** 65%. **Financial aid deadline:** January (call for date). The Archdiocese of San Francisco awards grants to eligible students living within the Archdiocese of San Francisco, Marin, and San Mateo. Additionally ICA offers many grants and scholarships. **Average grant:** $2,000. **Percentage of grants half-tuition or more:** 46%.

School's Mission Statement/Goals

"Immaculate Conception Academy, an all-girls Catholic school, offers a college-preparatory education in the Dominican tradition that promotes academic excellence, life–long learning skills and service to

God, family and community. A supportive and nurturing environment encourages a diverse student body to become women of faith, learning, community, leadership and vision."

What Sets School Apart from Others

"ICA is the oldest all girls' high school in the Archdiocese of San Francisco. Established in 1883, ICA continues to meet the challenge of graduating young women who can take their place in the 21st century. A low student/teacher ratio provides personal attention and guided mentoring that promotes self-esteem."• We offer the 'Flame Program,' which takes students with learning differences and ensures their entrance into selective colleges and universities. (Information is detailed above in Student Support Services.) At our On-Site College Admission Day in the fall, students are admitted to a college pending a successful completion of their senior year. ICA is currently one of the few private high schools that offer a full program in Home Economics, with Interior Design, Child Development, and Independent Living courses. In the past 4 years, ICA has had 5 Gates Millennium Scholarship Winners."

Academic Program

Courses offered (AP=Advanced Placement, H=Honors, (AP)=AP option, (H)=Honors option): **English:** English I-IV, English III (H), English Literature & Composition (AP); **History:** Ancient History, Modern World History (H), U.S. History (AP), U.S. Govt./Economics, U.S. Govt. & Politics, (AP); **Math:** Algebra IA, Algebra IB, Algebra I, Algebra II (H), Geometry, Pre-Calculus (H), Calculus AB (AP), Problem Solving, Statistics; **Science:** Integrated Science, Biology (H), Chemistry, Conceptual Physics, Physics, Human Physiology; **Foreign Languages:** Spanish I-III, Spanish Language (AP), Spanish Literature (AP), Spanish I-II Bilingual, French I-III, French IV (H); **Arts:** Dance I-II, Drama I-II, Art I-II, Digital Art, Piano; **Religion:** Christian Faith & Sacraments, Morality & Social Justice, Scripture Old/New Testament, Pursuit of Character; **P.E:** P.E., Health Education; **Other:** Academic Studies, Working with Young Children, Clothing I-II, Interior Design, Computer Programming, Computer Science (AP), Psychology, Developmental Child Psychology, Imaginative Writing, Language of Film, Publications. **Computer lab/training:** "Immaculate Conception is a wireless campus designed to meet the computer needs of the 21st century. We have two computer labs and a mobile computer lab for classrooms to perform interactive lessons with technology. All of our language classrooms have mini-computer labs where students are able to take advantage of enhancing their language skills through the world of computers. In the counseling center, students are able to use computers to meet their college preparation needs." **Grading:** A-F. **Graduation requirements:** 40 credits religion and English; 40 credits social studies; 30 credits math and science; 20 credits foreign language; 30 credits electives; 10 credits P.E./health and visual and performing arts; total of 240 credits. **Average nightly homework (M-Th):** N/P. **Faculty:** N/P. **Faculty ethnicity:** N/P. **Faculty selection/training:** N/P. **Teacher/student ratio:** 1:10. **Percentage of students enrolled in AP:** N/P. **Senior class profile (mean):** SAT N/P. GPA: N/P. **National Merit Scholarship Program:** N/P. **College enrollment (last class):** 100%; 82% in 4-year and 18% in 2-year. **Recent (last 4 yrs) colleges:** UC (Berkeley, Davis, LA, Santa Barbara, SD), CSU (Sonoma, Hayward, SF, SJ), Boston U, USF, Notre Dame de Namur U, Holy Names C, FIDM, Menlo, St. Francis C, Stanford, Xavier U-Louisiana, and St. Mary's C of Cal.

Other Indicators the School is Accomplishing its Goals
"The Class of 2008 was awarded over 3 million dollars in scholarships from non-profit organizations and institutions. Annually, Immaculate Conception Academy offers wonderful and exciting events for our students to advance their academic career. In the fall, ICA is one of the few Bay Area high schools that offers on-site College Admission Day, where over a dozen colleges and universities take college applications at the school site and provide students on the spot admissions pending successful completion of their senior year. Over 94 applications were submitted and processed at this event. Also, in the fall ICA provides students beginning their freshmen year with standardized test preparation. Tests are administered on National Testing Day, the Explore exam (administered by the ACT for 9th graders), PLAN (administered by ACT for 10th graders) and the PSAT examination (administered by the College Board). Results are reviewed with students in a group session to assist them in their skills in various academic areas. To further assist students, we offer an on-site SAT test preparation program. In addition, ICA hosts various fairs. In the spring semester, students are given an opportunity to participate in our College Fair and Health Fair where various organizations, institutions and colleges provide information about their programs. Through the Counseling Center, ICA provides students with several summer enrichment programs to enhance their skills in the areas of the arts, engineering, political science and more. These programs are located in the Bay Area and across the nation."

Campus/Campus Life
Campus description: Historic main building and two other buildings linked by the enclosed student park area. **Library:** Over 4,000 holdings; additional computer lab with Internet access; extensive research section. **Sports facilities:** Gymnasium. **Theater/arts facilities:** N/P. **Open/closed campus:** Closed. **Lunches:** Hot breakfast and lunch service. **Bus service:** N/P. **Uniforms/dress code:** Uniforms. **Co-curricular activities/clubs:** Student Government, Campus Ministry, Walkathon, Career Day, Spirit Week, Mini-courses, Health Fairs, Mother-Daughter Tea, Father-Daughter Night, Ambassador Club, Asian-American Cultural Society, Student Honorary Clubs – CSF/NHS, and BLOCK. S.A.V.E., Ecology Club, Film-Am Club, Black Student Union, 'Aina 'O

Hawai'i, Las Latina Unidas, Double XX Science Club, Yearbook, Choir. **Foreign exchange programs/internships:** N/P. **Community service:** Mandatory 25 hours minimum per year per student. (Types N/P)

Student Support Services

Counselor/student ratio (not including college counselors): 1:88. "We take an active role in our small school setting. The three counselors are an academic counselor (MA), a personal counselor (M.F.T), and a FLAME coordinator (M.Ed.)." **Counseling:** "ICA's Guidance Team provides individualized attention for all our students in order to ensure academic and personal success. Together with students and their families, we strive to assist all ICA students in reaching their goals. Our success is shown in our college track record." **Learning differences/disabilities:** "The FLAME program seeks to ensure that all students have the academic support and services that they need to reach their highest potential. The program includes collaboration with classroom teachers for special accommodations as specified in assessment; coordination of all administrative documentation relative to educational assessments; standardized testing, college application, and student personnel files; development of long-range programmatic planning. It is a resource for parents to help seek assessments of special needs. It provides individualized instruction in the areas of study skills, testing strategies, critical thinking skills, and interpersonal skills development."

Student Conduct and Health

Code of conduct: All students are expected to strive to live the philosophy of ICA, which indicates the challenge "to live meaningful Christian Lives". ICA's philosophy designates a "Spartan Code of Honor" to which the students strive to follow. **How school handles drug/alcohol usage:** N/P. **Prevention and awareness programs:** N/P.

Parent Involvement

Parent participation: "Parent Guild, socials, and fundraisers." **Parent/ teacher communication:** "Via telephone, e-mail, and/or by appointment." **Parent education:** N/P. **Donations:** "Parents are expected to support the school both financially and through volunteer hours."

Sports

Basketball, volleyball, softball, tennis, soccer, cross-country and cheerleading.

How Parents/Students Characterize the School

Parent response(s): "ICA is a school where my daughter found who she is. The school helped develop her leadership and spirituality." **Student response(s):** "I have made friendships that will last a lifetime and feel I have been given the tools with which to work. I have every confidence that I will continue to use those tools in college."

International High School

150 Oak Street
San Francisco, CA 94102
(415) 558-2084 *fax (415) 558-2085*
www.internationalsf.org

Jane Camblin, Head of School
Betsy Brody, Admissions Director, betsyb@internationalsf.org
Erin Cronin, Associate Director of Admission, erinc@internationalsf.org
Romy Ruukel, Admissions Coordinator, romyr@internationalsf.org

General

Coed day high school. Independent. Shares a campus with the French American International School (preK-8) and space with the Chinese American International School. Founded in 1962. Nonprofit, member CAIS, BAIHS, CASE, BAAD, ECIS, CIS, IBO. **Enrollment:** Approx. 328. **Average class size:** 15-18. **Accreditation:** WASC/CAIS and the French Ministry of Education. **School year:** 10-mo. calendar. **School day:** 8:10 a.m.-4:10 p.m. **Location:** Near the Civic Center, accessible by BART, CalTrain and Muni.

Student Body

Geographic breakdown (counties): 67% from San Francisco; 17% Alameda; 7% Marin; and 9% San Mateo. **Ethnicity:** 67% Caucasian (non-Latino); 13% Asian; 7% Latino; 6% African-American; 7% multi-ethnic. **International students (I-20 status):** 1%. **Middle schools (freshman):** Of 86 freshmen, 19% came from 12 public middle schools; 79% from 17 private, independent schools; 2% from 3 parochial schools.

Admission

Applications due: Mid-January (call for date). **Application fee:** $75. **Application process:** The school hosts open houses in the fall for parents and students to tour the campus and meet faculty and staff. Shadow visits are available for students from late September through December. Students visit the school and submit an essay, teacher recommendations, transcripts, and results of a standardized test. An admissions representative interviews each student. **No. of freshman applications:** 250 for approx. 40 places. **Minimum admission requirements:** Students are expected to have at least a B average, fairly strong standardized test scores (50% or above in independent school norms on SSATs, for example). Note: Prior study of a second language is not necessary for admission to the high school. Classes in the international track are taught in English and students may choose French, Mandarin or Spanish as their second language. German and Italian are available as a third language (or another language via a tutor). Applicants to the French section must be highly proficient in French. **Test required:** SSAT, ISEE, SAT 9, CTBS, CTP4, or STAR. **Preferences:** French American eighth grade students who meet admissions standards,

French nationals in the French program, and siblings (if appropriate). **"We are looking for** motivated learners who are interested in a global perspective on education." **What kind of student do you best serve?** "Students with curious minds who are capable of committing to a challenging program. Initiative, independent minds, and a passion for learning are unstated prerequisites."

Costs

Latest tuition: $27,670 payable in 1 or monthly payments. **Sibling discount:** None. **Tuition increases:** Approx. 4-6%. **Other costs:** One-time new student enrollment fee of $2,000. **Percentage of students receiving financial aid:** 23%. **Financial aid deadline:** Mid-January (call for date). **Average grant:** $15,500. **Percentage of grants of half-tuition or more:** N/P. French government aid is available to French nationals.

School's Mission Statement/Goals

"Guided by the principles of academic rigor and diversity, the French American International School offers programs of study in French and English to prepare its graduates for a world in which the ability to think critically and to communicate across cultures is of paramount importance."

Academic Program

"Students participate in one of two all-honors baccalaureate programs, the International Baccalaureate (IB) or the French Baccalaureate. Both baccalaureates are internationally recognized diploma programs that can earn students up to one year's credit at American and international universities. The IB is recognized as one of the most comprehensive honors programs taught in the United States and abroad." **Courses offered** (AP=Advanced Placement, H=Honors, (AP)=AP option, (H)=Honors option): "Because the IB is a comprehensive all honors program, AP courses are not offered; however, students are eligible to take AP exams in many of their courses. Both the IB and the French Baccalaureate offer rigorous academic programs, comprising the last two years of high school, in which students must study at least two languages, math, a laboratory science, a social science and a sixth subject of their selection, which may include another language, another science, arts, drama, music or additional social sciences. All IB Diploma candidates take Theory of Knowledge, a class that investigates the different ways of knowing and how knowledge, perception and investigation cut across all subject lines. Additionally, students produce a personally researched 4,000 word extended essay in an IB field of their choice. Students are expected to participate in the areas of public and community service, physical activities, and the creative and cultural arts." **Computer lab/training:** "Integrated into the school curriculum." (N/P lab) **Grading:** 0-7 for students enrolled in the IB program; 0-20 for those enrolled in the French Bac and classes in the French Track.

Only corresponding letter grades appear on transcripts. **Graduation requirements:** 4 years of English and math; 3 years of history/social studies (including one credit year of U.S. History), experimental science (encompassing at least two different lab sciences), and French or a second language other than French, or a first language other than English; 2 years of other academic domains such as a third science, a third language, a social science, a second art or further information technology; 1 year of the art disciplines, P.E., and 50 hours documented community service. Graduation also depends on satisfactory conduct and attendance records. **Average nightly homework (M-Th):** G9-10: 2 hours; G11-12: 2-4 hours. **Faculty:** 50 f/t, 9 p/t; 56% male, 44% female; 95% have master's degrees or foreign equivalents; 14% hold doctorate degrees. **Faculty ethnicity:** "Represent 11 nationalities." (N/P ethnicities) **Faculty selection/training:** "Faculty is selected from recruitment fairs both locally and internationally. Faculty is encouraged to participate in professional development workshops and trainings." **Teacher/student ratio:** 1:15. **Percentage of students enrolled in AP:** N/A (See information on IB, above). **Most recent senior class profile (mean)** SAT Math 610, SAT Critical Reading 623, SAT Writing 620. GPA: 3.62. **National Merit Scholarship Program:** 3 Semifinalists, 6 Commended Scholars. **College enrollment (last class):** 100%; 98% in 4-year, 2% in 2-year. **Recent (last 3 yrs) colleges:** Amherst U, Arizona SU, Art Institute of Chicago (3), Bard C (2), Barnard C (5), Bates C, Bennington C, Berklee School of Music, Boston U (4), Brown U, Bryn Mawr C (2), Bucknell U, Cal Poly-SLO (2), CSU-LA, Cambridge U (UK), Carleton, CesMed, Marseille, Columbia, Cornell U (3), Dickinson C, Embry-Riddle Aeronautical U, Emerson (3), Eugene Lang C (2), European School of Economics, Fordham U, George Washington U, Georgetown U, Hamilton, Harvard, Haverford C, Johns Hopkins U, Kenyon C (2), Lewis & Clark, Louisiana SU, Loyola Marymount, Macalester (2), Marlboro C, McGill (7), Middlebury (4), Mills C (3), Northeastern, Northwestern, NYU (6), Oberlin (6), Occidental C, Olin School of Engineering, Oregon SU, Oxford (UK), Oxford C of Emory, Pomona, Princeton, Regis U, Santa Clara, Sarah Lawrence (4), Smith C (2), SFSU (3), Skidmore (2), Stanford, Swarthmore (2), Syracuse U, Trinity C, U-Arizona (2), U-British Columbia, Université Bordeux II, UC (Berkeley (10), Davis (11), Irvine, LA (14), Riverside, SD (5), Santa Barbara (7), Santa Cruz (10)), U-Arizona (4), U-British Columbia (2), U-Chicago (2), U-Colorado at Boulder, U-Maryland-Baltimore County, UNC-Chapel Hill, U-Oregon, Penn (2), U-Pittsburgh, U-Puget Sound, U-Redlands, USF (4), USC (9), U-Texas-Austin, U-Washington (2), Vassar (6), Washington U-St. Louis, Wellesley (3), Wesleyan, Wheaton, Willamette, Worchester Polytechnic, and Yale (4).

Other Indicators the School is Accomplishing its Goals
"SAT II Tests: Mean Scores (Class of 2007): Literature: 631, Math I: 620, Math II: 625, Chemistry: 631, French: 731, and Spanish: 645."

Campus/Campus Life

Campus description: The school is located in the Hayes Valley neighborhood and within blocks of the Conservatory of Music, opera, ballet, Asian Art Museum, symphony, and government centers; 180,000 sq. ft. campus. The facilities include 5 science labs, a language lab, a technology lab, a gymnasium, and a rooftop deck. New facilities include a biotechnology lab, expanded college counseling and resource center, and a renovated library/media center. A new arts pavilion will include a new theater, recording space, digital arts/film studio and visual arts spaces. **Library:** On campus and also use of the San Francisco Civic Center library. The library contains 10,000 print volumes; 35 periodical subscriptions; 6 computers all with Internet access; 70 CD-ROMS; online catalog (OPAC); study space for 50. Open to students 8 a.m.-5 p.m.; 2 full-time librarians. **Sports facilities:** The gymnasium is 10,000 sq. ft. and has basketball and volleyball courts, a weight training room, team/locker rooms, restrooms, athletic director offices, bleachers, and scoreboards. **Theater/arts facilities:** Theater, performing and fine arts studios. **Open/closed campus:** Open. **Lunches:** Students bring their own lunches daily or visit nearby cafés. **Bus service:** The campus is 4 blocks from the Civic Center BART station, one block from the Muni streetcar station, and one block from the bus lines on Van Ness/Market. There is a direct connection between CalTrain and Van Ness Avenue. **Uniform/dress code:** None. **Co-curricular activities/clubs:** Clubs are student initiated and student run, and therefore vary from year to year. Recent clubs include: Gay Straight Alliance, Photography Club, student newspaper, Bake for Lives (student fundraising), Multicultural Students' Association, student council, Student and Faculty rock band, jazz and rock bands, chorus, after-school theater troupe, film club, league sports, etc. **Foreign exchange programs/internships:** The school organizes cultural and academic exchanges abroad for interested students in G9-11. Past trips have included Nicaragua, Germany, Beijing, Paris, Ethiopia, India, Russia and Tahiti. **Community service:** Required by the school and the International Baccalaureate. Students have collaborated with organizations such as Save the Children, San Francisco School Volunteers, The Rose Home, and Habitat for Humanity. Students have also assisted at senior centers, the SPCA, and local youth organizations. Recent international projects include building a school in Jemejem Legebatu, Ethiopia and building a pre-school in M'bour, Senegal. **Typical freshman schedule:** English Literature, Algebra I or II, U.S. History, Physics/Chemistry, Biology, a second language (Beginning French, Spanish, or Mandarin); one semester each of two of the following arts electives: Stagecraft, Theater Performance, Art, Film and Video or Music, P.E., and an optional third language (German, Mandarin, Spanish, or Italian).

Student Support Services

Counselor/student ratio (not including college counselors): 1:328. **Counseling:** "The guidance counselor runs a peer counseling group, and is available for individual support. Students are also assigned advisors to assist them in academic and non-academic matters. The Dean of Students oversees the advisory program, and each advisor is responsible for a group of approximately 20 students. The advisor oversees the group, monitors each student's progress, and is also the first point of contact for parent communication. Two college counselors begin formally working with students in G11 and meet individually with students and families to discuss college and university selection, application, and admission." **Learning disabilities/differences:** "International seeks to accommodate all the needs of enrolled students."

Student Conduct and Health

Code of conduct: "Expectations for student behavior apply on the Oak Street campus and whenever students represent the school on field trips, off-campus activities, or exchanges. Principles of conduct: Obey national and state law; act with regard for the safety of persons and property; conduct oneself as a responsible member of an academic community; respect the rights, dignity, and differences of every other person; and exhibit honesty and integrity at all times." **How school handles drugs/alcohol:** "Forbidden on campus. First offenders are suspended from classes for one week, complete 6 hours of community service, participate in peer counseling and receive a letter in their permanent file. A second violation results in expulsion from school." **Prevention and awareness programs:** "Provided at all grade levels as a part of the required health education curriculum, as well as special lunchtime presentations on issues pertinent to teenagers."

Summer Programs

Summer enrichment program course offerings include: Essay Writing, French, Spanish, Mandarin, Algebra, and Study Skills. Summer abroad programs include: language, theatre, and sports camps in France and an arts camp in Senegal.

Parent Involvement

Parent participation: 12 hours per year per family required. **Parent/teacher communication:** Parent/teacher conferences are held twice per year. Meetings with teachers/dean are held as necessary. **Parent education:** The Parents' Association sponsors seminars for parents, produces a monthly newsletter, and oversees volunteer committees in the areas of arts, sports, technology, and community service. Parents may attend monthly meetings with the principal, and parents may also become involved in the Parents' Coalition of Bay Area High Schools. **Donations:** "Encouraged and welcomed. Our parents are our best resource in terms of volunteerism as well as financial donors."

Sports
Through the BCL, students compete in soccer, basketball, golf, swimming, cross-country, tennis, volleyball, badminton, track and field, and baseball.

What Sets School Apart From Others
"The International High School is unique. We not only offer rigorous academics and an 'all-honors program,' but also are the only Bay Area school which provides a truly multilingual, multicultural, and student-centered education. We view our graduates as key players in a future world that will be characterized by rapid change and fierce competition. The education offered at International provides students with a multicultural understanding and the tools for success in the global village of the twenty-first century."

How Parents/Students Characterize School
Parent response(s): "I find my son's exposure to a more international environment very valuable. This is a unique education that I don't believe exists anywhere else in our area." "Besides receiving a world-class education, my daughter has blossomed as a person. She has discovered strengths and talents she had not previously known." **Student response(s):** "International is a good fit for me because it is 'international.' It allows me to study different languages, participate in exchanges, and keeps me challenged." "This is my ideal school. I like the academics and the pace of work. The people who I have met are great, and I'm having a wonderful time."

The Jewish Community High School of the Bay (JCHS)
1835 Ellis Street
San Francisco, CA 94115
(415) 345-9777 *fax (415) 345-1888*
www.jchsofthebay.org

Rabbi Howard Ruben, Head of School
Marcia Levin, Director of Admissions, mlevin@jchsofthebay.org

General
Coed Jewish high school (N/P % Jewish). Independent. Founded in 2000. **Enrollment:** 155, anticipated enrollment 250-400. **Average class size:** 15. **Accreditation:** WASC, member of NAIS, CAIS, PEJE, NAAJHS, SSATB, ISEE, BAAD, BAIHS, ISBOA, NASSP, CASE, BALD, ASCD, BATDC, BAISSC, WACAC, NACAC, SSBL. **School year:** Aug.-June. **School day:** 8:15 a.m.-3:20 p.m. **Location:** In the Western Addition, near Fillmore St. Muni buses 38 and 31 stop within two blocks of campus. JCHS arranges transportation for North Bay, East Bay and Peninsula students.

Student Body

Geographic breakdown (counties): 45% from San Francisco; 7% from Marin; 7% from the Peninsula; 41% from the East Bay. **Ethnicity:** N/P. **International students (I-20 status):** N/P. **Middle schools (freshman):** 62% came from 6 Jewish day schools; 21% from 11 public schools; 17% from 10 independent schools. 38 middle schools are represented in student body.

Admission

Applications due: January (call for date). **Application fee:** $75. **Application process:** Students visit campus and interview with a member of the admissions committee in the fall. Parents are advised to schedule this visit and interview in September, as space fills quickly. Applicants must submit student and parent application forms, teacher recommendation forms, standardized test scores, 7th grade (full year) transcript and 8th grade (1st semester/trimester) transcript. **No. of freshman applications:** 130 for 55 places. **Minimum admission requirements:** "Admission at JCHS is open to motivated students interested in a college preparatory education in general and Jewish studies with an extensive co-curricular program in athletics, art, music, dance and other electives." **Preferences:** "Students who self-identify as Jewish." **Test required:** SSAT or ISEE. **"We are looking for** students who are motivated, creative and accomplished with a connection to the community through service, leadership or observance." **What sort of student do you best serve?** "JCHS serves motivated Jewish students with a college preparatory curriculum, which offers a focus on the Jewish culture and tradition as well as extensive opportunities in athletics, community service, and visual and performing arts."

Costs

Latest tuition: $27,700 payable in 1, 2, 10 or 12 monthly payments. **Sibling discount:** None. **Tuition increases:** 7%. **Other costs:** $100 - $200 student trip fee. **Percentage of students receiving financial aid:** 31%. **Financial aid deadline:** February (call for date). **Average grant:** $16,000. **Percentage of grants of half-tuition grants or more:** N/P.

School's Mission Statement/Goals

"The Jewish Community High School of the Bay (JCHS) is a co-educational day school providing a rigorous, college preparatory curriculum in general and Judaic studies. We are committed to an extensive enrichment program, including the arts and athletics. JCHS serves the San Francisco Bay Community and is open to all Jewish students regardless of prior Jewish educational experience. JCHS is guided by the rhythms of the Jewish calendar, Jewish culture and tradition, and by an inextricable link to the land of Israel. Our goal is to provide our students with the education necessary to gain acceptance into the finest universities and to engage in lifelong Jewish learning, enabling our graduates to employ the skills and lessons taught within our walls to their lives within both the Jewish and the wider community."

Academic Program:
Courses offered ((H)=Honor option, (AP)=AP option, (A)=Advanced option): **Literature:** World Literature (A), American Literature (H); **History:** World History, American History (AP), Jewish History; **Math:** Algebra 1-2 (A), Geometry (A), Pre-Calculus (H); **Science:** Physics (A), Chemistry (A), Biology (AP); **Arts:** Studio Art 1: Elements of Art, Studio Art 2: Principles of Art, Mixed Media Sculpture, Graphic Design, Drawing and Painting, Theater Lab, Jazz Band, Voice Ensemble; **Health/P.E.:** Health and Wellness, P.E.; **Religion:** Tanach (Bible), Talmud (Rabbinic Literature); **Languages:** Modern Hebrew, French, Spanish. **Computer lab/training:** Desktop computers are available in the library. Laptops are available for students to check out; wireless connection throughout school. **Grading:** A-F. Progress reports at mid-quarter point; mid-semester letter grades; full evaluation with narrative at end of each semester. **Graduation requirements:** The core curriculum is: (1 credit = 1 semester) 7 credits of Humanities, including 4 credits of English, 3 of history (World History, U.S. History, Senior Seminar in History); 7 credits of math/science, including 3 math credits, 3 lab science credits and 1 math or science elective; 7 credits of Jewish Studies, including 3 Bible and literature credits, 2 Jewish study elective credits, 1 Jewish history credit and 1 Senior Seminar in Jewish Thought; 2 to 3.5 credits of Hebrew and world languages (electives in Spanish and French offered); credit of visual and performing arts; and 2 credits of health and P.E. **Average nightly homework (M-Th):** 2 hours. **Faculty:** 39; 35% male, 65% female; 75% hold advanced degrees (N/P degrees). **Faculty ethnicity:** N/P. **Faculty selection/training:** "Faculty are selected through an extensive interview and hiring process. On-going professional development; new faculty orientation." **Teacher/student ratio:** 1:5. **Percentage of students enrolled in AP:** N/P. **Senior class profile (mean):** SAT Math 578, SAT Critical Reading 605, SAT Writing 602. Average GPA 3.5. **National Merit Scholarship Program:** N/A. **College enrollment (last class):** 100% (N/P % 4-yr, 2-yr) **Recent colleges:** N/P.

Other Indicators the School is Accomplishing its Goals
"In recognition of the school's excellent program and faculty, JCHS received a full 6-year term of accreditation from the Western Association of Schools and Colleges (WASC) in spring, 2007."

Campus/Campus Life
Campus description: The school, which takes up nearly a city block in a residential neighborhood, is in a newly remodeled 62,000 sq. ft. building with an 11,000 sq. ft. Jerusalem stone courtyard. The campus includes a secure parking garage with free parking for students, faculty and visitors. **Library:** "Our very spacious and beautiful library is shared with the Bureau of Jewish Education Library and offers an extensive

general and Jewish collection of 25,000 volumes. We offer an online webpage, subscription databases for student use, project-based search strategy pages, and active student and parent book discussion groups." **Sports facilities:** The campus has a basketball court and uses the USF Koret Center facilities to host games and team practices. **Theater/arts facilities:** "Performing Arts Theater, seating 200 in a new state-of-the-art theater." **Open/closed campus:** Closed. **Lunches:** Kosher, organic salad and multi-ethnic hot entrée menu served 5 days per week. **Bus service:** Transportation service for Marin and East Bay students. **Uniforms/dress code:** No uniform (dress code N/P). **Co-curricular activities/clubs:** Yearbook, student government, Interfaith Teen Council, Village Project Tutoring Club, Social Club, Jam Band, Digital Media, drama productions three times per year, hip-hop dance club, BBQ club, STAND chapter, literary magazine, Opera Club. JCHS offers a variety of student activities including student dances, Prom, holiday parties, community events, annual Arts Evening, annual Science Symposium, student concerts, and Experiential Journeys throughout the U.S. and Israel. **Foreign exchange programs/internships:** "In development." **Community service:** "Community Outreach involvement at JCHS is required and incorporated into each year. Students engage the world in 3 ways: volunteering time to help and empower others in need, sharing and being generous with money and possessions and standing up for the rights of others and ourselves through protest and activism." **Typical freshman schedule:** World Literature, Math, Conceptual Physics, World History, Tanach, Hebrew and Study Hall. Electives in world languages, art, health or P.E. may be available. "Schedule is a modified block schedule. The JCHS academic program offers a context for our students' deepest questions and personal explorations. We believe that all classes, as well as co-curricular activities, provide a context for considering issues that pertain to our society, family, personal lives, self-esteem and ethical behavior. We hope that study and discussions both inside and outside of the classroom inform our students' moral development and strengthen their Jewish identity."

Student Support Services
Counselor-student ratio (not including college counselors): N/P. **Counseling:** Full-time School Counselor, Educational Support Director and College Advisor. Each student also has a faculty mentor and a grade-level dean to provide support. **Learning disabilities/difference:** N/P.

Student Conduct and Health
Code of conduct: "Deal honestly and truthfully in all matters; demonstrate respect for the common Jewish traditions that shape school life and of the diversity of belief and practice represented within our school and general community; act in a considerate and friendly manner toward classmates, faculty, staff and guests of the school; dress in a manner that communicates respect for oneself, the community and

the process of learning; respect the school buildings and property by keeping the campus attractive and litter free; when off campus, keep in mind that you represent yourself, your family and JCHS while participating in trips, athletic and academic teams, performances, and community service." **How school handles drug/alcohol usage:** "The possession and/or use of alcohol and other drugs not specifically prescribed by a doctor are illegal. Students at JCHS are prohibited from possessing, using or distributing tobacco or alcohol products and/or being under the influence of alcohol or other illegal drugs while on school grounds, at any school-sponsored activity (on campus or off campus), and riding on school buses. Students are not permitted to share or distribute any personal medications brought from home. Violation of this standard will result in possible suspension or expulsion in addition to police and/or counseling referral." **Prevention and awareness program:** "JCHS offers an extensive health curriculum that addresses these topics."

Summer Programs: N/P.

Parent Involvement

Parent participation: Parent Organization (PO) coordinates volunteerism for school events and evening meetings. **Parent/teacher communication:** Conferences as needed; quarterly grade reports; written narratives twice per year. **Parent education:** Regularly scheduled educational programs and parent meetings with administrators; college informational evenings; on-going learning opportunities and programs; weekly JCHS "The Week Ahead" newsletter e-mailed to the school community announcing upcoming school functions and holiday information. **Donations:** "JCHS encourages parents to support the school however possible (financial or otherwise) – many parents volunteer their time at school events."

Sports

"The interscholastic athletic program at JCHS provides the opportunity for athletes of all levels to build a strong set of values, including cooperation, sportsmanship, self-confidence, dedication and discipline. Students are encouraged to participate in sports or club teams, and approximatley 75% participate on a JCHS athletic team. Starting in 2008, JCHS will be competing in the newly formed PSAL and moving to California's Central Coast Section for all varsity sports. Club sports are also available in tennis, golf and Ultimate Frisbee."

What Sets School Apart From Others

"JCHS weaves together humanities, jewish studies, and math/science. We braid together that which is experiential, authentic, and experimental. We braid together a love of learning, the construction of a nourishing community, and the pursuit of justice and mercy. We braid together wisdom drawn from science, art, and the spirit. We braid together God, Torah, and Israel. It is a richly colorful and deeply complicated tapestry." — Rabbi Ruben, Head of School

How Parents/Students Characterize School

Parent response(s): "JCHS has exceeded our initial and very high expectations, and we feel privileged to be part of this vibrant and committed community of students and families. The best testimonial to the school is to hear the students themselves express their enthusiasm for learning, their closeness and respect for the faculty, and their sense of being valued as individuals by staff." **Student response(s):** "JCHS has been a great experience for me. I feel that taking Judaic Studies classes, learning Hebrew, and being part of a very supportive Jewish community has helped me grow both as a Jew and as a person. Before I came to JCHS, I knew that I was Jewish, but I did not fully understand what that meant. Keeping kosher or saying Kaddish meant nothing to me. Now I am able to place them in a certain context and know what they mean. The community at JCHS is very supportive. Students and teachers accept, support and challenge me to grow in all areas. For example, my English teachers have helped polish my writing skills, resulting in my participation in a national poetry contest after my freshman year. I have also worked with the administration to develop a recycling program, which has expanded to include a school-wide lunch compost program. Looking back and comparing who I was before JCHS to who I am now, and looking at my great friends and teachers here, I am very happy that I came to JCHS."

Junípero Serra High School

451 W. 20th Avenue
San Mateo, CA 94403
(650) 345-8207 *fax (650) 573-6638*
www.serrahs.com
padres@serrahs.com

Lars Lund, President
Randy Vogel, Admissions Director, rvogel@serrahs.com

General

Boys Catholic day school. (75% Catholic). Operated by the Archdiocese of San Francisco. Founded in 1944. Nonprofit. **Enrollment:** 990. **Average class size:** 25-26. **Accreditation:** WASC. **School year:** Mid-Aug.-late May. **School day:** 8:10 a.m.-2:55 p.m. **Location:** In San Mateo, 22 miles south of San Francisco, 9 miles north of Palo Alto; just off Hwy. 92, which intersects Hwys. 280 and 101.

Student Body

Geographic breakdown (counties): 98% from the Peninsula (from San Francisco through Palo Alto, including the coastal areas of Half

Moon Bay and Pacifica); 2% other Bay Area counties. **Ethnicity:** 66% Caucasian; 10% Hispanic; 6% Filipino; 7% Asian/Pacific Islander; 2% African-American; 9% multi-ethnic. **International students (I-20 status):** Less than 1%. **Middle schools (freshman):** 23 Catholic feeder schools in the county including St. Gregory (San Mateo), St. Matthew (San Mateo), Immaculate Heart of Mary (Belmont), Our Lady of Angels (Burlingame), St. Catherine (Burlingame), St. Dunstan (Millbrae), St. Robert (San Bruno), All Souls (So. San Francisco), St. Pius (Redwood City), St. Veronica (So. San Francisco), Mt. Carmel (Redwood City) and more than 35 public feeder schools including Crocker (Hillsborough), Bowditch (Foster City), Ralston (Belmont), Tierra Linda (San Carlos), Central (San Carlos), Abbott (San Mateo) and Burlingame Intermediate (Burlingame). (N/P # students from each).

Admission

Applications due: Mid-December (check website for exact dates). **Application fee:** $70. **Application process:** Applications are available online in early September. The school hosts an open house on the first Thursday of each December at 7 p.m. for boys in G6-8 and their families. Full day shadow visits may be scheduled during September-February. Appointments may be made online. Transcripts and recommendation forms from a middle school counselor or principal are needed by early February. Clergy recommendation forms are optional, though most applicants submit them. The form seeks a recommendation from any clergy member who knows the child, or alternatively asks for information on the applicant's spirituality. Applicants are interviewed in February, and decision letters are sent mid-March. **No. of freshmen applications:** More than 500 for 250 places. Seven new students were admitted to G10, 6 to G11. **Minimum admission requirements:** "We generally look for students who are at or above grade level in their testing with grades of As, Bs or Cs in academic subjects." **Test required:** The HSPT is taken at the school the second Saturday in January. **Preferences:** Catholic. **"We are looking for** students seeking a college preparatory education and who wish to participate in the school community." **What kind of students do you best serve?** "Our mission is to meet the needs of Catholic boys in San Mateo County; students who are above average academically are usually successful at Serra."

Costs

Latest tuition: $14,100, which includes the registration fee, paid in the spring. Payable in 1 (July), 2 (July and Dec.) or monthly payments (by direct debit). **Sibling discount:** None. **Tuition increases:** Approx. 7%. **Other costs:** Approx. $500 for textbooks. **Percentage of students receiving financial aid:** 22%. **Financial aid deadline:** Second week in February (check website for exact dates). **Average grant:** $4,000. **Percentage of grants of half-tuition or more:** 8%.

School's Mission Statement/Goals

"Junípero Serra High School is the Archdiocesan Catholic school educating the young men of San Mateo County. We are an academic high school, reflecting the cultural richness of San Mateo County with a strong college preparatory curriculum. Our mission is to develop the gifts and talents of each student and to foster Gospel values in an environment of academic excellence and mutual respect." • "Our Philosophy ... Empowered by parents, the primary educators of their children and the Archdiocese of San Francisco, Junípero Serra High School is a Catholic school participating in the educational ministry of the Church. Junípero Serra has the responsibility to provide an integrated ministry through the celebration of Word and Sacrament, the building of community and the promotion of service to the world in which we live. At Junípero Serra High School, the educational process, grounded in the Catholic tradition, affirms the dignity of the human person. The unique gifts and talents of each Junípero Serra student are developed in two complementary ways: first, through the fostering of intellectual capabilities, artistic creativity and physical skills and secondly, through the nurturing of spiritual, moral, psychological and social growth. Through an integration of faith, life and culture, each student is encouraged to look critically at the diversity and challenges of our society and to make responsible choices based on the Gospel values of justice and compassion. The purpose of Junípero Serra High School is to develop mature Christians, men of faith, wisdom, and service who, like Blessed Junípero Serra, find Christ in and bring Christ to the people with whom they live, work and serve."

Academic Program

Courses offered (AP=Advanced Placement, H=Honors, (AP)=AP option, (H)=Honors option): **English:** English 1-4 (H), English 1A-2A, Junior English, AP English Language and Composition, Senior Literature and Composition, Senior Writing, Creative Writing, Shakespeare, Publications 1-2, AP English Literature and Composition; **History:** World History 1-2 (H), AP U.S. History, Govt., AP American Govt. and Politics, Economics, California History, Cultural Anthropology; **Math:** Intro to Algebra, Algebra 1-2 (H), Geometry (H), Algebra 3-4, Algebra with Trigonometry (H), Trigonometry, Pre-Calculus (H), Calculus, Calculus AB-AP, Calculus BC-AP, Statistics, Business Accounting, Virtual Enterprise; **P.E.:** P.E.-Health, P.E. 2-3, P.E. Athletics; **Science:** Discovering Science (H), Chemistry (H/AP), Biology (H), Chemistry in the Community, Physics (H/AP), Advanced Biology (AP), Anatomy and Physiology, Introductory Astronomy; **Foreign Languages:** French 1-8, AP French Language, Spanish 1-4, 3-8 (H), AP Spanish Language, German 1-8; **Theology:** Intro to Church Scriptures and Spirituality, Intro to Morality/Moral Decision-Making, Jesus of History-Christ of Faith, Church History, Christian Lifestyles, Social Justice, Bioethics; **Arts:** Symphonic Band, Jazz Band, Guitar, Percussion, Men's Chorus, Mixed Chorus, Dramatic and Musical Theater Production, Advanced

Drama, Art, Advanced Art, Ceramics, Architectural Design, AP Art History, Films, Photography; **Computers:** Computer Literacy, Computer Programming, Advanced Computer Literacy, AP Computer Science; **Other:** Psychology, Yearbook, Publication. Coed classes: At Mercy High School in Burlingame, Art, Digital Photography, Anatomy and Physiology, American Sign Language; at Notre Dame High School in Belmont, French IV (H), AP French, Basic Art, Bioethics, Ceramics, Environmental Science In Action, Psychology, Sculpture, Economics, AP Art History, String Orchestra, AP Spanish. **Computer lab/training:** The school has two computer labs, one for students to use on their own, the other for class instruction; one with 30 PCs, the other with 32 PCs; 18 PCs are in the science labs, 32 in the library, 8 in the history lab and 1 in each classroom. The school computers are all networked, and all students have access and e-mail accounts. One semester Computer Literacy required. **Grading:** A-F, issued 6 times a year. **Graduation requirements:** Designed to meet or exceed the minimum admission requirements for the UC system: 4 years English and religion; 3 years social studies and math; 2.5 years science; 2 years of a foreign language; 1 year visual and performing arts; 1 year P.E., .5 year computer literacy; 80 hours of Christian Service. **Average nightly homework (Mon-Th):** G9-10: 3-4 hours; G11: 4 hours; G12: 2-4 hours. **Faculty:** 73; 77% male, 23% female; 58% hold master's degrees and 2% hold doctorates. **Faculty ethnicity:** 91% Caucasian; 6% Hispanic; 3% other. **Faculty selection/training:** "Faculty has teaching credentials and higher degrees. Periodic in-services are held throughout the school year, and continuing education and workshops are encouraged." **Teacher/student ratio:** 1:26. **Percentage of students enrolled in AP/exam pass rate:** 34%; pass rate 80%. **Senior class profile (mean):** SAT: N/P; GPA: 3.0. **National Merit Scholarship Program:** N/P. **College enrollment (last class):** 80% in 4-year, 20% in 2-year. **Recent (last 3 yrs) colleges:** Arizona SU, Berklee C of Music, Boston C, Boston U, Cal Maritime Academy, Catholic U-America, CSU (all campuses), Claremont-McKenna, Colby C, Columbia U, Cornell, Dartmouth, Duke, Fordham, Georgetown, Gonzaga, Harvard, Loyola-Marymount, Marquette, Menlo, NYU, Northeastern, Northwestern, Notre Dame de Namur U, Occidental, Oregon SU, Portland U, Pepperdine, Princeton, Regis, St. Mary's, Santa Clara, Seattle, SMU, St. John's, Stanford, Syracuse, Temple U, Texas Tech U, Tulane U, Villanova U, Washington U-St. Louis, Washington SU, Whittier C, UC (all campuses), U.S. Naval Academy, U-Arizona, U-Chicago, U-Colorado-Boulder, U-Hawaii, U-Illinois, U-Massachusetts, U-Michigan, U-Nevada-Reno, U-Notre Dame, U-Oregon, UOP, U-Portland, U-Puget Sound, USD, USF, USC, U-Texas, U-Vermont, U-Washington, and Willamette U.

Other Indicators the School is Accomplishing its Goals

"The success of our graduates in a wide variety of areas upon graduation from school" and "a willingness of students to work in and serve the community of which they are a part."

Campus/Campus Life

Campus description: The school has a 13-acre campus with a building complex that includes two stories of classrooms, science labs and offices; a chapel, auditorium and caféteria. **Library:** 14,000 volumes with an online catalog accessible through the school's website. Resources include more than 35 periodical subscriptions—both hardcopy and online. Supplementary online subscription databases: Infotrak, Facts. com, American Journey Online, Britannica Online Encyclopedia, SIRS Online Researcher, World's Best Poetry, and others. Several networked computers; study space for 80 students; open from 7:30 a.m.- 4 p.m.; full-time librarian with 2 part-time assistants. **Sports facilities:** The Kenneth Houle Athletic Complex includes outdoor basketball courts, a locker room, weight room and swimming pool, the Jesse Freitas Football Field and Track, the Dan Frisella Memorial Baseball Field, soccer field and gymnasium. **Theater/arts facilities:** 850-seat auditorium; at the back of the campus is an art building with drawing and painting studios and a music center; architectural design studio. **Open/closed campus:** Closed. **Lunches:** Students may purchase hot lunch daily. **Bus service:** SamTrans (public). **Uniforms/dress code:** "Casual pants, jeans in good condition, and walking shorts are permitted; sweats, overalls and military pants etc. are not allowed. Shirts must have collars or a full turtleneck and sleeves. School spirit T-shirts may be worn. No drug, alcohol, etc. messages allowed on clothing or backpacks. Hats are not allowed in the school building. No facial hair, hair longer than collar, dyed hair, piercings or tattoos allowed. Certain dress-up days for special occasions require buttoned collared dress shirt, tie, non-denim slacks and dress shoes." **Co-curricular activities/clubs:** More than 38 clubs including yearbook and a monthly newspaper. In both publications, students have the opportunity to contribute writing, photography or aid in design. **Foreign exchange programs/internships:** No formal program. **Community service:** All students are required to complete 80 hours of volunteer service with a nonprofit agency before graduation. Students participate in two blood drives, two annual holiday food drives, an Adopt-A-Family program and a toy drive for young cancer patients. Students are also "strongly encouraged" to participate in activities of their parishes. **Typical freshman schedule:** English, Algebra or Geometry, World History, Theology, foreign language (French, Spanish or German), and Discovering Science/Computer Literacy.

Student Support Services

Counselor-student ratio (not including college counselors): 1:240. **Counseling:** The school has four full-time counselors who engage in personal, academic and college counseling, as well as a staff member for the College and Career Center. College counseling begins freshman year. **Learning disabilities/differences:** "A learning resource specialist assists teachers and counselors of students with learning differences to make the necessary accommodations to help students achieve success in the classroom."

Student Conduct and Health

Code of conduct: "Besides prohibiting violations of the law, cheating and other honor code provisions, the code prohibits beepers, walkmen, and skateboards. **How school handles drug/alcohol usage:** "On first offense the student is subject to expulsion, though a student who has a clean record may be placed on probation if the violation did not involve drug or alcohol sales. On second offense, he is dismissed." **Prevention and awareness programs:** "Program for Student Assistance, Student Formation Programs, and one required parent formation/information night each school year."

Summer Programs

The school offers a coed summer recreational camp for ages 5-12; baseball, basketball, football and soccer mini-camps; a coed academic summer school program with enrichment for junior high students; enrichment and review for incoming students; and high school courses.

Parent Involvement

Parent participation: No requirement, although parents are invited to participate in the Mothers' Auxiliary, Fathers' Club, and Boosters' Club, all of which provide social, service, and fundraising activities for the school. Major yearly events include a Benefit Auction, Fashion Show, St. Patrick's Day Extravaganza, Crab Cioppino and Tri-Trip Dinner. **Parent/teacher communication:** Parent/teacher conferences, school website, and academic reports through e-mail. **Parent education:** The school hosts various orientation programs, college night programs, discussion of teenage issues, Back-to-School Night, and report card conference nights. **Donations:** "Each family is asked to make a yearly gift or pledge based on whatever is a comfortable amount for them to Junípero Serra's Parent Pledge Program. The amount donated by our families varies greatly."

Sports

Junípero Serra has 35 teams in 14 interscholastic sports competing in the WCAL in (fall) football, water polo, cross-country; (winter) basketball, wrestling, soccer, (spring) baseball, track, golf, swimming, tennis, volleyball, lacrosse, and crew. Most all sports offer three teams: freshman level, junior varsity and varsity competition. Student-athletes make use of on-site and off-site facilities and personnel, including a full-time athletic trainer and a full-time strength and conditioning coach. The school also offers intramural competition and sports-related clubs.

What Sets School Apart From Others

"Junípero Serra offers the best of both worlds. We allow our students to be themselves in an all-male environment where camaraderie, brotherhood and school spirit are much more commonplace than competition and fashion. We also enjoy a relationship with two sister schools: Mercy in Burlingame and Notre Dame in Belmont. This allows for healthy interaction and includes coed classes, retreats, club activities, performing arts and dances. With an enrollment of 990 students, we are small enough that our students do not get lost in the shuffle, but big enough to offer the same activities and course offerings of much larger schools. Junípero Serra places its students at various levels in our college preparatory program according to their needs and abilities. Outside of the classroom, our students are involved in a host of activities including music and drama productions, team sports, student publications, student government and numerous other clubs, while also serving in their community or parish. The school offers 'a good atmosphere for learning; a dedicated faculty (with sixteen alumni who have come back to teach); and a true sense of community including teachers, staff, students and their families.'"

How Parents/Students Characterize School

Parent response(s): "A quality education in a caring environment." "Students can thrive in a variety of areas." "Junípero Serra demonstrates the ability to reach out to all students." "Serra was a blessing for both our son and our family." "The ordinary hard-working family is recognized and valued." "Serra not only educates our sons, but helps them find out who they are capable of becoming." "An education based on values." "Serra High School is the best thing that has happened to my son. His personality and his self-esteem have blossomed. We really appreciate all that is going on there. Everything is so positive."
Student response(s): "Strong academics, athletics and extra-curriculars." "Good atmosphere and feeling of community." "Brotherhood is the heart of what it means to be a Padre." "Junípero Serra High School feels like home." "Great school spirit." "Serra bridges the gap between the students and the teachers to aid the learning process." "Serra is a place that allows people to be themselves." "Serra not only improves who you are, but who you will be." "Serra has truly prepared me for the next chapter in my life."

Kehillah Jewish High School
3900 Fabian Way
Palo Alto, CA 94303
(650) 213-9600 *fax (650) 213-9601*
www.kehillahhigh.org

Lillian Howard, Head of School
Alison Ruebusch and Mark Cahn, Principals
Marily Lerner, Director of Admissions, admissions@kehillah.org

General

Coed Jewish day high school (100% Jewish). Independent. Founded in 2002. Nonprofit, member CAIS, NAIS, BAAD, PAAD, BAIHS, SSATB, PEJE, RAVSAK. **Enrollment:** 110 to grow to 250 in 2015. **Average class size:** 10-15. **Accreditation:** WASC. **School year:** Late August to mid-June. **School day:** 8:30 a.m.-3:45 p.m. **Location:** Palo Alto near Hwy. 101; across the street from the Taube-Koret Campus for Jewish Life.

Student Body

Geographic breakdown (counties): 33% from San Mateo; 65% from Santa Clara; 1% from Alameda; 1% from Santa Cruz. **Ethnicity:** 95% Caucasian; less than 5% Latino, Asian, and African-American. **International students (I-20 status):** None. **Middle schools (freshman):** Of 35 freshmen, 50% came from 13 public middle schools; 13% from 4 private, non-parochial schools; 34% from 4 Jewish day schools, and 3% from home school programs.

Admission

Applications due: Second week of January (call for date). **Application fee:** $50. **Application process:** Students/parents interested in the school are encouraged to visit the school's website for the admissions event schedule and to call or e-mail to request view books and applications. The school's open houses (2 or 3 per recruitment season) allow families to meet students, parents, teachers and administrators and learn about the academic and student life programs. An interview is required as part of the admissions process. Shadow visits are scheduled on an individual basis from late October through January. **No. of freshman applications:** 60 (N/P places). **Minimum admission requirements:** Evidence of academic ability that fits with Kehillah's college-preparatory curriculum. **Test required:** SSAT. **Preferences:** Siblings. "**We are looking for** students who desire a quest for knowledge, truth, and meaning in a comprehensive program that blends the arts, sciences, mathematics, humanities and Jewish studies." **What kind of student do you best serve?** "Jewish students who are seeking an outstanding college preparatory program which engages the mind and the heart."

Costs

Latest tuition: $24,600 payable in 10 monthly payments. **Sibling discount:** None. **Tuition increases:** Approx. 5%. **Other costs:** Approx. $600 for books, $1,600 other fees. **Percentage of students receiving financial aid:** 40%. **Financial aid deadline:** Call for date. **Average grant:** $12,000. **Percentage of grants of half-tuition or more:** N/P.

School's Mission Statement/Goals

"Kehillah Jewish High School provides its students with an outstanding education that is immersed in Jewish values. It cultivates young adults who are critical, self-reliant, and integrated thinkers, and who will grow as responsible, committed members of the Jewish community and the world-at-large."

Academic Program

Courses offered (AP=Advanced Placement, H=Honors, (AP)=AP option, (H)=Honors option): N/P. "Kehillah offers a full schedule of UC-approved general and Jewish studies courses, including honors and AP for those who qualify. In addition, there is a large variety of elective courses available in Jewish and academic subjects, technology, visual and performing arts, and P.E." **Computer/lab training:** "Computer lab is available throughout the day, and technology classes are offered." **Grading:** A-F and written comments at the end of each quarter. **Graduation requirements:** A minimum of 27 course credits, including 4 years of literature, 3 years of mathematics, 3 years of science, 3 years of history, 3 years of modern Hebrew, 4 years of Jewish text courses, 1 year of Jewish history, 1 year of fine arts, 1 year of another elective and 1 year of P.E.; a minimum of 80 hours of community service. **Average nightly homework (M-Th):** Approx. 2 hours, although 6 weekly prep periods often allow students to complete all or part of their homework at school. **Faculty:** 24; 54% male, 46% female; 85% have advanced degrees. (N/P degrees). **Faculty selection/training:** "Our faculty is comprised of master teachers, experts in their disciplines who inspire their students to excellence. They foster critical and creative thinking as they guide their students in the exploration of great ideas and values. Our teachers also realize that educating a student is a partnership between the school and the home and pride themselves on accessibility to parents. Our teachers have a bachelor's degree and a teaching credential, or a master's or Ph.D. plus high school teaching experience." **Teacher/student ratio:** 1:10. **Percentage of students enrolled in AP:** N/P. **Most recent senior class profile (mean):** SAT Math 598, SAT Critical Reading 608, SAT Writing 602; GPA: 3.28 unweighted. **National Merit Scholarship Program:** 1 Semi-finalist; 1 Commended Scholar. **College enrollment (last class):** "100%." (N/P 4-, 2-year). **Recent (last 3 yrs) colleges:** "Our first three graduating classes have been admitted to over 120 colleges and universities, including Stanford, Yale, and every [UC] campus, NYU, Tufts, Duke, and Brandeis."

Other Indicators the School is Accomplishing its Goals

"In its accreditation report, WASC praised Kehillah for 'creating an environment where attention is paid to each student's performance, progress and challenges.'"

Campus/Campus Life

Campus description: "In 2005, Kehillah moved from San Jose to its permanent location in Palo Alto. Every classroom is equipped with an [interactive whiteboard]. The school facility has state-of-the-art science and computer labs. There is wireless Internet access throughout the campus, and all students are able to check out laptop computers for use during the school day. **Library:** "The library is spacious and in the process of developing a full digital and hard-copy collection of general studies and Jewish volumes." **Sports facilities:** The school is across from the Taube-Koret Campus of Jewish Life, and students will have access to its gymnasiums, swimming pools and an auditorium. **Theater/arts facilities:** Large art studio suitable for multiple art media. It includes a full dark room and a kiln. The facilities include a "Black box" theatre, large multi-purpose space for larger performances, a music/recording studio and a dance studio. **Open/closed campus:** Open for seniors and second semester juniors only. **Lunches:** Kosher dairy/vegetarian lunch program. **Bus service:** KJHS provides subsidized transportation from around the South Bay and North Peninsula. **Uniforms/dress code:** "Proper school attire at KJHS involves clothing that is neat, clean, respectful of self, and respectful of the learning environment and the study of sacred texts." **Co-curricular activities/clubs:** Student clubs and activities include Speech and Debate, Drama, Improvisational Comedy, Dance, Student Council, Hiking Club, GSA, Israel Club, Darfur Relief Club, Yearbook, Student Newspaper, and others to be developed as determined by student and faculty interest. **Foreign exchange programs/internships:** N/P. **Community service:** Students are required to perform 20 hours per year. "The students have a strong say in which community service area interest them. Every year a day is dedicated to having all students participate in community service projects throughout the community (e.g., Habitat for Humanity, work in soup kitchens, battered women shelters, beach clean-up, nursing home visits). In addition, each class takes a service-oriented class trip (e.g., Hurricane Katrina home repair in Waveland, Mississippi, wildfire prevention work in San Diego, youth conference on homelessness in Washington, D.C.). The culminating trip for seniors is a 3-week experience in Israel which also involves community service." **Typical freshman schedule:** World Literature, math, Hebrew, Jewish Text I, World History, Biology and an elective.

Student Support Services
Counselor/student ratio (not including college counselors): 1:110. **Counseling:** Counseling is provided by a guidance counselor. **Learning differences/disabilities:** "Accommodations in the classroom and extra time on tests are available for students with diagnosed learning differences."

Student Conduct and Health
Code of conduct: "KJHS is a 'Kehillah' – a Jewish community built on trust and respect for one another, safety, integrity, tolerance and inclusiveness. There are written policies regarding specific areas of student conduct." **How school handles drug/alcohol usage:** Zero tolerance. **Prevention and awareness programs:** "Assemblies and speakers on these topics throughout the school year."

Summer Programs: N/P.

Parent Involvement

Parent participation: "Not mandatory but encouraged through the Kehillah Parent Association (KPA)." **Parent/teacher communication:** Newsletter, conferences, written reports, report cards and informal status updates through e-mail and telephone. **Parent education:** "Offered on issues related to high school students." **Donations:** "Voluntary but we look for 100% participation."

Sports

Boys and girls basketball, soccer, tennis; girls volleyball. Teams are added according to student interest.

What Sets School Apart From Others

"Kehillah Jewish High School is the only Jewish independent high school in Silicon Valley. It offers excellent college preparatory academics, compelling Jewish studies, individual teacher attention, guidance and college counseling, and open access to electives and extra-curriculars, all in a warm and vibrant Jewish community."

How Parents/Students Characterize School

Parent response(s): "KJHS has rigorous academics, and getting good grades is important. But it's more than that; it's about asking the students who they are as human beings—what makes them tick, and how to nurture those qualities to serve not only themselves, but the community—locally, nationally, and internationally." **Student response(s):** "Kehillah really helped to prepare me for college. I felt really comfortable approaching my professors this (freshman) year in college because I had spent so much time with my teachers at Kehillah. I was able to handle the course load because I had developed really good study skills at Kehillah."

The King's Academy

562 N. Britton Avenue
Sunnyvale, CA 94085
(408) 481-9900 *fax (408) 481-9932*
www.tka.org

Bob Kellogg, Principal
Jackie LaFrance, Admissions, jlafrance@tka.org or x 222

General

Coed high school and middle school (G6-12). Founded in 1991. Christian. Nonprofit. **Enrollment:** Approx. 530 students in G9-12. **Average class size:** 23. **Accreditation:** WASC/ACSI. **School year:** Aug.-June.

School day: 8 a.m.-3 p.m. M, W; 8 a.m.-2:15 p.m. Tu, Th, F. **Location:** Fair Oaks exit off Hwy. 101 (Wolfe Road exit off Hwy. 280); the school is accessible by CalTrain (Sunnyvale Station) and by bus.

Student Body

Geographic breakdown (counties): 88% from Santa Clara; 9% from San Mateo; 3% from Alameda. **Ethnicity:** 51% Caucasian; 24% Asian; 4% Latino; 3% African-American; 18% multi-ethnic. **International students (I-20 status):** 5. **Middle schools (freshman):** 15% came from public middle schools; 85% from private, non-parochial schools. (N/P # schools).

Admission

Applications due: January 31. **Application fee:** $75. **Application process:** Applicant submits the application, which includes four references and an academic history, takes the entrance exam, and interviews with an Admissions Committee member. **No. of freshman applications:** 288 applications for 184 places. **Minimum admission requirements:** 65th percentile on all standardized tests. **Test required:** Math, Reading Comprehension, Vocabulary (last version Stanford Achievement Tests). **Preferences:** "A high-achieving student with a desire to learn." "We are looking for students with teachable hearts and coachable spirits, students desiring to have a stronger walk with the Lord." **What kind of student do you best serve?** "We best serve students with a consistent, above average academic record."

Costs

Latest tuition: $11,154 for full-time; $8,371 for part-time. **Sibling discount:** $600. **Tuition increases:** Approx. 7%. **Other costs:** Student fee of $750 covers books, yearbooks, academic field trips, graduation, etc.; re-enrollment fee of $175. **Percentage of students receiving financial aid:** 10%. **Financial aid deadline:** Mid-March (call for date). **Average grant:** 20-30% of tuition. **Percentage of grants of half-tuition or more:** 0.

School's Mission Statement/Goals

"The King's Academy is a Christ-centered college preparatory middle and senior high school for students who have teachable hearts and coachable spirits. We offer a loving family environment where students are encouraged to grow in their relationships with Jesus, their family, teachers and others. We are committed to developing God's best for each student spiritually, academically, morally and socially through every program and activity."

Academic Program

Courses offered (AP=Advanced Placement, H=Honors, (AP)=AP option, (H)=Honors option): **English:** Language Arts 6, Comp/Lit 7-8, English 9-12 (H/AP); **Math:** General Math, General Math 6-7, Pre-

Algebra, Algebra I, Geometry (H), Algebra 2 (H), Advanced Math (H), Business Math, Calculus (AP); **Foreign Languages:** 1A, 1B, 1-5 (Spanish, French), Greek; **Religion:** History of Ancient Israel, Biblical Ethics, Basic Bible, New Testament Literature, Understanding the Times and World Philosophy Seminar, Foundations of Spiritual Formation; **Science:** Physical Science, Physics (H), Biology (H/AP), Chemistry (H/AP), Anatomy & Physiology, Marine Biology, Environmental Science, Life Science, Pestilence & Civilization; **P.E.:** P.E., Weight Training, Basketball, Football; **History:** Ancient World History, Modern World History (H), U.S. History (H/AP), Government/Economics (H); **Computers:** Intro to Computers, Broadcasting, Computer Aided Design, Computer Applications, Intro to Computer Science (AP), Digital Video Production, Web Page Design, Digital Photography, Beginning Computer Programming; **Arts:** Beginning Drama, Drama Fundamentals, Advanced Drama, Beginning Band, Concert Band (Marching Band), Percussion (Winter Guard), Orchestra, Mixed Chorus, Royal Union-A Vocal Music Company, Music Leadership Workshop, Film Studies, Discovering Art, Modern Creative Art 1-2, Three-D Art 1-2, Advanced Art, Calligraphy, Ceramics, Beginning Dance, Intermediate Dance, Advanced Dance; **Other:** Intro to Psychology, Yearbook, Creative Writing, Peer Tutoring, Intro to Sports Medicine, Sewing 1-2, Retail Management, Student Council. **Computer lab/training:** Four computer labs, a large lab with 24 student workstations, a small lab with 16 student workstations, a computer center in the library with 28 student workstations, and a Multimedia Lab with 12 student workstations and full video broadcasting capabilities. The school also has a portable multimedia cart. Each classroom is wired to the school's data network and is equipped with a computer and printer for staff use. One-half year computer training required. (80 computers) **Grading:** A-F. **Graduation requirements:** 4 years English and history; 3 years math and science; 2 years foreign language and P.E.; 1 year visual/performing arts; 1 semester computers; 25+ units electives; 40 hours community service per year; 1 semester of Bible freshman and sophomore years and 1 year of Bible junior and senior years. **Average nightly homework (M-Th):** 2-3 hours. **Faculty:** 69; 41% male, 59% female; 26% hold master's degrees, 6% hold doctorates. **Faculty ethnicity:** 83% Caucasian; 7% Latino; 5% Asian; 2% African-American; 3% multiracial. **Faculty selection/training:** "Interview process after applying. Teachers must keep their credentials current." **Teacher/student ratio:** 1:24. **Percentage of students enrolled in AP:** 28%; pass rate 100%. **Most recent senior class profile (mean):** SAT Math 620, SAT Critical Reading 588, SAT Writing 581; GPA: N/P. **National Merit Scholarship Program:** 15. **College enrollment (last class):** 88% in 4-year; 12% in 2-year. **Recent (last 3 yrs) colleges:** Azusa Pacific, Bethany Bible C, Biola, CSU (Chico, Fresno, Fullerton, Hayward, Humboldt, Long Beach, LA, Northridge, Monterey Bay, Sacramento, SD, San Marcos, SJ, Sonoma, Stanislaus, Cal Poly-Pomona, Cal Poly-SLO), Cal Lutheran, Chapman, Colorado Christian, Colorado SU, Cornell, Concordia, Dartmouth, Dominguez Hills, Duke, Evangel, Florida SU,

George Fox U, Gettysburg, Gonzaga, Grove City C, Harvard, Hawaii Pacific, Johns Hopkins, Loyola Marymount, Manipal Medical U-India, Mary Baldwin C, MIT, The Master's C, Mount St. Mary's, Multnomah Bible C, NYU, Northeastern, Oregon SU, Occidental, Pacific Lutheran, Pepperdine, Portland U, Point Loma Nazarene, Princeton, Redlands, Rose-Hulman Ins. of Tech., St. Andrews (Scotland), St. Mary's, St. Olaf's, Santa Clara, Seattle Pacific, Simpson, Smith, Stanford, UC (Berkeley, Davis, Irvine, LA, Riverside, SD, Santa Barbara, Santa Cruz), U-Arizona, U-Colorado (Boulder), U-Hawaii, U-Miami, U-Michigan, U-North Texas, U-Oregon, UOP, U-Portland, USC, U-Washington, Valparaiso U, Vanguard, Villanova, Washington SU, Westmont, Wesleyan, Whitman, Whittier, Willamette, and Yale.

Other Indicators the School is Accomplishing its Goals

"Our school continues to grow even though it is expensive to send a child to a private school. Our students thrive in our nurturing environment as shown by our growing athletic program, our growing drama and music programs and our thriving service program. Reports from our alumni reveal an easy transition into college life and college academics. We consistently receive exceptional reports of our students' behavior when on trips with our school, at away athletic competitions, etc. Parents remark how pleased they are to see their child grow in maturity and leadership while they are at The King's Academy."

Campus/Campus Life

Campus description: The school is located in a former Sunnyvale public high school building of 40,000 sq. ft. surrounding a large community area. The school's facilities include chemistry, biology, physics and AP labs; 4 computer labs; a multimedia center; 2 art studios; a band room; a dance studio and gym. The grounds include a full-size football/soccer field, a softball field and a baseball field with batting cages. **Library:** Computer center (30 computers), open to students 8 a.m. - 4 p.m. **Sports facilities:** A 12,000 square foot gymnasium with locker and weight rooms and an auxiliary gym used mainly for wrestling and P.E. **Theater/arts facilities:** A 500-seat theater. Band and choral music rooms equipped with instruments. Art, dance and drama studios. **Open/closed campus:** Closed (open for seniors). **Lunches:** Available in the student store. **Bus service:** Public bus only. **Uniform/dress code:** "Modest dress code." (N/P description) **Co-curricular activities/clubs:** Activities include International Club, National Honor Society, National Junior Honor Society, California Scholarship Federation, California Junior Scholarship Federation, Equestrian Club, Tech Club, Fashion Club. **Foreign exchange programs/internships:** None. **Community service:** "'Servant Safaris' to build houses in Tecate, Mexico, rebuild houses in the Gulf Coast, repair houses in Kentucky, "share the gospel in Peru for high school students"; alternate service plan." **Typical freshman schedule:** English 9 (H), Ancient World History, Geometry (H), foreign language 2, Bible, Biology (H), P.E. and other elective.

Student Support Services

Counselor/student ratio (not including college counselors): 1:4. Counseling: "Academic and college counseling is available." **Learning differences/disabilities:** Student Support Services provides limited accommodations for students with documented learning disabilities. Peer tutoring program.

Student Conduct and Health

Code of conduct: "The school's behavior code, aside from standard provisions, requires students maintain a 'Christ-like attitude,' exercise common courtesy and respect, and refrain from dating relationships while on campus." **How school handles drugs/alcohol:** Suspension/ expulsion. **Prevention and awareness programs:** "Seminars, speakers. Spiritual life program provides one-on-one counseling/instruction as needed."

Summer Programs

Current offerings include sports camps for basketball, football, volleyball, wrestling, baseball, and tennis, as well as classes including Algebra I, Pre-Algebra, Intro to Bible, and Study Skills.

Parent Involvement

Parent participation: "Sixteen hours of service per year for Student Fee refund. Many parents volunteer above this amount." **Parent/teacher communication:** Two progress reports per semester not including semester report cards, report cards, parent/teacher conferences, A+ Board, website, e-mail. **Parent education:** Speaker Series, special parent nights for 7-12 grades. **Donations:** "Encouraged."

Sports

Girls compete in volleyball, tennis, soccer (JV, V), basketball (JV, V), softball (V), cross-country, track and field, and swimming; boys compete in volleyball, football (JV, V), tennis, soccer (JV, V), basketball (JV, V), baseball (JV, V), cross-country, track and field, wrestling and swimming.

What Sets School Apart From Others

"We offer a rigorous academic program in a Christian environment. While The King's Academy places high value on academic excellence, important growth occurs by building strong, Christ-centered relationships in and out of the classroom. In addition, the school offers a part-time high school program for students who are home-schooled. The student attends the school two days a week and is able to take advantage of programs such as sports and extracurricular clubs that are difficult to obtain in a home-school environment. Other programs that support home-schooling are also available."

How Parents/Students Characterize School

Parent response(s): "We strongly support the school's nurturing program. We feel well taken care of in such a caring environment." **Student response(s):** "I thoroughly enjoy the school and its activities. I feel extraordinarily connected to my teachers." "I feel that the school has helped develop my leadership as well as my academic potential. I have learned to reach beyond myself and to become a contributing member of society."

Lick-Wilmerding High School

755 Ocean Avenue
San Francisco, CA 94402
(415) 337-9990 *fax (415) 239-1230*
www.lwhs.org

Al Adams, Head of School
Lisa Wu, Director of Admissions, lwadmit@lwhs.org

General

Coed day high school. Independent. Founded in 1895. Nonprofit, member CAIS, NAIS, ASCD, NACAC, College Board, SSATB, ERB, POCIS, BAAD, ABC. **Enrollment:** Approx. 430. **Average class size:** 15. **Accreditation:** WASC/CAIS. **School year:** Aug.-May. **School day:** 8 a.m.-3:15 p.m. **Location:** At the intersection of Ocean, Geneva and Hwy. 280; across the street from City College; one block from the Balboa Park BART station and on Muni lines 9X, 29, 36, 43 and 49 and the J, K, and M street car lines.

Student Body

Geographic breakdown (counties): 70% from San Francisco; 2% from Marin; 8% from the Peninsula; 20% from East Bay. **Ethnicity:** 48% Caucasian (non-Latino); 15% Asian; 6% Latino; 5% African-American; 25% multi-ethnic; other 1%. **International students (I-20 status):** 1. **Middle schools (freshman):** 59 different schools: 26% from public middle schools; 59% from private, non-parochial schools; 15% from parochial schools. (N/P # schools)

Admission

Applications due: Mid-January (call for date). **Application fee:** $95. **Application process:** Families may attend one of four open houses scheduled for Saturday or Sunday afternoons in October through December. Reservations are necessary. Students may visit for two hours in the morning or afternoon on Tuesdays through Fridays beginning in October and ending in mid-December. Call after September 1 for an appointment. All students who have submitted an application are interviewed on one of two Saturdays in January. Lick uses the BAAD Teacher Recommendation Forms. **No. of freshman applications:**

725-800 (N/P # places). **Minimum admission requirements:** Trends are that "Successful applicants have A's and B's and are enrolled in honor classes if available. They exhibit strong writing skills in their personal statements and are highly recommended by their teachers." **Preferences:** N/P. **Test required:** SSAT or ISEE. "We are looking for academically talented students who are ready for independence and who are focused in the classroom; for students who are kind and passionate and who will contribute to the many activities on campus." **What kind of student do you best serve?** See prior statement.

Costs

Latest tuition: $30,700 payable in 3 or 10 payments. Flexible Tuition, depending on a family's ability to pay, ranges from $1,000 to $29,700. **Sibling discount:** None. **Tuition increases:** N/P. **Other costs:** Books and other fees are included in tuition; new students pay a $1,000 one-time facilities use fee. **Percentage of students receiving financial aid:** 42%. **Financial aid deadline:** Mid-January (call for date). **Average grant:** N/P. **Percentage of grants of half-tuition or more:** N/P.

School's Mission Statement/Goals

"Lick-Wilmerding High School inspires students to become self-directed, lifelong learners who contribute to our world with knowledge, skill, creativity, compassion, and can-do confidence. Toward this end, Lick-Wilmerding integrates a distinguished college preparatory curriculum with a distinctive program in the technical arts. As a private school with a public purpose, Lick-Wilmerding encourages participation in community service and is committed to developing innovative educational programs that will benefit students and teachers throughout the Bay Area. Lick-Wilmerding's purpose, built on the foundation of a diverse and inclusive community, is to develop qualities of the head, heart, and hands that will serve students well throughout their lives."

Academic Program

Courses offered (AP=Advanced Placement, H=Honors, (AP)=AP option, (H)=Honors option): **English:** English 1 (required in G9), English 2 (required in G10), AP Literature (required in G11), The Literature of Africa, Shakespeare and Mark Twain; **Foreign Languages:** French 1-5 (AP, H), Mandarin 1-2, Spanish 1-4 (AP, H); **History and Social Studies:** Discovery and Transition (required in G10), Technology and Power (required in G10), U.S. History H (required in G11), Senior Seminars, AP World History, Philosophy; **Math:** Algebra 1-2 (H), Inductive Geometry, Deductive Geometry, Pre-Calculus (H), AP Calculus AB, AP Calculus BC, Statistics (AP); **Performing Arts:** Acting Techniques 1, Advanced Acting Workshop, Directing/Dramatic Theory, Stagecraft, Playwriting and Performance, Chamber Orchestra (H), Big Band, Jazz Combo, AP Music Theory, Chamber Singers; **P.E.:** Body/Mind Education (required G9); **Science:** Biology (AP) (required in G9), Chemistry

(AP) (required in G10), Physics (AP), Interactions in Physics, Anatomy and Physiology, Brain and Behavior; **Art, Design and Technology:** Contemporary Media (required G9), Photography 1-2, Drawing & Painting, Architectural Design 1-2, Computer Science, Electronics; **Technical Arts:** Junior Project (required in G11), Jellis Block (required in G10), Glass 1-2, Fabrications 1-2, Woodworking 1-2, Wood Carving, Electronics 1-2, Jewelry/Metalsmithing 1-2; **Special Programs:** Independent Study, Teaching Assistant. **Computer lab/training:** 3 computer labs on campus. All freshmen are required to complete Contemporary Media, which includes instruction in MS Office Applications, HTML, iMovie, networking, and programming. AP Computer is also offered. **Grading:** A-F, issued at the end of each semester. Narrative comments are given at the end of the first and third quarters. **Graduation requirements:** 4 years English; 3 years foreign language (1 language or 2 years of 2 languages), history and math; 2 years technical arts; 2 years science and P.E. (or sport team participation); 1 year visual and performing arts; 1 semester computer, counseling. **Jellis Block:** Named for Jellis Wilmerding, benefactor of the Wilmerding School of Industrial Arts (1900), this block invokes the credo of that school which featured the application of students' skills and knowledge in the real world. During this culminating block of the year, Lick students will engage in hands-on application of what they know—often in public settings. Ranging from direct service opportunities to community-based student-action research, these projects will culminate in some form of public presentation or exhibition. Successful completion of Jellis Block is a graduation requirement for G10 and G11. **Average nightly homework (M-Th):** 2-3 hours. **Faculty:** 64; 46% male, 54% female; 71% hold master's degrees and 6% hold doctorates. **Faculty ethnicity:** N/P. **Faculty selection/training:** "Faculty is selected based on their education, teaching experience, educational philosophy, recommendations, interviews, and a teaching demonstration. In addition, candidates are assessed on their understanding of and desire to commit to the school's mission and vision. Teachers take classes, engage in the school's professional development program, and are active in a wide variety of professional organizations." **Teacher/student ratio:** 1:10. **Percentage of students enrolled in AP:** N/P; pass rate 90%. **Senior class profile (mean):** SAT Math 680, SAT Critical Reading 685, SAT Writing 687; GPA: 3.58 (unweighted). **National Merit Scholarship Program:** The past four classes included 37 National Merit Scholarship Finalists, 3 National Achievement Scholarship Finalists, 88 National Merit Commendations, 4 selected for National Hispanic Recognition Program. **College enrollment (last class):** 100% in 4-year colleges. **Recent (last 3 yrs) colleges:** [partial list] Amherst, UC-Berkeley, Cal Poly-SLO, U-Chicago, Columbia, Cooper Union, Duke, Harvard, MIT, McGill, UNC (Chapel Hill), Northwestern, Oberlin, Pomona, Reed, USC, Spelman, Stanford, Swarthmore, Vassar, Washington in St. Louis, and Yale.

Other Indicators the School is Accomplishing its Goals

"SAT II Mean Scores (last class) Biology 632, Chemistry 658, English Composition 630, English Literature 613, French 710, Korean 800, Math IC 619, Math IIC 698, Physics 635, Spanish 606, U.S. History 553."

Campus/Campus Life

Campus description: Lick-Wilmerding High School occupies the city block bounded by Geneva, Howth, Ocean and I-280. The buildings include a classroom building, science labs, theater, gymnasium, music room, the McCullough Library/Herbst Arts and Humanities Center (a facility that includes the library; humanities writing center; and art, drafting and design, and photography studios), and a new award-winning complex that opened in 2004 (a facility that includes the glass, wood, metal, jewelry, and electronic shops; a computer lab; physics lab; and caféteria). **Library:** The Jack McCullough ('25) Library is 7,100 sq. ft. and has seating for 100 students. It "is the campus nexus—effectively creating a library-centered school that through technology links students and faculty to the school's and the world's information resources." **Sports facilities:** On-campus gymnasium. Teams use athletic facilities at the City College campus, such as the all-weather track and eight lighted tennis courts, as well as nearby fields in Balboa Park. In 2008, the new Health and Wellness Center opened across the street from Lick. The $80 million complex features fitness rooms, weight rooms, and an Olympic-size swimming pool. Students have complete access to the facilities. **Theater/arts facilities:** A newly remodeled theater seats 430. The school also has a dance studio; art studio; drafting and design studio; photography studio (with darkroom); and glass, wood and fabrications shops. **Open/closed campus:** Open. **Lunches:** Caféteria provides hot lunch, sandwich, and salad bar options. **Bus service:** Public only. **Uniforms/dress code:** None. **Co-curricular activities/clubs:** All clubs are student run and initiated and thus vary from year to year. Last year, clubs included Admissions "Hospitality Club," Agape Christian Club, Black Student Union, Community Action Club, Drama Productions (Fall and Spring), Gardening Club, Gay Straight Alliance, Hapa Club, Jewish Student Union, Knitting Club, Latinos Unidos, Literary Magazine, M.E.A.T. BBQ Club, Middle East Discussion Forum, Movie Club, Paper Tiger (school newspaper), Student Council, "The Waves" A Capella Group. **Foreign exchange programs/internships:** N/P. **Community service:** "Based on the belief that 'volunteerism should be voluntary,' students are encouraged but not required to participate in community service. The school's full-time community service coordinator assists students in finding projects that match their interests and maintains extensive involvement with many community organizations, such as Rebuilding Together or elementary school tutoring programs." **Typical freshman schedule:** Biology, Contemporary Media, English I, world language (level depends on placement), Drafting and Design (one semester),

Body/Mind Education, math (depending on placement), visual or performing arts (i.e. Drama, Instrumental or Vocal Music, Photography, Studio Art), after-school sport or play (optional).

Student Support Services

Counselor/student ratio (not including college counselors): N/P. **Counseling:** Ninth graders are assigned an advising group of approx. 11 students with a faculty advisor who moderates and oversees each student's progress for the full 4 years. The advisor also serves as a first point of contact for parents. The counseling program includes peer counseling groups. Personal/family counseling is available if needed. Formal college counseling begins in the junior year with individual and family meetings. The school has 2 full-time college counselors. **Learning differences/disabilities:** The school has a Learning Strategies Center that offers "psycho-educational assessment as needed to students suspected of learning difficulties; provides consultation to students, parents, and teachers on learning differences; provides learning strategies, support and resources for all students; fosters understanding, respect, and appreciation for the wide and diverse range of skills and talents that we all bring to the learning process; maintains disability-related documents; determines eligibility for academic accommodations; and develops plans for the provision of such accommodations."

Student Conduct and Health

Code of conduct: "The school has standard rules regarding drugs, alcohol, tobacco, stealing, lying, plagiarism and harassment. It also insists on civility and that students respect the neighborhood and its residents." **How school handles drug/alcohol usage:** "The ultimate consequences of violating the prohibition against selling, distributing, possessing or being under the influence of illegal drugs or alcohol during school hours or at school events is typically suspension or dismissal from the school. Additionally, in certain cases, drug evaluation, rehabilitation, and other measures may be imposed." **Prevention and awareness programs:** N/P.

Summer Programs

Each summer the school offers alternating foreign language trips to a French-speaking and a Spanish-speaking country. Each trip provides a cultural immersion opportunity with touring and family home stays. Students in the Flexible Tuition Program are assisted with the cost of these trips.

Parent Involvement

Parent participation: "Lick encourages parents to attend student activities and to volunteer in school events through the Parents' Association in the following areas: Hospitality and Celebration; Social, education, and enrichment opportunities; fundraising/development;

Parent Association Meetings." **Parent/teacher communication:** Annual parent conference; bi-annual written comments; progress reports upon request; access to students' advisors; e-mail. **Parent education:** The Parents' Association holds monthly meetings that spotlight topics relating to parenting teenagers. Parents are invited to participate in the Bay Area Coalition of Parents. **Donations:** "Parents are expected to make a contribution to the Annual Fund, which supports the annual operating budget of the school. The school's goal is 100% participation in the Annual Fund."

Sports
Teams compete in the BCL. Girls compete in basketball (frosh/soph JV, V), soccer (JV, V), tennis (JV, V), volleyball (JV, V); boys in baseball (V), basketball (frosh/soph, JV, V), lacrosse (JV, V), soccer (JV, V); boys and girls in cross-country, track and field, and swimming; coed badminton (not BCL).

What Sets School Apart From Others
"L-W is best known for the economic, racial, and cultural diversity of its student body and its commitment to a well-rounded education for the 'Head, Heart and Hands.' Having been tuition free for the first 77 years, Lick takes its mandate to be accessible to students from all walks of life very seriously. The earnings on its endowment are dedicated almost exclusively to making the school more financially accessible. As a result, 42% of families participate in the Flexible Tuition Program. Lick is often described as being an unusually friendly place with an unpretentious student body." • "L-W is the only independent school in the nation which, in addition to its rigorous college preparatory program, also requires extensive work in the wood, metal, electronic and glass shops as well as in drafting/design. Three philosophical pillars support this technical arts program: (1) an understanding of and appreciation for fine craftsmanship, (2) the blending of the fine and technical arts, and (3) the integration of science and technology. The school's 'Head, Heart, Hands' philosophy is further enhanced by first-rate programs in theater, choral and instrumental music, dance and fine arts."

How Parents/Students Characterize School
Parent response(s): "The L-W community is friendly, informal, and very high-energy. Walk around the campus and you may hear a lively discussion emanating from an English seminar, a Duke Ellington tune being played by the Advanced Jazz Ensemble, and the hum of a circular saw being used in a Tech Arts workshop. You may also find students sitting in the hallway studying for a chemistry test or discussing the agenda for the Multicultural Alliance meeting later in the day. It's a school where learning takes place on many levels and people smile a lot." **Student response(s):** "Stepping through the doors of Lick-Wilmerding meant stepping into a world of possibilities. Most of the

experiences that I have had at Lick I never could have predicted my first day of high school, but that is the beauty of Lick-Wilmerding." "I learned that I was capable of doing things I never thought I could. One of Lick's strengths is the school's ability to push one's boundaries." "I believe that, through Lick's unique approach to education, I have found myself. I have learned to think independently and analytically since Lick's teachers expect their students to think as inquisitive young adults, as capable and eager citizens of the world. With their help, I have been able to realize the thrill of intellectual creativity." "High school is a precious time for growth and discovery; there will be triumphs and defeats, but it is important to know that Lick's faculty is there to guide you, and your friends are there to support you along the way."

Lisa Kampner Hebrew Academy High School

645 14th Ave.
San Francisco, CA 94118
(415) 752-7333 *fax (415) 752-5851*
www.hebrewacademy.com

Rabbi Pinchas Lipner, Dean
Pamela Vold, Director of Admissions, lisakampnerhebrewacademy@
yahoo.com

General

Coed Jewish day high school (100% Jewish). Independent. Founded in 1969. Nonprofit, member of Torah Umesorah. **Enrollment:** Approx. 90. **Average class size:** 15. **Accreditation:** WASC. **School year:** Sept.-June. **School day:** 8:30 a.m.-3:36 p.m. **Location:** In the Richmond District of San Francisco, accessible by Muni (street parking also available).

Student Body

Geographic breakdown (counties): 96% from San Francisco; 1% from Marin; 2% from San Mateo; 1% from Contra Costa. **Ethnicity:** 100% Caucasian (including Latino). **International students (I-20 status):** None. **Middle schools (freshman):** 55% came from 6 middle schools; 44% were continuing students from the Hebrew Academy lower and middle schools; 1% from 1 private, non-parochial school.

Admission

Applications due: Rolling. **Application fee:** $50. **Application process:** School visit and interview, application form, student essays, 3 references, and testing (administered at the school). **No. of freshman applications:** N/P. **Minimum admission requirements:** "Student must be Jewish by Jewish law or be willing to convert." **Test required:** School-administered achievement test. **Preferences:** Jewish students. "**We are looking for** students who will be happy in a small school, who value and respect the intellectual and spiritual life we offer." **What kind of student do you best serve?** "We want students who want to be active in and contribute to a learning community that has high intellectual and moral standards. We value a positive attitude towards learning, personal creativity, kindness and moral strength. We value students who want to contribute to their families, their community and the Jewish people."

Costs
Latest tuition: $15,900 payable in 2 or 12 installments. **Sibling discount:** "Case-by-case basis." **Tuition increases:** "Do not occur annually." **Other costs:** $300 for books, $600 building fund, $55 per month for electives and AP courses. "Generous need-based financial aid is available." **Percentage of students receiving financial aid:** 88%. **Financial aid deadline:** None. **Average grant:** N/P. **Percentage of grants of half-tuition or more:** N/P.

School's Mission Statement/Goals
"Our campus is a place for a learning partnership with the strong and simple family values of love and respect for one another. In a world of increasing turbulence, the Hebrew Academy is a safe place. Every student is valued for his or her own potential. We provide a morally structured but accepting environment. Our success rate is high: our students enter universities, Yeshivas, and careers of their choice. • Educating a child is a responsibility best shared between the home and school. The Hebrew Academy is a Jewish day school which strives to provide an excellent academic and Jewish education. We endeavor to expose our children to an intensive appreciation of their religious and ethical responsibilities. • The creation of the State of Israel is one of the seminal events in Jewish history. Recognizing the significance of the State and its national institutions, we seek to instill in our students an attachment to the State of Israel and its people as well as a sense of responsibility for their welfare. • Our goal is to develop knowledgeable, independent, proud Jews who will contribute to their Jewish and general communities. We are guided by the Biblical injunction: 'Train up a child in the way he should go and when he is old he will not depart from it.' (Proverbs 22:6)"

Academic Program
Courses offered ((AP)=AP option, (H)=Honors option): Secular core curriculum: Algebra I-II, Geometry, Pre-Calculus, Calculus (AP), U.S. History (AP), World History (AP), European History (AP), Govt (AP), Economics, English, English Literature & Composition (AP), English Language & Composition (AP), Physics, Advanced Physics (AP), Chemistry (H/AP), Biology (AP). All courses can be taken as honors courses. Call for current elective and non-core subjects, as they vary. Additional AP courses offered in Art History, U.S. Govt and Politics, Psychology. Judaic core curriculum: Tefillah (prayer), Hebrew Language, Torah,

Talmud, Gemorah, Jewish History, Jewish Laws & Customs. **Computer lab/training:** N/P. **Grading:** A+ to F. **Graduation requirements:** "UC admission requirements." **Average nightly homework (M-Th):** 2 hours. **Faculty:** 22 (8 f/t, 14 p/t); 45% men, 55% women; 15% master's degrees, 15% doctorate degrees. **Faculty ethnicity:** 100% Caucasian (non-Latino). **Faculty selection/training:** "BA or BS required plus further study and experience; interviews and recommendations required. Frequent evaluations." **Teacher/student ratio:** 1:4.5. **Percentage of students enrolled in AP:** 55%; pass rate 74%. "**Senior class profile (mean):** SAT N/P; GPA: 3.4. **National Merit Scholarship Program:** "Every graduating class has included Semifinalists" (N/P #). **College enrollment (last class):** "100% (N/P % 4-yr., 2-yr.). **Recent (last 3 yrs) colleges:** UC (Berkeley, UCLA, Davis, SD, Santa Cruz, Santa Barbara, Merced), USC, Stanford, Columbia, John Jay, USF, CSU (SF, Sacramento), Dominican U, Yeshiva U, SFCC, Skyline C, Diablo Valley C, Yeshiva Ohr Yerushalayem, and Jerusalem U.

Other Indicators the School is Accomplishing its Goals

"Graduates continue their commitment to Judaism and become productive members of the Jewish community. One hundred percent of graduates are accepted to college. We are very proud that a school our size has, from 2002 to 2008, a 50% acceptance rate at UC-Berkeley. In addition, our alumni never lose touch."

Campus/Campus Life

Campus description: The Hebrew Academy campus is a modern stucco building in a quiet residential neighborhood close to Golden Gate Park. **Library:** "Spacious and airy, with approx. 7,000 volumes that include secular works and Judaic works in both English and Hebrew." **Sports facilities:** Full-sized gymnasium/multipurpose room, outdoor basketball area. **Theater/arts facilities:** "Active, highly regarded drama program with annual productions on the Hebrew Academy stage." **Open/closed campus:** "Open campus for high school students is a privilege and requires parental and student contract." **Lunches:** Pizza, bagels, and hot dogs each available once a week. Snack bar. **Bus service:** Public only. **Uniforms/dress code:** Dress code requires boys to wear shirts with collars, neat pants (no shorts), and a yarmulke; girls wear modest attire, meaning a skirt below the knee and with no slits. Tops must not expose the midriff or collarbones and must have sleeves. **Co-curricular activities/clubs:** Varies. Can include drama, fine art, newspaper, debate, book discussion, tennis, basketball, women's self-defense, women's dance, philosophy club, chess club. **Foreign exchange programs/internships:** None. **Community service:** Required hours of community service include neighborhood cleanup, assistance at school functions, and volunteer service at Jewish service agencies. **Typical freshman schedule:** Morning: prayer, Hebrew language, 2 periods of Judaic studies. Afternoon: Physics, Algebra I or II, English, World History, elective or study hall.

Student Support Services

Counselor/student ratio (not including college counselors): N/P. **Counseling:** "Available from rabbinic staff, from secular principal, and from teachers." **Learning differences/disabilities:** "Handled on a case-by-case basis. The school is not equipped to handle serious learning differences."

Student Conduct and Health

Code of conduct: "Students are expected to behave in a moral and ethical manner in keeping with Jewish principles. Contract signed at the start of each school year." **How school handles drugs/alcohol:** Zero tolerance. **Prevention and awareness programs:** N/P.

Summer Programs: None.

Parent Involvement

Parent participation: Not required. Parents are asked to participate in fundraising activities. **Parent/teacher communication:** "Back-to-School Night, parent/teacher conferences, interim reports, private conferences with teachers and administration available." **Parent education:** Back-to-School Night. **Donations:** "Periodically requested."

Sports

"No organized sports teams at this time. Boys P.E., stressing basketball and informal basketball games, are held after school hours."

What Sets School Apart From Others

"The Hebrew Academy is a remarkable school with exceptional students. We provide a traditional and morally structured but accepting environment. Our success rate is high: our students enter universities, Yeshivas and careers of their choice. Our standards are high, and we look for students with the ability to reach their personal and academic goals. The relationships between faculty and students are unique in their depth, friendship and mutual respect. The Hebrew Academy is a school where academic, creative and personal potential are fulfilled and lifetime relationships are forged. Each student is part of a close knit and outstanding whole whose well-being is the focus of our highly trained and caring faculty."

How Parents/Students Characterize the School

Parent response(s): "Academically rigorous and outstanding. Everyone knows its reputation for getting its students into good universities." **Student response(s):** "Hebrew Academy is like a family; you feel the warmth and closeness the minute you walk through the front door." "I wish the Hebrew Academy were also a college."

Lycée Français La Pérouse

1201 Ortega Street
San Francisco, CA 94122
(415) 661-5232 *fax (415) 661-0246*
www.lelycee.org

Frédérick Arzelier, Headmaster
Isabelle Desmole, Director of Admissions, admissions@lelycee.org

General

Coed French immersion day high school (with middle school at same site and with pre-K-5 on other campuses in the city and in Marin). Founded in 1967. Nonsectarian. Nonprofit, member CAIS and WASC. **Enrollment:** N/P. **Average class size:** 15-20. **Accreditation:** French Ministry of Education and WASC. **School year:** Sept.-June. **School day:** 8:15 a.m.-3:50 p.m. **Location:** 19th Avenue and Ortega.

Student Body

Geographic breakdown (counties): 33% from San Francisco; 45% from San Mateo and South Bay; 20% from Marin and other North Bay counties; 2% from East Bay. **Ethnicity:** "The high school has 13 nationalities represented (35 nationalities in the whole school) including approx. 60% French-U.S.; 25% U.S.; 5% U.S-other; and 10% multi-ethnic."

Admission

Applications due: January 15. **Application fee:** $100. **Application process:** Visits by appointment and open houses are held throughout the year. (Check website). "Students coming from other French schools or the French system are automatically admitted to grade level based on their report cards. Non-French speaking students are welcome to apply up to the first grade." **No. of freshman applications:** N/P. **Minimum admission requirements:** None. **Test required:** None. **Preferences:** Siblings. "**We are looking for** students coming from a French educational system or who are already fluent in the French language." **What kind of student do you best serve?** "Students who are fluent in French and can follow a rigorous French curriculum."

Costs

Latest tuition: $16,670-$18,570 payable in 1 or 10 payments. **Sibling discount:** N/P. **Tuition increases:** Approx. 5%. **Other costs:** $100 registration fee; $1,000 one-time entrance fee per family. **Percentage of students receiving financial aid:** 25%. **Financial aid deadline:** N/P. **Average grant:** $2,000. **Percentage of grants of half-tuition or more:** N/P.

School's Mission Statement/Goals

"The Lycée offers the children of multiculturally-minded Bay Area families a rigorous curriculum focused on French-language immersion and academic excellence. Based on the French national system, this Pre-K through 12th grade program exceeds all requirements set by both France and the United States and provides full preparation for both European and North American colleges and universities. The diverse and international nature of our students and faculty fosters a spirit of community and respect that prepares our students to be responsible global citizens."

Academic Program

"The academic program is based on the French national curriculum augmented by courses in American History and English literature. Consistent with the French system of education, in high school, Lycée students choose one of three general areas of study, corresponding to the three most prestigious Baccalaureate diplomas: Literature (14 hours per week of humanities, philosophy, and languages), Economics and Sociology (6 hours per week of economics), or Sciences (18 hours per week of math and sciences). All courses are taught in French with the exception of U.S. History, English Literature, Spanish, Chinese and German." **Courses offered** (AP=Advanced Placement, H=Honors, (AP)=AP option, (H)=Honors option): **English:** English Literature (H), ESL; **Math:** Mathematics H; **Science:** Physics/Chemistry H, Biology/Geology H, Technology/Computer Science; **History:** Geography, Economics, U.S. History; **Languages:** French H, Spanish, German, Latin; **Arts:** Visual Art, Theater, Music. **Other:** P.E. **Computer lab/training:** The campus is equipped with both a computer lab and a teaching center dedicated to teaching on the Internet and taking advantage of the many French educational programs available through the Internet. **Grading:** "The Lycée uses the French system of grading on a scale of 0 to 20, complemented by written evaluations. The French system is more rigorous than American grading and is known and respected by American colleges and universities." **Graduation requirements:** "Set by French Ministry plus SF Unified School district." **Average nightly homework (M-Th):** G9-11: 2 hours, G12: 2.5+ hours. **Faculty:** 115 (N/P gender, degrees). **Faculty ethnicity:** N/P. **Faculty selection/training:** "The French Ministry of Education sends certified teachers from France 1-4 years, while other French teachers are hired locally. Yearly evaluations are held by French officials. English and U.S. History teachers hold California teaching credentials. In-service days are held on an on-going basis as well as continuing education." **Teacher/student ratio:** N/P. **Percentage of students enrolled in AP:** 30%; pass rate 95%. **Senior class profile (mean):** N/P; GPA: N/P. **National Merit Scholarship Program:** N/P. **College enrollment (last class):** N/P..

Other Indicators the School is Accomplishing its Goals

"The Lycée offers the college preparatory track of the French educational system. At the end of the 12th grade, students take the French Baccalaureate exam choosing from the three general areas of study (S-Science, L-Literature, or ES – Economic Science). In addition, the

Lycee offers the International Option of the French Baccalaureate (OIB), allowing them to continue on with excellent university studies in France, in other European countries, or in the U.S. Lycée students have a 93% pass rate (students in France have a 60% pass rate). Students entering the U.S. university system also take the PSAT, SAT and AP exams. Lycée students have received as much as one year's college credit for their scores on the Bac. The Lycée's goal is to awaken the desire for learning and equip the child with the tools to earn self-esteem through personal achievement."

Campus/Campus Life
Campus description: "Three campuses [for pre-K-12]. The buildings have been extensively remodeled for more classrooms, state-of-the-art labs in the secondary school, computer, a music room, an extensive library with a rooftop terrace on Ashbury campus (open only to the upper grades), and a greenhouse." **Library:** The secondary school library houses more than 10,000 print volumes, has computers with Internet access, and a videotheque. **Sports facilities:** Basketball court on Ortega. **Theater/arts facilities:** "Art studio and a beautiful auditorium on Ortega." **Open/closed campus:** Open if they have written permission from a parent. **Lunches:** Hot lunches may be purchased. **Bus service:** Round trip from the Peninsula and the North Bay. **Uniform/dress code:** No uniform. **Co-curricular activities/clubs:** Activities include theater, yearbook, multimedia (Internet), music, soccer, roller hockey, basketball and volleyball, table tennis, and student government. **Foreign exchange programs/internships:** N/P. **Community service:** Each class carries out a project such as volunteering at the Hamilton Center and the Haight-Ashbury Food Program, helping at the Randall Museum, visiting seniors in retirement homes, fundraising and clothing collection for projects in Latin America and Amnesty International. **Typical freshman schedule:** "Seven periods of 55 minutes each. A freshman would study, over the course of a week, music, art, computer science, drama, U.S. history, biology, physics/chemistry, Latin (an elective), history-geography, foreign language, P.E., math, French literature, and English literature."

Student Support Services
Counselor/student ratio (not including college counselors): N/P. **Counseling:** A full-time American college counselor, a full-time speech therapist and a part-time psychologist are on staff. An optional study hall is offered, and tutoring is available from other students upon parental request. **Learning disabilities/differences:** "A part-time school psychologist is available at the request of teachers or parents."

Student Conduct and Health
Code of conduct: "Standard." **How school handles drugs/alcohol:** N/P. **Prevention and awareness programs:** Students and teachers undergo a substance abuse awareness program each year.

Summer Programs: Lower grades only.

Parent Involvement
Parent participation: "Parents are expected to participate in fundraising by contributing financially to the Annual Appeal and volunteering, by assisting in organizing the annual auction and other school events. Parents are encouraged to serve on committees of the Board of Directors and to seek election to the Board or School Council. Many other volunteer opportunities are available including a French market on the Marin campus, translating, library help, etc." **Parent/teacher communication:** Students receive five report cards a year. Two parent/teacher conferences a year. One class council per trimester is held with all teachers, student delegates, parent delegates, and the administration. **Parent education:** Cross-cultural workshops; U.S. college panel discussions with alumni; lectures/discussions on bilingualism, communication, safety and other issues. **Donations:** "Parents are asked to participate in the annual giving campaign and several fundraisers."

Sports
"The regular sports curriculum includes roller hockey, table tennis, gymnastics, swimming, basketball and soccer among other activities. The Lycée participates in city-wide private school games with teams in basketball and volleyball."

What Sets School Apart From Others
"The Lycée belongs to a network of over 400 French schools worldwide and receives financial support from the French government. Founded in 1967 by parents, the Lycée is an academic institution accredited by the French Ministry of Education. The Lycée's students have access to any other French school at their own grade level. As a result of the high quality English curriculum, students are also qualified to enter an American school at or above their grade level and are fully prepared to enter European or North American colleges and universities."

How Parents/Students Characterize School
Parent response(s): "I believe that the Lycée is educating tomorrow's world leaders. Who else can be better prepared to face this international world than our own children, who at age eight can already tell us how a French person's approach is different from an American's and that neither one is better; they are just different." "The environment is so positive. It's obvious that the instructors have a vision. They are well prepared to carry out their mission, and they are secure in their role. I like the fact that my son's teachers have such excellent morale." **Student response(s):** "The Lycée's students are winners in the intellectual arena; the Baccalaureate scores every year are remarkable. In the social arena, the Lycée's theater workshop is always admired and congratulated by the American and French art communities. I realize

that many doors were opened to guarantee me a successful future. A graduate of the Lycée enters the world of work or higher education with incomparable potential ... and the Lycée gives us the keys to fully realize that potential." "It was at the Lycée that I discovered learning is wonderful. Just last year in my master's program at Stanford I noticed I often used the methods of analysis that I learned at the Lycée in philosophy class. Where else can you play the saxophone in a jazz group with the director, garden with the history/geography professor, spend hours arguing with the philosophy professor in a café, and finish school with 100% on the Baccalaureate?"

Marin Academy
1600 Mission Avenue
San Rafael, CA 94901
(415) 453-2808 *fax (415) 453-8905*
www.ma.org

Travis Brownley, Head of School
Dan Babior, Admissions Director, dbabior@ma.org

General
Coed day high school. Founded in 1971. Nonsectarian. Nonprofit, member CAIS, NAIS, BAIHS, BAAD, SSATB, CASE, ISEE/ERB. **Enrollment: 400. Average class size: 15. Accreditation:** WASC. **School year:** Aug.–June. **School day:** 8 a.m.-3 p.m. **Location:** Near downtown San Rafael, 12 miles north of San Francisco in Marin County. Accessible by Hwys. 101 and 580 (to Richmond Bridge and East Bay).

Student Body
Geographic breakdown (counties): 71% from Marin; 15% from East Bay; 12% from San Francisco; 2% from Sonoma. **Ethnicity:** 73% Caucasian (non-Latino); 7% Asian; 3% Latino; 4% African-American; 13% multi-ethnic. **International students (I-20 status):** 0%. **Middle schools (freshman):** 32% came from public middle schools; 67% from private, non-parochial schools; 1% from parochial schools. (N/P # schools)

Admission
Applications due: Mid-January (call for date). **Application fee:** $75. **Application process:** At the beginning of the eighth grade year, parents should contact the school to be put on the admission mailing list. Visits are scheduled from the last week of September through early January. Parents receive information regarding open houses and other events. Applications include parent and student sections, recommendations from current math and English teachers, a principal/guidance counselor recommendation (BAIHS forms), transcripts, and test scores. Applications can be made online. Parent portions of applications

are due in December; student interviews are then scheduled. **No. of freshman applications:** More than 470 for 108 places. **Minimum admission requirements:** N/P. **Test required:** SSAT, ERB/ISEE, CAT, or CTBS/Stanford Achievement Test. **Preferences:** None. "**We are looking for** students who demonstrate a love of learning and have the ability to pursue a challenging college preparatory curriculum that is balanced by participation in a broad array of activities outside of the classroom such as athletics, service, the arts, and outdoor education. Our students and faculty work together to create an environment in which every member of our community can take on the greatest possible challenges – and succeed at them." **What kind of student do you best serve?** "Academically able, active learners – motivated students who are interested in school and the world around them."

Costs
Latest tuition: $30,970 payable in 1 or 3 payments, or monthly with a $110 set-up fee. **Sibling discount:** None. **Tuition increases:** Approx. 6%. **Other costs:** Approx. $600-$900 for books, Mini-course, supplies and outings. **Percentage of students receiving financial aid:** 21%. **Financial aid deadline:** January (call for date). **Average grant:** $21,325. **Percentage of grants of half-tuition or more:** 76%.

School's Mission Statement/Goals
"Marin Academy asks every individual to think, question, and create in an environment of encouragement and compassion, and challenges each person to accept the responsibilities posed by education in a democratic society."

Academic Program
"The curriculum is rigorously college preparatory with highly developed requirements in all academic areas, plus the arts and P.E." **Courses offered** (AP=Advanced Placement, H=Honors, (AP)=AP option, (H)=Honors option): **English:** English I-II, Reading and Writing Poetry (H), Reading and Writing the Short Story (H), 20th Century Novel (H), Ethics and Values (H), Personal and Expository Writing: Creative Non-Fiction (H), African-American Literature (H), British Literature (H), A Room of One's Own: Women's Literature (H), That's Absurd (H), Journalism (H), Latino Literature (H); What the Dickens? (H), Shakespeare (H), Power and Resistance (H), Why War? (H), The Golden Gate (H); **Math:** Algebra I, Algebra II (H), Geometry (H), Finite Mathematics, AP Statistics, Pre-Calculus (H), AP Calculus AB, AP Calculus BC, Number Theory, Discrete Math, and Cryptography, Multivariable Calculus; **History:** World Civilizations, U.S. History, Modern World History (H), Senior Seminar: Technology and the Global Economy, Middle East Studies, Latin American Studies, Classical Studies–Greece, History, Culture and Identity, Religion and Politics,Senior Seminar: Justice in America, Russian History, (+ frequently offered electives such as African Studies, Classical Stud-

ies: Rome, Senior Seminar); **Science:** Biology, Chemistry, Physics, Advanced Biology (H), Geology, Human Anatomy and Physiology (H), Environmental Science (AP), Advanced Chemistry (H), Oceanography H, Advanced Physics with Calculus (H), Individual Investigation in Advanced Science; **Foreign language:** Spanish I-II, Spanish III (H), Spanish IV, Spanish IV AP Language, Spanish V (H), Spanish VI, French I-II, French III (H), French IV, French IV AP Language, French V(H), Japanese II-IV H; **Arts:** American Roots Music, Music of the World, Chorus/Vocal Workshop, Chamber Ensemble, Advanced Chamber Ensemble H, Jazz Band, Rock/Blues Ensemble, Chorus Band, Visual Arts I-II: Drawing and Painting, Visual Arts III: Drawing, Visual Arts III: Painting, Visual Arts IV: Drawing, Visual Arts IV: Painting, Visual Arts II: Ceramics, Visual Arts III: Ceramic Hand-building, Visual Arts III: Ceramic Wheel-throwing, Visual Arts IV: Advanced Ceramics, Visual Arts II: Photography, Visual Arts III: Photography, Visual Arts IV: Photography, Theater I-II, Theater III/IV: Company, Theater Independent Study, Dance I-IV; **P.E.:** Intramural Sports Program, Freshman Core Human Development, Aikido, Dance, Outdoor Education & Skills; **Other:** Peer Teaching Assistant Program, Independent Study. **Special programs:** Students may seek to graduate with an International Studies emphasis. This requires students take specific classes with a non-U.S. focus; take 4 years of French or Spanish or 3 years of Japanese; perform 20 hours of international studies outside the classroom; and, in their senior year, write a thesis or present a project. The school's mini-courses (one required a year) include 30-40 offerings for week-long experiential learning, often involving travel or community service. The school also has an Outings Program, involving weekends participating in various outdoor activities including backpacking, skiing, scuba, and rock climbing. Through the High School Honors Program, juniors and seniors, with approval, may take one course per semester at nearby Dominican College at a reduced rate. **Computer lab/training:** Computers and multimedia technology are available to faculty and students in most classrooms and in 4 labs located throughout campus. Over 100 computers are available to students, and all faculty are assigned laptops. Students are provided e-mail accounts, digital storage services and web publishing. The school supports a fiber optic network and a T-1 connection to the Internet. The school has a full-time Director of Educational Technology and a full-time technology specialist. **Grading:** A-F. **Graduation requirements:** Designed to exceed UC admission requirements; 4 years English; 3 years math (through Algebra II), history, lab science, one foreign language or, in exceptional circumstances, 2 years of two languages; 2 years fine arts and P.E.; one mini-course each year. **Average nightly homework (M-Th):** G9-12: 45 min.-1 hour per class meeting. Classes meet every other day. **Faculty:** 51; 39% men, 61% women; 67% hold advanced degrees. (N/P degrees) **Faculty ethnicity:** "20% people of color." (N/P ethnicities) **Faculty selection/training:** "Faculty selection is based on subject area expertise, reflected in the field, etc. The school is deeply interested in the professional growth of the faculty. Support is given for faculty to attend professional workshops, conferences, and seminars; continuing education for faculty including course work and advanced degrees; encouragement of faculty participation and leadership in local, regional, and national professional groups and task forces; professional in-service programs; the E.E. Ford Fellowship; professional development via curriculum expansion and development." **Teacher/student ratio:** 1:9. **Percentage of students enrolled in AP:** 37%; pass rate 80%. **Senior class profile (mean):** SAT Math 645, SAT Critical Reading 650, SAT Writing 675; GPA unweighted: 3.45. **National Merit Scholarship Program:** "23% of most recent class received National Merit Recognition." **College enrollment (last class):** [Last 2 years] 100%; 99% to 4-year, less than 1% to 2-year. **Recent (last 3 yrs) colleges:** American U, Bard, Bates, Beloit, Boston C, Boston U, Bowdoin, Brandeis, Brown, UC (Berkeley, Davis, Irvine, LA, Riverside, SD, Santa Barbara, Santa Cruz), CSU-LA, Cal Poly, Case Western, Claremont McKenna, Colby, Colgate, C of Charleston, U-Colorado (Boulder), Colorado C, Columbia, Cornell, Dickinson, Emerson, George Washington, Georgetown, Goucher, Harvard, Haverford, U-Hawaii, Johns Hopkins, Lake Forest C, Linfield, Loyola Marymount U, Macalester, MIT, McGill, Middlebury, Mount Holyoke, NYU, UNC-Chapel Hill, Northwestern, Oberlin, Occidental, U-Oregon, Parsons, U-Penn, Pitzer, Pomona, U Puget Sound, RISD, Rice, U-Rochester, Santa Clara, Santa Monica C, Sarah Lawrence, Scripps, Skidmore, USC, SMU, Stanford, Trinity C, Dublin, Tufts, Tulane, Vassar, U-Vermont, Wellesley C, Wesleyan, Whitman, Williams, and Yale.

Other Indicators the School is Accomplishing its Goals

"Our most meaningful indicator of how well we are accomplishing our goals is the correspondence we receive from students who have graduated Marin Academy. Testimonials abound about how well prepared students are for the academic demands of college, how socially confident they are, and how well-rounded they are compared to many of their peers. We also hear from alumni who have graduated college and are shaping their respective career paths. Once again, the influence of MA looms large in the descriptions of why students discovered certain paths that have become so fulfilling. One quote from a student who graduated several years ago is illustrative of MA's influence: 'After many years and many professions, I am a teacher. I realized that I had not received the same level of inspiration from any other piece of my life as I had from my teachers at Marin Academy. Now, I spend my days trying to live up to the standards they set for me.'"

Campus/Campus Life

Campus description: The school is situated on a 10-acre campus on a hillside in San Rafael, the former site of a military school. The campus's 12 buildings include Foster Hall, a three-story former private home circa 1870, which houses administration, college counseling offices, classes and caféteria. The Thacher Hall of Science has 4 lab-classrooms, a science library, a computer lab and an observation platform for experiments. **Library:** A new library with 20,000 volume capacity, multiple database access. **Sports facilities:** The Athletic Center, completed in 1998, has a gym, locker rooms, and training rooms. The old gym continues to be used as a gym and also a student center. The school grounds include a pool, a new field turf field for soccer, and lacrosse. **Theater/arts facilities:** The Visual Arts Center houses drawing and painting studios, photography labs (digital and traditional) and ceramics studio. The Music Building includes practice rooms and recording facilities. Our Performing Arts Center has a 235-seat theater, an 80-seat "Black-Box" theater, music studios, practice rooms, and dance studio. **Open/closed campus:** Open. **Lunches:** Food service available on a pay-for-item basis — organic, locally grown. **Bus service:** A private company provides van service to/from the East Bay, Southern Marin and San Francisco. **Uniforms/dress code:** "Marin Academy expects that students will dress in a manner that is appropriate for a school setting and that is not disruptive of the educational process. If a dispute over the appropriateness of clothing arises, the decision of the Head will be final." **Co-curricular activities/clubs:** Yearbook, athletics, school newspaper, literary magazine, Trust Council, Student Senate, dramatic and musical productions, senior projects, forensics, filmmaking, Model UN, Japanimation, Technology Club, Multicultural Action Coalition, Peace and Justice Coalition, the MA Eco-Council, and many others. **Foreign exchange programs/internships:** None. **Community service:** A Community Service Coordinator helps students find placement at Bay Area agencies ranging from food kitchens to beach clean-up, to tutoring at local schools. Some students organize their own projects such as food, book, and clothing drives, etc. **Typical freshman schedule:** 7 periods of approx. 80 minutes each (classes meet every other day), including English, math, World Civilizations, Human Development, foreign language, science, and an elective.

Student Support Services

Counselor/student ratio (not including college counselors): 1:200. **Counseling:** "The School Counselor offers 1:1 counseling for students and consults with parents. The Dean of Students oversees the counseling program and the general counseling environment of the school and also provides individual counseling. In addition, group counseling is provided from time to time as the students request it. Both the Dean of Students and the School Counselor hold advanced degrees in social work or psychology. All students are matched with an advisor and are part of an Advising Group. The advisor is an advocate for the students and advises them on the culture, standards, rules and academic and social lives of the school, and monitors the students' progress throughout the year. The class deans work closely with the advisors to help ensure the academic and personal well-being of each student. Marin Academy has a Director and Associate Director of College Counseling who work with students all four years. The assigned college counselor meets individually with each student and family beginning in the spring of the junior year. In addition, the school hosts a Junior College Night for students and parents, plus two college nights for seniors and their families. Approx. 100 colleges visit Marin Academy each year. Teachers are available for tutorials every other day to help students on an individual basis." **Learning differences/disabilities:** The school has a Learning Services Coordinator who works with parents and students when students with learning differences enroll. Students with special learning needs are granted extended time on tests if they have submitted documentation of educational testing by an approved specialist or institution specifically indicating the need for additional time.

Student Conduct and Health

Code of conduct: "Marin Academy is a small community, founded upon trust and mutual respect. The involvement and contributions of each individual play an integral part in the day-to-day functioning of the school as a whole. We want each student to recognize his/her responsibility for the welfare of the school and encourage all students to respect other individuals within the community and physical environment in which they work." **How school handles drugs/alcohol:** "It is the policy of Marin Academy that selling, distributing, possessing, using and being under the influence of illegal drugs or alcohol is prohibited on campus at any time, on or off campus during school hours, or during or before attendance at school-related events. Any violation of the policy goes directly to the Dean of Students. The sale or distribution of all illegal drugs or alcohol will result in immediate expulsion, barring extraordinary circumstances. A student found in the presence of, using, or in possession of an illegal drug or alcohol will not be allowed to attend school until he or she has undergone a clinical assessment for substance abuse with a mutually agreed upon professional counselor. The student and his or her family will further be required to follow the recommendations of the assessment in order for the student to re-enter Marin Academy. A second instance of use or possession of an illegal drug or alcohol will result in immediate expulsion, barring extraordinary circumstances." **Prevention and awareness programs:** "The human development curriculum is structured to provide students with up-to-date pertinent information about social issues, especially those that directly affect adolescents. These include developmental aspects of identity formation, nutrition, relationships, sexuality, and substance use."

Summer Programs

The school offers the Crossroads Program for selected underserved students from local public schools, G5–8.

Parent Involvement

Parent participation: Not required, though the Marin Academy Parents' Association seeks the involvement of all interested parents. **Parent/teacher communication:** Advisors, who meet with students once a week (each advisor is responsible for 10-12 students), are the first link between school and home. Advisors are in communication with the parents and will inform a student's teacher, if necessary, of any difficulties the child is having and any support that should be offered. Parents meet with the advisors on Parent Conference Day. Parents are also welcome to call individual classroom teachers (whom they will all meet at Back-to-School Night) at any time, as well as class deans, the Academic Dean, and the Dean of Students. All faculty and staff have voicemail and e-mail. **Parent education:** The Association holds monthly meetings with educational opportunities for parents, sponsors a scrip program, trains guides for admission tours, hosts gatherings for new parents, and assists with other events throughout the year. **Donations:** "MA parents contribute in many ways to the school through volunteerism and financial contributions. All levels of support are greatly appreciated."

Sports

Girls and boys play on varsity teams in volleyball, tennis, cross-country, water polo, basketball, softball, swimming, soccer, and track and field; girls compete in varsity volleyball; boys in varsity lacrosse, and baseball. Boys and girls engage in sailing; boys in golf; girls in softball and soccer (JV and V). Club sports in sailing and fencing. 75% of students participate in sports. Most teams compete in the BCL; teams have won over 30 league titles.

What Sets School Apart From Others

"While we believe that the preparation for college and adult life must begin in the classroom with a demanding academic curriculum, we are as much concerned with our students' personal growth as we are with their intellectual growth, and this concern is reflected in our commitment to the variety of challenging experiences which, taken as a whole, constitute a Marin Academy education. First and foremost, we are committed to academic excellence. In addition, our commitment to experiential education is reflected in everything we do outside the classroom at Marin Academy. We believe that many adolescents in our society are information-rich and experience-poor and that they need challenging experiences which will help them discover their sense of self and their essential humanity. We believe that students learn best in a relaxed, open, friendly school community — one based on respect and trust, where they are encouraged to take responsibility for their education and to be an integral part of the school's decision-making process."

How Parents/Students Characterize School

Parent response(s): "MA appreciates and celebrates every student as an individual. This characteristic is valued tremendously. This appreciation of individuality as well as difference continues through college and beyond. We will always be grateful to MA for providing this to our son and daughter." "MA is a perfect balance of academics, athletics and the arts." **Student response(s):** "I discovered the best of myself at MA. I know who I am and who I am capable of becoming. What I have appreciated the most is that MA let me be me while challenging my mind and body." "I have the confidence to try anything I want. The unique personal attention provided at Marin Academy fosters a spirit of independence and determination." "Marin Academy was the starting point at which I began to truly develop my intellect, my beliefs and values. It made me question the way things existed in my life and gave me a strong foundation on which I built while at college."

Marin Catholic High School

675 Sir Francis Drake Boulevard
Kentfield, CA 94904
(415) 464-3811 *fax (415) 461-7161*
www.marincatholic.org

Fr. Thomas Daly, President
Chris Valdez, Principal
Teri Hanley, Director of Admissions, thanley@marincatholic.org

General

Coed Catholic day high school (parochial, 65% Catholic). Founded in 1949. Nonprofit. **Enrollment:** Approx. 730. **Average class size:** 23. **Accreditation:** WASC. **School year:** Mid-Aug.-May. **School day:** 8 a.m.-2:55 p.m. **Location:** On Sir Francis Drake Boulevard, a main thoroughfare in Marin County, accessible by Golden Gate Transit buses. Approx. 15 minutes by car from the Golden Gate Bridge and 20 minutes from the Richmond Bridge.

Student Body

Geographic breakdown (counties): 94% from Marin; 2% from San Francisco; 2% from Sonoma; 2% from Alameda. **Ethnicity:** Approx. 82% Caucasian (non-Latino); 6% multi-ethnic; 7% Latino; 4% Asian; 1% African-American. **International students (I-20 status):** N/P. **Middle schools (freshman):** 50% came from Marin County parochial schools; 15% from private schools; 35% from public schools. (N/P # students).

Admission

Applications due: Priority filing date mid-December (check website). Applications are available and submitted online. **Application fee:** $75.

Application process: The school schedules student and parent visits from September through January each year. An Open House is held in October. Applications submitted by mid-December deadline receive priority. The mandatory HSPT is given on two dates in January. Interviews of parents and student are held in February, and decisions are mailed mid-March. **No. of fresmen applications:** 400 for 200 (# places N/P). **Minimum admission requirements:** N/P. **Test required:** HSPT. **Preferences:** N/P. **"We are looking for"** N/P. **What kind of student do you best serve?** "Marin Catholic students are college-bound young people interested in developing themselves as a 'whole person.' Marin Catholic seeks students who wish to become positive contributors to the school community, bringing with them their own unique talents and individual interests."

Costs

Latest tuition: $13,900 payable in 1, 2, or 10 payments. **Sibling discount:** None. **Tuition increases:** Approx. 4%. **Other costs:** Approx. $300 for books (new); used books also available. Tuition assistance is available to students who demonstrate need. **Percentage of students receiving financial aid:** 20%. **Financial aid deadline:** February 1. **Average grant:** N/P. **Percentage of grants of half-tuition or more:** N/P.

School's Mission Statement/Goals

"Marin Catholic serves young men and women in the Catholic tradition. Consistent with our Gospel values, we are committed to the education of the whole person. We provide a spiritual, academic, and extracurricular environment dedicated to imparting knowledge, values, and vision." • "We expect our students, through their experiences in the classroom and as active members of the school community, to develop the attributes of an educated person: responsibility, both personal and social; critical ability; appreciation for the beauty and complexity of the world around us. We hope to instill in our students the confidence that will empower them, as informed and compassionate individuals, to effect change in that world. We are committed to learning as a lifelong process."

Academic Program

Courses offered (AP=Advanced Placement, H=Honors, (AP)=AP option, (H)=Honors option): **Arts:** Art I-III, Drawing and Painting, Ceramics I & II, Photography I & II, Advanced Art & Portfolio, Beginning Acting, Advanced Acting, Drama Internship, Chorale, Symphonic Band, Music Technology, Jazz Ensemble; **Computer Education:** Computer Literacy, Graphic Design; **English:** English 9 (H), English 10 (H), American Literature (H), Post Modern American Literature, AP English, Senior Composition; **Language:** Spanish I-IV, AP Spanish, French II-IV, AP French, Italian I-V, Language Support Program; **Math:** Algebra I-IIC, Algebra 1-II, Accelerated Algebra 1, Algebra II (H), Geometry C, Geometry (H), Intro to Probability and Statistics,

Finite Math & Problem Solving, Precalculus (H), AP Calculus AB, AP Calculus BC, AP Statistics **P.E.:** Health/Movement Education, Weight Training **Science:** Biology 9 (H), Chemistry (H), Conceptual Physics, Marine Science, Physiology, Physics, AP Environmental Science, AP Biology, AP Physics, AP Chemistry, Science Internship **Social Studies:** Global Studies (H), Western Civilization (H), American Studies: U.S. History, AP U.S. History, AP U.S. Govt., Psychology (1 Sem), Economics (1 Sem), Modern American Society, AP Psychology, U.S. Government; **Theology:** Theology 9 (Introduction to Faith & Catholicism, Theology 10 (The Bible: Old and New Testament), Theology 11 (Christian Morality and Social Justice), Theology 12 (Intro to Theological Investigations, A Catholic Approach, Theology 12 (H) (Christian Literature). **Computer/ lab/training:** N/P. **Grading:** N/P. **Graduation requirements:** Students are required to pursue a course of study which includes enrollment in seven academic classes each year and which leads to the completion of a minimum of 260 total credits: 4 years English (40 credits); 4 years Theology (40 credits); 4 years social studies (40 credits) 2 years foreign language (20 credits), 1 year visual or performing arts (10 credits); 2 years science (20 credits); 3 years mathematics (30 credits) - including Algebra, Geometry and Intermediate or Advanced Algebra; 1 semester P.E. (5 credits); 1 semester computer education (5 credits); electives to complete the 260 credits required for graduation; Christian Service - 25 hours for each year enrolled at Marin Catholic; a retreat for each year enrolled at Marin Catholic and a Junior College Project. **Average nightly homework (M-Th):** 2-2 1/2 hours. **Faculty:** 58; 53% male, 47% female (N/P degrees). **Faculty ethnicity:** N/P. **Faculty selection/training:** N/P. **Teacher/student ratio:** 1:23. **Percentage of students enrolled in AP:** N/P. **Senior class profile (mean):** SAT N/P; GPA: N/P. **National Merit Scholarship Program:** N/P. **College enrollment (last class):** 95% in 4-year. (N/P % 2-year). **Recent (last 3 yrs) colleges:** American U, Arizona SU, Bentley C (2), Berklee C of Music, Boston C (5), CCA, Cal Maritime Academy, Cal Poly-SLO (28), Cal Poly-Pomona, CSU (Channel Islands, Chico (9), Fullerton, Northridge, Sacramento (2), San Bernardino, San Marcos (2), Carroll C (Montana), Chapman U (2), Claremont McKenna C, Colby, Colgate, Columbia, Cornell, Cornish C of the Arts, Davidson C, Denison, Dominican U (3), Duke, FIDM (SF), Fordham U, Franklin C (Switzerland) (2), Georgetown, Gonzaga (6), Hofstra, Iona C, Ithaca C, Kennesaw SU, Loyola Marymount U (10), Loyola U Chicago (2), Michigan SU, Middlebury, NYU (2), Northeastern U, (2), Northern SU, Northwestern, Oregon SU, Penn, Pennsylvania SU (University Park), Saint John's U (2), Saint Mary's C of California (5), SDSU (7), SF Conservatory of Music, SFSU (5), SJSU, Santa Barbara City C (4), Santa Clara (7), Santa Monica C, Seattle U (2), Sonoma SU (12), St. Mary's C of Maryland (2), Stanford (3), Stevens Institute of Technology, Texas Christian U, The Art Institute of California (SF), Catholic U-America, U-Arizona (11), Tufts, U.S. Coast Guard Academy (2), U.S. Naval Academy, UC (Berkeley (6), Davis (19), Irvine, LA (13), Riverside (2), SD (3), Santa Barbara (17), Santa Cruz (9)), U-Colorado at Boulder (18), U-Dallas (2), U-Denver, U-Nevada (Reno) (2), U-Notre Dame, U-Oregon (8), U-Pittsburgh, U-Redlands, USD (6), USF (7), USC (9), UOP, U-Utah, U-Washington, Utah SU, Vanderbilt, Villanova U (3), Virginia Polytechnic Institute and SU, Washington U (St. Louis), Wheaton, Whitman, Whittier C, Willamette U (2), Williams C, and Yale.

Other Indicators the School is Accomplishing its Goals

"The Marin Catholic curriculum is designed to provide a challenging, college prep experience for all of our students. Along with the development and enhancement of essential skills, the required course of study encourages exploration and self-evaluation. Successfully completing the academic program, which includes choosing the most rigorous course of study one can, qualifies students for admission to the most competitive colleges and universities. 100% of our graduates are accepted to college each year; 95%, traditionally, matriculate to four-year colleges and universities."

Campus/Campus Life

Campus description: The school has a 14-acre campus at the base of Mt. Tamalpais in Kentfield. The school includes a two-story school building, sports fields, performing arts center, gym, chapel, and new Student Education Center. **Library:** The library is equipped with state-of-the-art technology and has study spaces for 75 students. **Sports facilities:** Turf football field, baseball field and soccer field, track and gymnasium. Newly renovated locker rooms. **Theater/arts facilities:** Performing Arts Center and award-winning Wiegand Visual Arts Wing, which includes ceramic and photography studios. **Open/closed campus:** Closed. **Lunches:** The school cafeteria serves breakfast and lunch. Open from 7:45 a.m. to 3:15 p.m. **Bus service:** Daily to/from school. **Uniforms/dress code:** "Specific dress code is enforced." (N/P description) **Co-curricular activities/clubs:** Activities include Academic Decathlon (ACADEC), California Scholarship Federation, Cheerleading, Washington, D.C. Close-up, Drama Club, Earth Awareness Club, Emcee Echoes Student Newspaper, French Club, Intramural Sports, Italian Club, Mock Trial Team, National Honor Society, Rotary Interact Club, Student Government, Peace and Justice Club and Chess Club. **Foreign exchange programs/internships:** N/P. **Community service:** "An integral part of the educational experience at Marin Catholic is the 100 hours service component which has students live out the school mission of Faith, Knowledge and Service in their community." **Typical freshman schedule:** English 9 or English 9 Honors, theology, Algebra I or Advanced Algebra II, foreign language (Italian or Spanish), Global Studies or Global Studies Honors, Biology or Biology Honors, P.E. and computer literacy or arts elective.

Student Support Services

Counselor/student ratio (not including college counselors): 1:180. **Counseling:** The school assigns each student a personal and academic counselor with whom the student meets individually on a regularly scheduled basis. Parents, advisors, and students do academic planning each spring. Juniors and seniors receive individual and small group college counseling. **Learning disabilities/differences:** Marin Catholic admits students with documented learning disabilities who meet the school's admission criteria. Documented students may then enroll in the Academic Service Program, where they are expected to follow the school's college preparatory curriculum.

Student Conduct and Health

Code of conduct: "Basic to the philosophy of Marin Catholic is respect. We expect interactions between students, students and teachers, among staff members, and between parents/guardians and staff to be based on respect. Marin Catholic is committed to providing a safe, respectful environment for its staff and students. In addition to prohibiting illegal activity, the Code of Behavior provides sanctions for profanity/vulgarity/insolence, verbal harassment, denigrating speech and name-calling, and physical intimidation." **How school handles drugs/alcohol:** "If a student is found in possession of illegal substances, the substance and the student's car keys (if applicable) are confiscated, and parents/guardians are immediately notified. The student is subject to expulsion and possibly immediate suspension pending a meeting of the Disciplinary Review Board. Should the student be allowed to remain, he or she may be subject to random drug testing, an after-care program, and other disciplinary actions. The school may randomly use a 'breathalyzer' at school-sponsored events to ensure safety and sobriety." **Prevention and awareness programs:** The Health Education Coordinator provides educational programs and events for students and parents in the areas of drug/alcohol use and abuse, family communication, short-term therapeutic counseling, and other areas that pertain to adolescent health and wellness.

Summer Programs

The school hosts a month-long summer session (mid-June to mid-July) consisting of academic classes, fitness courses, and computer science courses. Incoming freshmen may take a class in study skills. Cost: Approx. $350 per class. Summer athletic camps are also available.

Parent Involvement

Parent participation: "None required, though parents are very active in the school." **Parent/teacher communication:** Formal report cards each semester and a school-wide web based information system allows parents and student to monitor academic progress in real time. **Parent education:** N/P. **Donations:** "Parents are asked to give to the annual fund."

Sports

"Marin Catholic has one of the most comprehensive athletic programs for young men and women in the Bay Area. Competing in the MCAL, Marin Catholic offers the rich athletic tradition which has allowed thousands of student-athletes to benefit from the lessons that athletic competition offers. The program consists of freshman, junior varsity and varsity team sports. Winter sports include: basketball, cheerleading/dance, cross-country skiing, sailing and wrestling. Spring sports include: baseball, golf, lacrosse, sailing, soccer (girls), softball, swimming and diving, tennis (boys), track and field, and volleyball (boys). Fall sports include: cheerleading, cross-country, field hockey (girls), football, golf (girls) soccer (boys), tennis (girls), volleyball (girls) and water polo.

What Sets School Apart From Others

"Marin Catholic High School is a Catholic, coeducational college preparatory school. As a school community, we strive to provide opportunities for growth academically, spiritually, and socially. The Marin Catholic curriculum is designed to provide a challenging and stimulating academic experience for all of our students." • "The spiritual program at Marin Catholic is the foundation of all our school programs. Students are required to complete four years of theology, participate in a retreat each year, and complete 100 hours of Christian Service. Our Campus Ministry Program invites students to become involved in the planning of liturgies, retreats, and other prayer services." • "The athletic and extracurricular program is as diverse and interesting as our student body, providing students with tremendous opportunities to enhance their high school experience. Over 90 percent of our student body participates in athletic or extracurricular activities."

How Parents/Students Characterize School

Parent response(s): "Marin Catholic offers young adults a supportive and positive environment in which they can learn and grow. The combination of a high quality, college prep curriculum with a strong, Catholic, faith-based social setting is truly a treasure to the community." **Student response(s):** "MC has provided me the opportunity to grow on a spiritual and intellectual basis. Surrounded by mentally stimulating academic courses, unbelievable athletics, a multitude of various clubs, and a caring faith community, I have been able to perform at my highest level."

The Marin School
100 Ebbtide Avenue, Suite 500
Sausalito, CA 94965
(415) 339-9336 *fax (415) 339-9337*
www.themarinschool.org

Barbara J. Schakel, Head of School
David Bralower, Director of Admission, dbralower@themarinschool.org

General
Coed day high school. Nonsectarian. Independent. Founded in 1980.
Nonprofit. Member BAIHS. **Enrollment:** Approx. 100. **Average class
size:** 8. **Accreditation:** WASC. **School year:** Sept.-June. **School day:**
8:20 a.m.-3:25 p.m. **Location:** In Sausalito, a suburb 5 miles north of
San Francisco in Marin County. Near Hwy. 101, assessable via Golden
Gate Transit.

Student Body
Geographic breakdown (counties): 74% Marin; 21% San Francisco;
5% East Bay. **Ethnicity:** 77% Caucasian (non-Latino); 10% Latino; 7%
multi-ethnic; 3% Asian; 3% African American. **International students
(I-20 status):** None. **Middle schools (freshman):** 43% came from 5
public middle schools; 48% from 7 private, non-parochial schools; 9%
from SF charter schools.

Admission
Applications due: Mid-January (call for date). **Application fee:** $75.
Application process: "The school accepts the BAIHS common parent application form and BAIHS common letters of recommendation.
Students also submit a student application specific to the school, a
transcript, and results of the admission test. As part of the application
process, students participate in a shadow visit and in a student interview. Other admissions activities include information events, parent
receptions, and parent tours. Decisions are mailed mid-March." **No. of
freshman applications:** 80. **Minimum admission requirements:** "The
school considers each applicant on an individual basis. Candidates
typically show strong academic potential and creativity, and an ability
to succeed in a college-preparatory curriculum." **Test required: SSAT.**
Preferences: None. "**We are looking for** students who are interested
in a strong academic program, who have potential, both academically
and creatively, and who would thrive in an environment where their
individuality is valued, their creativity encouraged, and their academic
success achievable." **What sort of student do you best serve?** "The
Marin School is seeking bright, creative students who are committed
to reaching their full potential in a challenging, college-prep environment. We welcome a range of students including those who are gifted
and those who may have some learning challenges. We also look for

students who enjoy extracurricular activities and who see the value of a small community."

Costs
Latest tuition: $30,900 payable in 1 or 2 payments (includes textbooks, yearbooks and a fall trip). Monthly payment plans or loans are available through an outside agency. **Sibling discount:** None. **Tuition increases:** Approx. 4-9%. **Other costs:** Approx. $100 for graduation and $100 for curriculum-related activities. **Percentage of students receiving financial aid:** 12%. **Financial aid deadline:** Mid-January (call for date). **Average grant:** $22,500. **Percentage of grants half-tuition or more:** 78%.

School's Mission Statement/Goals
"Our mission is to provide a collaborative learning environment that inspires creativity, integrity, and academic excellence."

Academic Program
Courses offered (AP=Advanced Placement, H=Honors, (AP)=AP option, (H)=Honors option): **English:** Survey of Literature, World Literature, American Literature (H), English Literature (H), Writers' Workshop, Journalism, Film as Literature 1,2; **Math:** Algebra I, Geometry (H), Algebra II/Trigonometry (H), Pre-Calculus, Calculus; **History/Social Sciences:** Geography, Modern World History (H), U.S. History (H), Government, Economics, Philosophy, Native American History, Politics and the Media, Resistance, Rebellion and Revolution, American and the Vietnam War, History of Rock and Roll; **Science:** Biology (H), Physics (H), Chemistry (H), Zoology, Astronomy; **Foreign language:** Spanish, French, Japanese; **Arts:** Basic Art and Design, Drawing and Painting, Advanced Drawing and Painting, Studio Art, Art History, Photography 1-3, Digital Photography, Drama 1-4, Jazz Band 1-4, Recording Class; **Technology:** Computer Science, Java 1-2, Robotics, Fabrication Laboratory, 3D Graphic Design and Animation; **Special Programs:** Each year students and teachers have various opportunities to travel to a foreign country. Trips have included Mexico, Spain, France, Ireland, Chile, Peru, Japan, Belize, Chile and Ghana. **Computer lab/training:** The school has a technology lab with 22 PCs. PCs are also available in the library and throughout the school, including in the film editing lab and the recording studio. The school also has a multimedia room that includes five Mac G-4 computers. Students have user accounts at school for Internet access for research. The school maintains an extensive website for home-school communication. **Grading:** A-F twice a year. **Graduation requirements:** Designed to meet UC admission requirements, 4 years English, 4 years history/social science, 3 years math, 3 years science, 3 years foreign language; 2 years P.E.; 2 years visual/performing arts, 3 years additional electives; 80 hours community service. **Average nightly homework (M-Th):** G9-10: 1.5-2 hours; G11-12: 2-3 hours. **Faculty:** 17; 65% male, 35%

female; 10% hold advanced degrees (N/P degrees). **Faculty ethnicity:** 100% Caucasian. **Faculty selection/training:** "Most hold valid teaching credentials. They are selected based upon experience, personality, talents and their ability to interact one-on-one with students. The school requires in-service training and encourages continuing education." **Teacher/student ratio:** 1:7. **Senior class profile (mean):** SAT Math 529, SAT Critical Reading 539, SAT Writing 518; GPA: 3.01. **College enrollment (last class):** 90% in 4-year, 10% in 2-year. **Recent (last 3 yrs) colleges:** Antioch, Bard, CCA, CSU (Chico, Humboldt, Long Beach, LA, Mont. Bay, Northridge, SF, SJ, Sonoma), Cal Poly-SLO, Dartmouth, Eckerd C, Goucher C, Hampshire, Emerson, Emery Riddle, Eugene Lang, Evergreen SU, Gonzaga, Hampshire, Harvey Mudd, Institute of the Arts, Kalamazoo, Lewis & Clark, Linfield, Massachusetts School of the Arts, Northern Arizona, NYU, School of the Visual Arts, Northwest C of Art, Pitzer, Pratt Institute, Reed, RPI, Rollins, Seattle U, St. Mary's, Skidmore, Syracuse U, Tulane U, UC (Berkeley, Davis, Irvine, LA, Riverside, Santa Barbara, Santa Cruz, SD), U-Denver, U-LaVerne, U-Oregon, U-Puget Sound, U-Redlands, USF, U-Southern Oregon, Washington C, Whittier, and Willamette.

Other Indicators the School is Accomplishing its Goals

"Enrollment has been increasing steadily over the last couple of years with the incoming 9th grade class being the largest in the school's history. Students continue to matriculate to great colleges and universities across the country. In the classroom, our students continue to be engaged in a number of exciting and rewarding projects/partnerships that help enhance the quality of their educational experience. Through The Marin School Writers' Series, students have engaged with both fiction and non-fiction authors, as well as poets, and have been published in journals for young writers, including Creative Communications, and the journal of the Marin Poetry Center. The TMS Film program has continued its relationship with the San Francisco Film Society and invited award winning filmmakers into the classroom to speak with students. Biology students, in conjunction with the Farallones Institute, have monitored sand crab populations at Muir Beach. Working with the California Academy of Sciences, biology students studied dock-fowling organisms in San Francisco Bay. In 2007, the school completed its first capital campaign. The funds raised will be used to expand some areas of our curriculum and to enhance the overall experience for our growing student population. In addition to the capital campaign, the administration also completed the TMS Strategic Plan to carry the school through the year 2013. At the beginning of the 2007 school year, we had the grand opening of our new TMS Performing Arts Center and Internet café. The performing arts center contains a 75-seat black box theatre with top-of-the-line lights and sound equipment. The space has a fully equipped recording studio as well as a film editing lab. The Internet Café serves as another space on campus for students to socialize/quietly work during the school day."

Campus/Campus Life

Campus description: "The campus consists of two buildings, totaling 15,000 sq. ft., including classrooms, science labs, administrative offices, library, art studio, dark room, performing arts center, multi-media room, technology lab and study rooms. The grounds include fields where students play basketball, soccer, softball, street hockey, tennis and flag football. Sausalito's Martin Luther King Gymnasium is located in an adjacent building." **Library:** 990 sq. ft.; 2,700 volumes, 25 journal subscriptions and 5 daily periodicals; 4 computers; study space for 24 students. Open to students from 8:30 a.m. to 4:15 p.m. most days. On-line catalog. Fully wired so students and faculty can access the library catalog, Internet, and school network from personal computers. Access available to many full-text and online databases. **Sports facilities:** The school uses a public gymnasium and on-site public playing fields and tennis courts. **Theater/arts facilities:** Performing Arts Center with recording studio, film editing studio, art studio, multimedia center with photography darkroom. **Open/closed campus:** Closed campus except for juniors and seniors who may leave for lunch. **Lunches:** No lunch service. Students may purchase lunch through outside provider. **Bus service:** Public. **Uniforms/dress code:** "Clothing must be school-appropriate." **Co-curricular activities/clubs:** Newspaper, yearbook, student council, literary publications, jazz band/recording studio, intramural sports, soccer, basketball, and various academic and cultural clubs. **Foreign exchange program/internships:** None. **Community service:** "Service hours required for graduation. Varies according to grade level." (N/P eamples) **Typical freshman schedule:** Six to seven classes of 50 minutes each, including five core classes plus P.E., Art, Drama, or Jazz Band.

Student Support Services

Counselor/student ratio (not including college counselors): 1:100. **Counseling:** "The Marin School employs a part-time emotional-growth counselor, as well as a college counselor. Each teacher acts as an academic mentor for 6-8 students. Advisors communicate with parents on a regular basis. All teachers meet twice a week to discuss the progress of each student in the school. With a 1:7 teacher-student ratio, teachers are able to work closely with students each day. Workshops are scheduled on alternate days to enable students to meet with each of their teachers. Weekly assignments are posted on the website, as are biweekly grade reports." **Learning differences/disabilities:** "The Marin School has a college-preparatory program, with strong academic and arts programs. We have a full-time educational specialist available to students, teachers, and parents. If there is a question about whether the program is appropriate for a given student with diagnosed learning differences/disabilities, the staff works individually with the applicant family to determine whether or not the school will be able to support the student's learning needs. The Marin School also recognizes that each student has a unique learning style and commits to providing an appropriate learning environment for each student."

Student Conduct and Health

Code of conduct: "The focus is on the rights of all members of the community: students, teachers, and staff. A spirit of community and personal responsibility is fostered, which results in mutual respect, a safe environment, and a sense of ownership for all." **How school handles drugs/alcohol:** "Staff monitors students closely. If a problem exists, the school is proactive in its response. This may include working with the family to find a treatment program. If the problem is severe enough, the student is dismissed. A written policy regarding drug and alcohol usage helps guide decisions." **Prevention/ awareness programs:** "An experienced counselor provides ongoing awareness programs for students and staff, and also sponsors programs designed to educate the students about making healthful choices."

Summer Program

Some students complete independent study work in the summer. Teachers sometimes offer SAT prep classes, art classes, and often, international travel.

Parent Involvement

Parent participation: "Parents are expected to support the school through volunteer participation and annual giving." **Parent/teacher communication:** Parents receive biweekly report cards on their children's progress. Advisors are in contact with parents by phone and e-mail. Parent/student/teacher conferences are held three times a year. **Parent education:** The Marin School Parent Association sponsors speakers of interest to the group. **Donations:** "Parents are expected to participate in annual giving."

Sports

The Marin School participates in the Small Schools Bridge League, affiliated with the North Coast Section. Teams include boys and girls soccer and boys basketball. Tennis and Ultimate Frisbee are also available. Students also engage in running, basketball, volleyball, soccer, flag football, and street hockey through the P.E. program and the intramural sports program.

What Sets School Apart From Others

"The Marin School offers a unique opportunity for all students. The small classroom environment fosters a high level of participation and engagement in learning. The 1:7 teacher/student ratio allows teachers to challenge each student individually so that individual potential is maximized. Most classes meet every other day with a discussion-based seminar on the class day and group and individual feedback on the workshop day. Classes are student-centered, and each student is encouraged to exercise his/her voice in discussion and debate.

This close relationship between students and teachers ensures the teachers a greater understanding of each student's learning style and talents or gifts. Because of the daily system, students quickly adapt strong organizational skills and the ability to advocate for themselves. Communication between school and home is a high priority, and the school's website provides daily academic statistics, bi-weekly reports, and weekly assignment posting for students and parents. The faculty meets twice a week to discuss student progress and problem-solve concerns. The outside-the-walls curriculum consists of our fieldtrip/ experiential ed opportunities. Because classes are small, faculty frequently organize curriculum-related field trips and outdoor adventures such as river rafting and wilderness backpacking. International travel is also an integral part of the school's program; students who participate in these trips spend part of the school year studying the culture of the country in preparation for a full experience."

How Parents/Students Characterize School

Parent response(s): "As proud parents of high school students at The Marin School, we feel compelled to share our secret: The Marin School is an outstanding option for bright, creative young people who are looking for a challenging college preparatory environment that nurtures their individuality, self discipline, and love of learning." "The one-on-one education is the best part of The Marin School. You cannot get a better situation. Students learn in the way learning is supposed to occur; it is enjoyable, fun, in-depth and held to a high standard of excellence." "The Marin School gives each of its students what every young adult deserves: support, stimulation, and an environment that encourages both self-expression and intellectual growth. Students leave our community knowing they can succeed." "No one can be lost, and there's tremendous support to assure that concepts covered are understood. In addition, the entire school atmosphere is designed to surround and embrace the students, celebrate their independent thinking, and encourage their exploration and discovery in many dimensions." "Teachers enjoy helping the students grow and thrive, and the small school environment enables the teachers to use their creative talents and energies to make The Marin School quite special." **Student response(s):** "The low teacher/student ratio provided a unique chance to get to know and become friends with many of my teachers. These circumstances resulted in a very close and personal environment. It seemed to me that the teachers received more respect from the students and that the students were more likely to do all of their work because they had a bond with the teacher. The teachers, in turn, knew each student on a personal level. They knew our abilities, strengths, and weaknesses." "The teachers did not just teach me the curriculum; they went beyond that and helped push my limits and go beyond what I thought my abilities were."

Menlo School

50 Valparaiso Avenue
Atherton, CA 94027
(650) 330-2000 *fax (650) 330-2002*
www.menloschool.org

Norman Colb, Head of School
Cathy Shelburne, Director of Upper School Admission, (650) 330-2000
ext. 2602, cshelburne@menloschool.org

General

Coed high school and middle school. Nonsectarian. Founded in
1915. Nonprofit, member CAIS, NAIS, BAIHS. **Enrollment:** 540 (high
school). **Average class size:** 15. **Student/teacher ratio:** 10:1. **Accreditation:** WASC/CAIS. **School year:** Aug.-June. **School day:** 8 a.m.-3 p.m.
Location: In Atherton, a suburb near Palo Alto. A school shuttle takes
students between campus and the Menlo Park CalTrain station at no
additional cost. Transportation available to and from the East Bay.

Student Body

Geographic breakdown (counties): 46% from San Mateo; 48% from
Santa Clara; 1% from San Francisco; 5% from other counties. **Ethnic-
ity:** 75% Caucasian (non-Latino); 12% Asian; 4% Latino; 4% African-
American; 5% multi-ethnic. **International students (I-20 status):** N/P.
Middle schools (freshman): N/P.

Admission

Applications due: Early January (call for date). **Application fee:** $85.
Application process: "Application, essay, visit, test." **No. of freshman
applications:** 350 for 70 places. (Newly admitted students make up
half of the ninth grade class of 140. Approx. 65 places are taken by
school's middle school students.) **Minimum admission requirements:**
N/P. **Test required:** ISEE. **Preferences:** N/P. **"We are looking for** bright
students with strong interests in and out of the classroom." **What kind
of student do you best serve?** N/P.

Costs

Latest tuition: $30,800 payable in 1 or 10 payments. **Sibling discount:**
None. **Tuition increases:** 5%. **Other costs:** $550 for books. **Percent-
age of students receiving financial aid:** 20%. **Financial aid deadline:**
Mid-January (call for date). **Average grant:** $13,000. **No. of grants of
half-tuition or more:** 126. **Percentage of grants of half-tuition or
more:** N/P.

School's Mission Statement/Goals

"Menlo School is dedicated to providing a challenging academic
curriculum complemented by outstanding fine arts and athletic programs. The school helps students develop positive values and nurtures

character development in a supportive environment that upholds the highest moral and ethical standards. Menlo's program encourages students to reach their fullest potential and to develop the skills necessary to respond intelligently and humanely to the complexities of a diverse world."

Academic Program

Courses offered (AP=Advanced Placement, H=Honors, (H)=Honors option, (AP)=AP option): **English:** English, including college-level electives such as British Literature, College Writing, Fiction Writing, Science Fiction, Shakespeare, 20th Century American Fiction, Comparative Literature; **History:** Intro to History, Western Studies, U.S. History, History and Social Science Electives (including Asian History, Intro to Law, Economics, Ancient Greece, Ancient Rome, Ideology and Power, Psychology); **Math/Computers:** Algebra I, Algebra II (H), Geometry (H), Pre-Calculus, Foundations of Calculus H, Computer Science AP, Statistics, AB Calculus (AP), BC Calculus (AP); **Science:** Physics, Chemistry & Biology, AP Physics B, AP Physics C, Electronics and Robotics, Chemistry (AP), Bio-Tech/Science Research; **Foreign Languages:** French I-III, French IV H, AP French Language, AP French Literature, Spanish I-III, Spanish IV H, AP Spanish Language, Spanish V Literature, Japanese I, Latin I-IV (H), AP Vergil, AP Latin Literature; **Arts:** Intro to the Arts, Freshman Seminar, Public Speaking, Writing, Studio Art, Advanced Art, AP Art Portfolio, Drama, Advanced Drama, Chorus, Select Chorus, Chamber Orchestra, Jazz Band, Music Theory AP, Jazz Dance, Advanced Jazz Dance. **Computer lab/training:** N/P. **Grading:** A-F. **Graduation requirements:** 4 years English; 3 years foreign language, history, math, and science (physics, biology, chemistry); 1.5 years fine arts; 20 hours of community service each year. **Average nightly homework (M-Th):** N/P. **Faculty:** 81 f/t and 12 p/t teachers and administrators; (N/P gender); 80% hold advanced degrees - 63 master's, 13 Ph.D.s and 1 JD. **Faculty ethnicity:** "13% of color." (N/P ethnicities) **Faculty selection/training:** "National searches are conducted. Advanced degrees are encouraged. Rigorous teacher evaluation process." **Teacher/student ratio:** N/P. **Percentage of students enrolled in AP:** 60%; pass rate: 70% of the scores were in the 4 to 5 range; 91% scored 3 or above. **Senior class profile (mean):** SAT Math 672, SAT Critical Reading 662, SAT Writing 661; SAT II scores: Lit 642, Math 1C 631, Math 2C 701, Am History 657, Bio-E 631, Chemistry 701, Physics 765, French 687, Latin 693, Spanish 693; GPA: 3.49. **National Merit Scholarship Program:** 18 students were Semifinalists; of these 17 became Finalists. Seven students from the last class were named Semifinalists. **College enrollment (last class):** (N/P % 2- and 4-yr). **Recent (last 3 yrs) colleges:** UC (Davis, Berkeley, SD, LA, Santa Barbara, Santa Cruz), U-Colorado, U-Oregon, USC, Santa Clara, U-Arizona, Stanford, Occidental, SMU, Cornell, Lewis & Clark, USD, NYU, Duke, Princeton, Claremont McKenna, Tufts, Bucknell, Vassar, Washington U, Brown, MIT, U-Michigan, Cal Poly-SLO, Willamette, Yale, Amherst, Dartmouth, Cal Poly-Pomona, and Harvard.

Other Indicators the School is Accomplishing its Goals
"New campus buildings housing all academic subjects."

Campus/Campus Life
Campus description: "The school, on 30 acres of treed property, has a middle school campus that is 4 years old and a state-of-the art high school academic complex new in fall of 2004." **Library:** 20,000 books, current magazines and newspapers, and VHS/DVD collection; wired for personal computers to access the Internet; 16 computers for student use in the Electronic Resource Room and an additional 21 computers in its multimedia room; open 7:15 a.m. to 7 p.m. Monday-Thursday and 7:15 a.m.- 5 p.m. on Fridays. **Sports facilities:** N/P. **Theater/arts facilities:** N/P. **Open/closed campus:** Open campus beginning in G10. **Lunches:** Cafeteria choices, included in tuition. **Bus service:** Free shuttle bus between camous and Menlo Park CalTrain station. **Uniform/dress code:** None. **Co-curricular activities/clubs:** 35 clubs, including Multicultural Awareness Club, Junior Statesmen of America, Junior Classical League, Literary Magazine, Cooking Club, Italian Conversation Club, Video Club, Chess Club, Ham Radio Club, Interact, Debate Club, Friends Club, Gay/Straight Alliance, The Neighborhood Math Club, Political Action Awareness Club, Photography Club, Robotics Club, Spanish Club, Menlo Modern Language Journal, Four From Earth, Indus Club, French Club, Team, Student Council, Art Club, Model United Nations. **Foreign exchange programs/internships:** None. **Community service:** "Numerous opportunities available through school community service office. 20 community service hours a year are required." **Typical freshman schedule:** "Five solids/arts rotation."

Student Support Services
Counselor/student ratio (not including college counselors): N/P. **Counseling:** "Personal, academic, and college counseling. One full-time school counselor focuses on mental/emotional health of students. Four full-time college counselors also assist students in academic advising. The school provides a full-time nurse." **Learning disabilities/differences:** "No formal program, but the Director of Academic Support Services assists students with special learning challenges."

Student Conduct and Health
Code of conduct: "The school functions on assumptions of trust and respect between and among students and faculty." **How school handles drugs/alcohol:** "Each discipline case is considered individually." **Prevention/awareness programs:** "Covered in regular student and parent education programs."

Summer Programs: N/P. Contact school.

Parent Involvement

Parent participation: "Very active Parent Association." **Parent/teacher communication:** Parents and teachers communicate through e-mail and teacher's individual telephone extension numbers. **Parent education:** "A faculty/parent committee organizes a full day of seminars for parents on typical adolescent issues." **Donations:** "Parents give generously in time and/or money to improve the school."

Sports

Through the Peninsula Athletic League and West Bay Athletic League, girls compete in cross-country, water polo, tennis, volleyball, basketball, soccer, golf, track, lacrosse, softball, and swimming; boys compete in cross-country, football, water polo, basketball, soccer, baseball, golf, swimming, tennis, track, volleyball, wrestling, and lacrosse.

What Sets School Apart From Others

"Outwardly relaxed and informal, inwardly focused and rigorous. Strong academics with emphasis in sports and arts, with encouragement to develop a sense of self and a love of learning by providing a broad spectrum of choices in curricular and extracurricular offerings."

How Parents/Students Characterize School

Parent response(s): "I admire the culture of Menlo which encourages students to take responsibility for their personal behavior and academic and extracurricular goals. Also, I'm proud to send my children to a school that values achievement in a wide range of areas, including academics, athletics, fine arts, and community service." **Student response(s):** "Menlo has enabled me to take on new challenges with the feeling that I can accomplish anything. It has given me the support that I need to explore, to question, and to move forward toward my dreams and my future."

Mercy High School

2750 Adeline Drive
Burlingame, CA 94010
(650) 762-1114 *fax (650) 343-5529*
www.mercyhsb.com

Ms. Laura M. Held, Principal
Mrs. Ellen M. Williamson, Director of Admission, ewilliamson@mercyhsb.com

General

Girls Catholic day high school (75% Catholic). Founded in 1931 by the Sisters of Mercy. Nonprofit. **Enrollment:** 500. **Average class size:** 24. **Accreditation:** WASC. **School year:** Late Aug.-early June. **School day:** 8:05 a.m.-3 p.m. **Location:** Between Hwys. 101 and 280, in the Burlingame hills, accessible using bus, BART, CalTrain, shuttle.

Student Body

Geographic breakdown (counties): 94% from San Mateo; 2% from San Francisco; 2% from Alameda; 2% from Napa/Contra Costa/Santa Clara/Solano. **Ethnicity:** 55% Caucasian (non-Latina); 10% Latina; 19% Asian; 16% multi-ethnic. **International students (I-20 status):** 0. **Middle schools (freshman):** 51 schools: 33% from public middle schools; 22% from private non-parochial schools; 45% from parochial schools. (N/P # schools).

Admissions

Applications due: Priority in early December; final in early January. **Application fee:** $65-$85 depending on application timing. **Application process:** The Admission Committee reviews each applicant based upon her (1) 7th and 8th grade transcripts for consistency and academic promise; (2) principal, 8th grade teacher, or counselor recommendations; (3) entrance examination results (exam given twice in January); (4) personal interview; and (5) clergy recommendation (optional). The Admission Committee meets in late February and finalizes acceptance in mid-March. **No. of freshman applications:** 300+. **Minimum admission requirements:** N/P. **Test required:** HSPT. **Preferences:** All being equal – Catholic school students, siblings, legacies. **"We are looking for** well-rounded students willing to commit to the Mercy tradition of academic excellence, hospitality, and service to others. Mercy High School encourages young women interested in a strong college prep curriculum to apply. Mercy High School, Burlingame, welcomes and admits students of any race, religion and national origin." **What kind of student do you best serve?** N/P.

Costs

Latest tuition: $15,325. **Sibling discount:** N/P. **Tuition increases:** N/P. **Other costs:** Registration $600; books $250 to $550; uniforms approx. $150-$250. **Percentage of students receiving financial aid:** 20%. **Financial aid deadline:** Early February. **Average grant:** N/P. **Percentage of grants half tuition or more:** 0.

School's Mission Statement/Goals

"Mercy High School, a Catholic college preparatory school, is dedicated to educating young women of all cultural and economic backgrounds for academic excellence, compassionate service, Christian leadership, global awareness, and lifelong learning. Rooted in Catherine McAuley's unique vision for women and the poor, Mercy High School is sponsored by the Sisters of Mercy. The faculty and staff work in collaboration with the Sisters of Mercy to create a Christian community which values hospitality and the dignity of each person. Mercy High School challenges its faculty, staff, and students to act with integrity and work for justice."

Academic Program

Courses offered (AP=Advanced Placement, H=Honors, (AP)=option, (H)=Honors option): **English:** English I-IV (H), AP English III, AP English IV; **Social Science:** AP U.S. History, AP American Government; **Math:** Algebra I (H), Geometry (H), Algebra II (H), Pre Calculus, Analysis/Calculus (H), AP Calculus; **Foreign language:** Spanish I-IV (H), AP Spanish IV, French I-IV (H), AP French IV, American Sign Language I – IV; **Science:** Biology 1(H), AP Biology, Chemistry (H), Physics (H), AP Physics, Forensic Science, Anatomy Physiology; **Arts:** Art I-III (H), Ceramics I-III (H), AP Studio Art; Chorale I, II, Advanced and Honors, Dance I-IV, Photography, Drama; Computer Science. **Computer lab/training:** Campus is fully networked. **Grading:** A-F. **Graduation requirements:** 4 years English and religion; 3 years social studies; 3 years math and science; 2 years foreign language; 1 year P.E. and fine arts; 1 semester computer science; 20 hours of community service per year. Graduation requirements are designed to meet or exceed the UC standards. **Average nightly homework (M-Th):** 2-4 hours. **Faculty:** N/P#; 10% male, 90% female; 57% hold master's degrees or higher. **Faculty ethnicity:** 87% Caucasian (non-Latino); 6% Latino; 4% Asian; 3% other. **Faculty selection/training:** "100% of teachers have credentials or master's degrees. All are required to take at least 3 semester units of continuing education every 3 years." **Teacher/student ratio:** 1:20. **Percentage of students enrolled in AP:** 35%; pass rate: N/P. **Senior class profile (mean):** SAT Math 538, SAT Critical Reading 567, SAT Writing N/P; GPA: N/P. **National Merit Scholarship Program:** 1 Scholar, 2 Commended. **College enrollment (last class):** 85% in 4-year, 15% in 2-year. **Recent colleges:** N/P.

Other Indicators the School Is Accomplishing its Goals

"Mercy High School is true to the school's roots in the Mercy tradition of excellence in education and leadership. Mercy graduates hold positions of importance such as United States Congresswoman and state Superior Court Judge. Mercy women are making significant contributions as doctors, nurses, CEO's and executive vice presidents, teachers, professors, administrators, lawyers, social workers, activists, philanthropists, Broadway actors, recording artists, and entrepreneurs. Mercy women are committed to giving back to their community, their world, and their school."

Campus/Campus Life

Campus description: Nestled in the Burlingame hills, the school is located on a 40-acre campus. Facilities in the high school complex include the historic Kohl Mansion, the two-story classroom "Wing," Russell Hall, Math Study Center, Reading Writing Center and Foreign Language Center, which supplement the library in Russell Hall, two multimedia labs and physics, chemistry, and biology labs. **Library:** 4,850 sq. ft; study space for 80 students, computers and laptops with Internet access; 75 periodical subscriptions; 12,000 print volumes; open to students 7:45 a.m.-4:30 p.m. **Sports facilities:** Grasilli Fitness Center, swimming pool, and tennis courts. **Theater/arts facilities:** Grassilli Dance Studio. **Open/closed campus:** Closed. **Lunches:** Caféteria with hot lunch service. **Bus service:** Public bus, SamTrans, Mercy shuttle from BART. **Uniform/dress code:** The required school uniform consists of a blue/black plaid knife pleat skirt, a polo shirt (long or short sleeves) with the school logo, pullover sweater/vest. Options include navy Bermuda shorts or navy slacks, various school sweatshirts, and navy or white turtleneck. **Co-curricular activities clubs:** California Scholarship Federation, National Honor Society, National Spanish Honor Society, National French Honor Society, Creative Writing Club, Girls Athletic Association, Heritage Council, Junior Statesmen of America, Bowling Club and Ski and Snowboarding Club (Coed/Tri-school), Ambassador Club, Students Against a Violent Society, Amnesty International, Cooking Club, Knitting Club, Philanthropy Club. **Foreign exchange program/internships:** None. **Community service:** Community service includes visiting the elderly, tutoring, coaching sports teams, donating blood, outdoor education, peer counseling and education camp counseling, volunteering at parish festivals, community service agencies, political campaigns, soup kitchens, or a local hospital. **Typical freshman schedule:** English I, Biology, mathematics, foreign language, religious studies, computer science, CORE and P.E.

Student Support Services

Counselor/student ratio (not including college counselors): N/P. **Counseling:** "Girls are assigned to a counselor during their freshman year with whom they will continue to consult until graduation. This arrangement has been very successful and allows a comforting 'constant' mentor. We are a close-knit community, and we work in conjunction with the students and the Academic Learning Team, which is comprised of the teachers, the counselor, and our administrators. If a student finds herself in academic difficulty, our Academic Learning Team will work together with the student and her parents to suggest alternatives and to bring our considerable support network to the table to help her improve. Students and parents are connected with our College Advisor early in their experience at Mercy in order to manage all steps in the college application process. Mercy students are able to visit with college representatives, on campus, as early as freshman and sophomore year." **Learning differences/disabilities:** "The Academic Mentoring Educational Support program works to support students who are able to manage the full academic program but may need some type of appropriate accommodation or support (limited space)."

Student Conduct and Health

Code of conduct: "While at Mercy or off-campus, students are expected to be respectful of themselves and others, and of the property of others. They are expected to show pride in Mercy by exhibiting considerate behavior and respect for Mercy and themselves. A student can expect

that disciplinary action will be taken if she is reported for misconduct on her way to or from school, at another school, or at a school
function." **How school handles drug/alcohol usage:** "If a student is
in possession of any illegal substance, the parents and or/guardians
will be notified and the school will take further appropriate action.
School action may be: expulsion, suspension, disciplinary probation,
referral to a substance abuse program, or a combination thereof."
Prevention/awareness programs: "We participate in the Community
of Concern program, a collaboration of high schools that provides
parents/students with information."

Summer Programs
Pre-high school (Tools for School) and a few high school academic
courses are offered in half or full days for one month during the
summer. High school students may take credit courses in math and
computer. For G6-12, Mercy offers a summer sports camp in four
one-week sessions (mid June-mid July). Students choose from half
or full days including volleyball, Tae Kwon Do, lacrosse, basketball,
swimming soccer, and water polo.

Parent Involvement
Parent participation: "There are many parent Fun Raisers and Fund
Raisers. Parents find that Mercy Burlingame is a place to be involved
and make new friends too. Parents are asked to donate 30 hours per
year for two-parent households; 15 hours per year for one-parent
households if they are not able to contribute monetarily." **Parent/
teacher communication:** "Grade-to-date reports are mailed to parents
twice a semester; in addition, parents are able to communicate with
teachers and the school administration through School-loop. Mercy's
website provides information for parents." **Parent education:** "Two to
three evening seminars each year for parents, touching upon areas of
youth/parent interest, such as college planning and stress reduction."
Donations: Parents are asked to give $900 per year.

Sports
Mercy students may try out for 26 athletic teams in the following 14
sports: water polo, tennis, cross-country, golf, volleyball, basketball,
soccer, softball, lacrosse, gymnastics, track, swimming, cheerleading,
and song leading.

What Sets School Apart From Others
"Mercy High School is one of thirty-nine schools throughout the
United States sponsored by the Sisters of Mercy. Located in the
historic Kohl Mansion, Mercy High School is a Catholic, college preparatory school for young women of all faiths. In the tradition of the
Sisters of Mercy, our students are encouraged to envision their future,
discover their talents, and grow in their faith through a challenging
and motivating curricular and co-curricular program. With a student

body of 500 young women, we provide a unique college preparatory community on the peninsula. Each girl is well known by her teachers and classmates, and is challenged to reach her greatest potential. Annually, 99% -100% of our graduates go on to outstanding colleges and universities throughout the country. Enhancing Mercy's exceptional environment for young women is the opportunity for our students to participate in a significant number of coeducational experiences through the Tri-School Program with Junipero Serra High School and Notre Dame Belmont. As members of the Tri-School community, our students take part in coed classes, retreats, service projects, student activities, performing and visual arts, as well as dances."

How Parents/Students Characterize School

Parent response: "Our expectations have not only been met, but greatly exceeded in a wide variety of ways. Our daughter has acquired maturity, self-confidence, and the desire to do well. ... The college prep program is outstanding. We are extremely pleased and impressed with the well-rounded curriculum." **Student response(s):** "Mercy has given me a taste of the various things the world has to offer. Because of this, I look upon my upcoming college experience with an anticipation to explore any realm of interest. Mercy has prepared me for the university lifestyle by showing me how to be independent, how to take the first step, and that a young woman can follow her dreams."

Mercy High School (San Francisco)

3250 19th Avenue
San Francisco, CA 94132
(415) 584-5929 *fax (415) 334-9726*
www.mercyhs.org

Dotty McCrea, Principal
Liz Belonogoff, Admissions Director, lbelonogoff@mercyhs.org

General

Girls Catholic day high school (63% Catholic). Founded in 1952. Non-profit, member WASC/WCEA and NCEA. **Enrollment:** 500. **Average class size:** 22. **Accreditation:** WASC/CAIS. **School year:** Late Aug.-May. **School day:** 8 a.m.-3:05 p.m. **Location:** Across from Stonestown Galleria, close to San Francisco State University. Accessible by Muni.

Student Body

Geographic breakdown (counties): 60% from San Francisco; 35% San Mateo; 4% from Contra Costa, 1% Sonoma. **Ethnicity:** 27% Caucasian; 23% Hispanic; 16% Asian; 16% Filipino; 5% African-American; 13% multiethnic. **International students (I-20 status):** 1%. **Middle schools (freshman):** 62% came from 31 K-8 Catholic elementary schools; 14%

from 7 private, non-parochial schools; 24% from 12 public middle/junior high schools.

Admission

Applications due: Mid-December (see website or call for date). **Application fee:** $80. **Application process:** Includes student essay, review of 7th and 8th grade transcripts, standardized test scores, HSPT results and confidential recommendation from applicant's school. **No. of freshman applications:** Approx. 400. **Minimum admission requirements:** "The admissions process is unique. Each student's attributes are valued and evaluated. No one quality is given preference over another. While strong academic performance is important, each student's essay, test scores, extra-curricular activities and recommendations are considered." **Test required:** HSPT. **Preferences:** None. "**We are looking for** college/university-bound, academically accomplished, socially aware young ladies." **What kind of student do you best serve?** "Girls who are interested in spiritual, intellectual, and creative growth opportunities. Girls who want to develop skills to become strong, independent women who can make a difference in the world."

Costs

Latest tuition: $12,500. **Sibling discount:** "Based on need." **Tuition increases:** Approx. 5-8%. **Other costs:** $225 book rental fee. **Percentage of students receiving financial aid:** 46%. **Financial aid deadline:** Call for date. **Average grant:** $2,500. "No. of tuition grants: 30." **Percentage of grants of half-tuition or more:** 11%.

School's Mission Statement/Goals

"The mission of Mercy High School-San Francisco is to educate women to serve in leadership roles and to instill the Mercy values of compassion, respect, and service. A Mercy education both challenges and fosters each student to share her gifts with the community, celebrate diversity, and defend social justice with competence and conscience."

Academic Program

Courses offered: "Courses in the following departments: Business/Computer Technology, English, Mathematics, P.E., Religious Studies, Science, Social Studies, Visual and Performing Arts and World Languages. There are 10 Honors classes and 16 AP classes. AP courses include: Calculus AB, Calculus BC, English Language, English Literature, Chemistry, Physics, U.S. History, French Language, Spanish Language, Spanish for Native Speakers, Spanish Literature, Studio Art (one-dimensional): Painting, Studio Art (two-dimensional): Ceramics." (N/P courses) **Computer lab/training:** N/P. **Grading:** A-F. **Graduation requirements:** "240 credits, 100 hours community service and participation in 2 Intersession courses." (N/P subjects) **Average nightly homework** (M-Th): G9: 2-3 hours; G10-12: 3-4 hours. **Faculty:** 43 f/t faculty members; 81% female, and 19% male; 22 p/t employees, 68% female, 22% male; 70% hold master's degrees; and 3% hold doctorates. **Faculty ethnicity:** N/P. **Faculty selection/training:** N/P. **Teacher/student ratio:** 1:20. **Percentage of students enrolled in AP:** N/P. **Senior class profile (mean):** N/P. **National Merit Scholarship Program:** "3-5 candidates each year." **College enrollment (last class):** "70% in 4-year, 30% in 2-year with plans to transfer to 4-year." **Recent colleges:** N/P.

Other Indicators the School is Accomplishing its Goals
"Ninety-nine percent of graduates go on to college. Mercy has more than 8,000 alumnae; 40-45 return for Career Day."

Campus/Campus Life
Campus description: The six-acre Mercy campus extends from 19th Avenue to Junipero Serra Boulevard and includes a three-story school building, extensive lawns, pavilion, multi-use athletic facility, tennis courts, gardens and statuary. In addition to classrooms, the building houses a library, chapel, resource center, cafeteria, science labs, technology centers, and counseling center. **Library:** More than 20,000 volumes; separate annex for individual as well as group study; open each school day from 8 a.m.-4 p.m. **Sports facilities:** The multi-use athletic facility includes full sports courts, separate locker and shower areas for home and visiting teams, curricular and co-curricular activity centers and outdoor tennis courts and prep shop. **Theater/arts facilities:** The Visual and Performing Arts Center has studios for ceramics, drawing, painting and dance, as well as a 470-seat theater. **Open/closed campus:** Closed. **Lunches:** A full service cafeteria is open daily from 7:30 a.m.-2 p.m. It also contains vending machines. **Bus service:** Public buses and streetcars. **Uniforms/dress code:** "The uniform includes plaid skirt, white blouse or white polo shirt, navy pants optional, navy sweater or vest. Shoes must be within guidelines. Monthly casual and dressy free-dress days are announced." **Co-curricular activities/clubs:** Anime, Math Club, Photo Club, Web Squad, Speech Club, Amnesty International, Green Club, Multicultural, Dolce, Literary Magazine, Yearbook, National Honor Society, Mercy Athletic Association, Performing Arts Association. **Foreign exchange programs/internships:** None. **Community service:** 100 hours required. (N/P examples) **Typical freshman schedule:** N/P.

Student Support Services
Counselor/student ratio (not including college counselors): 1:191. **Counseling:** "Mercy's counselors provide academic, personal, college, and career counseling." **Learning differences/disabilities:** "Mercy High School does not have a formal resource program for students with diagnosed learning differences. Admission of students with learning challenges is made on an individual basis."

Student Conduct and Health

Code of conduct: "The student handbook requires reverence and respect for self and others, prohibits racism and/or prejudiced behavior and harassment of any kind, and prohibits smoking on campus and within a half-mile of the school. No headphones, cell phones, or pagers." **How school handles drugs/alcohol:** "Any student found dealing in or selling drugs or alcohol will be expelled. Any student involved in possession or use of drugs or alcohol at school or during a school function will be sent home immediately in the company of a parent or guardian and is subject to expulsion. The Principal makes the final decision following consultation with counselors, the Dean of Students, the student and parents/guardians." **Prevention/ awareness programs:** "Drug and alcohol abuse prevention along with AIDS awareness programs are sponsored by the counseling department, the religion department, and student government."

Summer Programs

"Mercy offers a four-week coed academic summer program for students in G6-12 wishing to review, make up, or preview an academic course. It includes math, English, science, foreign languages, driver's ed, Internet Research, Introduction to High School Math and English, as well as SAT prep. Online classes are also available."

Parent Involvement

Parent participation: "Parents are encouraged to participate in the Parent Guild, which supports Mercy with volunteers as needed and with various annual fundraisers." **Parent/teacher communication:** "Report cards at each semester include grades, credits, and teachers' comments. Progress reports are sent mid-semester for all students. Parent/teacher conferences upon request." **Parent education:** The Counseling Department and the Parent Guild sponsor various programs with parenting/teen speakers throughout the school year. **Donations:** "Parents are asked to give a minimum of $350 as a tax-deductible contribution annually."

Sports

Students compete in the Private School Athletic League. Mercy offers volleyball, tennis, cross-country, basketball, soccer, track and field, and softball.

What Sets School Apart From Others

"Mercy High School-San Francisco is a small, safe, and caring environment with a college preparatory curriculum with Honors and Advanced Placement opportunities, an extensive visual and performing arts program, an advanced technology department, and an outstanding library. Mercy students can choose from over 40 elective courses, diverse club activities, and competitive athletic teams. The beautiful Mercy campus is easily accessible by public transportation. Mercy's campus has on-site parking for faculty, staff and visitors." • "Mercy sponsors a weeklong intersession every other year. Participation in two sessions is a graduation requirement. The purpose is to enrich the curriculum beyond the walls of the classroom into the greater community. Offerings have included theater performances, trips to Washington, D.C., backpacking trips, Oregon Shakespeare Festival, Northern and Southern California college campus tours, equestrian camp, shadowing a professional (medicine, business, education), foreign film study, off-shore marine life and biology. Each course has a separate fee; scholarships are available."

How Parents/Students Characterize School
Parent response(s): "In a recent parent survey, 97% of all parents surveyed rated Mercy good to excellent in meeting the spiritual, academic, and social needs of their daughters." **Student response(s):** "In a recent student survey, 80% of Mercy students rated both their educational experiences and student services (library, computer, and science labs, Resource Center, clubs, student government, assemblies) as good or higher."

Mid-Peninsula High School
1340 Willow Road
Menlo Park, CA 94025
(650) 321-1991 *fax (650) 321-9921*
www.mid-pen.com

Dr. Douglas C. Thompson, Head of School
Director of Admissions, ext. 108, info@mid-pen.com

General
Coed day high school. Independent. Founded in 1979. Nonprofit, member CAIS. **Enrollment:** Approx. 125. **Average class size:** 15. **Accreditation:** WASC/CAIS. **School year:** Sept.-June. **School day:** 9:30 a.m.-3:10 p.m. **Location:** In Menlo Park, accessible by local buses and CalTrain shuttle.

Student Body
Geographic breakdown (counties): 5% from San Francisco; 1% from Marin; 40% from San Mateo; 30% from Palo Alto and Menlo Park; 10% from Fremont/Union City; 14% from San Jose area. **Ethnicity:** 66% Caucasian; 5% Asian; 17% Latino; 9% African-American; 3% biracial. **Foreign student (I-20 status):** None. **Middle schools (freshman):** 60% came from public middle schools; 40% from private, non-parochial schools; none from parochial schools. (N/P # schools)

Admission

Applications due: Approx. January 15 (call for date). Rolling admissions throughout the year. **Application fee:** None. **Application process:** Interview, application, student shadow, letters of recommendation, grades/test scores. **No. of freshman applications:** 50 (# places N/P). **Minimum admission requirements:** "Each applicant is considered on an individual basis." **Preferences:** None. **"We are looking for** students who are motivated to do well; are looking for a school that fits their goals; and who want to work in a small, nurturing school environment—one in which students are well known, respected and happy." **What kind of student do you best serve?** "Students do well when they are a part of the team we have with our Core teacher program, learning to communicate with their teachers and parents for success. Students who want to work closely with teachers who care about them. Students who want individuality, to be celebrated and respected, and participate in our community of learners."

Costs

Latest tuition: Approx. $25,000. **Sibling discount:** 10%. **Tuition increases:** Approx. 5-7%. **Other costs:** Registration and student activities fee approx. $1,400. **Percentage of students receiving financial aid:** 25%. **Financial aid deadline:** Approx. January 15 (call for date). **Average grant:** N/P. **Percentage of of grants half-tuition or more:** N/P.

School's Mission Statement/Goals

"Mid-Peninsula High School, a community for learning, offers students a stimulating, nurturing, safe environment that empowers them to reach their full academic and social potential. As a small, caring, educational community, we work to strengthen relationships between students, their families, and the school. We recognize and understand unique learning styles and create flexible academic programs designed to meet each student's needs. It is our expectation that Mid-Peninsula High School students will become capable, self-directed individuals who care about themselves, their families, and their communities."

Academic Program

Courses offered: N/P. **Computer/lab training:** N/P. **Grading:** A-F. **Graduation requirements:** "Standard requirements based on California State Standards: 215 credits to graduate, 10 credits per one year class." **Average nightly homework (M-Th):** 30 min.-2 hours; study hall on campus with teacher tutoring available daily all year. **Faculty:** 18. (N/P gender, degrees) **Faculty ethnicity:** "African-American, Caucasian and Latino." (N/P %) **Faculty selection/training:** "Interview, rigorous referral and background check, current credential and/or degree(s) in field(s) applied for are required." **Teacher/student ratio:** 1:15. **Percentage of students enrolled in AP:** N/P. "All AP courses available online." **Senior class profile (mean):** SAT Math 518, SAT Reading 556, SAT Writing 520; GPA: 3.20 **National Merit Scholarship Program:** None.

College enrollment (last class): 90% (N/P 4- yr, 2-yr). **Recent colleges:** UC, CSU, UOP, Willamette U, CCA, and Academy of Art U.

Other Indicators the School is Accomplishing its Goals: N/P.

Campus/Campus Life

Campus description: New two-story building with large field/lawn. Two science labs for biology and chemistry/physics, a student center, and computer lab. **Library:** Teachers maintain resources in each subject area in classrooms. Enrichment Center with Internet access. **Sports facilities:** Full gymnasium and sports field. **Theater/arts facilities:** Art studio. **Open/closed campus:** Closed. **Lunches:** Students buy hot lunch from catered service. **Bus service:** Public. **Uniforms/dress code:** None. **Co-curricular activities/clubs:** Sports, art, drama, prom committee, peer counselors, yearbook, office aides, student barbecues. **Foreign exchange program/internships:** None. **Community service:** 10 hours per year or more required. (N/P examples) **Typical freshman schedule:** English 9, Art I, Algebra I, P.E., study hall, World Studies I.

Student Support Services

Counselor/student ratio (not including college counselors): N/P. **Counseling:** "Counseling is done by the Homeroom/Advisory (Core) teacher; one full-time counselor, also peer counseling." **Learning differences/disabilities:** "Speak with the Director of Admissions to determine if applicant meets the profile of the students with learning differences/disabilities that Mid-Peninsula accepts. We are a college preparatory high school; however, approximately 25% of our students have diagnosed learning differences. We are not a facility to work with Special Day Students. We do not have a certification to work with Special Needs students, but we accept many students with learning differences and disabilities and have a learning specialist to support and understand their accommodations in a preparatory environment. Most of these students go on to attend 2- or 4-year colleges."

Student Conduct and Health

Code of conduct: "Each student and family signs a code of conduct agreement." **How school handles drugs/alcohol:** "Student dismissal, recommend drug/alcohol evaluation and counseling. Expulsion/Zero Tolerance." **Prevention/ awareness programs:** "Recommend several local programs and counselors in the Bay Area."

Summer Programs

Five-week summer program. Students in G9-12 can earn 10 credits in English, math, history, government, and art.

Parent Involvement

Parent participation: "Monthly parent meetings. Parents plan events such as prom, Back-to-School evenings, and BBQs. They assist with mailings and community service and act as a referral for new parents." **Parent/teacher communication:** "Each parent has an advisor (core teacher) to speak with weekly all year." **Parent education:** N/P. **Donations:** N/P

Sports
Boys and girls basketball, volleyball; coed soccer, cross-country, and track; boys baseball; girls softball.

What Sets School Apart From Others
"Mid-Peninsula High School is distinguished primarily by its small size, which allows for a high degree of individual attention; for its flexibility of program, which encourages students to take charge of their own education; and for its Core program, which allows for intensive advising and constant interaction between students and their teachers."

How Parents/Students Characterize School
Parent response(s): "This school offers a safe, respectful and kind environment for my child." "We appreciate the flexible, supportive, unique, and creative atmosphere of Mid-Peninsula High School." "My child feels a special kind of support here." **Student response(s):** "I have a chance to get involved in anything I am interested in from sports to special committees." "I have less overall stress here. I feel like I can take charge of my learning. The teachers want you to succeed." "This is a great, nonjudgmental place. The programs are inclusive, and the school adapts to your needs." "This school is not pretentious, and the peer tutoring program is great."

Moreau Catholic High School
27170 Mission Boulevard
Hayward, CA 94544
(510) 881-4320 *fax (510) 581-5669*
www.moreaucatholic.org

Mr. Terry Lee, Principal
Ms. Tara Rolle, Director of Admissions, trolle@moreaucatholic.org

General
Coed Catholic day high school (parochial, 75% Catholic). Sponsored by Brothers of the Holy Cross. Founded in 1965. Nonprofit. **Enrollment:** Approx. 910. **Average class size:** 24. **Accreditation:** WASC. **School year:** Aug.-June. **School day:** Alternating schedule 8 a.m.-2:35 p.m. or 8 a.m.-2:15 p.m. **Location:** On Mission Boulevard in South Hayward, accessible by public transportation. Buses to the Hayward and South Hayward BART stations stop near the school.

Student Body

Geographic breakdown (counties): 97% from Alameda; 3% from Santa Clara and San Joaquin. **Ethnicity:** 27% Caucasian (non-Latino); 34% Asian; 12% Latino; 4% African-American; 23% multi-ethnic. **International students (I-20 status):** 3. **Middle schools (freshman):** 21% came from public middle schools; 35% from private, non-parochial schools; 64% from parochial schools. (N/P # schools)

Admission

Applications due: Mid-December (call for date). **Application fee:** $65. **Application process:** Applications are standardized within the Diocese of Oakland and are available in the fall. A parent information evening and open house are held in October. Students must take an admission test, and acceptance notifications are mailed in mid-March. **No. of freshman applications:** N/P. **Minimum admission requirements:** "Applicants are considered on an individual basis." **Test required:** HSPT. **Preferences:** "Siblings, legacies, and students whose families support the mission of the school." **"We are looking for** students who have a combination of character, willingness to learn and study, and a concern for others. Entrance requirements are not necessarily based solely on intellectual ability." **What kind of student do you best serve?** N/P.

Costs

Latest tuition: $11,544 payable in 10 or 12 payments. **Sibling discount:** None. Grants are available for families with two or more children. **Tuition increases:** 2-4%. **Other costs:** Books approx. $350 (they may be sold back at the end of the year, laptop (leased or purchased through school), materials fees for some classes. **Percentage of students receiving financial aid:** 20%. **Financial aid deadline:** Approx. February 4 (call for date). **Average grant:** N/P. **Percentage of grants half-tuition or more:** N/P. "Need-based financial aid and merit scholarships are available. The school offers the Father Moreau Catholic Scholarship, which is merit-based, and the Brother Gary Stone Scholarship which is merit- and need-based."

School's Mission Statement/Goals

"Moreau Catholic is dedicated to the legacy and values of the Congregation of Holy Cross and its founder Father Basil Moreau. We are a college preparatory school committed to outstanding achievement. As a community of faith, we prepare our students through academic, social, and spiritual learning experiences that form and transform them as they become responsible citizens of our global community."

Academic Program

"A comprehensive, college-preparatory curriculum designed to qualify graduates for entry into the University of California." **Courses offered:** N/P. **Computer lab/training:** "Two dedicated computer labs with 150 computers for students and 1:1 laptop program; one teacher technology lab with 6 computers and each teacher provided laptop. Academic courses are available through the Computer Science department." **Grading:** A-F. **Graduation requirements:** "270 units, including 4 years English; 3.5 years theology; 3 years math; 2 years social studies, science (life and physical), P.E., and foreign language; .5 year computer science; 80 hours community service. In addition, 12th graders must demonstrate achievement on the 12th grade level or above on a standardized achievement test in the areas of reading, language arts, and math. Students are tested in October and re-tested in January. Those not demonstrating proficiency receive an 'amended diploma' indicating this area of deficiency." **Average nightly homework (M-Th):** 2-3 hours. **Faculty:** N/P. **Faculty ethnicity:** N/P. **Faculty selection/training:** N/P. **Teacher/student ratio:** 1:18. **Percentage of students enrolled in AP:** 32%; pass rate: 64% received scores of 3 or above. **Senior class profile (mean):** N/P. **College enrollment (last class):** 77% in 4-year, 21% in 2-year. **Recent colleges:** N/P.

Other Indicators the School is Accomplishing its Goals

"Moreau Catholic was founded and is sponsored by the Congregation of Holy Cross. This religious congregation came to the United States and began its educational mission by starting a college in South Bend, Indiana — College of Notre Dame. The goal for every Holy Cross school is to educate the whole person. This means not only the intellect, but also the artistic, physical, social, and spiritual as well. Moreau Catholic continues that tradition by meeting the life needs of every individual student."

Campus/Campus Life

Campus description: "Situated on 14 acres in Hayward, the school has seven buildings. Besides the main building, which houses classrooms and the library and chapel, there are two gymnasiums, a student center, a center for the fine arts, and an auditorium." **Library:** 1,026 sq. ft.; study space for 75; 14 computers; online catalog; 75 periodical subscriptions, 15,000 print volumes; Internet access. Open to students 7:30 a.m.-4:30 p.m. **Sports facilities:** Two gymnasiums and sports playing fields. **Theater/arts facilities:** Center for fine arts and auditorium dedicated solely to fine arts performances. **Open/closed campus:** Closed. **Lunches:** N/P. **Bus service:** None. **Uniforms/dress code:** Apparel choices for male and female students include a choice of polo shirts or oxford type collared shirts, pants, shorts, skirts and skorts in khaki or solid dark colored cotton twill. **Co-curricular activities/clubs:** Activities include Academic Challenge Team, African-American Alliance, Asian Student Union, Band and Color Guard, California Scholarship Federation, Chess Club, Chinese Film Club, Competition Club, EarthWise, Food & Film Club, Hiking Club, Interact Club, Junior State, Kaisahan, Link Crew, Math Club, National Honor Society, Newspaper, Nuestra Gente, Okonome Anime, Polynesian Club, Portuguese Club,

Academic Challenge Team (Quiz Bowl Club), Ski & Snowboard Club, Step Club, Student Ambassadors, Student Government, Theater Club, Yearbook. **Foreign exchange program/internships:** Foreign exchange program with Funibashi, Japan, the sister city of Hayward, CA. **Community service:** 80-hour requirement fulfilled by providing service to nonprofit agencies. (N/P examples) **Typical freshman schedule:** English, visual and performing arts, foreign language or study skills, math, P.E., Theology, World History.

Student Support Services

Counselor/student ratio (not including college counselors): 1:226. **Counseling:** "Four full-time counselors provide academic, personal, and college and career counseling." **Learning disabilities/differences:** "Accommodations provided with official documentation."

Student Conduct and Health

Code of conduct: "In addition to prohibiting illegal conduct, the school prohibits habitual profanity or vulgarity and persistent violation of the dress code. In addition, students may be suspended or expelled for violations of the law or 'actions or attitudes directly contrary to the mission of the School.'" **How school handles drugs/alcohol:** "In the case of a discipline violation concerning drugs, including alcohol, the students may be required to undergo a professional assessment. Failure to undergo the assessment will result in the student's dismissal. The result of this assessment will be among the factors considered to determine the student's continued enrollment." **Prevention / awareness programs:** "Moreau Catholic High School is a member of the Northern California Community of Concern, a consortium of high schools which provides information and literature to parents and students. Individual, family counseling and assistance is provided."

Summer Programs

A summer school program is provided to incoming students who need to strengthen a skill such as math or English. There are a limited number of class offerings for current students needing to make up a course because of a non-passing grade as well as for enrichment.

Parent Involvement

Parent participation: "Parents are not required to give hours to the school; all such participation is voluntary." **Parent/teacher communication:** "The school uses Apple's Power School program: an online, real-time grade and attendance program. Both students and parents receive unique passwords that allow them to keep abreast of current grades and attendance as well as to access teachers through e-mail." **Parent education:** N/P. **Donations:** "Parents are encouraged to make donations to the annual fund."

Sports

"41 teams staffed by 59 coaches. Teams compete in the Hayward Area Athletic League. Boys play football, cross-country, basketball, soccer, badminton, baseball, golf, track and field, swimming, tennis, and volleyball; girls play tennis, cross-country, rally squad, volleyball, basketball, soccer, softball, badminton, swimming, and track and field."

What Sets School Apart From Others

"A Holy Cross education seeks to achieve three specific, but integrated goals: information, formation, and transformation. Information is comprised of the knowledge and skills communicated to students which is aimed at preparing them for life and work in the future. By formation, it is meant that the intellectual, social, and spiritual development of students is found in every aspect of school life. Finally, transformation is where the values and qualities of life which students are taught and encouraged to embrace will eventually lead the individual student to be an agent of change for the common good."

How Parents/Students Characterize School: N/P.

Notre Dame High School (Belmont)

1540 Ralston Avenue
Belmont, CA 94002-1995
(650) 595-1913 *fax (650) 595-2643*
www.ndhsb.org

Rita Gleason, Principal/President
Shyrl McCormick, Director of Admission, admissions@ndhsb.org

General

Girls Catholic day high school (75% Catholic). Founded in 1851. Nonprofit, member BAIHS. **Enrollment:** Approx. 630. **Average class size:** 24. **Accreditation:** WASC. **School year:** Aug.-June. **School day:** 8 a.m.-2:50 p.m. **Location:** On Ralston Ave. between Hwys. 101 and 280. The school provides a free shuttle in the morning from SamTrans bus stops on El Camino and Ralston, and Ralston and Alameda de las Pulgas, and the Belmont CalTrain station. The stops are a 10-minute walk from the school. Students with cars are assigned parking spaces.

Student Body

Geographic breakdown (counties): 96% from San Mateo; 1% from Marin; 1% from San Francisco; 2% from Santa Clara. **Ethnicity:** "28% minority." (N/P ethnic groups) **International students (I-20 status):** 0. **Middle schools (freshman):** 30% came from 16 public middle schools; 9% from 10 private, non-parochial schools; 61% from 19 parochial schools.

Admission
Applications due: Early January (call for date). **Application fee:** $50; transfer/late fee $100. **Application process:** N/P. Call for brochure. **No. of freshman applications:** 350 for 150 places. Five new students were admitted to G10, 3 to G11. **Minimum admission requirements:** "We do not accept students with Ds/Fs on 8th grade transcripts." **Test required:** HSPT. **Preferences:** Catholics, siblings, legacies. **"We are looking for** young women who demonstrate an aptitude and motivation to commit to a college preparatory program with a willingness to participate in religious and co-curricular activities." **What kind of student do you best serve?** "Young women who want to grow and develop in a challenging yet comfortable single gender environment."

Costs
Latest tuition: $14,950 payable in 12 payments. **Sibling discount:** None. **Tuition increases:** 3-8%. **Other costs:** $300-$600 for books; $300-$400 for uniforms. **Percentage of students receiving financial aid:** 25%. **Average grant:** $1,500. **Percentage of grants half-tuition or more:** N/P. "Honors at Entrance scholarships are based upon standardized test scores and strong academic records. They are renewable if the student maintains a 3.2 GPA. Citizenship scholarships (nonrenewable) are awarded to Catholic students from elementary schools who exemplify the values of the founders of the school, the Sisters of Notre Dame de Namur. Incoming alumnae daughters' scholarships (nonrenewable) are available to daughters of alumnae."

School's Mission Statement/Goals
"Notre Dame High School is an independent Catholic school dedicated to the educational mission of St. Julie Billiart and the Sisters of Notre Dame de Namur. We are a caring and compassionate community committed to justice and peace while developing responsible women of active faith, strong intellect, and Christian leadership. We develop the gifts and talents of each student and foster Gospel values in an environment of academic excellence and mutual respect."

Academic Program
"Students take a minimum of six classes each semester. In addition to classes offered at Notre Dame, students may take part in a Tri-School program, attending classes at Mercy High School in Burlingame (girls) and Junipero Serra High School in San Mateo (boys)." **Courses offered** (AP=Advanced Placement, H=Honors, (AP)=AP option, (H)=Honors option): **English:** English I -II(H), English III-British Literature (AP), English IV-World Literature (AP), Creative Writing; **Math:** Algebra I (Accelerated), Geometry (H), Advanced Algebra (H), Statistics, Functions/Statistics/Trigonometry, Pre-Calculus (H), Intro to Calculus, AP Calculus AB, Calculus BC, Advanced Mathematics Independent Study; **P.E.:** P.E. I, Aerobics, Self Defense, Beginning Dance A; **Religious Studies:** Hebrew Scripture, Living the Gospel, Faith and Morality,

Church History, Social Justice, Women in Relationships, Spirituality and Storytelling, Bioethics, World Religions, Retreat Leadership, and Ministry/Leadership/Service; **Science:** Human Biology, Biology (H/AP), Environmental Science in Action I-II, Physical Science, Chemistry (H/AP), Physics (H), Introduction to Sports Medicine; **Social Science:** World History (H), Modern World History (H), U.S. History (AP), U.S. Government, AP U.S. Government and Politics, Economics, Psychology; **Arts:** AP Art History, Beginning Art A/B, Intermediate Art A/B, Advanced Art, Honors Art, AP Studio Art, Sculpture A/B, Beginning Chorus A/B, Intermediate Chorus A/B, Advanced Chorus, Honors Chorus, Beginning Dance A/B, Intermediate Dance A/B, Advanced Dance, Honors Dance, In-Step Performance Team, Photography A/B, Video Production, Orchestra; **Computers:** Computer Applications, Web Page Design, Programming in C++, Introduction to Java Programming, Independent Study; **Foreign Languages:** French I-III, French III H, French IV, AP French Language, AP French Literature, Spanish I-III, Spanish III H, Spanish IV, AP Spanish Language; **Other:** Yearbook, Journalism, Driver's Ed. In addition, students may take Anatomy and Physiology, American Sign Language, Non-Darkroom Photography, Folk and Social Dance at Mercy High School, Burlingame; at Junipero Serra High School in San Mateo: Jazz Band, Advanced Band, Virtual Enterprise. Intersession, offered every other year, provides students with on- and off-campus experiences such as Yosemite Institute, Outdoor Education, family trips, and other activities. **Computer lab/training:** The school has two computer labs with 25 PowerMacs each. The library has 25 computers with Internet access and 25 iBooks available with wireless Internet access for classroom use. **Grading:** A-F. **Graduation requirements:** "Graduation requirements are designed to meet UC-Berkeley admission requirements. 240 credits are required including 4 years English and religious studies; 3 years math, science, social science; 1-2-year visual and performing arts (AP Art History or two sequential courses from either the visual or performing arts strand); 2-3 years electives; 2 years foreign language; 1 year P.E.; 100 hours community service." **Average nightly homework (M-Th):** 1.5 - 3 hours. **Faculty:** N/P #; 37% male, 63% female; 62% hold master's degrees. **Faculty ethnicity:** 92% Caucasian (non-Latino); 6% Latino; 2% Asian. **Faculty selection/training:** "The school requires faculty members to hold a teaching credential in their subject area and to attend 4 in-services per year. The school has a cooperative arrangement with Notre Dame de Namur University for high school teachers to take graduate courses." **Teacher/student ratio:** 1:15. **Percentage of students enrolled in AP:** 25%; pass rate 67.4%. **Senior class profile (mean):** SAT Math 545, SAT Critical Reading 532, SAT Writing 560; GPA: 3.0, (unweighted). **National Merit Scholarship Program:** Last year one student received the National Merit Award and five students were Commended. **College enrollment (last class):** 88% in 4-year, 12% in 2-year. **Recent (last 4 yrs) colleges:** American U, Arizona SU, Azusa Pacific U, Barnard, Boston C, Boston U, Bucknell U, Cal Poly-Pomona,

California Baptist U, CCA, Cal Institute of Technology, Cal Lutheran, Canada C, Carnegie Mellon, Carroll C, Chapman, SFCC, Claremont McKenna, Colgate, C of San Mateo, Columbia, Cornell, CSU (Chico, East Bay, Fullerton, Long Beach, LA, Northridge, Sacramento, Sonoma, SD, SF, SJ), Dartmouth, Dominican, Dublin City U, Emerson, Foothill, Fordham, Furman, George Washington, Gonzaga, Grinnell, Harvard, Harvey Mudd, Hillsdale, Hofstra, Howard, Johns Hopkins, Lake Forest, Lehigh, Lewis and Clark, Linfield, Loyola Marymount, Loyola (New Orleans), Marist, Marymount, Menlo, Mills, Mount St. Mary's, Northeastern, Northern Arizona, Northwestern, Notre Dame de Namur, Occidental, Oregon SU, Pepperdine, Providence, Purdue, Regis, SFAI, Santa Barbara City C, Santa Clara, School of Visual Arts, Scripps C, Seattle, Simmons C, St. John's, St. Louis, St. Mary's, Stanford, Syracuse, The Art Institute of California, FIDM, U-the Arts, Tulane, U-Arizona, U-British Columbia, UC (Berkeley, Davis, Irvine, LA, Merced, Riverside, SD, Santa Barbara, Santa Cruz), U-Colorado, U-Denver, U-Hawaii, U-Iowa, U-Manchester, U-Nevada, Notre Dame, U-Oregon, U-Pennsylvania, U-Portland, U-Puget Sound, U-Redlands, USD, USF, USC, U-Texas, UOP, University of Victoria, UVA, U-Washington, Vanderbilt, Wake Forest, Warren Wilson, West Valley, Whittier, and Yale.

Other Indicators the School is Accomplishing its Goals

"99-100% of graduating seniors enroll in college; 6-year WASC accreditation."

Campus/Campus Life

Campus description: The school occupies a three-story building built in 1928 and a two story extension built in 2003 on the former Ralston-Sharon Estate in Belmont, a suburban community between San Francisco and San Jose. The building, surrounded by 11.6 acres including lawns and wooded areas, borders the Notre Dame Elementary School and Notre Dame de Namur University. The high school building includes a dining room/soda fountain, technology center, a greenhouse, two gymnasiums, an outdoor swimming pool, cafeteria, and garden courtyard. **Library:** 3,850 sq. ft.; study space for 95 students; 70 periodical subscriptions; 12,222 print volumes; 26 computers with Internet access; online catalog. Open to students 7 a.m.-5:30 p.m. **Sports facilities:** Two gymnasiums (one seats 900, team rooms and lockers), an outdoor swimming pool, a softball and soccer field. **Theater/arts facilities:** Art room, ceramics lab, orchestra/chorus room, and TV studio. The school uses the university's theater. **Open/closed campus:** Closed. **Lunches:** Hot lunches are available daily in two locations on campus. **Bus service:** Van pick-up at El Camino/Ralston every morning at no cost. **Uniform/dress code:** Everyday uniforms: navy or khaki skorts, pants, or Capri pants, white blouse, white or navy polo shirts, navy fleece vest, school sweatshirts, tennis shoes. Formal dress: navy blue skort, white blouse, navy sweater, logo socks, and black, blue, or brown shoes. No more than two piercings per ear, no other visible body piercings, and no visible tattoos allowed. No shaved heads or unnatural dye colors. **Co-curricular activities/clubs:** The school shares social and other activities with Mercy High School in Burlingame (girls) and Junipero Serra High School in San Mateo (boys). This tri-school program provides coeducational experiences in academics, Campus Ministry, athletics, performing arts, and student activities. Approx. 65% of students are involved in student leadership. Organizations include California Scholarship Federation, National Honor Society, Mixed Chorus, Tri-Music Honor Society, In-Step, Literary Magazine, Link Crew, and SOS. Clubs include Ambassadors Club, Anime, Art Club, Bowling Club, Chess Club, Club SNDWICH, Culture Club, Ecology Club, Film Club, French Club, Hip Hop Dance Club, Improv Club, Italian Club, Jewelry Club, Junior State of America, Knitting Club, Middle Eastern Awareness Club, PATCH, Potterteers, Rock Climbing Club, Science Club, STAND, Unidas, Chorus, Tri-School Mixed Chorus, Literary Magazine, Yearbook, and Newspaper. **Foreign exchange program/internships:** None. **Community service:** A weekly bulletin lists opportunities. Group opportunities are provided by the Campus Ministry staff three times a semester. **Typical freshman schedule:** Religion, English, World History, math, science, foreign language, elective.

Student Support Services

Counselor/student ratio (not including college counselors): 1:160. **Counseling:** "The school has 4 full-time counselors, 2 full-time and 1 part-time campus ministers, an administrative assistant, and student peer tutors. Freshmen meet in small groups during their first quarter with a counselor or member of the Campus Ministry to ease the transition to high school and to learn of campus resources. Personal crisis counseling is available to students in need; the department also makes available printed materials on issues relating to adolescence, referrals to outside agencies, and counseling and mediation. For academic counseling, students meet once a year with a counselor to plan their schedule for the following year, and meet during the year on an as-needed basis. A college counselor and a scholarship coordinator assist students with college planning through visits with college representatives, college catalogs, and online college and scholarship information." **Learning disabilities/differences:** "The school admits five students who have special learning needs to the 9th grade each year. These students have their own counselor for their four years at Notre Dame to assist them through the school's academic program. Individual learning style compensations are also given. No accommodations are given, however, in terms of requirements. All students in the school, with or without learning disabilities/differences, are expected to complete all graduation requirements."

Student Conduct and Health

Code of conduct: "The school has a policy of academic honesty adopted from Stanford's Honor Code." **How school handles drugs/alcohol:** "On the first offense, the student is suspended for 3 days minimum and placed on probation. Student and parents must agree to a drug evaluation and mandatory drug testing; the student may not return to school until results are received by the school. For second offenses, the student is liable for immediate expulsion. Knowingly being present where alcoholic beverages or intoxicants are being used is prohibited by the school. Selling or dealing drugs on campus or at school-sponsored trips or activities results in immediate expulsion and police involvement." **Prevention/awareness programs:** "Campus Ministry presents Friday Nite Live, which promotes healthy living and drug and alcohol education. AIDS education is provided in religious studies classes. These issues are addressed at Parent Education Evenings."

Summer Programs

Notre Dame offers coed summer school for students entering G9-12 from mid-June to Mid-July. Classes include pre-high school courses in English and math, driver's ed, P.E., and sports camp. The academic courses are designed for students who need remediation, review, or to preview certain courses and are not for credit unless previously approved. Students may take 2 courses, each meeting 2.5 hours per day. The school also offers a summer enrichment program for girls entering G6-8.

Parent Involvement

Parent participation: "No mandatory hours. Parents are invited to be involved in a volunteer capacity." **Parent/teacher communication:** "Report cards are distributed 3 times each semester (6 per year). Only the semester grades are recorded on the permanent transcript. Parents may request mid-grading period progress reports." **Parent education:** "Monthly parent meetings on a wide range of topics relating to teenagers; grade level college planning evening meetings." **Donations:** "Parent Partnership Program: This voluntary pledge program reinforces the partnership formed between Notre Dame and the parent body. The expectation is that all families participate at some level in this 100% tax deductible commitment."

Sports

The school competes in the West Catholic Athletic League on the varsity, junior varsity, and freshman levels in cross-country, tennis, volleyball, water polo, basketball, golf, soccer, softball, swimming, and track and field. Cheerleading is a part of the athletic program, and the team competes on the varsity and junior varsity levels. There are more than 500 roster spots available for students on 23 teams.

What Sets School Apart From Others
"As a single-gender institution, Notre Dame, Belmont is committed to the development of responsible women of active faith, strong intellect, and Christian leadership. In our challenging academic environment, our young women separate academic concerns from social concerns, learn from a greater number of same-gender academic role models, and assume leadership positions without fear of upsetting gender stereotypes."

How Parents/Students Characterize School
Parent response(s): "Our daughter received a quality education in a caring environment. The single-sex environment contributed to her positive self-esteem and confidence. Thank you!" "Two daughters presently at ND, both happy and doing well. Couldn't ask for more than that!" "I wanted my daughter to get the best education along with a spiritual experience, and I believe deeply that NDHS gave her that!" **Student response(s):** "At Notre Dame we have sought out and discovered ourselves—our hopes and dreams, our values and faith, our courage and our love." "I have received a strong foundation at Notre Dame and gained precious life skills in analytical thinking. I am proud to be a Tiger and part of the Notre Dame tradition." "Notre Dame offers it all—engaging academics, spirited activities, and strong athletics. What I've learned in my time at Notre Dame will allow me to continue learning and competing in college and beyond."

Notre Dame High School (San Jose)
596 South Second Street
San Jose, CA 95112
(408) 294-1113 *fax (408) 293-9779*
www.ndsj.org

Mary Beth Riley, Principal
Diana Hernandez, Admissions, dhernandez@ndsj.org

General
Girls Catholic day high school. (63% Catholic). Founded in 1851. Nonprofit, sponsored by the Sisters of Notre Dame de Namur. **Enrollment:** 630. **Average class size:** 27. **Accreditation:** WASC. **School year:** Aug.-June. **School day:** 7:50 a.m.-2:45 p.m. (dismissal is 1:30 p.m. on Friday). **Location:** In downtown San Jose, near Hwys. 280 and 101, 5 blocks from San Jose State.

Student Body
Geographic breakdown (counties): 87% from Santa Clara County; 9% from East Bay counties; 4% other South Bay counties. **Ethnicity:** 38% Caucasian (non-Latina); 21% Filipina; 11% Hispanic; 10% Chinese;

9% Vietnamese; 8% Asian-Indian; 3% African-American; 1% multi-ethnic. **International students (I-20 status):** None. **Middle schools (freshman):** 20% came from 24 public middle schools; 32% from 15 private, non-parochial schools; 48% from 22 parochial schools. Schools include: St. John Vianney, St. John the Baptist (Milpitas), St. Martin of Tours (San Jose), St. Patrick (San Jose), Most Holy Trinity, St. Leo the Great, Challenger (San Jose, Palo Alto, Sunnyvale), Girls Middle School, Hillbrook.

Admission

Applications due: Late January (call for date). **Application fee:** $60. **Application process:** "Shadow dates may be scheduled for October through February. In early November the school holds an 8th Grade Day when interested students may visit the campus. An open house is held in late October for families of students currently in G6-8. Applicants may take the admission test at Notre Dame in early to mid-January or at any other school in the Diocese. The school does not use a clergy recommendation form though the application asks for religion and baptism dates, if applicable. The school uses the San Jose Diocesan 7th and 8th grade student report. Decisions are mailed mid-March." **No. of freshman applications:** Over 375 for 165 places. Four transfer students were admitted to G10, 2 to G11." **Minimum admission requirements:** "B average and grade equivalency or higher on HSPT. Transfer students must have a B average and be able to meet the requirements for graduation. Students are accepted to 12th grade only if they are moving to the area and were enrolled in a Catholic school." **Test required:** HSPT. **Preferences:** Catholic, daughters of alumnae, siblings. **"We are looking for** young women interested in: spiritual and social development, co-curricular activities, developing strong voice and social responsibility." **What kind of student do you best serve?** "Young women who are intellectually curious and value diversity and service."

Costs

Latest tuition: $12,650 with payment options available. **Sibling discount:** None. **Tuition increases:** Approx. 6%. **Other costs:** Additional cost for uniforms and books. **Percentage of students receiving financial aid:** 16%. **Financial aid deadline:** Late January (call for date). **Average grant:** $2,200. **Percentage of grants of half-tuition or more:** N/P.

School's Mission Statement/Goals

"Established in 1851, Notre Dame High School is a Catholic secondary school which educates young women in the tradition of the Sisters of Notre Dame de Namur, founded by St. Julie Billiart. Our primary mission is expressed in her words: 'Teach them what they need to know for life.' We provide a challenging college preparatory curriculum that integrates classroom learning with downtown educational opportunities in culture, science, and technology. We maintain an enrollment that allows faculty to know each student and to give special attention to individual, academic, and personal needs. We encourage students to participate in varied activities to discover skills and talents in the arts, athletics, student leadership, and community service. In our richly diverse student body, young women develop a respect and appreciation for other individuals and cultures. Together, faculty and students create a supportive, open-minded environment in which each young woman is encouraged to explore her creative potential, develop self-esteem, strengthen her relationship with God, enjoy nurturing friendships and grow in her ability to work with others and serve her community. We educate young women for success and leadership in a global and technological society. We prepare them to live as well-educated, self-confident and socially responsible women, sustained by religious faith and guided by spiritual values."

Academic Program

"In addition to the academic program offered by the school, juniors and seniors may, with permission, take classes at San Jose State." **Courses offered** (AP=Advanced Placement, H=Honors, (AP)=AP option, (H)=Honors option): **English:** English I-II (H), English III-IV AP, Shakespeare, Creative Writing, Writing for Publication, Film as Literature; **Math:** Algebra I-II (H), Geometry (H), Trigonometry/Pre-Calculus (H), Calculus AP, Calculus (BC), Practical Statistics; **Religious Studies:** Christian Scriptures; Faith, Values, and Lifestyles; Decision Making; Spirituality and Self; Women, Creativity, and Spirituality; World Religions; Peace and Justice; Gifts, Leadership, Spirituality; Contemporary Themes in Liberation; **Social Studies:** Global Studies, Modern World History, U.S. History (AP), U.S. Government (AP), Psychology (AP), Economics, Conflicts in the Modern World, Contemporary Social Issues; Technology: Internet & Applications, Web Design, Video Production; **Science:** Biology I-II, Biology AP, Chemistry (H), Physics (H/AP), Earth Science, Environmental Science AP, Robotics; **Language:** Spanish I, Spanish II-III (H), Spanish IV (AP), French I, French II-III (H), French IV AP; **Arts:** Intro to Visual Expression, Advanced Art, Photography, Advanced Photography, Ceramics, Advanced Ceramics, Drama I-II, Symphonic Band, Drama Special Projects, Technical Theater, Musical Theater, Yearbook I-II, Chorus; **P.E.:** P.E., Fitness for Life. **Special programs:** Internship program, Senior Honors Project, Peer Counselor Training. **Computer lab/training:** The school has two computer labs each with Pentium PCs. The school's computers are networked. **Grading:** A-F. **Graduation requirements:** 4 years English; 3.5 years social studies; 3 years math (including geometry) and lab science; 2 years foreign language; 2 semesters fine arts and P.E.; 7 semesters religious studies; community service. **Average nightly homework (Mon-Th):** G9-10: 2 hours; G11-12: 2.5-3 hours. **Faculty:** 50 f/t and 2 p/t faculty members; 10% are male, 90% female; 50% hold master's, 6% advanced degrees. **Faculty ethnicity:** 84% Caucasian (non-Latino); 16% non-Caucasian. **Faculty selection/training:** N/P. **Teacher/student ratio:** 1:13. **Percentage of students enrolled in AP:** 35%; pass rate N/P. **Senior class profile (mean):** SAT Math 580, SAT Critical Reading 560, SAT Writing 570; GPA: 3.2-3.39. **National Merit Scholarship Program:** In most recent year's class, 2 students were Finalists, 2 were Semifinalist, 20 were Commended; 6 National Hispanic Scholar. **College enrollment (last class):** 94% in 4-year, 6% in 2-year. **Recent (last 3 yrs) colleges:** UC (Berkeley, Davis, Irvine, LA, Merced, Riverside, SD, Santa Barbara and Santa Cruz), CSU (Humboldt, Long Beach, SD, SF, Cal Poly-Pomona, Cal Poly-SLO), Harvard, Brown, Boston C, MIT, Fordham, Chapman, U-Arizona, Drexel, Loyola, Lewis & Clark, NYU, U-Portland, Willamette, Wellesley, Loyola Marymount, Santa Clara, Scripps, St. Mary's, Stanford, Carnegie Mellon, USF, USC, Fordham, and Dartmouth.

Other Indicators the School is Accomplishing its Goals

"Internship programs place 25-50 students per year and provides job shadow opportunities. Immersion program expansion includes Tijuana house building, Tenderloin, El Salvador and School of the Americas trips. Notre Dames Reads program integrates themed reading annually for school community. Expanded summer school and summer camp programs."

Campus/Campus Life

Campus description: The campus encompasses a square-block in downtown San Jose. and includes a 3-story classroom building with new technology in the library/media center, science labs and computer labs; a 2-story classroom building with computer lab; a gym with a caféteria; and a separate 1-story student-life center with a student lounge, courtyard, counseling offices, art studios, and a chapel. Most classrooms have desks arranged in clusters to advance cooperative learning. The grounds include a grassy area with picnic tables. **Library:** 1,800 sq. ft.; 17,000 print volumes; 23 periodical subscriptions; 27 computers, fully integrated fiber optic network system, individual student data ports; study space for 94 students. Open to students from 7 a.m.-5 p.m.; online card catalog; full-time credentialed Library Media Specialist. **Sports facilities:** Gymnasium on campus. The school uses the swimming pool at San Jose State, nearby parks for soccer, and Bellarmine's facilities for track and field. **Theater/arts facilities:** Art studios for ceramics studio, painting/drawing studio, photography lab. **Open/closed campus:** Closed. **Lunches:** Morning snacks and hot lunches daily. **Bus service:** Public. **Uniforms/dress code:** Gray skirts, white school logo shirts, gray school sweatshirts for everyday; free dress on Fridays with jeans permitted, formal dress for liturgy days. No unnatural hair colors. **Co-curricular activities/clubs:** "The school's location permits students to walk on organized field trips to the San Jose museums, the Technology Center, Performing Arts Center, and other downtown cultural and educational venues. Leadership organizations include: Associate Student Body, Teaching, Advising & Serving our Community (TASC), Peer Ministry Leadership Team (PMLT); Clubs include: Technology Club, Amnesty International, California Scholarship Federation, Gospel Choir, Interact, Culinary Club, National Honor Society, Notre Dame Ambassadors, Peer Counseling, Peer Tutoring, Students Against Destructive Decisions, Black Student Union, Filipino Student Association, South Asian Student Association, Japan Club, Latinas Unidas, Vietnamese Sisterhood, Environmental Club, Future Business Leaders of America, Speech and Debate Team." **Foreign exchange program/internships:** "Teacher sponsored European travel every summer." **Community service:** "The school's Community Service Learning Program involves 10 hours of service in the freshman year, 15 hours sophomore year, 18 hours junior year, and a senior project presented to the community. Students fulfill the requirement through work with local agencies. During Easter Break, students may travel to Tijuana to build a house for a needy family." **Typical freshman schedule:** Six classes of approx. 45 minutes on Mon.-Wed.; 90 minutes on Th. and Fri. English I, Algebra I or Geometry, homeroom/break, Spirituality & Self/Hebrew Scripture, Global Studies, fine arts elective, P.E., lunch, French I or Spanish I, resource period.

Student Support Services

Counselor/student ratio (not including college counselor): 1:158. Counseling: "Each student is assigned a counselor who will meet with her throughout her high school years for academic advising. Students are encouraged to seek out and/or are referred for additional support for academic or personal difficulties. Trained peer counselors provide additional programs. Each student is assigned a teacher to act as mentor/advisor throughout her 4 years. The mentor meets with groups of 23 students Monday-Wednesday for 15 minutes and for 35 minutes on Friday. Tutoring in math is available daily in a math lab staffed by a teacher or an advanced senior student. The school has college counselors who begin assisting students in their sophomore year. All students use the college, career and scholarship computer program; students can access their files from any computer on campus." **Learning disabilities/differences:** "Testing and classroom accommodations are provided, as appropriate, for diagnosed students."

Student Conduct and Health

Code of conduct: "The code of conduct is commensurate to the expectations of a college preparatory Catholic high school." **How school handles drug/alcohol usage:** "For first offenses, suspension, parent conference, behavior probation, referral to school counselor or a drug and alcohol education program, possible expulsion, and police may be called. Second offenses will result in parent conference and ordinarily in expulsion." **Prevention/awareness programs:** "These issues, along with other women's health issues, are addressed through the mentoring program."

Summer Programs
Coeducational summer program that includes sport camps, academic classes, art classes, college application and SAT prep classes.

Parent Involvement
Parent participation: "No required hours, though the Notre Dame Parent Association is open to all parents—its main function is to support the school. Through the association, parents assist with a variety of school functions including drama, field trips, and sports." **Parent/ teacher communication:** "As needed." **Parent education:** "The Counseling Department schedules annual parent nights for each grade level that address development and parenting issues." **Donations:** "Parents are encouraged to participate in the Parent Giving Program and the Annual Fund Drive, along with other development/school events."

Sports
The school is a member of the West Bay Athletic League and competes in volleyball (frosh, JV, V), tennis (JV, V), cross-country (V), basketball (frosh, JV, V), soccer (JV, V), softball (V), track and field (JV, V), swimming (JV, V), lacrosse (JV, V), and golf (V).

What Sets School Apart From Others
"A 157-year tradition in downtown San Jose; Notre Dame education with focus on woman's voice and social justice; diverse student body; excellent fine arts; lab science program; proximity to downtown venues and SJSU."

How Parents/Students Characterize School
Parent response(s): "Academic excellence/rigor; caring school community; responsive faculty and administration; creativity of student work." **Student response(s):** N/P.

Orinda Academy
19 Altarinda Road
Orinda, CA 94563
(925) 254-7553 *fax (925) 254-4768*
www.orindaacademy.org

Ronald Graydon, Director
Admissions Office: admission@orindaacademy.org

General
Coed day high school with middle school (G7-12). Nonsectarian. Independent. Founded in 1982. Nonprofit, member of EBISA and BAAD. **Enrollment:** Approx. 125. **Average class size:** 10. **Accredita-**

tion: WASC. **School year:** Sept.-June. **School day:** 8:30 a.m.-3:25 p.m. **Location:** In Orinda, accessible by Hwy. 24 and BART.

Student Body
Geographic breakdown (counties): 1% from San Francisco; 30% from Alameda; 69% from Contra Costa. **Ethnicity:** 74% Caucasian (non-Latino); 12.6% Asian; 10% African-American. **International students (I-20 status):** 5%. **Middle schools (freshman):** 50% came from public middle schools; 50% from private, non-parochial schools. (N/P #, schools)

Admission
Applications due: Approx. January 15 (call for date). **Application fee:** $75. **Application process:** Admission test, middle school transcripts, three recommendations, and student interview. **No. of freshman applications:** 100 (# places N/P). **Minimum admission requirements:** "Students should be capable of succeeding in a college preparatory curriculum. Each student's profile is individually assessed." **Test required:** ISEE. **Preferences:** None. "We are looking for students who desire an excellent education to prepare them for college and students who will bring a wide range of talents and interests to our program, ranging from talents in music, art, drama, computers, to leadership and sports. It is important that each student enrich the Orinda Academy community." **What kind of student do you best serve?** "Students seeking a small college preparatory school where they can reach their potential to enter the finest universities. Small class size enables students to interact with their teachers, making for an engaging academic experience, as well as providing an ideal setting for students to ask questions, seek clarification, remain focused, and intellectually challenge themselves. Orinda Academy has the flexibility to challenge students seeking honors and AP courses, as well as assist students who excel in extra-curricular activities and will benefit from a less rigorous course load."

Costs
Latest tuition: $23,995. **Sibling discount:** None. **Tuition increases:** Approx. 2-5%. **Other costs:** Approx. $700 for books. **Percentage of students receiving financial aid:** 20%. **Financial aid deadline:** Feb. 8 (call for date). **Average grant:** $10,000. **Percentage of grants half-tuition or more:** 45%.

School's Mission Statement/Goals
"The mission of Orinda Academy is to help each student discover a love of higher learning; build a set of personal, ethical values; develop a respect for the natural environment; and foster an appreciation for the diversity of our multi-cultural world. A vital part of this endeavor includes engendering a healthy lifestyle, critical thinking skills, a co-operative learning environment, and a sense of academic and personal responsibility in all members of our school community. We assist each

student to reach his or her full potential as a successful, confident, self-reliant individual, prepared for the academic rigor of a university education. Orinda Academy believes three factors contribute to the success of Orinda Academy graduates: a challenging and engaging curriculum; a nurturing school environment; and regular communication among parents, students, and teachers."

Academic Program

Courses offered (AP=Advanced Placement, H=Honors, (AP)=AP option, (H)=Honors option): **English:** English I-IV(AP), American Literature (H), British and Western Literature (H), Women's Literature, Creative Writing, Journalism; **Math:** Math A through Calculus II; **Science:** Earth Science, Environmental Science, Biology (H), Advanced Biology, Physics, Chemistry; **History and Social Sciences:** Geography, U.S. History (H), Western Civilization, Civics, Economics; **Foreign Languages:** Spanish I-IV (AP), French I-IV; **Computers:** Beginning Computers, Computers, Multi Media, Yearbook, Web Design; **Arts:** Chorus, Intro to Theater, Drama, Beginning Art, Advanced Art, Studio Art. **Computer lab/training:** "Mac-lab and multimedia program." **Grading:** A-F. **Graduation requirements:** 4 years of English; 3 years of math, social science and P.E.; 2 years of science; 1 semester of health; 1 year of foreign language or fine arts. **Average nightly homework (M-Th):** 1-3 hours. **Faculty:** 19; 5 with graduate degrees. (N/P gender, degrees) **Faculty ethnicity:** N/P. **Faculty selection/training:** N/P. **Teacher/student ratio:** 1:9. **Percentage of students enrolled in AP:** N/P. **Senior class profile (mean):** SAT Math 559, SAT Critical Reading 578, SAT Writing 572; GPA: 3.2. **National Merit Scholarship Program:** "Semifinalists and Commended Scholars." **College enrollment (last class):** 95%, 84% at 4-year. **Recent (4 yr) colleges:** UC (Berkeley, LA, SD, Santa Barbara, Davis, Santa Cruz, Irvine, Riverside), USF, St. Mary's, Santa Clara, Dominican C, Cal Lutheran, UOP, U-Redlands, Evergreen, Puget Sound, Willamette, Lewis & Clark, Lindfield, U-Oregon, U-Southern Oregon, CalArts, Expression College For Digital Arts, Brown, Barnard, Clark, Drew, Dickinson, Ithica, Connecticut C, Mayville, Loras, & Wheaton C, C of Santa Fe, U-Aberdeen, and U-Sterling (Scotland).

Other Indicators the School is Accomplishing its Goals

"Eighty-four percent of Orinda Academy graduates attend 4-year colleges and universities. We have been tracking our graduates for over 20 years, and they are very successful at top universities and graduate schools throughout the world. Twenty percent of our graduates attend the University of California system. We have had numerous graduates attend UC-Berkeley. Our graduates frequently return to our campus, emphasizing how well they are prepared for university academics. Though Orinda Academy is a small college preparatory school, our graduates are comfortable in intimate private universities and large public universities of 40,000 students."

Campus/Campus Life

Campus description: "Orinda Academy is located in the Orinda hills with views of the surrounding hills. The campus is divided among 3 large buildings with adjacent sports fields and basketball courts." **Library:** "An electronic library through the Internet in addition to a small on-site library with easy walking access to the new Orinda Public Library." **Sports facilities:** "Sports fields and basketball courts." **Theater/arts facilities:** "New art studio. The school also utilizes the new Orinda community theater for dramatic productions." **Open/closed campus:** Closed except for seniors. **Lunches:** "Offered through an outside caterer. Healthy snacks such as sandwiches, salads, and fruit are available in the school store." **Bus service:** None. **Uniforms/dress code:** None. **Co-curricular activities/clubs:** Student Action Club, Political Action Club, Anime Club, Movie Club, Chess Club. Clubs vary from year to year. **Foreign exchange program/internships:** None. **Community service:** Minimum of 40 hours required for graduation (examples N/P). **Typical freshman schedule:** English I, Geography/World History, Algebra/Geometry, Spanish/French, Earth Science, P.E., electives in computers, art, drama, and music.

Student Support Services

Counselor/student ratio (not including college counselors): 1:10. **Counseling:** "Academic and college counseling is ongoing throughout the student's academic career, with help in course selection, testing, college planning and placement. College representatives and college advisors are invited to the school for further assistance." **Learning differences/disabilities:** "We accommodate students with learning style differences who can succeed in a college preparatory curriculum. Our small class size lends itself to helping all students reach their potential. Our staff is well versed in teaching to different learning styles."

Student Conduct and Health

Code of conduct: "Students and staff at Orinda Academy are expected to treat each other with respect. Orinda Academy does not tolerate inappropriate behavior and has a no-tolerance policy regarding sexual harassment, violence, and drugs." **How school handles drugs/alcohol:** "Zero tolerance/expulsion." **Prevention/awareness programs:** "In the semester-long sophomore health class, students are educated in drug/alcohol abuse prevention and AIDS awareness, with speakers brought in from throughout the Bay Area."

Summer Programs

Courses include Algebra I, Geometry, Algebra II/Trigonometry, US History and English for G9-12. Middle school courses include a Basic Skills Review class for G7-9.

Parent Involvement

Parent participation: "The school has an active Parents Group which plans social events, graduation ceremonies, workshops and fundraising events." **Parent/teacher communication:** "Continuous communication is integral to the Orinda Academy logo – parents, students, teachers working together. Three parent/student/advisor conferences a year. Progress reports are sent home every two weeks for every student in the school to ensure students and parents alike are kept abreast of student performance." **Parent education:** "The school invites speakers to give workshops on topics such as college planning, financial aid, and learning styles." **Donations:** "The school encourages families to donate $500 each year."

Sports

Competitive sports teams in soccer, basketball, baseball, and softball. The school also offers P.E. courses in hiking, tai chi, yoga, weight-training, team sports, and dance.

What Sets School Apart From Others

"Orinda Academy is a college preparatory school where all students can succeed. The small class size enables students to work to their potential. Classes are often taught in a seminar style setting, with many hands-on projects and field trips to enrich the understanding. Student academic course loads are flexible allowing students to take a curriculum ideally suited to their needs, aptitudes, ambitions, and extracurricular activities. Orinda Academy also provides Math & Science Labs and Writing Labs offering one-to-one tutoring for students needing additional academic assistance. No one falls through the cracks at Orinda Academy. Orinda Academy provides excellent support for students with communication between parents, students and teachers. Orinda Academy students come from all over the Bay Area and around the world from small, independent elementary schools as well as larger public elementary schools.."

How Parents/Students Characterize School

Parent response(s): "It is a wonderful, small private school with an excellent program for college preparation, a truly gifted staff and a diverse student population." "Orinda Academy has completely prepared our son for college – not only academically but also in his self-confidence." "Orinda Academy is small, but neither one of our kids would have traded Orinda Academy because of what they are getting academically and personally." "During every college interview, our son repeatedly spoke of the great teachers at Orinda Academy and how they taught him to really think and examine issues." **Student response(s):** "Orinda Academy incredibly changed my life. I am not quite sure that I would be writing to you from a wonderful college had I never attended Orinda Academy." "I was completely prepared for UC-Berkeley. All the essays I wrote at Orinda Academy made college writing easy." "I am getting a full graduate scholarship to study chemistry at Washington U in Saint Louis. It wouldn't be possible if it weren't for Orinda Academy."

Pinewood School

26800 Fremont Road
Los Altos Hills, CA 94022
(650) 941-1532 *fax (650) 941-4727*
www.pinewood.edu, info@pinewood.edu

Mark Gardner, Principal
Laurie Wilson, Dean of Students, lwilson@pinewood.edu
Dafna Brown, Director of Admissions, dbrown@pinewood.edu

General
Coed day high school with middle school (G7-12). Nonsectarian. Founded in 1959. Nonprofit. **Enrollment:** 300. **Average class size:** 15-20. **Accreditation:** WASC. **School year:** Sept.-June. **School day:** 8 a.m.-3 p.m. **Location:** In the suburban residential community of Los Altos Hills, just south of Palo Alto, off Hwy. 280. Pinewood is 40 miles south of San Francisco and 15 miles north of San Jose.

Student Body
Geographic breakdown (counties): 75% from Santa Clara; 25% from San Mateo. **Ethnicity:** N/P. **International students (I-20 status):** 1%. **Middle schools (freshman):** 66% came from the school's middle school; 24% from public middle schools; 8% from private, nonparochial schools; 1% from parochial schools. (N/P #, schools)

Admission
Applications due: Approx. January 15 (call for date; late applications are reviewed on a space-available basis). **Application fee:** $50. **Application process:** "Prospective students and parents may visit the campus on Mondays beginning October 1. They may observe classes and meet and talk with students, teachers, and the school administration. Campus informational tours are given at 10:30 a.m. No appointment is necessary. Prospective students are encouraged to spend a day shadowing a current student, going to classes, and experiencing school life. Shadowing may be scheduled November through March. The application process includes an interview, entrance exam, transcripts, two teacher recommendations, personal essay, parent essay, and completed application form." **No. of freshman applications:** 80 for 20 places. Five new students were admitted to G10; 1 to G11; none to G12. **Minimum admission requirements:** "No specific cut-off—combination of grades, scores, and recommendations." **Test required:** ISSE. **Preferences:** None. "**We are looking for** those students who are strong academically, but who also want to be part of an educational environment that values and encourages creative expression, athletic participation and community involvement. The school motto is 'Pinewood is the Difference,' and faculty and students take pride in making this a reality. All students are expected to accept and support a standard of behavior that stresses commitment, honesty, kindness, conservative standards

of dress, appearance, language and moral conduct." **What kind of student do you best serve?** "The student who is a willing, positive and active participant in the opportunities provided—students who want personal involvement with their education, their teachers and their fellow students do best at Pinewood."

Costs

Latest tuition: $21,210. **Sibling discount:** N/P. **Tuition increases:** Approx. 5%. **Other costs:** $900 book/activity fee. **Percentage of students receiving financial aid:** 1%. **Financial aid deadline:** Approx. January 15 (call for date). **Average grant:** N/P. **Percentage of grants of half-tuition or more:** 0.

School's Mission Statement/Goals

"Pinewood School seeks to create an educational environment where students may acquire academic stamina, intellectual maturity, self-esteem and a high standard of behavior. Our goal is to provide students with the skills necessary for success in school and beyond through a strong college preparatory curriculum that emphasizes the importance of reading, writing, computation, communication, critical thinking and problem-solving skills. • We believe learning should be a positive and rewarding experience that challenges students to achieve their highest potential. Classes are small, allowing for individual instruction and attention and promoting student diversity and self-expression. This fosters open communication and rapport between students and teachers. Outside the classroom students are given opportunities to express themselves through a number of extracurricular activities designed for both group and individual involvement. The importance of these activities is stressed and student participation is actively encouraged and supported. • At Pinewood, it is our hope that students will take advantage of the opportunities afforded so that they become self-motivated, disciplined, responsible citizens prepared to lead a life of purpose, dignity and concern for others."

Academic Program

"As a college preparatory school, Pinewood's standard curriculum path is designed to meet the minimum course requirements of highly selective colleges and universities. Many students, however, follow the school's honors and AP curriculum paths." **Courses offered** (AP=Advanced Placement, H=Honors, (AP)=AP option, (H)=Honors option): **English:** Genre of Literature, American Literature, British Literature (H), World Literature, AP English Literature and Composition, Writing Techniques I, Writing Techniques II-III, College Writing, Yearbook, Journalism; **Math:** Algebra I-II, Geometry, Statistics, Mathematics-Selected Topics, Pre-Calculus with Trigonometry (H), AP Calculus I (AB), AP Calculus II (BC); **Speech:** Oral Communication; **History:** World History I-II, U.S. History (AP), American Government (H), World Geography, Economics; **Computer Science:** Computer Applications, Web Page Design; **Science:** Biology (AP), General Chemistry, Chemistry (H), General Physics, AP Physics, Astronomy, Biotechnology, Anatomy; **Social Science:** Psychology, Sociology, Philosophy, Leadership; **Foreign language:** Spanish I or II, Spanish III, Spanish IV (H), Spanish V (H/AP), French I-II, French III, French IV (H), French V (AP); **Arts:** Art History (AP), Studio Art I-II, Basic Drawing, Theater Arts, Humanities, Art Theory/Practice I-II, Theater I-II, Music History and Theory I-II; P.E. **Computer lab/training:** Computers are available for student use and instruction in the computer lab, library, and science and math classes. A laptop cart equipped with 15 computers is also available for use in any classroom. **Grading:** A-F (4.0 scale + for honors/AP courses). **Graduation requirements:** 4 years English/literature and history (including 1 semester of art history); 3 years foreign language, math, and science; 2.5 years writing; 2 years P.E.; .5 year oral communication, computer literacy, and economics. **Average nightly homework (Mon.-Thurs):** G9: 3 hours; G10-12: 3 hours (plus additional homework for honors and AP courses). **Faculty:** N/P #; 50% male, 50% female; 47% hold master's degrees. **Faculty ethnicity:** N/P. **Faculty selection/training:** "Faculty members are selected based on their resumes, recommendations, personal interviews with members of the administration, and in-class teaching demonstrations. Teaching credentials are not required; all faculty members are expected to teach in their major field. Pinewood holds several in-service meetings throughout the year, and teachers are encouraged to pursue continuing studies often with the financial support of the school administration." **Teacher/student ratio:** 1:7. **Percentage of students enrolled in AP:** 33%; pass rate 86%. **Most recent senior class profile (mean):** SAT Math 668, SAT Critical Reading 663, SAT Writing 668; GPA: 3.51. **National Merit Scholarship Program:** In most recent year, 7 students were Commended. **College enrollment (last class):** 95% in 4-year, 5% in 2-year. **Recent (4 yrs) colleges:** Included Harvard, Stanford, Princeton, MIT, UC (Berkeley, LA, Santa Barbara, Santa Cruz, SD), Pomona, Brown, Whitman, Carnegie-Mellon, SMU, USC, Northwestern, Cornell, Occidental, Duke, Whittier, Vassar, U-Colorado, Santa Clara, U-Wisconsin, Boston U, Cal Poly-SLO.

Campus/Campus Life

Campus description: "The campus, housing G7-12, consists of one 2-story building and several 1-story buildings arranged around a wide open area of playing fields. Classrooms, offices, labs (biology, chemistry and physics), an art studio, and a small theater open to the courtyard area; the 2-story building houses the gym, a student union/study hall, and additional classrooms." **Library:** 1,090 sq. ft.; 5,000 print volumes; 20 periodical subscriptions; 5 computers with Internet access; online catalog; study space for 35 students. Open to students from 7:45 a.m.-4:15 p.m.; full-time librarian. **Sports facilities:** Gymnasium, 4 tennis courts, basketball standards, and a soccer field. **Theater/arts facilities:** The school has a theater that opens to the courtyard. **Open/closed**

campus: Closed campus except for seniors, who may leave for lunch. **Lunches:** Hot lunches and bag lunches; miscellaneous snacks are also available. **Bus service:** None. **Uniforms/dress code:** "The dress code prohibits clothes advertising drugs, alcohol, tobacco, etc., any visible non-ear piercings, and midriffs, tanks, etc." **Co-curricular activities/clubs:** Interact Club (affiliated with Rotary International), National Honor Society, French Honor Society, Spanish Honor Society, Art Honor Society, speech and debate team, yearbook and newspaper, plays, musicals, student government, service clubs. **Foreign exchange program/internships:** Summer internship program for juniors and seniors. **Community service:** 20 hours required each year. (N/P examples) **Typical freshman schedule:** Eight periods of approx. 45 minutes each, including English, writing (1 semester), history (1 semester), math, science, French or Spanish, computers (1 semester), communications, music (1 semester), P.E.

Student Support Services

Counselor-student ratio: N/P. **Counseling:** "In junior high, college counseling begins with students and parents becoming acquainted with general college requirements and planning high school classes to meet those requirements. Starting the junior year of high school, the college advisor assists in all phases of the college admission process. Juniors take a semester-long college preparation class. Teachers offer tutoring throughout the day and after school for students who wish to pay for the service. A math lab, staffed by a math teacher and selected students from the National Honor Society or a Math Honor Society, is open daily to students. The school also has a Foreign Language Workshop staffed by teachers and honor students. Regarding personal counseling, students are encouraged to talk to members of the administration or their teachers." **Learning disabilities/differences:** "Students with mild, diagnosed learning differences function well at Pinewood. They are permitted to have extended testing time and to take oral exams as deemed necessary by an educational counselor. Pinewood does not offer any special programs for students with learning differences."

Student Conduct and Health

Code of conduct: "Standard." **How school handles drug/alcohol usage:** "Depends on specific circumstances. Zero tolerance for drug/alcohol use at school functions. Other interventions/counseling will depend on student and situation." **Prevention and awareness programs:** "Discussed in depth in various class curricula," as well as a 2-week program each year for G7-10.

Summer Programs

The Pinewood summer program is open to the public. Various enrichment and academic camps are offered from approximately mid-June through August.

Parent Involvement
Parent participation: "Limited to special events like the Jamboree, Golf Classic, Auction Dinner, sports programs and theatrical productions." **Parent/teacher communication:** "No scheduled conferences; conferences may be requested by parents, teachers or the administration at any time during the year. Parents are invited to communicate with all teachers and administrators in person, by phone, and by e-mail; they also have access to their child's grades and attendance through the Internet." **Parent education programs:** "Member of Common Ground series." **Donations:** None.

Sports
Girls cross-country, track and field, swimming, volleyball, tennis, soccer, basketball, softball and golf; Boys cross-country, track and field, swimming, soccer, basketball, tennis, golf, football, and baseball.

What Sets School Apart From Others
"Small size, caring attitude, relaxed, friendly, and pleasant environment where students seem happy to be a part of it."

How Parents/Students Characterize School
Parent response(s): "I love Pinewood! I cannot imagine a better environment, both socially and academically, for my two boys. I know that they will look back fondly at their time at P-dub." **Student response(s):** N/P.

Presentation High School
2281 Plummer Avenue
San Jose, CA 95125
(408) 264-1664 ext. 2441 *fax (408) 266-3028*
www.pres-net.com

Mary Miller, Principal
Dina Collins, Director of Admissions, dcollins@pres-net.com

General
Girls Catholic day high school (77% Catholic). Founded in 1962. Nonprofit. Operated by the Sisters of the Presentation. **Enrollment:** 752. **Average class size:** 28. **Accreditation:** WASC. **School year:** Sept.-May. **School day:** 7:45 a.m.-2:40 p.m.; block schedule. **Location:** In the Willow Glen residential neighborhood of San Jose, near Hwys. 280, 101 and 87.

Student Body
Geographical breakdown: N/P. **Ethnicity:** 65% Caucasian (non-Latina); 13% Latina; 5% Filipina; 3% Chinese; 3% Vietnamese; 1% Japanese;

1% Black; .05% Korean; .05% Persian; 8% multi-ethnic. **International students (I-20 status):** N/P. **Middle schools (freshman):** Presentation students come from more than 105 feeder schools; 16% came from public middle schools; 16% from private, non-parochial school; and 66% from parochial schools (# schools N/P). Among the represented feeder schools are St. Christopher, St. Francis Cabrini, St. John Vianney, Holy Family, St. Martin (San Jose), St. Catherine and St. Lucy.

Admission

Applications due: Late January (call for date). **Application fee:** $65. **Application process:** Presentation hosts an admissions open house during which parents and prospective students may visit the campus and meet faculty, coaches, and students. On Seventh Grade Day, seventh grade students attend Mini-Classes and a special assembly produced by Presentation students, and have an ice cream social. Placement tests are held in January. Eighth grade transcripts are due in early February, and acceptance letters are mailed mid-March. **No of freshmen applications:** 385 for 200 places. **Minimum admission requirements:** N/P. **Test required:** HSPT. **Preferences:** N/P. **"We are looking for"** N/P. **What kind of student do you best serve?** N/P.

Costs

Latest tuition: $9,485, payable in 1, 2, 4 or monthly payments. **Sibling discount:** None. **Tuition increases:** N/P. **Other costs:** N/P. **Percentage of students receiving financial aid:** N/P. **Financial aid deadline:** End of January (call for date). **Average grant:** 50%. **Percentage of grants half-tuition or more:** N/P.

School's Mission Statement/Goals

"Presentation High School is a secondary school for girls whose purpose and direction flow from the teaching mission of the Catholic Church and the educational ministry of the Sisters of the Presentation. As such, Presentation High School strives to permeate the entire educational process with the vision of life found in the Gospels. It endeavors to enable each student to integrate the acquisition of human knowledge and skills with her growing experience of life and the world and with her total development as a Christian person. The school recognizes that it shares with the family and the Church and the state in the total work of education. In particular with the family, which is the primary educator, the school must enter a fruitful partnership. The school, however, assumes responsibility for using its unique resources to bring about its stated purposes. In order to be faithful to its purposes, the school recognizes that the following beliefs must be the foundation upon which all goals, objectives, programs and procedures are developed and are continually evaluated: That education consists in harmonious development of the whole person—her religious, intellectual, volitional, aesthetic, emotional and physical powers; [that] although faith is a gift from God, one's faith is capable of growth and development and must be nurtured to maturity in harmony with the stages of human development; [that] Gospel values are best taught and internalized in the supportive atmosphere of a Christian community where the professional educators and staff along with the students evidence commitment to school goals and Gospel values; [that] the work of education is the work of empowering individuals to reach their full potential as human beings, to make responsible decisions as individuals and members of the larger community and to assume their full stature in today's society; [that] the school is an active institution which must be a dynamic force in bringing about the implementation of Christian principles in the social sphere."

Academic Program

"Students take a minimum course load of five classes per semester and may enroll in up to seven. Presentation graduation requirements are designed to satisfy those of the state of California and the UC and CSU systems." **Courses offered** (AP=Advanced Placement, H=Honors, (AP)=AP option, (H)=Honors option): **Computers:** Computer Applications I-II, Java, Desktop Publishing, Web Page Design, Business Economics, Business Law; **English:** English 9; English 9 Accelerated; English 10 (H); Speech (Beginning, Intermediate and Advanced); Adolescent in Literature; American Literature; British Literature; Contemporary Writing; Literary Analysis; Death in Literature; Expository Writing; God in Modern Literature; Literary Biographies; Literary Interpretation; Literature, Culture, and Identity; Modern Novel; Modern Playwrights; Shakespeare; Women Writers; English I-IV H/AP; The Individual and Society; **Arts:** Acting I-II, Art History and Appreciation, Film History and Appreciation, Music History and Appreciation, Dance I-II, Piano Keyboarding I-II, Ceramics I-II, Drawing and Painting I-II, Graphic Production I-II, Jazz Choir I-IV, Musical Comedy Production I-II, Photography I-II; **Math:** Algebra I, IA, IB, Accelerated Algebra I, Geometry (H), Algebra II (H), Computer Programming C++, Statistics, Trigonometry, Pre-Calculus (H), Calculus I, Calculus II (H/AP); **Language:** French I, II-III (H), French IV-V (H/AP), Spanish I, II-III (H), Spanish IV-V (H/AP); **P.E:** Indoor Sports, Outdoor Sports, P.E. Health, Aerobic Crosstraining and Strength Development; **Religion:** Understanding Your Faith/Religion, The Gospels: The Call to Christian Responsibility Religion, Christian Ethics, Christian Lifestyles, Christian Marriage, Scripture, Media and Cultures, Church History, Social Justice, Women of Faith, World Religions; **Science:** Intro to Science, Biology I (H), Biology II (H/AP), Chemistry (H), Physics (H), Bioethics, Earth Science, Environmental Science, Human Anatomy and Physiology; **Social Studies:** World History, Cultures, and Geography; Accelerated World History; U.S. History (H); Civics (H); California History; Economics (H); Microeconomics (H/AP); Macroeconomics (H/AP); Global Women's Issues; Modern History; Psychology (H/AP). **Computer lab/training:** The school utilizes an Ethernet network. The computer to student ratio is 1:4 and gives students the opportunity to access the web through a T-1 connection. Curriculum-based software is networked and is available throughout any one of the 3 major labs. Each of the major computer labs has 32 or more IBMs. There are satellite labs in the library and in the modern language department with HP machines. Each of the labs has laser printers, and the 3 major labs have LCD projection, allowing teachers to display lessons on screen through the computer. Computer basics required for graduation. **Grading:** N/P. **Graduation requirements:** 220 credits minimum required: 4 years English; 3.5 years religious studies (including .5 year ethics) and social studies including .5 year civics; 3 years math; 2 years same foreign language; 1 year P.E., lab science (+ 2 years other science) and fine, applied or performing arts; .5 year computer basics; an additional semester of art or technology. A minimum of 5 classes per semester is required. **Average nightly homework (M-Th):** G9: 2 hours; G10-11: 3-4 hours; G12: 3 hours. **Faculty:** 45; 21% male, 79% female; 62% hold master's degrees. **Faculty ethnicity:** N/P. **Faculty selection/training:** "All faculty have California state credentials and are teaching in their subject area. Each must acquire 30 professional growth units per year." **Teacher/student ratio:** 1:28. **Percentage of students enrolled in AP:** 19%; pass rate: 65% received scores of 3 or better. **Senior class profile (mean):** SAT: N/P; GPA: 3.33. **National Merit Scholarship Program:** Last year, 5 Commended students, 4 Semifinalists and 4 Finalists. **College enrollment (last class):** 100%; 87% in 4-year, 13% in 2-year. **Recent colleges:** N/P.

Other Indicators the School is Accomplishing its Goals: N/P.

Campus/Campus Life

Campus description: The campus includes a one-story building containing classrooms and offices, a theater and classroom complex, (which includes a newly equipped computer lab), an athletic complex, and a Christian Life Center with a chapel. The outdoor area includes sports fields. **Library:** Open to students from 7:30 a.m.-4 p.m. The library has a satellite computer lab and electronic access to the Santa Clara County libraries. **Sports facilities:** A gymnasium, weight room, dance studios and locker rooms, tennis courts and a softball field. **Theater/arts facilities:** 250-seat theater with a recording studio, dressing and make-up rooms, a studio art room and a ceramics room. **Open/closed campus:** Closed. **Lunches:** A breakfast and lunch service is provided. **Bus service:** Public. **Uniforms:** Required. **Co-curricular activities/clubs:** Dance, Drama, Speech and Debate, Campus Ministry, Student Government, and over 20 other clubs. **Foreign exchange program/internships:** N/P. **Community service:** "The Community Involvement organization is the largest club on campus and offers many opportunities for students to become involved in service-related activities." **Typical freshman schedule:** An entering freshman can take up to 7 courses per semester. Most freshmen will take 6 classes each semester: English, World History, math, religion and electives.

Student Support Services

Counselor/student ratio (not including college counselor): 1:130. **Counseling:** "Each student has an assigned counselor with whom she meets regularly. Counselors help students prepare for college, keep track of academic progress and requirements, and provide personal counseling as needed. At the beginning of her freshman year, each student is assigned a mentor with whom she will work over her four years at Presentation. Mentoring groups—28 to 34 students—meet once a week for general information, study skill instruction, and college and scholarship information. Mentors also meet with each of their mentees at least once a semester to discuss the student's academic progress, future goals, abilities and interests, and to provide guidance in these areas." **Learning differences/disabilities:** "We work with identified students and provide accommodations with extended time and peer and math tutor availability."

Student Conduct and Health: N/P.

Summer Programs

"Presentation High School offers summer sports camps in volleyball, basketball, softball, soccer and tennis. The Conservatory of the Arts at Presentation (CAP) is a 5-week, intensive program that offers performing arts education for boys and girls ages 11-18. The Study Skills Workshop is a 1-week workshop for incoming 9th graders to help them make a smooth transition to high school."

Parent Involvement: N/P.

Sports

Presentation competes in the West Catholic Athletic League in basketball, cross-country, golf, soccer, softball, swimming and diving, tennis, track and field, volleyball, field hockey, and water polo.

What Sets School Apart From Others: N/P.

How Parents/Students Characterize School: N/P.

The Quarry Lane High School

6363 Tassajara Road
Dublin, CA 94568
(925) 829-8000 *fax (925) 829-4928*
www.quarrylane.org

Dr. Sabri Arac, Headmaster
Candice McGraw, Admissions Director, cmcgraw@quarrylane.org

General
Coed day high school. Independent. Founded in 1991. Proprietary. **Accreditation:** WASC, NIPSA. **Enrollment:** Approx. 50, expanding to 400. **Average class size:** 17. **School year:** 9-mo. calendar (180 instructional days). **School day:** 8 a.m.-3:30 p.m. **Location:** In the East Bay accessible by school bus or BART.

Student Body
Geographic breakdown (counties): 55% from Alameda; 45% from Contra Costa. **Ethnicity:** 44% Asian; 43% Caucasian (non-Latino); 7% African-American; 6% Latino. **International students (I-20 status):** 10%. **Middle schools (freshman):** N/P.

Admission
Applications due: N/P. **Application fee:** $75. **Application process:** "Application form, student essay, parent statement, teacher recommendations, copy of transcripts, ISEE scores." **Test required:** ISEE. **No. of freshman applications:** 25 (# places N/P). **Minimum admission requirements:** N/P. **Preferences:** N/P. **"We are looking for** a motivated student from a family who values high quality education." **What kind of student do you best serve?** "Those students who strive for success in school and in life."

Costs
Latest tuition: $18,460. **Sibling discount:** None. **Tuition increases:** Approx. 3-5%. **Other costs:** Approx. $900 for books, $500 other fees. **Percentage of students receiving financial aid:** 10%. **Financial aid deadline:** N/A. **Average grant:** $5,000. **Percentage of grants of half tuition or more:** N/P.

School's Mission Statement/Goals
"The mission of The Quarry Lane School is to create an atmosphere which inspires a lifelong love of learning and nurtures each child to reach his or her fullest potential–emotionally, socially, academically, and physically–in order to assume responsibility as a future citizen of the world."

Academic Program
Courses offered (AP=Advanced Placement, H=Honors, (AP)=AP option, (H)=Honors option): "7 AP courses, 6 Honors courses." (N/P courses) **Computer lab/training:** "Fully operational computer lab with training provided." **Grading:** "4.0; AP credit 5.0." **Graduation requirements:** 4 years English; 3 years math (4 years recommended); 3 years science; 4 years social studies; 2 years of 1 foreign language (3 years recommended); 1 year visual and performing arts; 2 years P. E., 1 year of health. **Average nightly homework (M-Th):** 90 min. **Faculty:** 36. (N/P gender, degrees) **Faculty ethnicity:** 53% Caucasian; 14% Hispanic/Latino; 29% Middle Eastern/Indian/Asian; 4% African

American. **Faculty selection/training:** "Professional recruiting practices as well as industry job postings solicit qualified faculty and staff. Paneled interview process ensures right 'fit.' A 2-week training period in summer, assignment of mentor teacher and ongoing professional development train qualified faculty and staff." **Teacher/student ratio:** 1:10. **Percentage of students enrolled in AP:** 40%; pass rate N/P. **Senior class profile (mean score):** "N/A." **National Merit Scholarship Program:** "N/A." **College enrollment (last class):** "N/A."

Other Indicators the School is Accomplishing its Goals
"The Quarry Lane School is a candidate for the International Baccalaureate Diploma Program."

Campus/Campus Life
Campus description: "Ten acres among the rolling hills of the East Bay is the backdrop for facilities including a 71,000 sq. ft. Upper School building with modern physical science, life science and earth science laboratories, a new library, a computer laboratory, and 33 instructional classrooms." **Library:** N/P. **Sports facilities:** A full size indoor gymnasium, an outdoor running track, soccer field and tennis court. **Theater/Arts facilities:** Visual arts studio. **Open/closed campus:** Closed. **Lunches:** Optional hot lunch program. **Bus service:** Yes. **Uniforms/dress code:** Yes. (Description N/P) **Co-curricular activities/clubs:** Band, chess, drama, leadership and various clubs based on interest such as California Scholastic Federation, National Scholastic Federation, Academic Decathlon, National Forensic League, Robotics Club, Science Bowl, and International Club. **Foreign exchange program/internships:** None. **Community service:** "A huge focus school wide, imbedded in the Leadership curriculum." (Examples N/P) **Typical freshman schedule:** Spanish I/II, Geometry, Biology, P.E., Leadership, English I, History, 1:50-3:30 – Electives.

Student Support Services
Counselor/student ratio (not including college counselors): N/P. **Counseling:** N/P . **Learning differences/disabilities:** N/P.

Student Conduct and Health
Code of conduct: "Quarry Lane has a clearly stated behavior code and set of standards to which it holds all students accountable." (Description N/P) **How school handles drugs/alcohol:** No tolerance policy. **Prevention and awareness programs:** "Red Ribbon Week." (N/P description)

Summer Programs: None.

Parent Involvement
Parent participation: "QLS has a formal parent association. We offer numerous opportunities to volunteer school-wide as well as within

individual grade levels." **Parent participation:** "70%." **Parent/teacher communication:** "Through e-mail, Edline, school website. **Parent education:** N/P. **Donations:** N/P.

Sports: Basketball, volleyball, soccer, cross-country, tennis, and golf.

What Sets School Apart From Others

"Quarry Lane creates an environment in which the student feels challenged, supported and nurtured. We believe in educating the whole child and giving each student every opportunity for success. The Quarry Lane School celebrates internationalism. We take advantage of every opportunity to celebrate the multiple cultures in our school community—through festivals, class presentations, assemblies, projects and more. We are a perfect candidate school for the International Baccalaureate Program."

How Parents/Students Characterize School

Parent response(s): "The classes are small; the parents are involved; the teachers love their jobs. The kids are bright, polite, imaginative and support each other. The faculty is highly qualified and knows each student's strengths and weaknesses. " **Student response(s):** N/P.

Sacred Heart Cathedral Preparatory

1055 Ellis Street
San Francisco, CA 94109
(415) 775-6626 *fax (415) 292-4186*
www.shcp.edu

Dr. Kenneth Hogarty, Principal
Timothy M. Burke, Director of Admission, admissions@shcp.edu

General

Coed Catholic day high school (73% Catholic). Founded in 1874 as Sacred Heart High School. In 1987, the boys school merged with Cathedral High School, a girls school founded in 1852. Owned by the Archdiocese of San Francisco and directed by the De La Salle Christian Brothers and Daughters of Charity. Nonprofit. **Enrollment:** Approx. 1,250. **Average class size:** 26. **Accreditation:** WASC. **School year:** Late Aug.-early June. **School day:** 7:55 a.m.-2:20 p.m. **Location:** In the northern part of San Francisco near the Civic Center, opposite St. Mary's Cathedral near Van Ness Avenue. Accessible by three Muni bus lines running along Van Ness Avenue, and BART a few blocks away.

Student Body

Geographic breakdown (counties): 85% from San Francisco; 15% from San Mateo. **Ethnicity:** N/P. **Middle schools (freshman):** N/P.

Admission

Applications due: Approx. late November for freshmen and mid-May for transfer students (call for date). **Application fee:** $75. **Application process:** "The school holds an open house in November. Half-day visits are scheduled for potential applicants from mid-September through late November. Notifications are mailed mid-March." **Minimum admission requirements:** "Decisions are based on grades in G7-8, standardized test scores, HSPT scores, and teacher/principal recommendations." **No. of freshman applications:** Approx. 1,000 for 320 places. **Test required:** HSPT. **Preferences:** Siblings, legacies, Catholics and students from Catholic schools. **"We are looking for** young men and women of excellent character who show promise of benefiting from and succeeding in the school's challenging program of academics and activities." **What kind of student do you best serve?** "SHCP serves the students from diverse backgrounds who are interested in a well-rounded college preparatory education built on the philosophy and vision of our founders."

Costs

Latest tuition: $12,800 payable in 1, 2, or 10 payments. **Sibling discount:** None. **Tuition increases:** 5-7%. **Other costs:** $1,200 registration fee; books approx. $400 per year. **Percentage of students receiving financial aid:** 25%. **Financial aid deadline:** Call for date. **Average grant:** N/P. **Percentage of grants half-tuition or more:** N/P.

School's Mission Statement/Goals

"Inspired by the Daughters of Charity and the De La Salle Christian Brothers, in partnership with families, Sacred Heart Cathedral Preparatory's mission is to provide the finest education in an inclusive Catholic community of faith. We prepare our students to become service-oriented leaders with a commitment to living the Gospel."

Academic Program

Courses offered (AP=Advanced Placement, H=Honors, (AP)=AP option, (H)=Honors option): **Religion:** Scripture I-II, Church History I-II, History of Christian Art, Ethics, Human Sexuality, Living and Dying, Comparative Religions, LaSallian/Vincentian Leadership, Prayer and Spirituality, Religious Themes in Literature and Films, The Life and Times of Jesus, Senior Seminar 1,2; **English:** English I-VI (H), English 7,8 AP Literature and Composition, Journalism 1,2, Modernism, Frankenlit: What does it mean to be human?, World Literature, Speculative Fiction, Shakespeare, The Golden Age of Athens, Irish Literature; **Math:** Math Enhancement I-II, Algebra I-II (H), Geometry I-II, Advanced Algebra I-II, Advanced Algebra and Trigonometry I-II, Trigonometry I, Probability and Statistics I, Statistics I-II, Statistics (AP), Pre-Calculus I-II, Calculus I-IV(AP); **Science:** Earth Science, Biology 1,2, Biology (AP), Chemistry 1,2, Chemistry (H/AP), Marine Biology, Physics I-II, Physics (AP); **Social Science:** World History 1,2,

U.S. History 1,2, U.S. History (H/AP), Civics, American Government and Politics (AP), Economics, Government and Politics (AP), California and San Francisco History, Psychology (AP), Sociology, Modern America I, U.S. Homefront: Mid-20th Century I, Race and Culture I; **Arts:** Art I-VI, Art History (AP), Studio Art (AP), Acting, Advanced Acting, Music Appreciation, Digital Photography and Design, Concert Band, Concert Choir I-VI, Chamber Ensemble I-IV, Women's Choir, Movement I-II, Instrumental Music I-II, String Ensemble, Music Theory (AP); **Languages:** French I-VIII (H/AP), Spanish I-VIII (H/AP), Advanced Spanish in the Real World, Japanese I-VIII (AP), American Sign Language I-VI, Mandarin I-VI. **Other:** Health, Computer Applications, Library Skills, Office Assistant, Life Fitness, Developmental Coaching Theory I-II. **Computer lab and training:** The school has a computer lab with 37 IBM terminals. **Grading:** A-F. **Graduation requirements:** 4 years English and religion; 3 years math and social science; 2 years science (including biology and chemistry) and language other than English; 1 year visual and performing arts; 1 semester P.E/Health. **Average nightly homework (M-Th):** 2-3 hours. **Faculty:** 95 lay teachers, 2 teaching Christian Brothers, and 2 Daughters of Charity; 58% male, 42% female; 37 hold master's degrees, and 5 hold doctorates. **Faculty ethnicity:** N/P. **Faculty selection/training:** "All faculty hold BA degrees and teaching credentials." **Teacher/student ratio:** 1:14. **Percentage of students enrolled in AP:** 22%; 70% passed with a score of 3 or above. **Senior class profile:** N/P. **National Merit Scholarship Program:** N/P. **College enrollment (last class):** 100%; 92% 4-year, 8% 2-year. **Recent (last 4 yrs) colleges:** American U, U-Arizona, Arizona SU, Boston C, Biola U, Boston U, Cal Poly-Pomona, Chapman, U-Colorado, Cornell, CSU (Chico, East Bay, Fresno, Fullerton, Long Beach, Sacramento, SLO, Humboldt, SD, SJ, Sonoma, SF), Catholic U-America, Dominican, Emerson C, Emory U, FIDM, Fordham, Holy Names, C of the Holy Cross, La Salle U, Loyola Marymount, Loyola U-Chicago, Loyola U-New Orleans, McGill U (Canada), Menlo C, Northern Arizona U, Notre Dame de Namur, Northwestern, Occidental C, U-Oregon, Pace, Pepperdine, Parsons, U-Portland, Santa Clara, Saint Mary's C, Tennessee SU, UC (Berkeley, Davis, Irvine, LA, Merced, Riverside, Santa Cruz, SD), U-Notre Dame, U-Nevada (Las Vegas, Reno), UOP, U.S. Air Force Academy, USC, USF, U-Washington, Willamette, and Yale.

Other Indicators the School is Accomplishing its Goals
"SHCP has an increasingly high applicant base, a very low attrition rate, and an innovative administration and faculty."

Campus/Campus Life
Campus description: The campus spans two city blocks. Its four buildings house classrooms, two chemistry and four biology labs, a computer lab, a library, a weight room, a new Student Life Center which accommodates 1,500 students, a second gymnasium and a sports field, and chapel. **Library:** "12,000 sq. ft." **Sports facilities:** Two gymnasiums, a

2,300 sq. ft. weight room, fitness center, multipurpose playing field. **Theater/arts facilities:** A 1,500-seat Student Life Center. **Open/closed campus:** Closed. **Lunches:** Students may purchase lunches daily from the school dining room. **Bus service:** Public. **Uniform/dress code:** No dyed hair or tattoos, no earrings for boys. Girls may wear the school skirt, slacks or pants that are not jeans. Boys wear slacks, pants or school shorts other than jeans. Girls and boys wear the SHCP school polo shirt only. **Co-curricular activities/clubs:** N/P. **Foreign exchange program/internships:** Through an endowed scholarship program, students may travel and study abroad with faculty members during the summer and Christmas and Easter vacations. **Community service:** "Through the Campus Ministry program and religion classes, students choose from a variety of opportunities." (Examples N/P) **Typical freshman schedule:** "A typical school day includes seven 48-minute class periods, from 7:55 a.m.-2:20 p.m." (N/P classes)

Student Support Services
Counselor/student ratio (not including college counselors): N/P. **Counseling:** "The school's Counseling Department provides academic, personal, and college counseling to all students. Peer counseling is done by a small, select group of students under the direction of a faculty member. In conjunction with college counseling, the school provides career counseling to assist students in developing realistic career plans and means of implementing them." **Learning disabilities/differences:** Full-time Academic Resource Specialist.

Student Conduct and Health: N/P.

Summer Programs
"Sacred Heart Cathedral's Summer Program is designed to serve the youth of San Francisco and the Bay Area with academic enrichment and sports and fitness opportunities for boys and girls ages 8-14. Summer in the city will challenge young people inside and outside of the classroom. The unique schedule allows a student/camper to spend the entire day at SHCP by mixing and matching programs."

Parent Involvement
Parent participation: "No required hours, but parents are encouraged to be involved in the Parents' Association, Boosters Club, and a variety of activities." **Parent/teacher communication:** "Parents receive student grades twice a semester (every 9 weeks), and may request informal progress reports from the student's counselor." **Parent education:** "Programs are offered through the counseling office." **Donations:** "Parents are asked to be involved in the Parent Pledge Program."

Sports
Through the West Catholic Athletic League, boys compete in basketball, baseball, cross-country, football, golf, soccer, tennis, track and

field, volleyball, and wrestling; girls in basketball, cross-country, golf, soccer, softball, swimming, tennis, track and field, and volleyball. The school offers intramural basketball, volleyball, and coed kick ball.

What Sets School Apart From Others

"We have a nurturing and caring environment where individual respect is fostered on a daily basis. This is based on the teachings of St. John Baptist de La Salle and St. Vincent de Paul."

How Parents/Students Characterize School

Parent response(s): "I have had a very good experience at SHCP. I love the community and all that it has to offer my son. The academics are challenging, but there are also balances. They offer so many extra-curriculars that everyone can find their nitch." "My daughter has thoroughly enjoyed her learning experiences at SHCP, and the faculty and school environment have helped her academically, socially and spiritually. I could not imagine a better school for my child." "As an alumna and parent, I have always supported SH/SHCP 100%. I continue to be pleased with the teachers, staff, coaches and environment surrounding the students at this great institution operating in the center of the city." **Student response(s):** "The teachers, staff, students, and fellow classmates have made me feel very comfortable at SHCP. The friends I made here are people I can count on in my future endeavors. In all honesty, I could not imagine going to another school around the Bay Area." "I thoroughly enjoyed my experiences at SHCP and felt it was the best possible education."

Sacred Heart Preparatory

150 Valparaiso Avenue
Atherton, CA 94027
(650) 322-1866 *fax (650) 326-2761*
www.shschools.org

James Everitt, Principal
Carl Dos Remedios, Admission Director, admission@shschools.org

General

Coed Catholic day high school (70% Catholic). Independent. Founded in 1898 by the Religious of the Sacred Heart. Nonprofit, member CAIS, NAIS. **Enrollment:** 530. **Average class size:** 15. **Accreditation:** WASC/CAIS, Sacred Heart Network. **School year:** August-June. **School day:** 7:50 a.m.-3 p.m. **Location:** On the border of Menlo Park and Atherton, 33 miles south of San Francisco, 2 miles north of Palo Alto.

Student Body

Geographic breakdown (counties): 83% from San Mateo; 16% from Santa Clara; 1% from East Bay. **Ethnicity:** 74% Caucasian (non-Latino); 10% multi-ethnic; 8% Asian; 6% Latino; 2% African-American. **International students (I-20 status):** 0. **Middle schools (freshman):** N/P.

Admission

Applications due: Early January (call for date). **Application fee:** $75. An application fee waiver is available for those students for whom the application fee would be a hardship. **Application process:** "Applicants may request an application by calling the admission office in late August. Financial aid applications may also be obtained through the admission office. Open houses are held in the fall and winter for students and their families. Interested families should call the school early in the fall to schedule a full-day campus shadow visit for the applicant as there are a limited number of appointments available. Applications must be on file prior to the shadow visit as applicants are interviewed on that day. The school uses BAIHS recommendation forms for Principal/Counselor and Math/English teacher recommendations. Up-to-date middle school transcripts are also required." **No. of freshman applications:** 420 for 135 places. There were 5 new students admitted to G10; 2 to G11; 0 to G12. **Minimum admission requirements:** "Applicants are considered on an individual basis." **Test required:** HSPT. **Preferences:** Catholics, alumni, siblings. **"We are looking for** very well-rounded, hardworking, enthusiastic students who will appreciate the gift their parents are giving them with a Sacred Heart education." **What kind of student do you best serve?** N/P.

Costs

Latest tuition: $26,885. Payment plans are available. **Sibling discount:** None. **Tuition increases:** Approx. 6-8%. **Percentage of students receiving financial aid:** 35%. **Financial aid deadline:** Approx. January 15 (call for date). **Average grant:** $6,500. "180 need-based grants." **Percentage of grants half-tuition or more:** 18%.

School's Mission Statement/Goals

"Every Sacred Heart School offers an education that is marked by distinctive spirit, an education concerned for each student's total development: spiritual, intellectual, aesthetic, emotional, and physical. As a Sacred Heart School, Sacred Heart Preparatory emphasizes serious study, social responsibility, and lays the foundations of a strong faith. Five goals and criteria encompass the holistic nature of a Sacred Heart education. We seek to educate students toward: 1) a personal and active faith in God; 2) a deep respect for intellectual values; 3) a social awareness which impels to action; 4) the building of community as a Christian value; 5) personal growth in an atmosphere of wise freedom. These goals seek the development of persons who are knowledgeable, questioning, thoughtful and integrated. A Sacred Heart education provides students with a cognitive sense of values, allowing students to develop leadership skills, knowledge of responsibility, and a sense of community based on mutual respect."

Academic Program

Courses offered (AP=Advanced Placement, H=Honors, (AP)=AP option, (H)=Honors option): **Religious studies:** Intro to Religious Studies, Christian Scriptures, History of Christianity, Personal Ethics: Moral Decision-Making, Social Ethics: The Search for Justice, Ethics and Technology, Philosophy of Religion, Prayer and Meditation, **World Religions:** The Search for Meaning, Relationships; **English:** Literary Genius, U.S. Literature, World Literature & British Classics (AP), Creative Literature, The Art of the Essay, Exploring Poetry (H), Literature & Cinema (H), Shakespeare (H), Literature of Revolution (H), The Short Story (H), The Naturalist as Writer (H), AP English Literature IV; **Social Science:** Global Studies, History of the U.S. (AP), World Civilization, American Diplomacy, AP History of Art, AP U.S. Government, History of Africa, History of Middle East, Economics (H), Psychology, and Media and Culture; **Math:** Algebra I, II, Geometry (H), Algebra II/Trig (H), Functions, Statistics and Trigonometry, Pre-Calculus (H), Intro to Probability & Statistics, Intro to Fractals & Chaos, AP Calculus AB, AP Calculus BC, AP Statistics; **Science:** General Biology, Biology (H/AP), Chemistry (H/AP), Marine Biology, Anatomy and Physiology, Physics (H/AP); **Foreign language:** French I-IV (H), AP French Language, Latin I-V (H/AP), Spanish I-V (H/AP), Spanish for Spanish Speakers I-II; **Arts:** Intro to Art, Art I, Drawing/Painting, Sculpture, Ceramics, AP Art, Photography I, Advanced Photography, Survey of Computer Design Multimedia, Chorus, Instrumental Ensemble, Jazz Band, AP Music Theory, Drama I-VI, Rehearsal & Performance, Student Directing Project, Dance I-II, Communications; **Computer Science:** Intro to Computer Science, Survey of Computer Graphics, AP Computer Science I/AB; **P.E.:** P.E. I-II: Weight Training, Court Sports, Aerobics, Field & Water Sports. **Other:** Yearbook, Journalism I-II. **Honors programs:** "Opportunities for interdisciplinary course work of independent projects are encouraged." Programs include U.S Literature Honors Seminar, Sophomore Religious Studies Seminar, World Civilization Honors Seminar (History III), and Independent Honors Program for seniors. **Computer lab/training:** The school has two computer labs. All classrooms have computers with Internet access and all students have e-mail accounts. **Grading:** A-F twice a year. **Graduation requirements:** "Designed to meet UC requirements, 4 years English and social science; 3.5 years religious studies; 3 years math, science and a foreign language; 1.5 years fine arts; 1 year P.E.; a justice project; and a charity project for community service." **Average nightly homework (M-Th):** 3 hours. **Faculty:** N/P #, gender. 65% hold master's degrees and/or advanced degrees. **Faculty ethnicity:** 88% Caucasian (non-Latino); 5% Latino; 5% Asian; 2% multi-ethnic. **Faculty selection/training:** "Teachers attend workshops, conferences, symposia, seminars and university extension courses. Many faculty also receive grants from outside organizations to pursue summer work connected with their teaching. While most of our faculty already have master's degrees and/or teaching credentials, teachers are encouraged and supported in their endeavors to earn these degrees while they are on the staff at SHP. There are also numerous occasions during which issues of pedagogy are addressed on campus by the entire teaching community: early-morning meetings, summer workshops, in-service days, department retreats, etc." **Teacher/student ratio:** 1:15. **Percentage of students enrolled in AP:** 50%; pass rate: 21% of the scores were 5; 46% were 4 or 5; 78% were 3, 4, or 5. **Most recent senior class profile (mean):** SAT Math 584, SAT Critical Reading 596, SAT Writing 616; GPA: 3.48. **National Merit Scholarship Program:** 5 Semifinalists, 14 Commended and 1 National Achievement Semifinalist. **College enrollment (last class):** 95-100% in 4-year, 0-5% in 2-year with the intent of transferring to 4-year. **Recent (last 4 yrs) colleges:** Babson C, Bucknell U, CSU (Chico, Cal Poly-SLO, Hayward, SD and SJ), Case Western Reserve, C of William and Mary, Dartmouth, DePaul, Drew, Fordham, George Washington, Gonzaga, James Madison U, Lafayette C, Loyola U-Chicago, Loyola U-New Orleans, New Mexico SU, Nottingham Trent, Pomona, Regis, Saint Louis U, St. Mary's C of Cal, UC (Berkeley, Davis, Irvine, LA, Santa Barbara, and SD), U-Miami, U-North Carolina, Vanderbilt, Xavier U-Louisiana, USC, Stanford, Santa Clara, U-Arizona, Pepperdine U, U-Colorado, U-Washington, Bowdoin, Brown, Duke Loyola Marymount, NYU, Princeton, U-Denver, U-Oregon, U-Pennsylvania, USD, and Washington U (St. Louis).

Other Indicators the School is Accomplishing its Goals: N/P.

Campus/Campus Life

Campus description: At the center of the 64-acre campus is the main building, built in 1898 as a girls boarding school and convent. The three-story building houses offices, classrooms, a chapel, computer lab, and a library. In addition to the Performing Arts and athletic building, three other buildings house classrooms, science, physics, math and chemistry labs; campus ministry; a library; computer labs; counseling offices and a 400-seat auditorium. **Library:** 18,000 print volumes; automated catalog; periodicals, newspapers, and reference databases online; 2 teaching areas; 30 student computers with Internet access; seating for 120; new 10,000 sq. ft. facility opened in 2001. Open 7:30 a.m.-5 p.m. Mon.-Th.; 7:30 a.m.-4 p.m. Fri. Three staff members; two full-time librarians; active research skills program for G9-10. **Sports facilities:** Include a Sports Center with a gym, a dance studio, weight room and locker rooms; an Aquatic Center with an Olympic-sized pool; a football field; a tennis complex with eight courts and an all-weather track and new field house." **Theater/arts facilities:** Performing Arts Center seating 350. **Open/closed campus:** Closed. **Lunches:** Hot lunch menu daily. **Bus service:** A shuttle service to/from the CalTrain station. **Uniforms/dress code:** "Girls and boys may wear pants, including jeans (but not including athletic pants); walking shorts; t-shirts (absent inappropriate messages). Girls are required to wear dresses or skirts on liturgy days. They are not allowed to wear at any time: halter tops, tank tops, or midriff tops. Boys, for liturgy days, wear dress pants, collared shirts, and ties. Boys' hair may not extend over the collar and they may not have beards or moustaches. Only one ear stud is allowed for boys. No extreme dyed hair, tattoos, or piercing other than ears." **Co-curricular activities/clubs:** More than 30 clubs – all with faculty moderators or student representatives.(Examples N/P) **Foreign exchange program/internships:** "The school has a network exchange program with Sacred Heart Schools in the U.S. and abroad." **Community service:** "In order to graduate, all students must complete 20 hours of service for the Sacred Heart Community, a charity project and a justice project. The Sacred Heart Community requirement is designed to familiarize younger students with the school and its rituals and to educate them in their responsibilities to the community. A charity project revolves around 20 hours of direct service in response to immediate needs in order to cultivate the virtues of compassion and mercy. A justice project 'responds to structural injustice and empowers people to help themselves, thus forming in a Sacred Heart student the virtue of solidarity.' Students fulfill these requirements through various programs, including 3-day trips to San Francisco to assist in homeless shelters and other services, housebuilding in Mexico, environmental justice programs in Yosemite, working in soup kitchens, tutoring, coaching, organizing prayer vigils and benefit concerts, and/or educating the public about various justice issues. Students act as tutors in Redwood City elementary schools and on a literacy project in East Palo Alto and intern with social service agencies such as the Boys and Girls Club and Packard Children's Hospital. Students choose projects that interest them at a volunteer fair held each September." **Typical freshman schedule:** Religion, math, English, history, science, P.E., fine arts, foreign language.

Student Support Services

Counselor-student ratio (not including college counselor): 1:215. **Counseling:** "The school has four college counselors who, along with the academic advisors, work with students in college planning. College counseling begins freshman year with a parent/student college night. Some freshmen take the SAT II subject exams. Sophomores take the PSAT; some take the SAT II. Students are encouraged to attend a Case Study Workshop and College Fairs. Juniors are required to meet monthly in the spring to develop college and career options. Parents and students meet on a college night in the fall, and a Case Study Workshop is held in the Spring. Students take the PSAT/National Merit Scholarship Qualifying Test in the fall and the SAT I and II, ACT and AP exams in the spring. Seniors have required individual meetings and class meetings all year to assist in college and career choices. They take the entrance exams in the fall and AP exams in the spring. The school has one full-time personal counselor." **Learning disabilities/differences:** "We have a full-time learning specialist and a Center for Student Success to support all of our students."

Student Conduct and Health
Code of conduct: "The school requires students and parents to sign an honor code promising to maintain honest, respectful relationships with all members of the Sacred Heart community; not copy/share homework; never plagiarize another's work; and uphold the policies and goals of Sacred Heart Prep." **How school handles drug/alcohol usage:** "Zero tolerance (immediate dismissal) for using or selling drugs or alcohol on school grounds or at school-sponsored events." **Prevention/awareness programs:** "A health education program for freshmen will be part of the P.E. curriculum and will focus on nutrition, body awareness, drug and alcohol awareness, and HIV/AIDS awareness."

Summer Programs
Numerous sports, aquatics and summer camps are offered.

Parent Involvement
Parent participation: No required hours. **Parent/teacher communication:** Parent/teacher conferences are held at the end of the first quarter. **Parent education:** "The Parents' Association has a networking program for parents." **Donations:** N/P.

Sports
"More than 70% of the student body participates in competitive interscholastic sports, including tennis, cross-country, volleyball, water polo, basketball, soccer, softball, track and field, football, golf, baseball, swimming, and lacrosse."

What Sets School Apart From Others
"Sacred Heart Preparatory places an emphasis on spiritual and moral development as much as academic excellence."

How Parents/Students Characterize School: N/P

Saint Elizabeth High School
1530 34th Avenue
Oakland, CA 94544
(510) 532-8947 *fax (510) 532-9457*
www.stliz-hs.org

Sister Mary Liam, O.P. Principal
Norma J. Mondy, Admissions Director, nmondy@stliz-hs.org

General

Coed Catholic day high school (N/P % Catholic). Founded in 1921. Nonprofit. **Enrollment:** Approx. 250. **Average class size:** 18. **Accreditation:** WASC/WCEA. **School year:** Aug.-June. **School day:** 8 a.m.-2:42 p.m. **Location:** In the historic Fruitvale district of Oakland, accessible by BART.

Student Body

Geographic breakdown (counties): N/P. **Ethnicity:** 45% African-American; 40% Latino; 8% Asian/Pacific Island; 2% Caucasian; 1% Native American; 4% multi-ethnic. **Middle schools (freshman):** 28 different elementary schools. (N/P %, schools)

Admission

Applications due: January (call for exact date). **Application fee:** $75. **Application process:** "High School Placement Test, satisfactory grades from prior two years, recommendation of teachers and principal, interview with parent and student, ability to successfully complete the available curriculum, proven record of good citizenship, effort, and attendance." **No. of freshman applications:** N/P. **Minimum admission requirements:** N/P. **Preferences:** N/P. **"We are looking for":** N/P. **What kind of student do you best serve?** N/P.

Costs

Latest tuition: $9,000 payable in 10 payments. **Sibling discount:** Yes. **Tuition increases:** N/P. **Other costs:** Approx. $350-500 for books, $650 registration fees. **Percentage of students receiving financial aid:** 51%. **Financial aid deadline:** January (call for exact date). **Average grant:** $1,500. **Percentage of grants of half tuition or more:** N/P.

School's Mission Statement/Goals

"Saint Elizabeth High School is a coeducational Catholic Diocesan high school founded in the spirit of Saint Francis and Saint Dominic serving a diverse student population from Oakland and surrounding communities. We are committed to fostering self-esteem and preparing students for college, challenging them to live and proclaim the Gospel message, achieve academic success and secure skills necessary for a life lived according to God's plan."

Academic Program

Courses offered (AP=Advanced Placement, H=Honors, (AP)=AP option, (H)=Honors option): **Math:** Pre-Algebra, Algebra IA, IB, I, II, Geometry, Trigonometry, Pre-Calculus, Calculus AB; **Language Arts:** Composition, Advanced Composition, Literature, Experiencing Literature, American Literature, World Literature, English Literature (AP), Oral Communication, Literature in Film, Creative Writing, Journalism, Introduction to Drama; **Science:** Physical Science, Biology, Advanced Biology, Chemistry, Physics, Anatomy and Physiology; **Foreign Languages:** Spanish I-III, AP Spanish; **Religion:** Catholic Christianity, Religions of North America; **Social Sciences:** World Cultures, U.S. History, Civics and Economics, Psychology; **Arts:** Art and Culture, Drawing and Design, Advanced Painting; **Computer Science:** Graphic Design. **Computer lab/training:** N/P. **Grading:** A-F. **Graduation requirements:** 260 units. **Average nightly homework (M-Th):** 3 hrs. **Faculty:** 27; 4% Ph.D., 30% with master's degrees. (N/P gender) **Faculty ethnicity:** N/P. **Teacher/student ratio:** 1:11. **Percentage of students enrolled in AP:** N/P. **Senior class profile:** N/P. **National Merit Scholarship Program:** N/P. **College enrollment (last class):** 98%; 62% 4-year, 36% 2-year. **Recent (last 4 yrs) colleges:** Arizona SU, CSU, Clark Atlanta U, Dillard U, Dominican U, Embry Riddle Aeronautical U, Florida A&M, Grambling SU, Hampton U, Holy Names C, Howard U, Johnson C. Smith, LaVerne, Loyola Marymount U, Mills C, NYU, Prairie View A&M, Rutgers U, Saint Mary's C of C, Santa Clara, Spelman C, Southern U, Stilman C, Texas Southern U, Tuskegee, UC, U-Central Florida, U-Portland, USF, and Xavier U (New Orleans).

Other Indicators the School is Accomplishing its Goals: N/P.

Campus/Campus Life
Campus description: N/P. **Library:** N/P. **Sports facilities:** N/P. **Theater/arts facilities:** N/P. **Open/closed campus:** N/P. **Lunches:** N/P. **Bus service:** N/P. **Uniforms/dress code:** N/P. **Co-curricular activities/clubs:** Campus Ministry, Black Student Union, Art Club, Charity Club, Drama Club, Latino Club, Pacific Island Asian Club, Trails Club, Science Club, and Youth Empowerment System, California Scholarship Federation, and National Honor Society. **Foreign exchange programs/internships:** N/P. **Community service:** N/P. **Typical freshman schedule:** N/P.

Student Support Services
Counselor/student ratio: N/P. **Counseling:** "Academic counselors and college counseling are available to all students. The counseling office also administers standardized tests. Tests administered annually are the High School Placement Test (prospective freshmen), National Educational Development Test (current freshmen), PLAN preparation for the ACT (sophomores), PSAT preparation for the SAT (juniors), ACT with writing and SAT practice tests (seniors). All juniors and seniors are assisted with preparation and registration for the ACT with writing, the new SAT, and SAT II. Individual counseling is also available. Group counseling is available for women's issues, men's issues, grieving, coping with stress and anger management. Through the Youth Empowerment System (YES) team, selected students are trained to help with peer conflict resolution as a service to the whole school community. The campus ministry program offers pastoral, moral, and spiritual support." **Learning disabilities/differences:** N/P.

Code of Conduct and Health: N/P

Summer Programs: N/P

Parent Involvement
Parent participation: N/P. **Parent/teacher communication:** "Parents are able to use PowerSchool to access their student's grades online." **Parent education:** N/P. **Donations:** N/P/

Sports
Member of the Bay Shore Athletic League, the Bay Football League, North Coast Section, and California Interscholastic Federation. Boys and girls basketball, cross-country, soccer, track, volleyball; Boys football and baseball; girls softball.

What Sets School Apart From Others
"Saint Elizabeth High School is a Catholic Diocesan high school that accepts, proclaims and gives witness to the Gospel of Jesus Christ. The community of Saint Elizabeth High School believes: education has the power to liberate; parents are the primary educators of their children; students are ultimately responsible for their education; teachers in partnership with parents are the facilitators of learning; students from all socio-economic backgrounds, religious beliefs and academic abilities should have access to a Catholic education; students are vested with dignity, worth and value and are empowered by God to attain their potential and to contribute in a positive way to church and society; education is not isolated but interdependent with local, national and global communities."

How Parents/Students Characterize School: N/P.

Saint Francis High School
1885 Miramonte Avenue
Mountain View, CA 94040-4098
(650) 968-1213 ext. 430 *fax (650) 968-1706*
www.sfhs.com

Kevin J. Makley, President
Patricia I. Tennant, Principal
Mike Speckman, Director of Admissions, mispeckm@sfhs.com

Coed Catholic day high school (70% Catholic). Founded in 1955. Sponsored by the Brothers of Holy Cross, South-West Province. **Enrollment:** 1,600. **Average class size:** 28. **Accreditation:** WASC. **School year:** Aug.-June. **School day:** Alternating block schedule, 7:45 a.m. -2:30 p.m. **Location:** On the border of Mountain View and Los Altos, a suburb on the San Francisco Peninsula just south of Palo Alto.

Student Body

Geographic breakdown (counties): 28% from San Mateo; 61% from Santa Clara; 11% from Alameda. **Ethnicity:** 2.4% African American; 18.4% Asian; 63.3% Caucasian; 1.1% Hawaiian/Pacific Islander; 7.5% Latino; 6.8% multi-ethnic. **International students (I-20 status):** 0. **Middle schools (freshman):** "The school draws students from more than 120 middle schools. Approx. 60% of students are from parochial schools." (N/P schools)

Admission

Applications due: Mid-January (check website for date). **Application fee:** $65. **Application process:** The school hosts an open house in October for interested families. Applicants must take the HSPT entrance/placement exam, submit 7th and 8th grade reports from their current school, and provide a Roman Catholic Baptismal Certificate to qualify as a Catholic student. Faculty members interview all applicants mid-January through early February. Decisions are mailed in March. **No. of freshman applications:** 1,200 for 420 places. **Minimum admission requirements:** Admission criteria include 1) 7/8th grade grades; 2) HSPT entrance/placement exam; 3) teacher recommendation; 4) activity profile; and 5) interview. **Test required:** HSPT. **Preferences:** N/P. "We are looking for well-rounded students with high expectations who want to be challenged and grow spiritually, intellectually, and socially." **"What kind of student do you best serve?"** N/P

Costs

Latest tuition: $12,200. **Sibling discount:** None. **Tuition increases:** 7%. **Other costs:** N/P. **Percentage of students receiving financial aid:** 10+%. **Financial aid deadline:** February 1. **Average grant:** $6,000. **Percentage of grants of half-tuition or more:** N/P.

School's Mission Statement/Goals

"In the tradition of the Catholic Church and the spirit of Holy Cross, Saint Francis High School is committed to providing the finest college-preparatory program in an inclusive family environment, encouraging students to achieve their highest potential through:
• Spiritual development, which expresses their Christian values in the convictions of their heart and the actions of their hands;
• Intellectual development, which translates their knowledge and skills into independent and creative thinking;
• Social development, which transforms their activities and experiences into leadership in and service to the community.
Our students become Holy Cross men and women who are uniquely prepared for college, service and leadership. Holy Cross men and women are people of integrity who discover their God-given talents, respect the dignity of every person, celebrate family and bring hope to others."

Academic Program

The school has an alternating block schedule with 85-minute classes. One day there are four classes, and the following day, three classes with a collaboration period. The curriculum is "an academically challenging college preparatory program. Accelerated and honors classes are offered in all the traditional disciplines. An extensive elective program in the visual and performing arts and a strong art technology curriculum offer a variety of courses to meet the needs of the school's diverse and talented student body." **Courses offered** (AP=Advanced Placement, H=Honors, (AP)=AP option, (H)=Honors option): **Religious Studies:** Religious Studies I, New Testament, Living the Life, Moral Issues, Social Justice, Christian Vocation, World Religions, Contemporary Christian Spirituality, Christianity & Philosophy; **English:** English 1, 2 (H), English 3, AP Language, AP Literature, World Literature; Senior English Selectives: Contemporary American Authors, Sports in Literature, Film as Literature, AP English Literature, Mystery and Detective Fiction; English Electives: The Short Story, Creative Writing, Irish Literature, Speech 1, Argumentation and Debate, Advanced Speech and Rhetoric, Journalism 1; **Foreign Languages:** French 1-4, AP Language, AP Literature; German 1-4, AP Language, 5 Honors; Spanish 1-4, 3 Honors, AP Language, AP Literature; Chinese 1-2 (plans for a four-year program); **Social Studies:** World History & Geography (H), U.S. History: Colonial America to Civil War; AP European History, U.S. History (AP), U.S. Government, AP Government; Sophomore Selectives: Behavioral Psychology, Introduction to Economics, Facing History and Ourselves; Social Studies Electives: History and Politics of the Olympics, Contemporary World Problems, AP Psychology, Case Studies in Modern Africa and Asia, Case Studies in Human Rights, AP Macroeconomics, Psychology 1-2, Economics 1, Leadership; **Computer Science:** Computer Literacy, Computer Programming (AP); **Math:** Algebra 1 (H), Algebra 1-a/b, Geometry (H), Descriptive Geometry, Intermediate Algebra, Algebra 2, Advanced Algebra/Trig Honors, Applied Mathematics, Statistics, Trigonometry/Analytic Geometry, Precalculus (H), AP Statistics, Calculus, AP Calculus-AB, AP Calculus-BC; **Science:** Earth Science, Biology (H/AP), Chemistry (H/AP), Chemistry in the Community, Physics (H/AP), Sports Medicine and Exercise Science, Marine Biology, AP Environmental Science; **Arts:** Drama 1-4, Basic Design and Drawing 1, Graphic Arts, Advanced Digital Photography, Drawing & Composition 2, Painting 1-2, 3-D Design, Ceramics 2, Band Tech, Band 1-5, Jazz Ensemble, Percussion Ensemble: Steel Drums, Choir 1-4; **P.E.:** P.E./Health, Advanced Team Sports, Advanced Strength and Conditioning. **Computer lab/training:** "Mobile computers and six dedicated labs, a campus-wide wireless network, multimedia resources in each classroom and high-speed Internet access. The graphic arts lab has high-end workstations, theatrical lighting and blue-screen technology. Each student is provided an e-mail account. Computer literary required for graduation." **Grading:** A-F. **Graduation requirements:**

230 semester units, including 4 years religious studies and English; 3.5 years Social Studies; 3 years math and science; 2 years foreign language; 1 year visual or performing arts; .5 years P.E.; demonstrated computer literacy; and 50 hours community service. **Average nightly homework (M-Th):** N/P. **Faculty:** 109; 51% have advanced degrees (N/P gender, degrees). **Faculty ethnicity:** N/P. **Faculty selection/training:** N/P. **Teacher/student ratio:** 1:15. **Percentage of students enrolled in AP:** 26%; pass rate: 24% scored 5 or higher, 53% scored 4 or higher, 77% scored 3 or higher. **Most recent senior class profile (mean):** SAT Math 587, SAT Critical Reading 581, SAT Writing 596; GPA: N/P. **National Merit Scholarship Program:** The latest class had 16 finalists, and 33 Commended students. **College enrollment (last class):** 94.5% in 4-year, 4.9% in 2-year. **Recent (last 4 yrs) colleges:** Include Boston C, Cal Poly-SLO, Dartmouth, Georgetown, Harvard, Notre Dame, Princeton, Santa Clara, Stanford, UC-Berkeley, UCLA, USC, and Yale.

Other Indicators the School is Accomplishing its Goals
"Twice recognized since 1991 by Department of Education as a 'National School of Excellence. Numerous teachers, coaches, and students have earned national and local recognition and awards."

Campus/Campus Life
Campus description: "The school's campus is spread over 26 acres along a creek at the Los Altos/Mountain View border in a residential neighborhood. Students move from classroom to classroom as they would on a college campus. Popular places for students to gather include three student centers, located centrally at Moreau Hall, and the quad, which provides picnic tables and abundant space for students to eat, study, and spend time together. The school also provides sacred places for students to explore their faith. The Brothers' Chapel is available for prayer services, and the Saint Joseph Prayer Garden is an inspiring space for reflection." **Library:** "The Brother Eamon Shaffer Library is open from 7:15 a.m.-5 p.m. and houses a computer lab. The circulation system is fully automated with a web-based catalog system and provides online access to research databases." **Sports facilities:** "The 5,000-seat all-weather turf Ron Calcagno Stadium is used for field hockey, football, soccer and track programs. Baseball teams play in the Chris Bradford Stadium, which has 800 seats and an indoor batting facility. The Angelo A. Aguiar Athletic Complex contains three locker rooms as well as a modern training facility, which is staffed on a daily basis by a certified trainer. The Holy Cross Aquatic center is a 50-meter pool and the basketball and volleyball teams compete in Raskob Memorial Gymnasium. The tennis teams practice and play at Cuesta Tennis Center that is adjacent to the campus. Shoreline Golf Links in Mountain View is the home course of the golf teams." **Theater/arts facilities:** "The school provides three fine arts labs, a modern graphic arts lab, a dedicated band and choir rehearsal space, and a small theater and classroom space for the drama program. Saint

Francis broke ground in the spring of 2008 on the Performing Arts Center and Graham Theater, a facility with modern sound, stage amenities and seating for more than 400 people." **Open/closed campus:** Closed. **Lunches:** N/P. **Bus service:** Morning bus service is available from the Mountain View Caltrain station. **Uniform/dress code:** "Dress code." (Description N/P) **Co-curricular activities/clubs:** More than 50 clubs and 75 student events held each year. Activities include ASB, Band, Chess Club, CSF, Drama, Foreign Language Honor Society, Forensics, International Club, Intramurals, Monogram, Multicultural Art Club, NHS, newspaper, Peer Helpers, Poetry Club, Radio Club, Robotics, Students Opposed to Drugs and Alcohol (SODA) Service Club, Interact, Shakespeare Club, Spirit Commission, Spirit Groups, Stand Up, Speak Up, Stock Market Club, Technology Club, Voices of Hope and Yearbook. **Foreign exchange program/internships:** "Saint Francis provides immersion opportunities for students around the world. In the most recent school year, 135 students and faculty participated in eight worldwide immersion programs to Chile, Brazil, El Salvador, New Orleans, Sherman Oaks, San Jose, the Coachella Valley in southern California and the Tohono O'odham Indian Reservation in Arizona." **Community service:** "The Holy Cross Service Program is a graduation requirement that encourages the development of the social conscience by placing students in direct contact with various populations of people in need. Empowering students to bring hope to others, they will work with people who are developmentally disabled, small children, elderly, and economically poor. While students are required to complete a minimum of 50 hours of service in our program, most exceed this requirement. Annually, Saint Francis students contribute over 50,000 hours of community service." **Typical freshman schedule:** Religion 1, English 1 (H), math, World History/Geography (H), foreign language, science or elective, P.E.

Student Support Services

Counselor/student ratio (not including college counselors): N/P. **Counseling:** "The Saint Francis Guidance and Counseling Department has nine professionally trained counselors on staff to provide academic, college and personal counseling services. A distinguishing strength of the department is the model of assigning students one counselor to work with throughout the entire high school experience. This connection nurtures students as they transition through the academic and social aspects of high school. Additionally, this 4-year relationship makes the college counseling process more personal, enabling students to find the best individual college fit." **Learning disabilities/differences:** "Saint Francis High School provides access services to academically qualified students with disabilities. Types of disabilities include medical, physical, psychological, attention-deficit and learning disabilities. Reasonable accommodations are provided for document-qualified students to minimize the effects of a student's disability and to maximize the potential for success."

Student Conduct and Health

Code of Conduct: "The Saint Francis faculty and administration believe in academic honesty and the principle of the honor code. Students are expected to do their own homework, to test without external resources, and to submit original work for all assignments. Saint Francis students are also expected to deny all requests to copy from their own work. Violation of this principle is subject to suspension from school and further disciplinary and academic penalties." **How the school handles drugs/alcohol usage:** "As a Catholic coeducational high school and a Holy Cross school, Saint Francis High School respects and promotes the dignity and worth of each human being. The use and abuse of alcohol and drugs is incompatible with the mission and philosophy of the school. Saint Francis High School expects students to avoid any use, involvement, or possession of alcohol and drugs. The Guidance and Counseling Department will refer any student who initiates help on their own to a guidance counselor who specializes in drug and alcohol counseling." **Prevention/awareness programs:** "Saint Francis High School is a satellite of the Northern California Community of Concern whose mission is to support member school communities in the prevention of the use and abuse of alcohol, tobacco, and other drugs by our students. To this end, the NCCC provides an environment in which member schools share resources, work collaboratively, and develop partnerships in the areas of parent/staff education, peer helping, and curriculum development."

Summer Programs:

The Freshman Experience for incoming Saint Francis freshmen; high school classes for enrichment or credit, including SAT and ACT prep; Advanced Sports Camps for G4-9; Sports and Activity Camp for ages 6-12.

Parent Involvement

Parent participation: "Parents are invited to become involved in the school's Men's and Women's Clubs. Parents organize and participate in events including annual parent-student events, the Lancer Auction, and Christmas at Our House held each holiday season. They work on projects from monthly mailings to concessions for sporting events." **Parent/teacher communication:** "Saint Francis High School is a community where educators, students, and parents work in unison to create a rich learning environment. The school understands that communication between home and school is integral to student achievement and encourages collaboration between parents, students, teachers, and counselors. To that end, the school employs electronic tools to provide information regarding academic responsibilities and progress." **Parent education:** "The school offers several seminars each year to help educate parents. The Guidance and Counseling Department sponsors several evenings throughout the year including:

a freshman/sophomore parent night focused on selecting appropriate courses with an eye toward college; a sophomore parent meeting discussing appropriate curfews, peer pressure and teen parties; and junior and senior college parent nights explaining the college search, application process, and financial aid." **Donations:** N/P.

Sports

Member of West Catholic Athletic League fielding 62 teams in 16 different sports including boys baseball, basketball, cross-country, football, golf, soccer, swimming and diving, tennis, track and field, volleyball, water polo and wrestling; girls basketball, cross-country, field hockey, golf, gymnastics, soccer, softball, swimming and diving, tennis, track and field, volleyball and water polo. "The school prides itself on 116 Central Coast Section Championships and over 200 League Championships."

What Sets School Apart From Others

"Saint Francis High School is a diverse, coeducational, Catholic, college preparatory school centrally located in Mountain View, California, and focused on educating the whole person in the tradition of Holy Cross. With a proven reputation for excellence in academics, athletics and the arts, Saint Francis prepares students for the rigors of college and the challenges of global citizenship. Saint Francis is a uniquely vibrant and spirited community where students are motivated by high expectations and enduring Christian values, and where every student has an opportunity to excel spiritually, intellectually, and socially. Saint Francis takes prides in its inclusive, family atmosphere. Students, parents, faculty, staff,and administrators work together in the tradition of Holy Cross to create a welcoming community that supports the growth and success of every student."

How Parents/Students Characterize School

Parent response(s): "Saint Francis truly educates the whole body, heart, and mind. It is coed, multi-racial, and multi-religious and so there is tremendous diversity in the classroom discussion and outside activities. There is a curriculum and activity for every student. My son made lifelong friends and had such a phenomenal high school experience that he now wants a college experience similar to that offered at Saint Francis. The school took a smart, shy kid and turned him into a very bright, confident speaker and leader. My son has received a phenomenal education that has prepared him for the most selective colleges."
Student response(s): "You are making the best decision to come to Saint Francis. There is the social aspect, the spiritual aspect, and the intellectual aspect, and you are going to have an awesome time."

St. Ignatius College Preparatory

2001 37th Avenue
San Francisco, CA 94116
(415) 731-7500
www.siprep.org

Mr. Patrick Ruff, Principal
Mr. Kevin M. Grady, Director of Admissions, admissions@siprep.org

General

Coed Catholic day high school. (82% Catholic) Founded in 1855 by
Jesuits. Nonprofit. **Enrollment:** Approx. 1,450. **Average class size:** 26.
Accreditation: WASC. **School year:** Aug.-June. **School day:** 8:30 a.m.-
2:20 p.m. **Location:** At 37th Avenue and Quintara, one block west of
Sunset Boulevard, in the Sunset District. Accessible by the 29 Muni
bus line and the L-Taraval Muni streetcar.

Student Body

Geographic breakdown (counties): Approx. 42% from San Francisco;
17% from Marin; 37% from San Mateo; 4% from the East Bay. **Ethnicity:** Approx. 61% Caucasian (non-Latino); 12% Latino; 12% Asian;
9% Filipino; 4% African-American; 2% multi-ethnic. **International
students (I-20 status):** None. **Middle schools (freshmen):** 65% from
parochial schools; 16% from public middle schools; 19% from private,
non-parochial schools. (N/P # schools)

Admission

Applications due: Mid-November (check website for exact date). **Application fee:** $75. **Application process:** St. Ignatius holds a Sunday
afternoon open house in the fall typically the second Sunday in November. Applications available online only and include student and
parent essays. **No. of freshman applications:** 1,250 for 350 places.
Transfers to G10-11 are considered on a space available basis. **Minimum admission requirements:** "Students should be progressing in
academic subjects commensurate with ability and should perform well
enough on the entrance exam to indicate capability of achievement in
a rigorous college preparatory course of study." **Test required:** HSPT.
Preferences: Qualified Catholics, legacies, siblings, and first generation
college bound applicants. "**We are looking for** academically talented,
spiritually open and active participants." **What kind of student do
you best serve?** "Students who are looking for the total package—a
rigorous college preparatory school, a Catholic school, and a school
with a wide range of co-curricular activities. Students must be open
to the spiritual dimension of the school."

Costs

Latest tuition: $15,500 payable in 10 payments. **Sibling discount:**
None. **Tuition increases:** N/P. **Other costs:** Registration fee of $550;

approx. $450 for books. **Percentage of students receiving financial aid:** 19%. **Financial aid deadline:** N/P. **Average grant:** $3,740. **Percentage of grants half-tuition or more:** N/P.

School's Mission Statement/Goals

"St. Ignatius strives to develop young women and men of competence, conscience, and compassion through an integrated program of academic, spiritual and extra-curricular activities. St. Ignatius seeks to develop students who strive toward the Jesuit ideal of the magis: a thirst for the more, for the greater good, for the most courageous response to the challenges of our time in the fullest development of students' talents, and for a lifelong disposition to serve."

Academic Program

"St. Ignatius offers a college preparatory curriculum representing a combination of courses fundamental to the Ignatian spirit of education, and including every aspect of the St. Ignatius experience: religious, social, and psychological, as well as academic. The kind of student St. Ignatius is striving to form is open to growth, intellectually competent, religious, loving, committed to doing justice, and capable of leadership. Students are required to enroll in 6 classes each semester." **Courses offered** (AP=Advanced Placement, H=Honors, (AP)=AP option, (H)=Honors option): **Computers:** Computer Applications, Computer Science AP; **English:** 9th,10th and 11th English (H), AP English, Modern American Authors, Shakespeare, Mythology, Fiction into Film, Burning Illusions, Women in Literature, Nature/Nexus, Dramatic Literature and Poetry, Literature and Composition; **Arts:** Art and Architecture I-II, Studio Art I-II, Sculpture: III-Dimensional Mixed Media, Photography I, Dance I-II, Acting: Scene Study, Advanced Acting, Music Appreciation, Survey of Early American Jazz, Beginning Band/Orchestra, Intermediate Band, (by audition: Acting/Drama Workshop, Musical Theater Workshop II, Dance Workshop, Mixed Chorus, Advanced Vocal Ensemble, Symphonic Orchestra, Jazz Band, String Quartet, Dixieland Band, Independent Study: Music Ensemble); **Foreign language:** French I-IV (A,H,AP), Spanish for Spanish Speakers, Spanish I-IV(A,H,AP), AP Spanish Literature, Latin I-IV (H), AP Latin, German II, Japanese I-III, Japanese IV(H); **Math:** Algebra I, II (H), Geometry (H), Pre-Calculus A,B (H), Math Analysis, Problem Solving Strategies, Intro to Trigonometry, Calculus (AP), Calculus AB; **P.E.:** General, Weight Training and Fitness, Recreational Sports, Competitive Sports, Beginning/Intermediate Aquatics; **Religious Studies:** Hebrew Scriptures, Christian Scriptures, Sacraments & Relationships, Morality and Social Justice, The Gospel & Jesus, The Search for Spiritual Meaning, Value and Belief, Liturgy and Worship, History of the Church, Ministry, Faith: A Universal Reflection (Major World Religions); **Science:** Biology (H/AP), Chemistry (AP), Engineering, Science Research Project, Physics (H/AP), Human Anatomy & Physiology, Environmental Science, Astronomy; **Social Sciences:** World History I, II, American

History (AP), American Government (H/AP), History of California, European History, Economics, Intro to Psychology, Psychology A,B (AP). **Computer lab/training:** N/P. **Grading:** A-F. **Graduation requirements:** 100 hours community service; 4 years English and college preparatory electives; 3.5 years religious studies; 3 years math and social science; 2.5 years science; 2 years same foreign language; 1 year fine arts and P.E. **Average nightly homework (M-Th):** G9: 2.5 hours; G10: 3.5 hours; G11-12: 4.5 hours. **Faculty:** 164; 52% male, 48% female; 54% hold master's degrees; and 5% hold doctorates. **Faculty ethnicity:** N/P. **Faculty selection/training:** N/P. **Teacher/student ratio:** 1:16.4. **Percentage of students enrolled in AP:** 40%; pass reate: 72% received scores of 3 or above. **Senior class profile in 2007 (mean):** SAT Math 605, SAT Critical Reading 617, SAT Writing 627; GPA: 3.31. **National Merit Scholarship Program:** Six finalists in latest year's class. **College enrollment (last class):** 100%; 94% in 4-year, 6% in 2-year. Of the 94%, 38% enrolled in UC universities and 16% in Jesuit universities. **Recent (last 4 yrs) colleges:** American U, Auburn U, Bethamy C, Boston U, Brown, Bryn Mawr, CSU (Cal Poly-SLO, Cal Poly-Pomona, Chico, Long Beach, Sacramento, SD, SF, SJ, Sonoma), Canada C, SFCC, C of Marin, C of San Mateo, Columbia, Cornell, Cuesta C, Dartmouth, Fairfield U, Foothill C, Fordham, Georgetown, Gonzaga, Harvard, Howard, Loyola Marymount, MIT, Marymount C, Morehouse C, Northern Arizona U, NYU, Northeastern, Occidental, Pomona, Princeton, Purdue, Reed, Regis U, Santa Barbara CC, Santa Clara, Santa Monica CC, Marymount C, Seattle U, Skyline C, St. Mary's, Stanford, Syracuse, Tulane, U-Arizona, U-Colorado, U-Maryland, U-Nevada, Notre Dame, U-Oregon, Oregon SU, Penn, U-Portland, U-Puget Sound, USD, UVA, U-Washington, UC (Berkeley, Davis, Irvine, LA, Riverside, SD, Santa Barbara, Santa Cruz), U.S. Air Force Academy, USC, USF, Vanderbilt, Villanova, Wellesley, West Valley JC, Willamette, and Yale.

Other Indicators the School is Accomplishing its Goals

"Advanced Placement pass rate in 2007 was 80.0% for 1,235 exams taken by SI students."

Campus/Campus Life

Campus description: The 11.5-acre campus includes three buildings housing classrooms and administration, an indoor swimming pool, two theaters, a music hall, two gymnasiums, cafeteria, chapel and sports facilities. **Library:** 18,000 print volumes; 80 periodical subscriptions; 3 librarians. It is available to students daily from 7:30 a.m.-5 p.m. Mon.-Thur. and until 3:30 p.m. on Fri. **Sports facilities:** Gymnasium, indoor swimming pool, full-size football field, four tennis courts, baseball diamond and practice cages, soccer field, and track. **Theater/arts facilities:** Two theaters. **Open/closed campus:** Closed. **Lunches:** May be purchased at the school cafeteria. **Bus service:** Charter service available from San Mateo and Marin Counties. **Uniform/dress code:** "The dress code can be summed up in two words: polo shirts." **Co-curricular**

activities/clubs: All freshman are required to choose at least one activity (*=those that satisfy freshman requirement). Clubs and activities include: A.A.A.S. (Association of African-American Students), Ambassador Club, Asian Students Coalition, Art & Publicity Committee*, Band*, Big Brothers & Sisters, Cycling Club, Block Club, California Scholarship Federation, Cheerleaders, Chess Club, Christian Life Community*, Computer Club*, Democratic Youth Rally, Drama Club*, Ignatian (Yearbook), Inside SI (newspaper), Irish Club, Italian Club, Junior Statesmen of America, Latino Club, Liturgy Club, Orchestra*, Social Justice, Rally Committee, Science Club*, Service Club, Speech and Debate*, Spirit Club, Student Council, Video Yearbook*, Wildcat Welcoming Club, and Young Republican Club. **Foreign exchange program/internships:** No formal programs. **Community service:** "The community service program has two directors and offers hundreds of community service opportunities, including work in parishes, hospitals, day care and recreation centers, convalescent homes, and summer schools and camps. At least 50 hours must be spent working with a disadvantaged segment of society." **Typical freshman schedule:** English 100, Algebra I, French I, P.E., Religious Studies 110, Biology (5 periods of 50 minutes each, 50-minute lunch).

Student Support Services
Counselor/student ratio (not including college counselors): N/P. **Counseling:** "The school has 12 counselors, including a full-time academic support service coordinator and three college counselors. The counselors provide individual and academic counseling; alcohol and drug counseling; assistance with transition to high school; assistance with SAT, SAT II and AP exam preparation; and career and college counseling." **Learning disabilities/differences:** "The school accepts some gifted students with mild, documented learning disabilities. Through its Academic Support Services program, such students are given reasonable accommodations such as extended time on major exams, etc."

Student Conduct and Health
Code of conduct: N/P. **How school handles tobacco/drugs/alcohol usage:** "No smoking within five blocks of campus. For a first violation of rules against possession, use, or sale of alcohol, illegal drugs or controlled substances at school or at a school-sponsored event or activity, the student is automatically suspended, placed on disciplinary probation for at least three months, and required to undergo alcohol/drug assessment, substance abuse counseling, and a treatment program; the student is also required to perform work for the school. Any subsequent violation within the student's four years may result in expulsion. All athletes and fine arts participants who are found to have been using alcohol or drugs on or off campus during the season are prohibited from further participation." **Prevention/awareness programs:** "The required freshman P.E. course includes drug and alcohol education components."

Summer Programs
SI offers academic, half-day summer school for students entering G8-9 (English, math, computer skills, and electives). Limited high school course offerings are available.

Parent Involvement
Parent participation: N/P. **Parent/teacher communication:** "Report cards are sent to parents twice each semester. Parents may arrange parent-teacher conferences with an individual teacher or a conference with the student's counselor at any time." **Parent education:** N/P. **Donations:** "The school has a parent pledge program. Parents who are able to make tax deductible contributions yearly to offset the difference of approx. $2,000 in the cost of education versus tuition are asked to do so."

Sports
More than 60 interscholastic teams including boys cross-country, football, water polo, volleyball, tennis, basketball, soccer, wrestling, baseball, crew, golf, lacrosse, swimming, diving, tennis, track and field, and volleyball; girls cross-country, water polo, field hockey, volleyball, tennis, basketball, soccer, softball, crew, swimming, diving, lacrosse, and track and field. In addition, intramural sports are played during the lunch period.

What Sets School Apart From Others
"Jesuit philosophy, total education, and forming, to paraphrase the words of Father Pedro Arrupe, S.J., 'men and women for and with others.' St. Ignatius High School's Profile of the Graduate at Graduation is a statement of academic abilities and personal characteristics the school seeks to instill in its students by the time of graduation. The school seeks to graduate students who are open to growth, intellectually competent, religious, loving, and committed to doing social justice, and who are committed to the pursuit of leadership growth. • SI's retreat program presents students with special opportunities for personal growth, spiritual reflection and community building."

How Parents/Students Characterize School
Parent response(s): "SI offers something for every student." **Student response(s):** "Students describe SI as a 'family' with a great sense of community."

St. Lawrence Academy

2000 Lawrence Court
Santa Clara, CA 95051
(408) 296-3013 *fax (408) 296-3794*
www.saintlawrence.org

Christie Filios, Principal
Anne Eubanks, Assistant Principal
Anna Moore, Director of Admissions, amoore@saintlawrence.org

General

Coed Catholic day high school. (70% Catholic) Founded in 1975, operated by Saint Lawrence Parish and Education Center in the Diocese
of San Jose. Nonprofit. **Enrollment:** 350. **Average class size:** 21. **Accreditation:** WASC. **School year:** Late Aug.-June. **School day:** 8:10
a.m.-2:45 p.m. **Location:** In an urban residential area a few blocks
from Lawrence Expressway and El Camino Real.

Student Body

Geographic breakdown (counties): 92% from Santa Clara; 2.5% from
the East Bay; 4.5% from San Mateo; 1% other. **Ethnicity:** Approx. 45%
Caucasian (non-Latino); 28% Asian; 15% Latino; 7% multi-ethnic;
5% African-American. **International students:** 0%. **Middle schools
(freshman):** 70 class came from 32 elementary and middle schools.
(N/P %, type)

Admission

Applications due: Early February (call for date). **Application fee:**
$65. **Application process:** "An open house is held in November for
students and parents. Interested 8th grade students may schedule a
shadow visit for a morning during October – January. Students submit an application by early February for priority consideration. In
January, students take the Diocese admission examination at any of
the schools in the Diocese he or she is considering. The Diocese 7th
and 8th grade school report is submitted by the elementary/middle
school, and teacher evaluations are required. Students applying for
the school's special program for students with learning disabilities
should contact the school for additional admission information." **No.
of freshman applications:** 250-300 for 100 places. **Minimum admission
requirements:** "C average. Most students falling in the 50th percentile
or above on the High School Placement Test (HSPT) will be considered for admission." **Test required:** HSPT. **Preferences:** "Students
who have attended Catholic elementary schools in the Diocese of
San Jose; students whose applications are received first; eighth grade
graduates of St. Lawrence Middle School; students whose parents are
parishioners of St. Lawrence the Martyr Church." "**We are looking
for** well-rounded students who are successful in the classroom and
contribute to their community." **What kind of student do you best**

serve? "We serve average and above average students who are looking for a small, family environment. We like to work as a team with students and supportive parents."

Costs

Latest tuition: $11,480 payable in 1 payment (2% discount if paid in full by July 1) or 10 payments. **Sibling discount:** Tuition is $10,540 for a second child; $9,990 for a third. **Tuition increases:** Approx. 3%. **Other costs:** $500 for registration; $400 in fees; additional costs for uniforms, textbooks, materials. **Percentage of students receiving financial aid:** Approx. 25%. **Financial aid deadline:** Early February - call for date. **Average grant:** $2,000. **Percentage of grants half-tuition or more:** 0.

School's Mission Statement/Goals

"St. Lawrence Academy is a Catholic college preparatory community committed to the mission of Jesus Christ. Striving to create a caring family environment, we share our Christian beliefs with all students regardless of race or creed. We nurture our community through prayer, worship and service. In cooperation with students and parents, we seek to encourage our students' moral and spiritual potential; to recognize the uniqueness and dignity of the individual; to develop intellectual, emotional, social and physical growth; to instill a sense of integrity, self esteem, and self-discipline; and to encourage them to achieve to their fullest potential. Throughout the curriculum we promote the growth of the whole student in a school with a diverse population. We empower the students to become responsible leaders who will fully share their gifts and talents with family, church and their immediate and global communities."

Academic Program

"Academically, the Academy follows the guidelines of the Univeristy of California in addition to the guidelines established by the Diocese." **Courses offered** (AP=Advanced Placement, H=Honors, (AP)=AP option, (H)=Honors option, Z=also offered in Zacchaeus Program for learning disabilities): **English:** English I-II (Z), American Literature (Z), World Literature (Z), English (H/AP), British Literature, Yearbook, Study Skills, Creative Writing, Film as Literature, Sports in Literature, Oral Communications; **Math:** Intro to Algebra, Algebra I, Algebra II, Geometry, Pre-Calculus, Calculus AB (AP), Accounting, Business Math, Trigonometry/Statistics; **Religion:** I Introduction to Catholicism, II Introduction to Sacred Scriptures. III Church History/ Social Justice, IV Christian Lifestyles, World Religions; **Social Sciences:** World History (Z), U.S. History (AP, Z), Government (Z), Economics (Z), Psychology, Sociology; **Science:** Integrated Science (Z), Biology (Z), Chemistry (H), Physics (H), Accelerated Biology, Anatomy and Physiology, Ecology; **Foreign language:** Spanish I-III, Spanish IV-V (H), French I-III, French IV-V (H), American Sign Language 1-2; **Arts:** Keyboarding/Computers,

Chorus, Drama/Theater Arts 1-2, Art 1-2, Computer Graphics, Digital Photography, Visual Technology, Music Appreciation, Studio Arts; **Other:** P.E., Civil and Consumer Law, Marketing/Careers, Journalism, Finance. **Special programs:** The school offers the Zacchaeus Program, a special program for students with documented learning disabilities (see Student Support Services section). **Computer lab/training:** "The school has a one-to-one educational computer initiative which provides a laptop for each student and faculty member." **Grading:** A-F. **Graduation requirements:** 4 years English; 3 years of math; 3.5 years religion; 3 years social science including world history, U.S. history, government and economics; 2.5 years science; 2 years of one foreign language; 1 year visual and performing arts and P.E.; 3.5 years of electives; .5 year computers/keyboarding. Graduation requirements are designed to meet UC minimum admission requirements. **Average nightly homework** (M-Th): G9: 1-1.5 hours; G10: 2 hours; G11: 2-2.5 hours; G12: 2.5-3 hours. **Faculty:** 33; 45% male, 55% female; 55% of the faculty hold master's degrees. **Faculty ethnicity:** 73% Caucasian (non-Latino); 9% African-American; 6% Latino; 6% Asian; 6% multi-ethnic. **Faculty selection/training:** "The school follows the Diocese guidelines on teacher credentials." **Teacher/student ratio:** 1:15. **Percentage of students enrolled in AP:** N/P. **Senior class profile:** SAT: N/P; GPA: "40% of student body maintain a GPA of 3.0 or higher." **National Merit Scholarship Program:** N/P. **College enrollment (last class):** "99% (N/P 4-yr, 2 yr)." **Recent colleges:** N/P.

Other Indicators the School is Accomplishing its Goals: N/P.

Campus/Campus Life

Campus description: "The high school is housed in a one-story building with two wings of classrooms and labs. The school has a new gym and two outdoor pools in a courtyard. The school houses two new science labs and a counseling center. The pavilion area of the school has been recently refurbished." **Library:** N/P. **Sports facilities:** "New gymnasium with two outdoor pools; batting cages; access to state-of-the-art facilities in Santa Clara County." **Theater/arts facilities:** Stage in Community Center. **Open/closed campus:** Closed. **Lunches:** Hot lunches are available daily. **Bus service:** Public. **Uniforms/dress code:** Uniforms. **Co-curricular activities/clubs:** Student Government and Leadership, Associated Student Body & Government Class Officers, Homeroom Representatives, National Honor Society, California Scholarship Federation, Board Game Club, Drama Group, Improv Team, Japan Homestay Club, Student Ambassadors, Culinary Club, Spanish Club, French Café, Literary Guild, Roller Hockey, Peer Helpers, Amnesty International, FAST, Movie Club. **Foreign exchange program/internships:** "Two-week program with Junshin High School in Nagasaki, Japan." **Community service:** All students are required to complete 25 hours of community service each year. **Typical freshman schedule:** Six 50-minute periods a week of English, Algebra I, Introduction to Catholicism, Spanish or French, keyboarding, Integrated Science, and either P.E., drama, chorus, or art.

Student Support Services
Counselor/student ratio (not including college counselors): 1:175. **Counseling:** "Two full-time counselors plus one part-time. The principal, vice principal, and campus minister also provide personal, academic, college and career guidance." **Learning disabilities/differences:** "The school offers the Zacchaeus Program, a distinctive program for students with mild learning disabilities. The program accepts 15 freshmen per year. Students are offered learning accommodations in all courses and specialized courses in some subject areas."

Student Conduct and Health
Code of conduct: "In order to create a quality, value-based education and maintain a positive learning environment for our students, all members of the St. Lawrence Academy community must work together to support the mission and philosophy of the school. Therefore, it is a condition of enrollment that a student behave in a manner, both on and off campus, that is consistent with the principles and philosophy of St. Lawrence Academy as determined by the school in its discretion." **How school handles drugs/alcohol:** N/P. **Prevention/awareness programs:** N/P.

Summer Programs: None.

Parent Involvement
Parent participation: Parents are required to give 10 hours of their time to the school each year. **Parent/teacher communication:** "Report cards four times a year; official parent conferences once a year and requested parent meetings as needed. Teachers are available through phone, voice, and e-mail. Student grades are available on the Internet 24 hours a day for parent and student viewing. Parent-Teacher Group monthly newsletter. Daily announcements sent to parents through e-mail." **Parent education:** "Parent evenings focusing on educational needs, college planning, financial aid, scheduling and student issues are offered each year." **Donations:** "The school asks that parents contribute the equivalent of one year's tuition over the four years their child attends the school."

Sports
The school is a member of the Private School Athletic League and is eligible for Central Coast Section Playoffs. Girls play on varsity teams in basketball, soccer, softball, tennis, cross-country, swimming, track and field and volleyball; boys on varsity teams in baseball, basketball, football, soccer, swimming, track and field, tennis, golf, cross-country and volleyball.

What Sets School Apart From Others

"St. Lawrence Academy is the most ethnically diverse high school in the Diocese of San Jose. The school is a success-oriented high school that values the individual. We are committed to a college prep curriculum with academic excellence, as well as diversity in the classroom. Through the educational process, we attempt to inspire and instill positive values in our students. It is unique in its provision of a program especially for students with learning disabilities. Our learning environment provides excellent student support: fully accredited strong academic program, small class sizes, math and reading labs with study skills emphasis, counselors on staff, a mentoring program, crisis intervention team, disciplinary review board, extra curricular activities, and student community outreach program."

How Parents/Students Characterize School: N/P.

Saint Mary's College High School

1294 Albina Avenue
Berkeley, CA 94706
(510) 559-6240 *fax (510) 559-6277*
www.saintmaryschs.org

Brother Edmond Larouche, F.S.C., President
Peter Imperial, Principal
Lawrence Puck, Director of Admission, lpuck@stmchs.org
Linda Yaris, Assoc. Director of Admissions, lyaris@stmchs.org

General

Coed Catholic day high school (N/P % Catholic). Founded in 1863. Nonprofit, member WASC, WCEA. **Enrollment:** 600. **Average class size:** 28. **Accreditation:** WASC, WCEA. **School year:** Aug.-June. **School day:** 8 a.m.-3 p.m. M, Th. and Fri.; 8 a.m.-2:10 p.m. Tu. and Wed. **Location:** 13-acre campus in North Berkeley accessible by bus, and a short walk from the North Berkeley BART station.

Student Body

Geographic breakdown (counties): 53.7% from Alameda; 31.3% from Contra Costa; 15% from other counties. **Ethnicity:** 35% Euro-American; 28% African-American; 10% Asian/Pacific Islander; 13% Latino/Hispanic-American; 15% multi-ethnic. **International students (I-20 status):** None. **Middle schools (freshman):** Freshman students come to Saint Mary's from a variety of 45 different Bay Area middle schools including parochial, private, and public schools. (N/P %, schools)

Admission

Applications due: Early January (check website for date). **Application fee:** N/P. **Application Process:** Application, 7th and 8th grade academic information (grades, progress reports, standardized test scores), teacher and/or Principal recommendations, the student interview, and HSPT scores. **No. of freshman applications:** Approx. 400 for 160 spaces. **Minimum admission requirements:** "Freshman entrance requirements are not based exclusively on the student's academic achievement, but also on a combination of his/her personal character, attendance, behavior, citizenship, and other related factors." **Test required:** HSPT. **Preferences:** "Faith, legacy, and feeder school are taken into consideration." **We are looking for** academically qualified, enthusiastic students who are ready to challenge themselves to participate in and contribute to an inclusive community and who see the Saint Mary's experience as a positive choice for themselves and their personal, spiritual, and academic goals." **What kind of student do you best serve?** "Saint Mary's serves students who are academically ready for a college preparatory program. We also are building a community of learners who are ready to share, to contribute, to challenge themselves, and to grow intellectually, and spiritually."

Costs

Latest tuition: $12,540, payable in 1, 2, 10 or 12 payments. **Sibling discount:** None. **Tuition increases:** 3-7%. **Other costs:** Books approx. $400. **Percentage of students receiving financial aid:** 27%. **Financial aid deadline:** Approx. February 6th (call for exact date). **Percentage of grants of half-tuition or more:** N/P.

School's Mission Statement/Goals:

" ....Essentially, we at Saint Mary's seek to educate the whole person, promoting the intellectual, spiritual, and physical development of each student through rigorous academic and co-curricular programs. We recognize the dignity of each student in a caring, moral environment. We affirm intellectual commitment and academic excellence, and we encourage students to assume personal responsibility for their education. For Saint Mary's students, education is created, not passively received. Students discover themselves and their world by actively engaging their peers, their teachers, and their whole community in intellectual and moral inquiry, in order to develop critical and independent thinking. We give special attention to raising an awareness of the poor and oppressed in our society, and to demonstrating this concern and sensitivity through Christian service. We believe students thrive in an atmosphere of mutual respect in an orderly and supportive environment. We expect students who come to Saint Mary's to give, to share, to contribute, to challenge, and to grow. As graduates, they are expected to be young men and women who will be lifelong learners and responsible, moral, productive citizens, and active members of their communities. Saint Mary's, through shared Lasallian spirituality, is committed to interdependence with the broader communities of the Bay Area, the nation, and the world. As we create community, we promote and honor diversity, be it racial, economic, ethnic, or social. We are a community in which learning occurs within the framework of Catholic Christian values, one which views all things with the eyes of faith."

Academic Program

"Saint Mary's offers a challenging college preparatory curriculum, providing students with a vital and comprehensive educational program, including a full offering of visual and performing arts, a variety of electives, honors and Advanced Placement classes. The school offers Advanced Placement (AP) in all academic subject areas for qualified students. All college preparatory courses are approved by the University of California. Each year the curriculum is evaluated in light of the school's philosophy, current state education requirements, college/university requirements and guidelines, and students' needs." **Courses offered:** N/P. **Computer lab/training:** "Saint Mary's supports a fully wireless dual-platform campus environment. Each faculty member is provided a Powerbook laptop. The school employs a full-time educational technologist to support multi-media and technology based learning throughout the curriculum. Powerschool, an information system, provides students and families with current academic assessment and school information." **Grading:** N/P. **Graduation requirements:** 4 years English; 3 years math, 3 years science, 3 years social studies, 2 years international language, 1 year visual and performing arts, 1 year P.E./heath, and 4 years religious studies. **Average nightly homework (M-Th):** 2-3 hours. **Faculty:** 44; 45% female, 55% male; 30% of faculty/school leadership hold master's or doctorate degrees. **Faculty ethnicity:** "35% faculty of color"; 65% are Catholic, two of whom are Christian Brothers. (N/P ethnicities) **Faculty selection/training:** "All have bachelors degrees in their areas; average number of years teaching experience is 14 years. Regular faculty in-service workshops and professional growth opportunities are provided to our faculty." **Teacher/student ratio:** 1:18. **Percentage of students enrolled in AP:** N/P. **Senior class profile:** N/P. **College enrollment (last class):** "100% are accepted into 4-year colleges and universities." **Recent colleges:** N/P.

Other Indicators the School Is Accomplishing its Goals

"A regular assessment process from WASC and from the internal leadership team evaluates Saint Mary's success based on our learning outcomes. We believe that a Saint Mary's graduate will: 1) understand what it means to be a mature Catholic in today's society; 2) be familiar with the personal, communal, and spiritual means available for continuing to become a well-integrated person; 3) have an appropriate foundation for college-level courses and for lifelong learning and possess skills to pursue such ends; 4) be actively engaged as the primary agent of his/her learning; understand diversity and seek to build community amid diversity; 5) honor the presence of God in self and others; and finally, 6) puts faith to work through service, especially to the poor and the oppressed."

Campus/Campus Life

Campus description: "Saint Mary's park-like campus is located in North Berkeley on a 13-acre site in a quiet residential neighborhood, making school a safe and easily accessible place for students and their families. The center is the academic quadrangle in which students move between several classroom buildings during the course of the day. The campus features impressive views of the San Francisco Bay, the Berkeley hills, and the U.C. Berkeley campus." **Library:** "More than 12,000 volumes, newspapers, magazines, Internet data bases." **Sports facilities:** "New $6 million state-of-the-art athletic complex, new all weather track and playing field; 8,700 sq.ft. multipurpose gymnasium and 7,300 sq.ft. practice gymnasium/auditorium." **Theater/arts facilities:** Multipurpose theater/performing arts auditorium. **Open/closed campus:** Closed, upper division students have off-campus privileges for lunch only. **Lunches:** Available for purchase. **Bus service:** "Carpools, a dedicated AC Transit Direct Bus Line 688. The North Berkeley BART station is a short walk from the campus." **Uniforms/dress code:** No uniforms. "The school expects that its students demonstrate modesty and good taste in their appearance and enforces a student dress/appearance code." **Co-curricular activities/clubs:** "The Student Activities Program encourages leadership, school unity, and community service through various clubs and student government. Students are encouraged to participate in co-curricular activities to expand their education and add to their social experience and growth. There are no ethnic/culture clubs at Saint Mary's that divide students." **Foreign Exchange program/internships:** None. **Community service:** "Saint Mary's integrates community service with academic coursework in its Service Learning program. Other programs such as Campus Ministry and Enrichment Week provide students with a variety of other opportunities to undertake various food and clothing drives for charitable needs." **Typical freshman schedule:** Every freshman takes a full 7 classes: English, math (Algebra 1 or Geometry), P.E. & Health, international language (Spanish or French), Biology, Religious Studies, and visual and performing arts (Music, Dance, Drama, Chorus or Art).

Student Support Services

Counselor/student ratio (not including college counselors): 1:157. **Counseling:**" Three full-time Student Counselors, one full-time College Counselor." **Learning disabilities/differences:** "Saint Mary's provides limited services for students with documented learning disabilities to minimize the impact of disability and maximize opportunities to forward their education. However, the school does not have a specialized program that supports students with learning disabilities/differences. Students are encouraged to locate specially designed programs of support or tutoring to ensure academic success."

Student Conduct and Health

Code of Conduct: "Students enrolled at Saint Mary's assume personal responsibility for their behavior and must represent themselves and their school well. Students are obliged to be respectful, considerate, and supportive of fellow students, teachers, and staff." **How school handles drugs/alcohol:** "Saint Mary's recognizes the many problems that challenge students and their families. Problems with drugs/alcohol are serious, and Saint Mary's makes every effort to assist students and their families who are interested in working to resolve any problems they may have. Confidentiality is observed. Saint Mary's has a zero tolerance level for those who profit from other people's addictions." **Prevention/awareness programs:** "The school's freshman health course discusses these and many other issues; they are also discussed in other academic areas of the program."

Summer Programs

The school offers an academic four-week summer school program for incoming freshmen if required as a condition of acceptance, with follow-up academic after-school support during the school year. Other summer school offerings vary from year to year depending on student need. Four weeks of summer co-ed basketball camp on campus are offered in June and July.

Parent Involvement

Parent participation: "Saint Mary's relies on strong parent involvement and support, although the school does not have a required number of parent participation hours. Every parent and family is a member of the Parents' Association. The purpose of the Parents' Association is to promote a spirit of community, enrich the students' educational experience by partnering with the administration, faculty, and staff; help in ensuring the intellectual, spiritual, social, and physical well-being of the students; and to encourage and support the Lasallian philosophy and character at Saint Mary's. The Parents' Association hosts monthly meetings and provides many opportunities for parents to volunteer for various school activities and programs." **Parent/teacher communication:** "PowerSchool." **Donations:** N/P.

Sports

Saint Mary's is a member of the Bay Shore Athletic League Division IV and North Coast Section within the California Interscholastic Federation. Saint Mary's offers 31 competitive athletic teams in 20 sports: cross-country, track and field. For boys and girls, golf, volleyball, soccer and tennis; girls softball, boys baseball, football, and lacrosse.

What Sets the School Apart from Others

"Saint Mary's is noted for the deep and powerful influence of the De La Salle Christian Brothers, their mission and values, which ensure the quality and character of the school. Our curricular program is enhanced by special programs such as: Service Learning, Critical Thinking initiatives, The Freshman Experience, Enrichment Week, Career Day, and Community Block. The Freshman Experience takes education out of the classroom, providing students with a four-day inter-departmental unique learning experience involving science, social studies, service learning and campus ministry. Enrichment Week is a one-week mini-course in March when faculty meet with students in a variety of learning opportunities outside the classroom involving a mix of academic, travel, college/career exploration, community service, recreational or individual internship classes. Career Day is a one day program providing students with an opportunity to consider and explore future career possibilities. Community Block are groups of 19-24 students and their faculty group leader who meet once a week, in a less structured environment, with a developmentally appropriate curriculum."

How Parents/Students Characterize the School
Parent response(s): "The hidden jewel of the East Bay." "The best thing that ever happened to my child ... much of who he is and who he will be is because of the time he spent at Saint Mary's." "You can test the true measure of a school by listening to the students—they will tell you the true story. My children always felt that they received an excellent education and preparation for college and wouldn't trade their time at Saint Mary's for anything." **Student response (s):** N/P.

Salesian High School
2851 Salesian Avenue
Richmond, CA 94804
(510) 234-4433 *fax (510) 236-4636*
www.salesian.com

Fr. Nick Reina, SDB, President & Director
Mr. Timothy Chambers, Principal
Dina Trombettas, Admission Director, dtrombettas@salesian.com

General
Coed Catholic day high school (68% Catholic). Operated by Salesians of Don Bosco. Founded in 1960. Nonprofit. **Enrollment:** 585. **Average class size:** 26. **Accreditation:** WASC. **School year:** Aug.-June. **School day:** 8 a.m.-2:50 p.m. **Location:** On the border of the urban communities of San Pablo and Richmond, 6 miles from the Richmond Bridge leading to Marin County, and 14 miles north of the SF Bay Bridge.

Student Body
Geographic breakdown (counties): 95% from Contra Costa; 4% from Alameda; 1% from San Francisco. **Ethnic breakdown:** 24% Latino; 23% Filipino; 23% European-American; 20% African-American; 8%

Asian/Pacific Islander; 2% Native American. **International students (I-20 status):** 1%. **Middle schools (freshman):** 10% came from 5 public middle schools; 25% from 4 private, non-Catholic school; 70% from 9 Catholic schools.

Admission

Applications due: Mid-December (check website for date). **Application fee:** $75. **Application process:** Online applications are available in September on the school website. An open house is held on the first Sunday of November. Recommendations from principal, math, and English teachers are due in February. Applicants are interviewed in February. **No. of freshman applications:** 295 for 150 places. **Minimum admission requirements:** 7th & 8th grade grades, recommendations from English and math teachers, personal interview." **Test required:** HSPT. **Preferences:** N/P. **"We are looking for"** N/P. **What kind of student do you best serve?"** N/P.

Costs

Latest tuition: $10,540. **Sibling discount:** None. **Tuition increases:** Approx. 8% year. **Other costs:** $725 registration, yearbook and capital improvement fee. **Percentage of students receiving financial aid:** 28%. **Financial aid deadline:** Mid-December (check website for date). **Average grant:** $4,000. **Percentage of grants of half tuition or more:** N/P.

School's Mission Statement/Goals:

"Salesian High School is a Catholic, college preparatory high school that educates young men and women to develop into good citizens for the betterment of society and the glory of God. Salesian combines the experience of church, school, playground, and home in a supportive, caring, family environment according to St. John Bosco's philosophy of reason, religion and kindness. Salesian High School intends: to educate students from diverse socio-economic backgrounds; to encourage students to develop their unique gifts and abilities; to value the innate talents and dignity of all students; to develop self-worth within each individual and respect for one another in a Christian community of faith, love and fellowship; to collaborate with all members of the Salesian family — students, parents, administrators, teachers, staff, alumni/ae and benefactors; to celebrate the school's rich diversity of race, ethnicity, religion, and/or socio-economic background."

Academic Program

Courses offered (AP=Advanced Placement, H=Honors, (AP)=AP option, (H)=Honors option): **English:** English I-III, English III (H), English IV (AP); **Math:** Intro to Algebra, Algebra I-II, Geometry, Algebra with Trigonometry (H), Intro to Calculus (H/AP), Calculus AB, AP Calculus BC, Independent Study, Statistics; **Religion:** Path Through Catholicism, The Hebrew and Christian Scriptures, Sign and Symbol, Christian Morality, Social Justice, History of Christianity, World Religions, Christian Lifestyles; **Social Sciences:** World History, U.S. History (AP), Government (H), Economics (H), Psychology; **Science:** Biology (AP), Chemistry (H), General Science, Physics, Anatomy, Environmental Science; **Foreign Languages:** Spanish I-III, Spanish A (accelerated), AP Spanish, French I-IV; **Arts:** Art I-II, Art Appreciation, AP History of Art; **Computer education:** Intro to Computers; **P.E.:** Health, P.E. **Computer lab/training:** The school has two computer labs with PCs. **Grading:** A-F. **Graduation requirements:** 230 semester credits including 4 years religion and English; 3 years math and social science; 2 years foreign language, science, and P.E./health; 1 year of a visual or performing art. Students must complete 20 hours community service per year. **Average nightly homework (M-Th):** G9-10: 2 hours; G11-12: 3 hours. **Faculty:** N/P. **Faculty ethnicity:** 89% Caucasian (non-Latino); 8% Latino; 2% African American. **Faculty selection/training:** N/P. **Teacher/student ratio:** 1:26. **Percentage of students enrolled in AP:** 25%; pass rate: N/P. **Senior class profile:** N/P. **National Merit Scholarship Program:** In the most recent class, 1 student was a Semi-finalist, 1 was Commended. **College enrollment (last class):** 75% in 4-year, 25% in 2-year. **Recent (last 4 yrs) colleges:** UC (Berkeley, Davis, Irvine, LA, Riverside, Santa Barbara, Santa Cruz, SD), CSU (Cal Poly-Pomona, Cal Poly–SLO, Chico, Fresno, Hayward, Sacramento, SD, SF, SJ, Sonoma), Cal Baptist C, Cal Maritime Academy, St. Mary's, Santa Clara, Stanford, USF, Westmont, C, Dillard U, Fordham, Georgetown, Eastern New Mexico SU, Humber C of Toronto, Keio U (Japan), Liberty U, Marymount (NY), Spelman, Stevens Institute of Technology, U-Arizona, U-Loyola (MD), U-North Carolina-Chapel Hill, Utah SU, Villanova, Georgetown.

Campus/Campus Life

Campus description: The school, a former Salesian seminary, is located on an 11-acre park-like campus at the end of cul-de-sac. The main building of the campus is a three-story art deco building housing classrooms, offices, and science labs. The four additional campus buildings include a library/multimedia center/caféteria/college placement office, the Salesian residence, and the Salesian Boys and Girls Club. **Library:** 1,000 sq. ft.; 20 computers with Internet access; study space for 25; open to students 9 a.m.-5 p.m.; full-time librarian; 9,500 print volumes; Athena online catalog. **Sports facilities:** "Gymnasium and locker rooms. The outdoor area includes a soccer field, baseball field, and a brand new track and field. The school uses the Contra Costa College swimming pool." **Theater/arts facilities:** Gymnasium/theater. **Open/closed campus:** Closed. **Lunches:** Hot lunches are served in the caféteria. **Uniforms/dress code:** "Students must wear a school name polo shirt, pleated pants, walking shorts or skirts. The dress code prohibits jeans; sweats; clothes with drug, alcohol, etc. messages; hooded clothing; denim; camouflage; midriff shirts, etc. No visible tattoos, beards or goatees; no more than one ear piercing per ear (two for girls); no bandanas, hats, or excessive unnatural hair colors; no beepers, cell phones or electronic devices." **Co-curricular activities/clubs:** AAAK, ASB Council, Asian Pacific Islander, Band, Campus Ministry, Cheerleaders, Chorale, Class Councils, Drama, Faith Families, Garden Club, Honor societies, Italian Club, Japanese Animation Club, Latino Club, Literary Magazine, Tabard, Animation Club, Mystery Players, Newspaper, Recycling Club, Yearbook. **Typical freshman schedule:** 6 periods of 45 minutes each long block 2 days/week, 90 minutes each of religious studies, English, world history, math, P.E., health, foreign language.

Student Support Services
Counselor/student ratio (not including college counselors): 1:125. **Counseling:** "Students receive college counseling beginning in 9th grade. Personal counseling is also available. After-school math labs are open to all students." **Learning disabilities/differences:** N/P.

Student Conduct and Health
Code of conduct: "Standard." **How school handles drug/alcohol usage:** "Zero tolerance." **Prevention/ awareness programs:** "Addressed in the 9th grade drug and alcohol program."

Summer Programs: "Academic classes are available."

Parent Involvement
Parent participation: "Parents are required to give 40 hours of their time to the school each year." **Parent/teacher communication:** "Two parent/teacher conferences are scheduled during each year. Additional conferences are available upon teacher or parent request." **Parent education:** N/P. **Donations:** N/P.

Sports
Football, cross-country, tennis, volleyball, soccer, basketball, track and field, swimming, baseball, softball, golf. The school is a member of the California Interscholastic Federation and a charter member of the Alameda Contra Costa Athletic League.

What Sets School Apart From Others:
"Our vision is to be the leading Catholic college prep school in the Bay Area providing a safe, welcoming, and nurturing environment for a diverse student body in the Salesian tradition."

How Parents/Students Characterize School: N/P.

San Domenico Upper School

1500 Butterfield Road
San Anselmo, CA 94960
(415) 258-1905 *fax (415) 258-1906*
www.sandomenico.org

Dr. Mathew Heersche, Head of School
Risa Oganesoff Heersche, Director of Upper School Admission
and International Student Relations, rheersche@sandomenico.org

General
Girls Catholic day and boarding high school (31% Catholic). Indepen-
dent. Founded in 1850 by the Dominicans. Nonprofit, member, CAIS,
NAIS, BAIHS. **Enrollment:** 150. **Average class size:** 12. **Accreditation:**
WASC/CAIS. **School year:** Aug.-June. **School day:** 8:10 a.m.-3:05 p.m.
Location: Approx. 20 miles north of San Francisco. The Golden Gate
Transit bus stops on campus; the school provides transportation from
the East Bay, San Francisco, and Marin Counties.

Student Body
Geographic breakdown (counties): 48% from Marin; 9% from San
Francisco; 1% from San Mateo; 16% from Alameda; 1% from Santa
Clara; 2% from Contra Costa. **Ethnicity:** 62% Caucasian (non-Latino);
29% Asian; 1% Latino; 7% African-American; 1% multi-ethnic. **International students (I-20 status):** 20%. **Middle schools (freshman):** 21%
came from public middle schools; 67% from private, non-parochial
schools; 12% from parochial schools. (N/P # schools)

Admission
Applications due: Early January (call for date). **Application fee:** $100.
Application process: Open house in November. "Student shadows
and parent tours are held from September through the first week
in January. Visiting students shadow a student through morning
classes. Parent tours are conducted by admissions personnel. The application consists of an information form, parent and student essays,
academic transcripts, recommendations, and admission test scores."
No. of freshman applications: 150 for 40 places. **Minimum admission
requirements:** "Each application is considered based on individual
merits." **Test required:** Either SSAT, HSPT, or ISEE. **Preferences:**
None. "**We are looking for** academically motivated students who value
the advantage of a small school setting, diversity of student body, and
involvement in school life and activities." **What kind of student do
you best serve?** "Above average students."

Costs
Latest tuition: $27,000 day, $39,500 for boarding. **Sibling discount:**
None. **Tuition increases:** Approx. 5%. **Other costs:** Approx. $300 for
books. **Percentage of students receiving financial aid:** 35%. **Financial

aid deadline: Early January (call for date). **Average grant:** N/P. **Percentage of grants of half-tuition or more:** N/P.

School's Mission Statement/Goals

"In the Dominican tradition of truth, we celebrate diversity, recognizing God's presence in ourselves and all creation. We explore and develop the unique gifts of each individual in mind, heart, body and spirit. We inspire inquiry and provide a strong academic foundation for lifelong intellectual growth. We recognize what it means to be human in a global community and respond with integrity to the needs and challenges of our time. • In the spirit of the above founding mission, San Domenico provides a cutting-edge curriculum which prepares female leaders for the 21st century. San Domenico has four over-arching goals for its students: -To prepare women for college. Graduates will continue their studies confident of their knowledge and of their essential habits of mind. • To prepare engaged, purposeful young women for full participation in the life of their society by empowering them emotionally, morally, and socially to contribute their interests and talents to improving their world. • To ready young women for the challenges of adult life, which necessitates that they be self-assured, self-reliant and realistic about the demands facing women in society.- To promote Dominican values so that young women seek the truth not as an abstraction but as a way of life characterized by charitable acceptance of others, by candor and honesty, by proclaiming what is good and by opening themselves to the rich variety of spiritual and intellectual meaning."

Academic Program

"The San Domenico curriculum trains the mind for thinking critically, analytically, and interpretively; develops skills for articulate and engaged reading, speaking, and writing. This establishes modes of intellectual inquiry. The arts, such as music, painting, ceramics, sculpture, dance, and drama centrally enhance the San Domenico experience." **Courses offered** (AP=Advanced Placement, H=Honors, (AP)=AP option, (H)=Honors option): **English:** English 9,10, ESL: Literature and Composition, ESL: Language Arts, American Literature, Language and Composition (AP), World Literature, Gothic Literature, Study of Fiction, Newcomers, English Literature and Composition (AP); **Languages:** French I-V (AP), Spanish I-V (AP); **Math:** Integrated Mathematics I-III (H), Pre-Calculus (H), Calculus (AP), Statistics (AP); **P.E.:** Health/P.E., Riding, Tennis, Sports Teams; **Humanities and Religion:** World Religion, Religion and the Arts, Sociology of Religion, Hebrew and Christian Scriptures, Ethics, Intro to Philosophy, Social Justice; **Science:** Conceptual Physics, Biology (AP, H), Chemistry (AP, H), Physics (AP), Environmental Science (AP), Teachers Assistant in Sciences; **History:** World History, Europe and the Modern World, U.S. History (AP), Issues in American Democracy, International Relations, ESL: World History; **Arts:** Music History and Performance, Music

Conservatory Program (private musical instrument instruction in piano, harpsichord, voice, recorder, harp, guitar, violin, viola, cello, bass, clarinet, flute, oboe, and bassoon), Dance, Orchestral Conducting, Flute Choir, String Quartet, Orchestra de Camera, Virtuoso Program, San Domenico Singers, San Domenico Chamber Singers, Theater Arts I-IV, Art I-III, Ceramics I-IV, Drawing/Painting I-III, Photography I-II, Printmaking I-IV, Studio Art (AP, H), Visual Arts, History of Art, Dance I-IV, Dance Ensemble. **Computer lab/training:** "All students learn computer skills as part of Freshman Foundations. The school's library, computer labs and classrooms are equipped with PC's and laptops." **Grading:** A-F. "Progress reports are issued mid-first quarter and academic update reports at any time the teacher feels concern or extra praise is in order. Deficiency notices for students attaining C- or below." **Graduation requirements:** 4 years of English and religious studies; 3 years of math, foreign language, social studies, and lab science; 2 years visual/performing arts; 2 years P.E.; 1 year health; 50 hours community service. **Average nightly homework (M-Th):** G9-10: 30 min. per course; G11-12: 40 min. per course. **Faculty:** 37; 40% male, 60% female; 81% hold advanced degrees in their fields. **Faculty ethnicity:** N/P. **Faculty selection/training:** "Professional development is important to us and all faculty are encouraged to attend seminars, classes and trainings each year." **Teacher/student ratio:** 1:8. **Percentage of students enrolled in AP:** 73%; pass rate: 69% scored 3 or higher. **Senior class profile (mean):** SAT Math 614, SAT Critical Reading 595, SAT Writing 604; GPA: 3.54 (unweighted). **National Merit Scholarship Program:** 2 Semifinalists and 2 Letters of Commendations. **College enrollment (last class):** 100% enrolled in 4-year. **Recent 4 yrs) colleges:** American, Amherst, Boston C, Boston U, Barnard, Bowdoin, Bryn Mawr, Bucknell, Cal Poly, Sonoma, SD, Carnegie Mellon, Chapman, Claremont McKenna, Colburn, Columbia, Dominican, Drexel, Duke, Eastman School of Music, Emerson, Eugene Lang, George Washington, Hamilton, Hampshire, Harvey Mudd, Indiana U, Jacobs School of Music, Johns Hopkins, Lake Forest, Lewis and Clark, Loyola U, Loyola Marymount, Macalester, Manhattan C, Manhattan School of Music, MIT, Mt. Holyoke, New England Conservatory of Music, NYU, Northeastern, Northwestern, Oberlin, Occidental, Ohio SU, Oregon SU, Parsons, Penn SU, Pratt Institute, Reed, RISD, Roger Williams, SF Conservatory of Music, Santa Clara, Scripps, Seattle, Skidmore, Smith, Stanford, Trinity C, Trinity U, Tufts, U.S. Naval Academy, U-British Columbia, UC (Berkeley, Davis, LA, Merced, SD, Santa Barbara, Santa Cruz, Riverside), U-Dallas, U-Denver, U Illinois, U Oregon, U-Penn, U-Puget Sound, U-Rochester, USD, USF, USC, U-Washington, U-Wisconsin, Wellesley, Wheaton, Whitman, Whittier, Willamette, and Yale.

Other Indicators the School is Accomplishing its Goals:

"SAT II Average scores: Writing 610 (includes ESL), Math II 690, History 680, Chemistry 640, Literature 630."

Campus/Campus Life

Campus description: "The school, spread over 515 acres in the hills of Marin County, has separate buildings housing the library, chapel, music conservatory, art room, dining hall, classroom facilities, three residence halls, administration buildings, an athletic center and concert facility. A one-acre organic garden and a creek run through the campus." **Library:** A separate building of 20,500 sq. ft. housing 22,424 volumes. Ten computers available for student use; 50 print subscriptions; online database. **Sports facilities:** The school has an athletic center with a training room, locker rooms, offices as well as a full regulation basketball court with bleachers. In addition, the campus has an Olympic-sized swimming pool, riding stables, six tennis courts, equestrian center, basketball courts, softball diamond, cross-country trail, jogging, hiking, biking and riding trails. **Theater/arts facilities:** Hall of the Arts concert facility with a dance studio, practice rooms for music instruction, and display areas for art as well as a 300-seat performance center. **Open/closed campus:** Closed campus except for seniors and 2nd semester juniors during free periods. **Lunches:** Full service caféteria with lunches included in tuition. **Bus service:** Included in tuition. **Uniforms/dress code:** "Students choose from a casual wear uniform wardrobe that includes skirts, khaki pants, polo shirts and sweatshirts." **Co-curricular activities/clubs:** "The key to our activities is our student government. The students plan spirit rallies, spirit week, Big/Little Sister events, class meetings, guest speakers, fundraising and community service. Social events include trips to Disneyland, Tahoe, Monterey as well as local theme parks. On-campus activities include movie overnights, talent show, health and wellness days, international day and Earth Day. Two open dances in addition to a Winter Formal at a local golf club and a Jr./Sr. Prom in San Francisco. The school year begins with a trip and activity for each grade. Clubs include yearbook, literary magazines, Student Council, Free to Grow (environmental and organic gardening club), photography, French Club, Guitar Club, International Club, Poetry Club, Social Justice Club, model United Nations, and Film Club. Spring Discovery is a week-long alternative learning experience involving extensive hands-on study of topics not normally taught in class. The freshmen concentrate on service, self-defense and CPR/First Aid classes. The sophomores participate in a nature exploration trip to Santa Catalina Island; juniors and seniors participate in week-long offerings such as a historical and literary trip to Boston, kayaking in Baja and Florida, cooking and sewing classes, theater and dance programs, immersion programs, and leadership camp, with new programs added each year. Art is central to San Domenico. Students enter local art shows, the theater arts produces several productions and the music students perform throughout the year. **Foreign exchange program/internships:** N/P. **Community service:** "Freshman have a week of community service opportunities each spring, including working in food banks and environmental clean-up projects. The student body as a whole participates in Adopt-a-Family at Christmas, UNICEF Halloween collections, Special Olympics, Marin Human Race and Pennies for Peace, as well as gathering money and items to send to countries that are impoverished, war torn or victims of natural disaster. Juniors and seniors choose a ROSE project, (Real Opportunity Service Education) a two-year, 50-hour program with one service agency that allows for in depth commitment to service and exploration of social justice issues." **Typical freshman schedule:** "Three periods of Freshman Foundations every day (English, history, religion, drama and art) which include group work and presentations as well as integrated learning. Students also learn computer skills including Power Point skills. The other 4 periods include math (integrated I or II), foreign language, Conceptual Physics and Health/P.E."

Student Support Services
Counselor/student ratio (not including college counselors): 1:150. One full-time personal counselor, peer counseling. **Counseling:** One full-time college counselor, Learning Center, Director of Counseling, Peer Counseling, Mentoring, College Counselor, health class. **Learning differences/disabilities:** N/P.

Student Conduct and Health
Code of conduct: "Honor Code signed by all students, faculty, and staff. Student participation on Honor Council. School rules, published in the handbook and Student Planner apply at school and at school-sponsored events. No tolerance community." **How school handles drugs/alcohol:** "Smoking on school grounds is punishable by detention and possible probation. Referral to smoking cessation programs for multiple offenses. Violation of the rule against drug/alcohol use/sale/possession is punishable by dismissal. Students merely present where alcoholic beverages, non-prescribed drugs, or tobacco are being used are liable for disciplinary action as well." **Prevention/awareness programs:** "Guest speakers to the entire community on issues of sleep, healthy foods, eating disorders, smoking, drugs, etc. Many guest speakers are used in the Freshman Health classes including representatives from local teen health clinic, Marin AIDS speakers, nurses, and other medical professionals."

Summer Programs
Summer programs in cooking from the garden, foreign language, summer arts intensive, music, riding, science discovery, web page design, and health and wellness for young women.

Parent Involvement
Parent participation: "No participation hours are required. All parents are involved in the Parents' Service Association. Parents attend pot luck dinners on campus. Evening speakers are featured through the school's Global Responsibility Forum. The school also has an annual

fundraiser, a Mother/Daughter Tea, Father/Daughter Sports Day and a dinner. Parents serve on the School Board and Board committees and in a parent advisory group, ABACUS (Advisory Board and Council to the Upper School). Two class parents, hospitality chair and a U.S. PSA Vice President organize parent events." **Parent/teacher communication:** "New parent orientations and the Back to School Day and Luncheon are attended by most parents. There is a monthly newsletter, a weekly e-mail communication and schedule, as well as letters as needed to keep parents informed. Formalized reports on student progress include report cards, progress reports, interim reports, academic updates, and deficiency reports." **Parent education:** "The school hosts parent education evenings on teen issues and decision making topics. We also mail copies of interesting articles or tell parents of interesting events, books and websites that relate to parenting and education." **Donations:** "Parents are encouraged to participate to the extent possible."

Sports
Girls compete in volleyball, basketball, soccer, tennis, swimming, track and field, cross-country, softball, badminton and riding. San Domenico is a member of the Bay Counties League.

What Sets School Apart From Others
"Since 1850, the all-girls San Domenico Upper School has offered generations of young women a distinctive education and unique opportunity to develop their creativity and passions while exploring new interests. At San Domenico, each young woman in partnership with a caring faculty takes personal responsibility for her academic preparation for college and for lifelong growth. The Upper School's blend of tradition and innovative college preparatory curricula teaches the essential habits of mind and prepares young women for leadership roles. As a religiously and culturally diverse student body of local and international students, San Domenico young women develop a global perspective. The Upper School concentrates on the unique gifts of each individual in a community where support for one another is highly valued. With a teacher to student ratio of 1:8, each student is engaged everyday in her education. Moreover, with a dedicated day and boarding faculty, the level of personal interaction is actually 1 to 1. Within the Dominican Catholic tradition, San Domenico strives to deepen each girl's unique gifts of mind, body, and spirit, while education for truth — epitomized in the Upper School motto veritas — is guided by the practice of study, reflection, and action. At San Domenico each young woman nurtures her spirituality. The range of proficiencies and passions is such that students dedicate themselves not just to the humanities and sciences but also to pre-professional music training, drama, and dance. Graduates attend colleges and universities around the country both private and public. Typically, a graduation class will send one third of the class to UC Berkeley and UCLA and two thirds to

private colleges and music conservatories. A Dominican education is an education for life — one that empowers each young woman to become independent, self-confident, and eager to question and explore."

How Parents/Students Characterize School

Parent response(s): "My daughter has gained self-esteem, self-aware-ness, and self-confidence through the academic and co-curricular programs offered at San Domenico." "The school offers a special kind of personal care to each girl." "San Domenico is like our second fam-ily." **Student response(s):** A student wrote this about San Domenico School on her college application: "To study in an international high school with great diversity is a significant experience that helps me understand and appreciate diversity. The student body in my high school has both external and internal diversity. Externally, we are living with people from all different races, cultures, and family back-grounds. Internally, each student has her unique thoughts and talents. Some are artists and musicians while some others are athletes; some are scholars with great ideas, while some are activists who carry out the actions. Living in a community with great diversity has taught me how to respect others' identities and how to collaborate with others to improve my community."

San Francisco University High School

3065 Jackson Street
San Francisco, CA 94115
(415) 447-3104 *fax (415) 447-5801*
www.sfuhs.org

Michael Diamonti, Head of School, mike.diamonti@sfuhs.org
Karen N. Kindler Director of Admission and Financial Aid, karen.kindler@sfuhs.org

General

Coed day high school. Nonsectarian. Independent. Founded in 1973. Nonprofit, member CAIS, NAIS, BAIHS. **Enrollment:** 389. **Average class size:** 15. **Accreditation:** WASC/CAIS. **School year:** Sept.-June. **School day:** Approx. 8 a.m.–2:30 p.m. **Location:** Pacific Heights/Pre-sidio Heights, a residential neighborhood in the northern part of San Francisco, accessible by the 1, 3, 24, and 43 Muni bus lines.

Student Body

Geographic breakdown: 72% from San Francisco; 20% from North Bay; 3% from East Bay; and 5% from the South Bay. **Ethnicity:** "38% of color." (N/P ethnicities) **International students (I-20 status):** N/P. **Middle schools (freshman):** 46 schools in the Bay Area: 21% from public; 72% from private, non-parochial schools; and 7% parochial schools. (N/P # schools)

Admission

Applications due: Mid-January. **Application fee:** $75. **Application process:** "University sponsors three admission open houses in the fall for 8th grade and prospective transfer families. Campus visits are from September through December and are strongly recommended. The application process includes the completion of a Student Statement, submission of transcripts, SSAT, a Parent Statement, as well as teacher and counselor recommendations. Applicants are also required to interview with a member of the Admission Committee. Decisions are mailed mid-March." **No. of freshman applications:** Approx. 500 (N/P # places). **Test required:** SSAT. **Minimum admission requirements:** N/P. **Preferences:** "Some preference is given to siblings and also to children of alumni." **"We are looking for** highly motivated students who have demonstrated the ability to pursue an academically demanding secondary school program. Successful applicants will have a combination of intellectual skills and personal qualities which will enable them to become effective members of the school community. While we value academic skills and innate talent, we also look for a desire to learn, a willingness to take risks, a curiosity about the world, a sense of compassion, a concern for others, and a commitment to the life of the mind. Successful applicants will be able to demonstrate that their education is not something that they are coming to obtain, but something that they are willing to create." **What kind of student do you best serve?** "Students who desire to learn more, to take risks and to reflect more deeply. Students who are interested in working in a collaborative environment and enjoy close faculty mentoring. Students that have a strong interest in interacting and learning with classmates of diverse backgrounds, perspectives, and talents are also a vital part of the UHS community."

Costs

Latest tuition: $29,750 payable in 1, 2, or 10-payments. **Sibling discount:** None. **Tuition increases:** 3-7%. **Percentage of students receiving financial aid:** Approx. 23%. **Financial aid deadline:** Mid-January (BAIHS schedule). **Average grant:** $18,985. **Percentage of grants of half-tuition or more:** N/P.

School's Mission Statement/Goals

"University High School welcomes students of demonstrated motivation and ability to engage in an education that fosters responsibility and the spirited pursuit of knowledge. We are a school where adults believe in the promise of every student, and together we build and sustain a community of diverse backgrounds, perspectives and talents. UHS challenges each individual to live a life of integrity, inquiry and purpose larger than the self."

Academic Program

Courses offered (AP=Advanced Placement, H=Honors, (AP)=AP option, (H)=Honors option): **Arts:** Non-Western Civilization: A History of the Arts (required), Studio Art AP, Art History AP, Beginning Instrumental, Jazz Ensemble, Chamber Orchestra, Camerata, Chorus, Ceramics I-III, Drawing I-II, Film I-II, Painting I-III, Photography I-III, Storytelling Beyond the Page, Electronic Music Studio, Jazz Combo, Acting I-II, Theater Production I-II, Music Theory AP, Technical Theater I-II, Musical Theater Productions. **English:** English I-II (required), Writing Workshop, Semester Seminars include: A Literary Madness, Literature and Philosophy, 19th Century American Literature, 19th Century British Literature, Poetry, Russian Literature, Shakespeare, Then and Now, The Bible, Haunting the American Imagination, Illuminations, Invisible Cities, Contemporary Literature of China and Japan, Literature of the Absurd, 20th Century American Novel, Short Story, and South African Literature. **Foreign Languages:** Mandarin I-IV, French I-III, Spanish I-III, Latin I-II, French AP Language, French AP Literature, Advanced French Seminar, Spanish AP Language, Spanish AP Literature, Advanced Spanish Seminar, Advanced Latin: Catullus AP, Advanced Latin: Vergil. **History:** Non-Western Civilization (required), U.S. History AP (required), Modern European History AP, Economics AP, Africa, American Lives, The African American Historical Experience, Jewish History Through Literature, Psychology, Making History. **Math:** Math I, Math II (H), Math III, Computer Science AP, Pre-Calculus H, Descriptive Statistics, Pre-Calculus for Social Sciences, Differential Calculus H, AB Calculus AP, BC Calculus AP, Multivariable Calculus, Statistics AP, Non-Euclidean Geometry, Chaos Theory, Discrete Mathematics, Cryptography, Linear Algebra. **Science:** Biology I-II and Chemistry I-II (required), Human Physiology, Chemistry AP, Physics, Physics-C AP: Mechanics, Physics-C AP: Electricity and Magnetism, Microbiology, Advanced Biology: Molecular Genetics, Advanced Chemistry, Environmental Science AP, Marine Biology, Astronomy: Solar Systems, Astronomy: Cosmology; **Interdepartmental Offerings:** Psychology; Independent Programs: Career Internships, Teaching Assistants, Tutorials, Alternative Education, Off-Campus Volunteers, Research Projects, Senior Seminars, Senior Project. **Computer lab/training:** "University High School is a wireless campus. A fiber-optic computer network links every classroom, and office in the school. Three computer labs offer both Windows-based PCs and Apple Macintosh computers. The science program uses networked laptop and desktop stations in its laboratories. There are 100 computers on campus and three laptop carts. Every student has access to school computers and personal e-mail accounts." **Grading:** A-F and written comments. **Graduation requirements:** "Designed to match UC admission requirements, 4 years English and P.E.; 3 years math and foreign language; 2 years lab science, history and fine art; 20 hours community service each year and participation in a class project." **Average nightly homework (M-Th):** N/P. **Faculty:** 64; 48%

male, 52% female; 77% hold advanced degrees. **Faculty ethnicity:** "23% faculty of color." (N/P ethnicities) **Faculty selection/training:** "We conduct national searches for qualified candidates. ... [V]irtually all have substantial previous teaching experience. In addition to their myriad duties as teachers, advisors, club leaders, coaches, and committee members, University faculty members systematically take time for their own professional growth. With the assistance of a sizable professional development fund, faculty attend and present papers at regional and national conferences, travel abroad during the summers, and remain actively involved in their own study and scholarship." **Teacher/student ratio:** 1:8. **Percentage of students enrolled in AP:** N/P (total of 467 exams); pass rate: 91% percent scored 3 or above and 78% scored 4 or above. **Most recent senior class profile (mean)** SAT Math 677, SAT Critical Reading 677, SAT Writing 682. Median GPA: 3.47 (unweighted). **National Merit Scholarship Program:** 12 students are expected to be NMSQT Semifinalists, and 19 are expected to be Commended. **College enrollment (last class):** 100% in 4-year. **Recent (last 4 yrs) colleges:** "The largest numbers of students have enrolled at Brown, Columbia, Harvard, NYU, Stanford, UC Berkeley, UCLA, Yale, and Johns Hopkins."

Other Indicators the School is Accomplishing its Goals

"SAT II Tests: Mean Scores (+ number of takers in last class): U.S. History 651 (46), Biology (Molecular) 740 (1), Chemistry 743 (28), French 697 (16), Japanese 700 (2), Latin 707 (2), English Literature 654 (37), Math I 647 (9), Math II 714 (43), Physics 630 (1), Spanish 698 (24)"

Campus/Campus Life

Campus Description: "The campus is located in the Pacific Heights/ Presidio Heights neighborhood of San Francisco, in the northern part of the city. The newly expanded and refurbished campus now spans four city blocks and is fully ADA compliant. The original 1917 Italianate building was designed by renowned architect, Julia Morgan. The campus includes six science labs, student lounges, language lab, three art studios, and a wet darkroom." **Library:** 7,500 sq. ft. (N/P volumes, etc). **Sports facilities:** Outdoor tennis and basketball courts, gymnasium, and changing rooms. The school uses the following on- and off-campus facilities and locations: University High School gymnasium, Paul Goode Field, Julius Khan, Presidio Golf Course, USF-Negoesco Field, USF-Koret Center, USF-Benedetti Field, USF-Memorial Field, Kezar Stadium, Boys and Girls Club, Golden Gate Park Tennis Club, Golden Gate Park Polo Fields, Mountain Lake Park, Alta Plaza Park, and Treasure Island. **Theater/Arts Facilities:** "500-seat state-of-the-art auditorium with a technical mezzanine with professional lighting and catwalks, a 'Juliet' balcony, optimum acoustical designs, cutting edge audio and visual technologies, and digital and computer capabilities. A spacious painting and drawing studio with plenty of natural light, a ceramics studio with 10 pottery wheels, three outdoor kilns and a large indoor work area, a photography studio equipped with a wet darkroom and 14 enlargers, a sound room for film production, an image library with thousands of digital and slide images, a collection of 35-mm cameras, digital cameras, lighting equipment, digital video cameras for student use, and additional gallery space with potential for a rooftop sculpture garden. Two new soundproof music classrooms which are specifically designed spaces to house University's larger ensembles and more intimate chamber groups, state-of-the art practice modules, electronic music/24 track ADAT recording studio, ample storage for our collection of instruments (including five pianos, two synthesizers, and a variety of woodwind, brass, string, and percussion instruments), and a music library that houses our expansive collection of sheet music." **Open/closed campus:** Open. **Lunches:** Full service caféteria. **Bus service:** Public. **Uniform/dress code:** "Casual." **Co-Curricular Activities/Clubs:** Amnesty International, Animal Rights Club, Asian Awareness Club, Astronomy Club, Biking Club, Cartoon Coalition, Community Service Committee, Chess Club, China Table, Debate Club, Devil's Advocate (school paper), Disney Club, Gadget Club, Gay Straight Alliance, Global Action Club, Green Club, Hope Cures Club, Math Pirates, Meditation Club, Monday Movie Madness, M.O.R.E. (Moving on Racial Equality), N.O.W. (National Organization of Women), Outdoor Education Club, Positive Social Action, Retrospect (school yearbook), Russian Club, School Council, Schmooze with Jews, Science Club, Social Capital and Food Club, Scrabble Club, Society for the Exploration of Mechanical Phenomena, Vox (school literary magazine). **Foreign exchange program/internships:** "Founding member of School Year Abroad; participates in Main Coast Semester and CityTerm. University aids students in identifying summer work and volunteer opportunities. The community service learning program and school academic departments announce opportunities throughout the year." **Community service:** "Community Service Learning Program is a four-year educational process that supports students as they work to expand and strengthen their communities and learn about related issues. This is a unique two-pronged approach: Not only do our students roll up their sleeves and participate in helping to improve their city but they also get to explore the public policy and social issues related to their service work. University's Community Service Learning courses are integrated into its daily program schedule. A sampling of sophomore classes that are connected with University's Community Service Learning Program: AIDS, Arts in Education, Basic Human Needs, Biodiversity, Literacy and Bilingual Education, Urban Youth Sports, Education Now!/Summerbridge. University offers many opportunities to serve the San Francisco community such as: Edgewood Family Center, Florence Crittendon Services, Golden Gate National Recreation Area, J.D. Randall Museum, John Swett Alternative Elementary School, Martin de Porres, The Names Project, Newcomer High School, Pets Unlimited, Project Open Hand, Russian American Community Services, Ruth Anne Rosenberg Adult Day Health Center,

St. Anthony's Foundation and Sutro Elementary School." **Typical freshman schedule:** 6 classes. (N/P courses)

Student Support Services
Counselor/student ratio (not including college counselors): 1:389. **Counseling:** "The school has a licensed counselor who meets with students or parents at their request and who holds evening meetings for parents on developmental issues. The Director of College Counseling meets individually with students and their parents beginning junior year and also works with the class as a whole." **Learning Disabilities/differences:** "In the fall of 2008, UHS opened a Learning Center, a space in which students can study, work in small groups, and/or make use of one of several learning-related software programs. Under the guidance of the Learning Specialist, students are encouraged to utilize the Learning Center and its resources to understand their learning styles and strengthen their study strategies."

Student Conduct and Health
Code of conduct: N/P. **How school handles drugs/alcohol:** N/P. **Prevention and Awareness Programs:** "The school offers a required semester-long course on teen health issues for sophomore students. The course covers a myriad of teenage health topics, including drugs, alcohol, tobacco, contraception, STIs, stress, sleep, nutrition, body image, media literacy, teen rights, gender, GLTB issues, and relationships. This class is team taught by senior peer advisors, with the Health Educator facilitating and providing resources. The purpose of this course is to present facts and information, as well as to provide a setting for lively discussion, for students to share views and opinions, consider how to handle relevant situations, and ask questions about a variety of health related subjects. The class meets twice a week, once in small discussion groups and again as a whole class for panels, presentations, and films."

Summer Programs
For six weeks in the summer, the school hosts Summerbridge, a tuition-free academic enrichment program for talented sixth, seventh, and eighth graders from the local public and parochial schools.

Parent Involvement
Parent participation: "All families are asked to go beyond the dollar gifts and contribute through the many opportunities organized by the Parents' Association, including committee and staffing work at the annual Decorator Showcase. The Parents' Association has over 20 committees that encompass a variety of responsibilities, ranging from student activities to enhancing the school life of the faculty to sponsoring and staffing the ever-popular Decorator Showcase. Each year, the parents of UHS collectively give hundreds of hours of time in countless ways that serve to enrich the lives of their children and play

a vital role in maintaining the sense of community in which parents can stay connected to the school as well as to other parents." **Parent/teacher communication:** "Faculty are quite accessible to parents." **Parent education:** "The Parent Advisory Board works with the Office of the Dean of Students and the Health Office to offer programs and seminars for the parent body. These seminars include topics ranging from health, college counseling, and intellectual/academic development." **Donations:** "Last year, the school had approximately 90% participation in the Annual Fund, with an average gift of $1,745."

Sports
Boys soccer, cross-country, basketball, baseball, fencing, golf, lacrosse, swimming, tennis, track; girls field hockey, tennis, volleyball, cross-country, basketball, lacrosse, soccer, softball, swimming, and track. Coed teams in badminton and club sailing.

What Sets School Apart From Others:
"It would be difficult to find another high school in the Bay Area which offers the highly personalized education and depth of learning that speaks to each student's individual needs in the way that University does. The curriculum represents a combination of required courses and a rich selection of electives aimed at meeting the needs and interests of a diverse student body, and a variety of opportunities to pursue independent programs of study. Further, University's co-curricular programs are integrated into our daily program schedule, thereby making it easier for students to fully participate and engage in a balanced educational experience. We are dedicated to helping our students achieve a healthy balance between academics, the arts, and athletics. University is about more than individual accomplishment; our students are committed to working with the faculty and each other on achieving a purpose larger than the self."

How Parents/Students Characterize School
Parent response(s): "My child has thrived at UHS. The teachers are incredibly caring and make the learning process a positive experience." "Parent participation is a wonderful way to get involved in the school. It's welcomed and appreciated but never demanded." "The school takes the issues of diversity, equity, and social justice seriously. The board of trustees, administration, faculty, students and parents are collaboratively involved in making the UHS experience a positive one for all students." **Student response(s):** "I am now a sophomore at UHS and it just keeps getting better." "The students are very friendly, and the academic and extra-curricular sides are excellent." "I learn so much from my teachers every day, but I know that my teachers are also interested in learning from me and welcome new knowledge with open arms. I love the relationships and friendships that I have with adults throughout this school, and I know it has been one of the most important reasons for my success at UHS."

San Francisco Waldorf High School

470 West Portal Avenue
San Francisco, CA 94127
(415) 431-2736 fax (415) 431-1712
www.sfwaldorfhighschool.org

Dave Alsop, Interim Head of Administration
Saudia Lawrence, Director of Admission, slawrence@sfwaldorf.org
Nick Wong, High School Dean

General

Coed day high school. Independent. Nonsectarian. Founded in 1997. Nonprofit, member BAIHS, AWSNA. **Enrollment:** Approx. 140. **Average class size:** 12-15. **Accreditation:** WASC/AWSNA. **School year:** Sept.-June. **School day:** 8:20 a.m. to 3:25 p.m. Accessible by SF Muni, Golden Gate Transit, and BART.

Student Body

Geographic breakdown (counties): 65% from San Francisco; 21% from Marin and North Bay; 4% East Bay; 10% from South Bay. **Ethnicity:** "28% of diverse ethnicity." (N/P groups) **International students (I-20 status):** 1-3%. **Middle schools (freshman):** N/P.

Admission

Applications due: Approx. January 15 (call for date). **Application fee:** $75. **Application process:**" In addition to the application, transcript, and teacher recommendations, students are required to visit for one day and participate in an interview with parent(s), submit a self-portrait and an academic work sample, and attend an open house. BAIHS common application forms and schedules are used." **No. of freshman applications:** 75-100 (N/P # places). **Minimum admission requirements:** N/P. **Test required:** None. **Preferences:** None. "**We are looking for** students who are willing and prepared to: challenge themselves academically; explore the arts; serve their community; move their bodies in healthful ways; and meet the world and engage themselves fully in it with a desire to make it a better place. We seek students who are eager to think imaginatively, to look at each issue they encounter from as many sides as possible, to see information and knowledge in both historical and contemporary contexts, and to take up the responsibilities of modern world citizenship." "**We are looking for** individuals who are curious, unafraid of making mistakes and learning from them, and who have the capacity to work through the struggles of becoming an adult." **What kind of student do you best serve?** "We best serve students who appreciate academic rigor; are interested in exploring the arts, music, and social issues; and who desire to involve themselves in community service, to contribute to the extracurricular life of the school and to become responsible citizens of the world."

Costs

Latest tuition: $24,700. Sibling discount: 10%. Tuition increases: Approx. 4.5-8%. Other costs: Approx. $200 for books, $200 tuition insurance fee, $500 sports fee, $150 supplies, $15 Parent Association dues, $10 accident insurance. **Percentage of students receiving financial aid: 37%. Financial aid deadline:** Mid-Jan. (call for date). **Average grant:** $5,000. **Percentage of grants of half-tuition or more:** 40%.

School's Mission Statement/Goals

"Our purpose is to provide Waldorf education in San Francisco for children from early childhood through high school. At San Francisco Waldorf School, academic excellence, social responsibility, and the recognition of each individual's gifts are the guiding educational ideals. The curriculum integrates the student's developmental needs with intellectual and artistic skills. Our deeply committed faculty works together to foster each student's sense of self-reliance, concern for community, and moral purpose. The student's educated, disciplined imagination will be the foundation for leadership into the future. • Goals of the High School: The goal of the high school is to support developing adolescents in achieving their full humanity intellectually, artistically, emotionally, and socially. A phenomenological approach encourages careful observation and independent thinking in course work. We want our students to know what they think, not what they are supposed to think. Using a broad, art-imbued curriculum, we strive to inspire our students to become responsible, compassionate, self-confident adults with a sense of global community who will be able to act out of freedom, work with respect for others, and use resources with social consciousness in their lives."

Academic Program

"San Francisco Waldorf High School offers a rigorous college preparatory curriculum that integrates ethical values and creative exploration into all subjects. Grounded in the classics, academic courses at San Francisco Waldorf High School expose students to the great ideas of mankind, the events that shaped civilizations, the beauty of mathematics, the power of the arts, and the phenomena of the natural world. Our academic program provides exposure and mastery of a broad range of ideas in math, art, science, and the humanities. By offering a wide variety of subjects, Waldorf students have the opportunity to discover their own unique strengths and talents, giving them the self-confidence to succeed in all areas of their education. The Waldorf curriculum is carefully crafted to guide students through various stages of their intellectual and personal development. Students learn to observe, compare, analyze, synthesize, question, and imagine alternatives. They debate ethical issues in science, history, and literature. They engage in abstract mathematical reasoning, as well as hands-on laboratory experiments. They consider ideas from multiple perspectives and appreciate the value of diversity. Learning through multiple methods results in a solid understanding of complex concepts and develops valuable skills that students will use throughout their lives." **Courses offered:** N/P. **Computer/lab training:** N/P. **Grading:** "Narrative evaluations are given after every main lesson and at the first quarter and end of semesters; unofficial transcripts and GPAs are given at the end of G10, 11, and 12. In G9, there is a pass/no credit system of grading; in subsequent years, GPA's are figured based on a 4.0 system." **Graduation requirements:** 4 years English, math, art, music, foreign language and movement/P.E./outdoor education; 2 years world history; 1 year U.S. History, cultural studies, biology, physics, physical science, chemistry, aesthetics (poetics, history of music, history of architecture, art history); 4 weeks internship in business or with nonprofits; 20 hours per year of community service plus 5 weeks (160 hours) of Project Week and Work Week community service during G9-11. **Faculty:** N/P. **Teacher/student ratio:** Approx. 1:6. **Percentage of students enrolled in AP:** N/P. **Most recent senior class profile (mean):** SAT Math 575, SAT Critical Reading 608, SAT Writing 590; GPA: N/P. **National Merit Scholarship Program:** In the past 3 years, 4 Finalists, 2 Semifinalists, and 3 students Commended. **College enrollment (last class):** [Last 4 years] 95% have enrolled in college, with a few taking a year off to travel or work. (N/P 4-yr, 2 yr) **Recent (last 4 yrs) colleges:** (partial list) American, Antioch, Bard, Bennington, Berkelee School of Music, Boston, Brown, CSU (Cal Poly, Fresno, Chico, Humboldt, Maritime Academy, SF, SLO) Colby-Sawyer, Cornell, Emerson (Boston), Eugene Lang, Evergreen, FIDM, Georgetown, George Washington, Goucher, Haverford, Ithaca, John Hopkins, Kenyon, Lewis and Clark, Loyola Marymount, Middlebury, Mitchell, Northeastern, NYU, Oberlin, Reed, SFAI, Sarah Lawrence, Smith, Trinity, Tufts, UC (Berkeley, Davis, LA, Santa Barbara, SD, Santa Cruz), UOP, USF, Wellesley, Wesleyan, Whitman, Whittier, and Willamette.

Campus/Campus Life

Campus description: "Located on 1.66 acres in a residential neighborhood, the 23,000 sq. ft. facility houses nine classrooms and three state-of-the-art science labs. It is within easy walking distance of local West Portal businesses and is easily accessible by car or public transportation. The school is registered with the U.S. Green Building Council as a LEED (Leadership in Energy and Environmental Design) Project, and is striving to reach the Gold level of Certification." **Library:** N/P. **Sports facilities:** Multipurpose room. **Theater/Arts facilities:** Two dedicated art studios. **Open/closed campus:** N/P. **Lunches:** N/P. **Bus service:** Public. **Uniforms/dress code:** "Casual." **Co-curricular activities/clubs:** Include Amnesty International, Technology Club, Key Club, The View (yearbook), Literary Magazine, Environmental Club, Drama Club, Peer Counselors, Theater Tech Crew, German Club, Spanish Club, Model UN, Dance Club. **Foreign exchange program/internships:** "The school has an active international exchange program with Waldorf schools in Spain, Germany, Peru, Argentina, and Colombia. Since the inception of the Exchange Program in 1998, the school has hosted some 3 dozen students from other countries." **Community service:** "Students select their own nonprofits to which they offer their services (10 hours each year), such as Glide Memorial, the Food Bank, Laguna Honda Hospital, and Central Gardens. They also provide 10 hours of service annually to the high school and its affiliates. In addition, students work during Project Week with such organizations as the National Park Service in Yosemite, The Presidio's Natural Resources Center, the Marine Mammal Center in Sausalito, Dharma Publishing (restoring sacred texts), Golden Gate Park's Arboretum, and local neighborhood groups cleaning graffiti and establishing Drug Free Zones." **Typical freshman schedule:** N/P.

Student Support Services

Counselor/student ratio (not including college counselors): 2:120. **Counseling:** "College and Career counselors assist students in determining what they are looking for in a college or career, defining the criteria, and examining their true passions." **Learning differences/disabilities:** "Our Individualized Learning Committee provides support and oversight for students with learning differences, establishing Individualized Learning Plans and serving as liaisons with faculty, family, and outside professionals. Students with educational assessments who qualify for admittance are granted extra time for testing or other accommodations and are supported with individual tutoring from teachers and outside tutors."

Parent Involvement

Parent participation: "Parents are encouraged to volunteer in the life of the school community, the Parents Council, the Parents' Coalition of Bay Area High Schools, and to contribute to annual fundraising." **Parent/teacher communication:** "Parents may contact teachers during school hours." **Parent education:** "Class sponsors offer a number of parent evenings each year to address the students' work and discuss parenting issues." **Donations:** N/P.

Sports

The school participates in the Bay Area Conference, Bay Counties League West and offers, for boys and girls, soccer, basketball, cross-country, and track and field; volleyball for girls and baseball for boys.

What Sets School Apart From Others

"We value education that does not teach to the test, but rather develops each student's innate capacities of imagination, thinking, and action. The majority of our classes are taught in blocks, which allows students and teachers to delve deeply into a subject, usually using original source material rather than textbooks. Our school is small and possesses a wonderful collegial environment, an ideal setting for adolescents to receive the education and social support they need to prepare themselves for their adult tasks in the global community. 'SFWHS Student Learning Expectations': Over their school career, we expect that students will develop capacities of active, creative thinking; sensitive, compassionate feeling; and self-directed, purposeful activity. Thinking: Students should be able to: assimilate and organize ideas and knowledge in a living, imaginative way; apply analytic and synthetic thinking to observed phenomena; communicate clearly and effectively, both orally and in writing; solve problems creatively; live in and work on difficult questions without expecting an immediate solution. Feeling: Students should be able to: show reverence for all forms of life; listen with interest and respect; experience the essence of common human striving through the discipline of the fine arts; appreciate and celebrate the diversity of human beings, and the uniqueness of each individual; be conscious of and care about global human needs. Willing: Students should be able to: set and achieve goals based on their ideals; commit themselves to developing their fullest capacities; integrate their education experience into the practical aspects of daily life; demonstrate sound judgment and values in the affairs of life; initiate positive social activity. We expect that by integrating these capacities within themselves, our graduates will have gained a measure of self-knowledge, an interest in self-development, and a positive, healthy orientation to the world."

How Parents/Students Characterize School: N/P.

Sonoma Academy
2500 Farmers Lane
Santa Rosa, CA 95404
(707) 545-1770 *fax (707) 636-2474*
www.sonomaacademy.org

Janet Durgin, Head of School
Mary Jo Dale, Director of Marketing and Enrollment,
maryjo.dale@sonomaacademy.org

General
Coed day high school. Nonsectarian. Independent. Founded in 2001. Nonprofit, member of NAIS, POCIS, CASE, BAISHA, BAAD, NBOA, ISBOA, NACAC, WACAC, BAISCC. **Enrollment:** Approx. 200. **Average class size:** 12. **Accreditation:** WASC. **School year:** Aug.-May. **School day:** 8 a.m.-3:30 p.m. **Location:** In Santa Rosa, accessible by bus from some areas.

Student Body

Geographic breakdown (counties): 84% from Sonoma; 5% from Marin; 9% from Napa, 1% Mendocino, .5% Lake. **Ethnicity:** 83% Caucasian (non-Latino); 1.5% Asian; 6.6% Latino; 2.5% African-American; 4% multiracial, 1.5% Pacific Islander, 1% Middleeastern. **International students (I-20 status):** 0. **Middle schools (freshman):** 60% came from 22 public middle schools (18% of those from 7 public charter); 30% from 3 private, non-parochial schools; 8% from 3 parochial schools.

Admission

Applications due: Mid-January (call for date). **Application fee:** $75. **Application process:** Includes application, essay, teacher recommendations, interview, and admission test. **No. of freshman applications:** N/P. **Minimum admission requirements:** "Each student is considered based on individual profile. Typically, we select motivated students with solid academic records and teacher recommendations who have the ability to communicate in their essay and interview." **Test required:** SSAT. **Preferences:** None. **"We are looking for** students who want to be a part of a learning community where challenge, working hard, creativity, support, and opportunity are the cornerstones." **What kind of student do you best serve?** "Students who want to be actively involved participants in their education."

Costs

Latest tuition: $28,500. **Sibling discount:** None. **Tuition increases:** Approx. 8%. **Other costs:** Approx. $1,650 book/materials/technology fee (which includes laptop loaner). **Percentage of students receiving financial aid:** 40%. **Financial aid deadline:** Mid-January (call for date). **Average grant:** 60% of tuition, books, and fees. **Percentage of grants of half-tuition or more:** N/P.

School's Mission Statement/Goals

"Sonoma Academy calls on its students to be creative, ethical, and committed to learning. The school nurtures inspiring teachers and engages with the surrounding community; its students communicate across cultures as they prepare to become leaders in a dynamic world."

Academic Program

Courses offered: Humanities: Humanities I: English 101 and History 101, Humanities II: English 201 and History 201, Humanities III: AP English Language and Composition and U.S. History, African Studies, AP English Literature and Composition, The Art of the Essay, Cooperation and Conflict in Eastern Europe, Creative Fiction and Nonfiction, Grit and Reverence: Environmental Literature of North America, Introduction to Economics, Making History: Seminar in Historiography and Research, Surface Tension: American Literature 1945 to the Present; **Math/Science:** Math-Science 1: Biology with Algebra I, Physics with Algebra II, Biochemistry 1: Biology, Geometry: Architecture,

Geometry: Proof, Biochemistry II: Chemistry, Biochemistry II: Honors Chemistry, Algebra II: Modeling, Precalculus, Honors Precalculus, AP Calculus AB, AP Chemistry, AP Physics C, AP Statistics, Introduction to Engineering, Natural History of California Mountains and Deserts, Oceanology; **World languages:** French I-IV, AP French Language, Spanish I-IV, AP Spanish Language; **Arts:** Foundation Arts: Visual, Foundation Arts: Performing, Foundation Arts: Music, Advanced Studio, Approaches to Contemporary Theater I & II, Digital Photography, Filmmaking for the Actor, The History of Western Music, Mosaics, Music Theory for the Musician, Performance Studio, Shakespeare in Performance, Studio I. **Computer lab/training:** Wireless laptop computers are given to each student. **Grading:** A+ - F, quarterly. Grades for interscholastic sports, P.E. classes, and exploratory classes are O (Outstanding), VG (Very Good), S (Satisfactory), NI (Needs Improvement), and U (Unsatisfactory). **Graduation requirements:** "A minimum of 26 credits. 4 credits of English and 3 credits of history and social science, including U.S. History; 3 credits of math, including Geometry and Algebra II; 3 credits of science, including two core lab sciences; world languages: completion of a Level III course in at least one world language; Arts: 2 credits; participation in an interscholastic sport or enrollment in a P.E. class during every term of enrollment with some possible exceptions; participation during every year of enrollment in Connections (SA's community service and study abroad program); 2 exploratory courses each quarter of enrollment; participation in Health and Wellness program during every year of enrollment." Intersession: participation during every year of enrollment. **Average nightly homework (M-Th):** Approx. 3 hours. **Faculty:** 19 f/t faculty members, 88% hold advanced degrees (N/P gender, degrees). **Faculty ethnicity:** "Of the 42 faculty and staff, 23% are people of color." (N/P ethnicities) **Faculty selection/training:** "SA hires highly qualified instructional staff, giving preference to those with advanced degrees. Ongoing professional development is comprehensive. Twice a year, two teacher training professionals review goals with individual teachers, observe classes, and provide feedback. For two hours every other week, faculty spend time engaged in reflective practice and collaboration on such topics as writing across the curriculum and using portfolios in the classroom. SA provides financial support and time off for teachers to attend local and national conferences and to visit peer schools." **Teacher/student ratio:** 1:10. **Percentage of students enrolled in AP:** 66%; pass rate: 80% scored 3 or higher; 54% scored 4 or 5. **Senior class profile (mean):** SAT Math 591, SAT Critical Reading 640, SAT Writing 634; GPA: N/P. **National Merit Scholarship Program:** One Letter of Commendation. **College enrollment (last class):** "100% accepted at multiple colleges of their choice." (N/P 4-yr, 2-yr). Of that group, 96% enrolled in college; 3% chose to travel or postpone their studies for other reasons. **Recent (last 4 yrs) colleges:** Brown, Cal Poly, Columbia, Dartmouth, Duke, Scripps, Skidmore, Smith, Stanford, Swarthmore, UC (Berkeley, Davis, LA, Santa Cruz), and Wesleyan.

Other Indicators the School is Accomplishing its Goals

"When surveyed about how well SA prepared them for college in a number of skill areas, 98% of our alumni said they were prepared in thinking/analytical skills (85% very well prepared); and 96% said they were prepared to be creative (70% very well prepared); 98% prepared for analytical writing (61% very well prepared); and 99% expressing views verbally, 96% prepared in terms of leading others; and 96% prepared for creative writing."

Campus/Campus Life

Campus description: "Sonoma Academy's new campus, on a 34-acre site in southeast Santa Rosa, includes a main building with a gymnasium, classrooms, and office spaces; a classroom building with science labs and a student lounge, and library; a Black Box Theater, all-weather soccer/lacrosse playing and practice fields, an amphitheater and an organic teaching garden. **Library:** "More than 10,000 volumes. Students access the numerous online catalogs of other libraries. The physical library is open to students whenever they are at school, and supervised by a professional librarian." **Sports facilities:** Gymnasium with seating for 810 people, training room, regulation-size athletic field and practice field. **Theater/arts facilities:** Dance studio, painting pavilion, ceramics studio, digital media studio, Black Box theater with seating for 150, music classroom and practice rooms. **Open/closed campus:** All students are required to sign in and out. At the start of the school year, juniors may apply for the privilege of leaving campus during free periods and lunch. Seniors in good standing have off-campus privileges at the start of the school year. **Lunches:** Students provide their own lunches or those with off-campus privileges purchase lunches from local establishments. **Bus service:** Available from some areas. **Uniforms/dress code:** "Students must use good judgment and dress appropriately. Clothing must be neat, clean, and in good repair, and may not have emblems or slogans that are obscene or that represent drug, alcohol, or tobacco products." **Co-curricular activities/clubs:** At the start of the school year interested club leaders seek out advisors to work with them on continuing or developing clubs. Current groups include: Amnesty International, Anime Club, Book Club, Diversity Club, French Club, Interfaith Club, Newspaper, Queer/Straight Alliance, Ride Club, SA Film Club, Spanish Club, Storytelling Club, Outdoor Leadership, and Yearbook. Students also participate in the Student Leadership Council (SLC) and the ALL-Stars (admissions representatives), through which they facilitate community meetings, interview applicants, represent the school at school fairs and open houses, plan and implement school-wide events, and help with new student orientation and Welcome Day. Seniors apply for positions as Health and Wellness Teaching Assistants to facilitate freshmen small groups for the year. Students may also serve on the Judicial Honor Council (convened for disciplinary infractions), and produce and act in the theater/music program. **Foreign exchange/internships:** Connections is a program that aims to provide students an opportunity to apply what they learn in the classroom to real life situations in their local and global communities. The program has sponsored trips to China, Costa Rica, France, Japan, Honduras, Mexico, Thailand, Russia and Nicaragua. The program arranges a minimum of three travel/study trips each year, and all students are eligible to participate, including those receiving financial aid. Travel is scheduled during school breaks and at Intersession each January, when students and teachers engage in intensive two-week study of a single subject. **Community service:** Through the Connections program, all Sonoma Academy students participate in volunteer or community service projects. **Typical freshman schedule:** All freshmen are enrolled in an interdisciplinary course in the humanities for which they earn full-year credit in both English and World History. They also take an interdisciplinary math-science course that includes Biology and Algebra I or II. Each freshman takes Foundation Arts, which is a combination of visual and performing arts and music, either French or Spanish, and participates in the school's Connections program and its Health and Wellness program. Each quarter, all students take two elective exploratory courses and are required to participate in either a P.E. class or interscholastic sports.

Student Support Services

Counselor/student ratio (not including college counselors): 1:100. **Counseling:** Sonoma Academy has two licensed professional counselors, available at the school 5 days per week. Counseling services for individual students and small groups are available for a limited number of sessions. Each student has a pair of faculty advisors who meet regularly with a group of 8 to 10 advisees. Advisors monitor the social and academic progress of their advisees, explain school policies, discuss community issues, review grades and comments, assist in course selection, and serve as a resource and support for their advisees. **Learning differences/disabilities:** "When staff, students, or parents suspect a learning disability, the family is referred to a learning specialist or may seek one on their own. The school has an on-site learning specialist/ Educational Support Coordinator who works with both students and faculty to develop appropriate learning and teaching strategies for students with learning differences."

Student Conduct and Health

Code of conduct: "Major School Rules: (1) Students are expected to act with respect, honesty, and integrity. We expect students to be honorable in all aspects of school life, including their academic work. (2) Students are expected to respect community property and the property of others. Theft, defacement, or vandalism of any school/personal property is not allowed. (3) Students are expected to maintain a safe environment. Students may not bring guns, knives, or any other weapons to school, any school function, or on any school trip, and must refrain from behavior that causes physical or emotional harm to others in the school community. (4) Students are expected to be drug, alcohol, and tobacco free on the school campus, prior to or at school functions, school field trips, or functions held at or sponsored by other schools. Distributing and/or selling illegal or prescription drugs or alcohol will subject a student to immediate dismissal, as well as criminal prosecution. If there is reasonable suspicion by the faculty or administration that a student has a substance abuse problem, or if a student violates the rule stated above, that student will be referred for a mandatory drug or alcohol evaluation. Students are expected to conduct themselves at all times and all places in a manner that is consistent with Sonoma Academy's reputation and the health and safety of all community members." **How school handles drugs/alcohol:** Provided above. **Prevention/awareness programs:** "Students are required to participate in Health and Wellness education during every year of enrollment. The program covers a broad range of topics dealing with the theme of developing a student's ability to make well-informed and responsible decisions regarding health and personal development."

Summer Programs: Summer math course.

Parent Involvement

Parent participation: "Every parent is a member of the Sonoma Academy Parents' Association (SAPA). This group helps to connect parents, support school activities, and develop strong relationships with teachers, advisors, and staff. The full SAPA group meets monthly in the morning. Subgroups like the Coyote Club (athletic boosters) and the Fine Arts groups are important liaisons with the school and also directly support students, providing snacks during performance rehearsals or organizing barbecues for athletes after home games. There are parent representatives for each class year who organize socials and also faculty appreciation events." **Parent/teacher communication:** Grades are recorded at the end of each quarter. At midterm of every quarter, each student receives a brief progress report with possible recommendations but no grade. At the end of each quarter, grades and narrative reports are mailed home to parents. Parent/student conferences with advisors are held after the first quarter, and parents are invited to call the advisor at any point to schedule an individual meeting. Parents gain an understanding of classes during Back to School Night in the fall, at which they sign up for parent/advisor conferences. After this initial formal meeting, parents are urged to contact teachers and advisors directly at any time through phone or e-mails. A weekly e-newsletter keeps parents up to date on school life by providing event reminders, news of changes, requests, congratulations, and breaking news. The school's website has calendars of school events, weekly photos, news, and a special parent section. **Parent education:** In addition to the above, the school sponsors a once-per-term parent education event that is open to the public. **Donations:** "Sonoma Academy is supported each year by the generous contributions of parents, grandparents, and friends. As of April of the last academic year, 86% of SA's parent body had contributed to the year's annual fund drive. In 2008, the parent fundraiser earned $400,000 for the school."

Sports

The school is a member of Coastal Mountain Conference, NCL II South, and Marin County Athletic League (lacrosse). The school fields boys and girls teams in soccer and cross-country running in fall, boys and girls basketball in winter, and lacrosse and track and field in spring. Teams play on regulation-size fields on the school's campus.

What Sets School Apart From Others

"Interdisciplinary curriculum: At the center of the Sonoma Academy curriculum are required interdisciplinary humanities (English and history) and mathematics/science courses for students in the freshman, sophomore, and junior years. Incoming freshmen and sophomores are also required to take an interdisciplinary foundation arts course each semester, choosing among (two of the following three) visual, music, or theater. Courses appear on the transcript as paired courses, indicating that one credit is earned for each discipline for the year. Interdisciplinary courses meet for 80 minutes a day all year long. The extended class periods promote student-centered learning and in-depth study. The interdisciplinary curriculum allows students to learn concepts in context. • Personal attention and support: Teachers have measurable involvement with students on a coordinated, consistent basis. There are two advisors per 8 -10 students, and they meet biweekly. Also, teachers meet weekly as a group to discuss individual students and their progress. • Integrated Techology: All students and teachers are given laptop computers and use them within the school's wireless environment for research, problem solving, and communication."

How Parents/Students Characterize School

Parent response(s): "SA has outstanding faculty, a real commitment to knowing each student and making each of them feel unique, while at the same time part of a very cohesive community. When my daughter talks about her teachers, she exudes enthusiasm and respect." "I feel lucky that my daughter is at a school that nourishes her creativity, is encouraging her to be a critical thinker, and is helping her to see herself as part of a bigger community and world." "It is said that if you can teach kids to love learning, all else will follow. SA faculty not only convey this love, but offer an amazing integration of imagination and the discipline of thinking." "My son's favorite thing about SA is the relationship between the students and teachers. There is a bond, so he feels that he is part of the class, not just an observer." **Student response(s):** "Even at Stanford University, I feel far more prepared than any of my classmates, especially in writing, discussion, and creative thinking. I also feel that SA prepared me to look for interesting opportunities and not just to focus on the schoolwork." "SA is a place for each student to find themselves and develop into people who could very well change the world. I learned that every person has the power to truly make a difference." "Not only did SA give me excellent preparation for college, it was a wonderful experience in itself. I learned so much; I made great friends; I traveled to France, Costa Rica, and Thailand, and I discovered new interests."

Stuart Hall High School

1715 Octavia Street (at Pine)
San Francisco, CA 94109
(415) 345-5811 *fax (415) 931-9161*
www.sacredsf.org

Gordon Sharafinski, Head of School
Anthony Farrell, Director of Admission and Financial Aid,
farrell@sacredsf.org

General

Boys Catholic day high school. (45% Catholic). Founded 2000, affiliated with Schools of the Sacred Heart. Independent. Nonprofit, member WASC, CAIS, NAIS, BAIHS. **Enrollment: 165. Average class size: 16. Accreditation:** Network of Sacred Heart Schools, WASC/CAIS. **School year:** Late Aug.-June. **School day:** 8 a.m.-3 p.m., 2:30 p.m. dismissal on Friday. **Location:** Lower Pacific Heights residential area, three blocks from Japantown, four blocks from Fillmore St., accessible by the 1, 2, 3, 4, and 22 Muni lines, and all Muni and Golden Gate Transit lines running on Van Ness Avenue.

Student Body

Geographic breakdown (counties): 74% from San Francisco; 16% from Marin; 5% from the Peninsula; 5% from the East Bay. **Ethnicity:** 57% Caucasian; 19% Asian; 5% Hispanic; 7% African-American; 12% multi-ethnic. **International students (I-20 status):** 3. **Middle schools (freshman):** 50% from private independent schools; 34% from private parochial schools; 16% from public middle schools. Over 35 schools are represented. (N/P schools)

Admission

Applications due: First week in January (call for date). **Application fee:** $75. **Application process:** "Shadow visits and interviews (required) are conducted October through January on Monday, Thursday, and Friday mornings. Parent tours are given on Monday and Friday mornings. Open houses are held in October and November for students and their families. Students must submit an application, teacher recommendations, standardized test scores, and a student essay."

No. of freshman applications: Approx. 200 (N/P # places). **Minimum admission requirements:** "Applicants must currently be working to the best of their ability and have a strong record with regard to good citizenship and social skills." **Test required:** HPST or SSAT. **Preferences:** N/P. "**We are looking for** young men who want to be engaged in their education by taking on a strong academic program and leadership roles within the school community." **What kind of student do you best serve?** "Students who want to be active in their school program; engaged with their classmates and teachers; involved in co-curricular activities, athletics, service, and leadership."

Costs
Latest tuition: $29,200 payable in 1 or 2 or 10 payments. **Sibling discount:** None. **Tuition increases:** Approx. 4-5%. **Other costs:** $300-$600 for books. **Percentage of students receiving financial aid:** 35%. **Financial aid deadline:** First week in January (call for date). **Average grant:** $14,550. **Percentage of grants half-tuition or more:** 52%.

School's Mission Statement/Goals
"The Schools of the Sacred Heart in the United States, members of a world-wide network, offer an education that is marked by a distinctive spirit. Stuart Hall High School, a Sacred Heart school, commits to the individual student's total development: spiritual, intellectual, emotional, and physical. Stuart Hall High School emphasizes serious study, sportsmanship, artistic discovery, social responsibility, and faith development. All schools of the Sacred Heart commit themselves to educate to: a personal and active faith in God; a deep respect for intellectual values; a social awareness which impels to action; the building of community as a Christian value; and personal growth in an atmosphere of wise freedom."

Academic Program
"Every student is enrolled in a challenging, enriching academic program and is an active participant in his own education. The learning that takes place, both in and out of the classroom, is a collaborative process between faculty and students. The administration, faculty, and student body are committed to intellectual honesty and leadership development and students are treated seriously as scholars and leaders. Each freshman and sophomore student is required to take a minimum of seven courses for credit each semester, while juniors and seniors must take a minimum of six courses for credit." Course offerings (A= Advanced, AP=Advanced Placement, H=Honors, (AP)=AP option, (H)=Honors option): **Theology:** World Religions, Sacred Texts, Ethics and Morality, Social Justice; **English:** English I-II (A), American Literature (H), World Literature, English Literature and Composition (AP); **History:** History I-II, U.S. History (AP, H), Government (AP), Economics, European History (AP), Psychology; **Foreign Languages:** French I-IV, French Language (AP), Spanish I-IV, Spanish Language

(AP), Latin I-IV, Latin Literature (AP); **Science:** Biology (A, AP), Chemistry (A, AP), Physics (H), Anatomy and Physiology, Environmental Science (AP); **Math:** Algebra I-II (A), Geometry (A), Pre-Calculus, Calculus, Trigonometry and Data Analysis, Calculus (AP: AB & BC); **Computer Science:** Technology and Design I-II, Programming I-II, Computer Science (AP); **Arts:** Instrumental Music, Independent Study, Art I-II, Advanced Art I-II, Photography. **Computer lab/training:** "1:1 student-laptop ratio and unlimited access to a computer on campus; all computers are linked to the Internet. Technology is integrated throughout the curriculum. One year of computer science is required." **Grading:** A-F. **Graduation requirements:** 4 years English, history, math and theology; 3 years lab science and foreign language; 2 years P.E.; 1 year fine arts, and computer science; 75 hours community service. Requirements are designed to satisfy UC admission standards. **Average nightly homework (M-Th):** 2-3 hours. **Faculty:** 30; 33% female, 67% male; 75% have advanced degrees. **Faculty ethnicity:** N/P. **Faculty selection/training:** "We look for teachers who are knowledgeable in their subject areas; who have a strong commitment to education; who desire small classes for interactive learning; who want to support students outside of the classroom through athletics, service, or club activities; who will accept and embrace the goals of a Sacred Heart education; who understand the benefits of teaching in a single sex environment; and who have the desire and ability to engage students in the classroom. Faculty members take advantage of the school's full support for professional development by attending conferences and workshops." **Teacher/student ratio:** 1:7. **Percentage of students enrolled in AP:** N/P. **Most recent senior class profile (mean):** SAT Math 591, SAT Critical Reading 591, SAT Writing 583; GPA: N/P. **National Merit Scholarship Program:** 10 Commended students. **College enrollment (last class):** 100% (N/P 4-yr, 2-yr). **Recent (last 4 yrs) colleges:** Bowdoin, Brown, UC (Riverside, Davis, Irvine, Santa Cruz, Berkeley, SD), CSU (SF, Humboldt, SJ, SLO), Cornell, Stanford, Fordham, Columbia, Kenyon, USD, Tulane, Loyola Marymount, Middlebury, Reed, Boston C, Colgate, Harvard, Rice, Vanderbilt, Georgetown, and USC.

Other Indicators the School is Accomplishing its Goals

"Academic scholarships, extensive community service, and athletic success."

Campus/Campus Life

Campus description: "Located in a newly renovated facility, the school includes classrooms, science and computer labs, art studio, library, and a full-court gymnasium. It has total technological accessibility through a wireless network, and an enclosed outdoor courtyard." **Library:** 2,000 hard cover volumes; 3,000 electronic journals; 200 electronic newspapers; plus accessibility to two other libraries located throughout a 4-school campus. **Sports facilities:** On-site gymnasium, weight room. **Theater/arts facilities:** "New state-of-the-art 300-seat theater."

Open/closed campus: Open. Lunches: Lunch program option. Bus service: Public. Uniforms/dress code: "Casual dress." Co-curricular activities/clubs: "Extensive co-curricular activities are offered, including coed activities with Convent High School, student government, drama, instrumental music, and clubs." Foreign exchange program/internships: N/P. Community service: "Students fulfill 75 hours of community service as a three-year requirement through a variety of activities relating to the elderly, the environment, the handicapped, the sick, the economically disadvantaged, and the newly immigrated. A Social Justice course senior year links seniors with a service site in the neighborhood." Typical freshman schedule: English I (advanced option), Theology I, History I, French, Spanish, or Latin, Algebra I (advanced option), Biology (advanced option), Technology and Design I (1 semester), Intro to Art (1 semester), and Health and Wellness I.

Student Support Services

Counselor-student ratio (not including college counselors): 1:165. Counseling: One counselor and one college counselor. In addition to professional counselors on staff, faculty provide academic counseling and advising to students. The Head of School, Dean of Students and Advisors provide academic counseling and advising to students. During the freshman year, students take the National Education Development Test. Freshmen and sophomores have one group presentation each year by the college counselor and meet individually with a college counselor as well. Sophomores and juniors take the PSAT in the fall. The juniors have weekly group meetings and individual sessions with a college counselor during the spring semester, and take the ACT, SAT I, and SAT II in the spring. Seniors continue to meet with the college counselor, both individually and in group sessions, and take the ACT, SAT I, and SAT II again in the fall. Learning disabilities/differences: "Support for students who are able to be successful as part of a mainstreamed program."

Student Conduct and Health

Code of conduct: "The Code of Ethics discussed in the Student Handbook focuses on respect for others, respect for others' property and school property, respect for education, and school spirit." How school handles drugs/alcohol: "Drug and alcohol usage or possession will not be tolerated and will result in serious punishment of either suspension or dismissal. This policy will be in effect whether a student is on campus or attending a school-sponsored function." Prevention/awareness programs: "Programs facilitated throughout the academic year."

Summer Programs

Stuart Hall High School offers a three-week co-curricular summer school program. Enrichment and accelerated courses are open to students from other Bay Area high schools as well.

Parent Involvement
Parent participation: "Parents are invited to participate through the Parents' Association as volunteers for various events and activities. No required hours." **Parent/teacher communication:** Formal reports are sent to parents four times a year. Formal parent/teacher conferences take place once each semester. Other evaluations are given as needed. **Parent education:** "Frequent seminars are offered through the Parents' Association." **Donations:** N/P.

Sports
Stuart Hall students compete through the Bay Counties Athletic League in basketball, lacrosse, soccer, baseball, golf, tennis, track, and cross-country. Fencing competes against AAA and BCL teams.

What Sets School Apart From Others
"A strong academic program for young men that utilizes San Francisco and all the resources the city has to offer. An education program that addresses the needs of male adolescents and provides an opportunity to explore personal, spiritual, and ethical values. A small-school environment that emphasizes individualized instruction, leadership opportunities, and a values-based education. Member of the Network of Sacred Heart Schools and partner with Convent of the Sacred Heart High School."

How Parents/Students Characterize School
Parent response(s): "I think this school is the perfect balance of school, student, and community. It offers my son a close-knit family-like community. The program really focuses on how guys learn and provides a place for the boys to thrive." **Student response(s):** "We get a healthy balance between academics, co-curricular and social involvement. As a guy, the environment of SHHS allows me to be a better student than I might be elsewhere. The courses are taught in a way that interests boys and keeps us focused. We are able to easily get involved in athletics, leadership, and all kinds of school activities. Because of our relationship with Convent High School, we have the best of both worlds—all guys in school and plenty of opportunities to meet girls outside of school."

The Urban School of San Francisco
1563 Page Street
San Francisco, CA 94117
(415) 626-2919 *fax (415) 626-1125*
www.urbanschool.org

Mark Salkind, Head of School
Bobby Ramos, Director of Admissions, bramos@urbanschool.org

General

Coed day high school. Independent. Founded in 1966. Nonprofit, member CAIS, NAIS, BAAD. **Enrollment:** Approx. 350. **Average class size:** 13. **Accreditation:** WASC/CAIS. **School year:** Sept.-June **School day:** 8:10 a.m.-2:45 p.m. **Location:** In Haight-Ashbury between Masonic and Ashbury, just a few blocks from Golden Gate Park. The school is accessible by 6, 7, 21, 33, 43, 71 Muni bus lines.

Student Body

Geographic breakdown (counties): 72% from San Francisco; 16% from Marin; 7% East Bay; 5% from South Bay. **Ethnicity:** 73% Caucasian, 27% multi-ethnic. **International students (I-20 status):** N/P. **Middle schools (freshman):** Approx. 75% came from private, non-parochial schools; approx. 25% from public and/or parochial middle schools. (N/P # schools)

Admission

Applications due: Mid-January (call for date). **Application fee:** $100. **Application process:** "Families should request an admissions packet online or by telephone in August before the start of the student's eighth grade year. Students are encouraged to schedule a half-day visit, which includes a tour of the campus with a current Urban student and an opportunity to observe classes. Students should also schedule an interview; interviews are offered several days a week after school. Visits and interviews are available on a first come, first served basis and begin in late September. The school hosts three open houses for prospective families in the fall, which provide opportunities to meet students and faculty and learn more about the school's program. To make a reservation for an open house, return the request card found in the admissions packet. Open house reservations are required and are accepted in the order received." **No. of freshman applications:** Approx. 600 (N/P # places). **Minimum admission requirements:** N/P. **Test required:** SSAT. **Preferences:** N/P. "We are looking for curious, caring, enthusiastic students who have the capacity for success in a challenging academic and co-curricular program." **What kind of student do you best serve?** "The Urban School seeks students who will actively and generously involve themselves in the life of the school and who are able to learn from a wide range of experiences, both in and out of the classroom. The school draws girls and boys from public and private schools in San Francisco, the East Bay, and Marin and strives to reflect the ethnic, racial, and socioeconomic diversity of the Bay Area among its students and faculty members."

Costs

Latest tuition: $28,000 payable in 2 or 10 monthly installments. Loans are available through outside companies. **Sibling discount:** None. **Tuition increases:** 6.3%. **Other costs:** $725 for books and materials and $725 for laptop use fee. **Percentage of students receiving financial**

aid: 22%. **Financial aid deadline:** Mid-January (call for date). **Average grant:** $22,084. **Percentage of grants half tuition or more:** N/P.

School's Mission Statement/Goals

"The Urban School of San Francisco seeks to ignite a passion for learning, inspiring its students to become self-motivated, enthusiastic participants in their education – both in high school and beyond."

Academic Program

"Urban organizes the school year using a block system rather than a conventional semester system. The block schedule allows for more concentrated, less fragmented learning than does a traditional high school schedule. The intensive block format enables students and teachers to focus on each area of study in greater depth and approach the material in a variety of ways. The block schedule divides the academic year into three, 12-week terms: fall, winter, and spring. Students take four intensive classes every term and most classes last for one or two terms. These classes meet for 70-minute periods with one 2-hour period per week. Due to longer class periods, a term-long class is equivalent to a semester course, and a two-term class is equivalent to a year-long course. **Courses offered** (AP=Advanced Placement, H=Honors, (AP)=AP option, (H)=Honors option): Honors classes are offered in all academic areas; Advanced Placement courses are offered in AB Calculus, Chemistry, and Studio Art. Extra-curricular AP exam preparation is offered in BC Calculus, literature, Physics, French, and Spanish. **English:** Writing and Thinking; Composition: American Voices and Greek Literature; Shakespeare; Medieval Literature; Latin American Literature; American Romanticism; Biblical Literature; Advanced Composition; Advanced Shakespeare: Kings and Fools; French Novels from the Romantic Period; Classicism, Romanticism, and Modernism; Joyce and Wolf; Russian Literature: Dostoevsky and Chekhov; Modern American Literature: The Odyssey at Home; 19th Century British Literature; Faulkner; AP English; **History:** 20th Century History, Civil War, Recent America, Globalization: Savior or Monster?, History of Women in America, History of South Asia, Revolutionary Europe, Russia and Eastern Europe, Peacemakers, Crime and Punishment, Constitutional Law, America Transformed (1865-1929), Telling Their Stories: Oral History Archives Project (Holocaust), African History, Comparative Religion: Our Search for Meaning, The American Revolution and the Constitution 1763-1820, History of England, Great Britain, and Ireland, Modern China; **Languages:** Spanish I-V, French I-V; **Arts:** Acting I-II: Comedy/Popular Theater, Peer Education Theater Ensemble, One-Acts (Senior Spring Seminar), Theater Productions, Circus Techniques, Intro to Chorus, Urban Singers, Music Theory, Jazz Band, Advanced Music Theory and Composition, Music Theory II: Composition/Electronic Music, Senior Recital/Music Theater Project; Studio Arts: Drawing, Painting, Printmaking, Bookmaking, Alternate Processes in Photography, Video

Production and Film History, Sculpture, AP Art; **Math and Computer:** Math I-III, Programming and Math, Functions, Maps, Space, Infinity, Advanced Math, Calculus, AP Calculus (AB), AP Calculus (BC); **Science:** Fundamentals of Biology, Human Biology, Physics: Motion, Physics: Waves and Energy, Inventions, Advanced Environmental Science, Ornithology, Marine Biology, Chemistry, Advanced Topics in Biology: Neurobiology, Advanced Topics in Biology: Genetics, Advanced Physics: Electricity & Magnetism, Advanced Mechanics, Astronomy, AP Chemistry. **Community service learning projects:** Freshen Group Project, 10th Grade Issues and Action, 11th and 12th Grade Project; Senior Options: California Studies, Network, Senior Spring. **Computer lab/training:** "Urban's approach to technology is purposely holistic: technology skills and related computer projects are integrated within the daily curriculum. All incoming students are issued state-of-the-art laptop computers for school and home use and all students learn computer programming as part of the required math sequence, multimedia presentation software in English and History, and data analysis programs when working with electronic probes and sensors in their science classes." **Grading:** "Urban believes that in a graded environment, students come to see education as a means to an end—getting good grades, rather than as an end in itself. Urban chooses to use narrative reports in evaluating students' work and academic progress. Students receive extensive written evaluations for each course every six weeks. One of Urban's chief goals is to prepare students for the next steps in their formal education; therefore, grades are recorded on a transcript for the purpose of college admissions. These grades are not available to students or parents. Instead, students and parents receive the grade point average at year's end. Juniors and seniors may receive their grade point average more often as they undertake the college admissions process." **Graduation requirements:** "22 credits are required for graduation, distributed across the curriculum. One credit is equivalent to a yearlong course." (N/P classes) **Average nightly homework (M-Th):** 45 min.-1 hour per subject. **Faculty:** 36; 50% female, 50% male; 55% hold advanced degrees and median years of total experience is 14 (N/P degrees). **Faculty ethnicity:** "14% faculty of color." (N/P ethnicities) **Faculty selection/training:** "Faculty searches are conducted nationally and Urban looks for teachers with expertise in a particular area. Prospective teachers should be passionate about their subject areas and enthusiastic about the educational philosophy of the school. Urban strives to hire teachers who are familiar with independent schools: accustomed to individualization in teaching, collaboration with colleagues, writing narrative reports, staying in close contact with families, and becoming involved with students outside the classroom setting. In addition to collaboration among teachers at Urban, faculty members attend local and national workshops and conferences, as well as enroll in courses and degree programs to further develop their skills." **Teacher/student ratio:** 1:8. **Percentage of students enrolled in AP/exam pass rate:** N/P. **Senior class profile (mean):** N/P.

National Merit Scholarship Program: N/P. **College enrollment (last class):** 99%.(N/P 4-yr, 2-yr) **Recent (last 4 yrs) colleges:** "The top six schools attended by the largest number of students are: NYU, Oberlin, Stanford, UC Berkeley, Vassar, and Wesleyan."

Other Indicators the School is Accomplishing its Goals

"Urban School was one of three independent schools nationwide to receive a 2004 Leading Edge Award in Technology by the National Association of Independent Schools. In recent years, Urban's boys and girls varsity basketball teams finished undefeated in league play and both won the BCL-West League Championships. The varsity girls basketball team won a Division Championship and was a Nor Cal Semi-Finalist. • Urban is among the first independent schools in the Bay Area to integrate technology throughout the curriculum by initiating a student laptop computer program. • Urban has been awarded a Certificate of Merit from the Council for Religion in Independent Schools; a Certificate of Honor for its Community Service Learning Program from the Board of Supervisors; the Excellence in Community Service Hunger Award by the Council for Spiritual and Ethical Education; and the Outstanding Achievement Award for Most Productive Blood Drive High School."

Campus/Campus Life

Campus description: "Urban is located in a residential neighborhood in a three-story building that houses classrooms, art studios, science labs, a library, and a black box theater. Our new 20,000 sq. ft. building includes eight new classrooms, four new science labs, faculty and staff office space, dedicated classrooms for music and performing arts, and a new student center." **Library:** The Herbst Library is composed of two parts: the physical library has 13,000 volumes and workspace for students; the virtual library providing access to numerous databases, Web links and thousands of periodicals and reference resources. **Sports facilities:** Athletic practices and games are held at the neighboring St. Agnes Gymnasium and on the playing fields of the San Francisco Park and Recreation Department. Urban van service is provided to and from athletic practices and games. **Theater/arts facilities:** Black box theater; art, printmaking, and ceramic studios; music and performing arts classrooms in new facility. **Open/closed campus:** Open. **Lunches:** On-site food service. **Bus service:** Urban van service is provided for athletic practices, field trips, and class trips. The school is accessible by several Muni bus lines. **Uniforms/dress code:** "Casual; however, students are expected to use good judgment and dress appropriately for a school setting. They may not wear clothes showing emblems or slogans that are profane or that represent drugs, alcohol, or tobacco products." **Co-curricular activities/clubs:** "Urban has over thirty different student clubs. New clubs may be established if there is sufficient interest among a group of students. Urban's Outdoor Trips Program introduces students to backpacking, kayaking, river rafting, skiing, and biking. In addition, each grade level takes a trip during the school year that offers students and teachers an opportunity to interact in a unique way outside the classroom. Students and faculty also plan a variety of special activities for the whole community. Last year's clubs and activities were Aim High Tutoring, Animation Club, Biking Club, Brown Bag Lunch (Theater), Chamber Ensemble, Chess Club, Circus Club, Community Outreach Club, Cooking Club, Dance Committee, Diversity Day Planning, Environmental Club, Foreign Film Club, French Club, Gay/Straight Alliance, Junior State of America, Kool Creative Club, Knitting Club, Martial Arts Club, Model United Nations, Multicultural Alliance for Diversity, Peer Resources, Poetry Society, Recycling Club, Science Club, Spanish Club, Student Admissions Committee, Student Committee (Student Government), Students of Color, Tech Club, and Urban Fan Club." **Foreign exchange/internship programs:** "Network is an exchange program offered through the Network of Complementary Schools. Urban students may elect any Network program at no additional cost for tuition or board." **Community service:** "Urban has been nationally recognized for its Service Learning Program, whereby all students are required to take a course called 'Project' that instills a sense of connection and responsibility to the larger community. Over their four years, students learn about the neighborhood, local government, health issues, service organizations, and community involvement. In G11-12, students work in communities throughout the Bay Area as interns and/or apprentices or engage in a service activity." **Typical freshman schedule:** "Intensive classes meet seven times every two weeks. In Week One, students have three 70-minute periods and one 2-hour period; in Week Two, two 70-minute periods and one 2-hour period. Elective classes meet three times each week for two 70-minute periods and one 50-minute period."

Student Support Services

Counselor/student ratio (not including college counselors): 1:250. **Counseling:** "Upon entering Urban, students are assigned a faculty advisor who is the liaison between student, school, and family. Students meet with their advisors in weekly group advising meetings and in individual meetings to review and plan their academic progress. The advisor is also available to discuss areas of concern and offer counsel and support. Equally important to students' personal growth are their relationships with peers. Urban trains a group of students in leadership and peer counseling skills. These students educate their peers about specific health issues and work to develop a Peer Education theater piece, which serves as a catalyst for discussions with freshmen, sophomores, and their parents on important adolescent issues. Urban also builds a strong partnership with parents in order to challenge and support each student consistently. Advisors call families periodically during the school year to discuss their child's progress and program." **Learning disabilities/differences:** "Reasonable accommodations can be made on an individual basis; however, there is no learning specialist on site."

Student Conduct and Health

Code of conduct: "Standard." **How school handles drugs/alcohol:** "The school forbids the use, sale, distribution, or possession of illegal drugs or alcohol. Students found using, in possession of, or under the influence of illegal drugs or alcohol at any time in the school building, off campus during school hours, and at any school-related trip, activity, or event will be suspended and will be required to undergo a substance abuse assessment. Second violations may result in expulsion. Sale or distribution of illegal drugs or alcohol will result in immediate expulsion. Smoking is prohibited on campus and in the surrounding off-campus neighborhood, and at all school sponsored events." **Prevention/awareness programs:** "Integrated throughout school program."

Summer Programs

Urban hosts "Aim High," a tuition-free summer enrichment program for middle school students from low-income families.

Parent Involvement

Parent participation: "Though not required, parent participation is expected, as volunteering is the best way to feel connected to a school community. When families enroll at Urban, parents automatically become members of the Parents' Association. Activities and events organized and/or supported by parent volunteers include Admissions Open Houses, Annual Spring Auction, Parent Networking Evenings, Parents' Diversity Committee, Library Administrative Support, Sports Banquet, Graduation, an all-night 'Safe and Sober' Grad Night Party, clerical support to administrative offices, and faculty recognition." **Parent/teacher communication:** "A faculty advisor is the liaison between student, school, and family. Advisors call families periodically during the school year and are the first contact for parents with questions about their child's progress and program." **Parent education:** The Parent Board organizes meetings for each grade level to discuss parenting issues with school administrators. **Donations:** "We encourage our parents to make Urban their highest philanthropic priority while their child is a student here. Annual Fund gifts to the school range from $10 to more than $10,000. While leadership gifts help to ensure the school's economic vitality, a gift of any amount is important and appreciated, for it demonstrates the donor's commitment to Urban. We ask each person to participate at a level appropriate for his or her circumstances. Last year, parent participation reached 96%."

Sports

"Urban is a member of the Bay Area Conference and the Bay Counties League-West. Urban fields teams in the following sports: boys cross-country (V, JV), girls cross-country (V, JV), boys soccer (V, JV), girls volleyball (V, JV), girls tennis (V, JV), boys basketball (V, JV, frosh/soph), girls basketball (V, JV, frosh/soph), girls soccer (V, JV), track and field (V), boys tennis (V), baseball (V), golf (V), softball (V), boys volleyball (V), dance team, and fencing. Students must participate in any of an array of physical activity classes taught at Urban or in an approved off-campus program. Some activities offered include: yoga, fencing, rock climbing, dance, capoeira, swimming, and off-season conditioning."

What Sets School Apart From Others

"The Urban School of San Francisco seeks to ignite a passion for learning. With an imaginative academic program that combines a college preparatory curriculum with community service, fieldwork, and internships, Urban inspires its students to become self-motivated, enthusiastic participants in their education."

How Parent/Students Characterize School: N/P

Valley Christian High School

100 Skyway Drive, Suite 110
San Jose, CA 95111
(408) 513-2400 *fax (408) 513-2424*
www.vcs.net

Dr. Joel Torode, Head of School
Scott Wessling, Admissions Director, swessling@vcs.net

General

Coed Christian day high school. Independent. Founded in 1960. Nonprofit, member ACSI. **Enrollment:** 1,215. **Average class size:** 25. **Accreditation:** ACSI/WASC. **School year:** Aug-May (173 instructional days). **School day:** 7:40 a.m.-2:25 p.m. **Location:** In South San Jose accessible by public transportation.

Student Body

Geographic breakdown (counties): N/P. **Ethnicity:** 60% Caucasian (non-Latino); 15% Asian; 12% Latino; 5% African-American; 8% multi-racial. **International students (I-20 status):** 4%. **Middle schools (freshman):** 8% from public middle schools; 7% from private, non-parochial schools; 81% from parochial schools. (N/P # schools)

Admission

Applications due: Late January for G9, approx. mid-February for G10-12. **Application fee:** $70. **Application process:** Completed application, recommendations, admissions/placement testing, and personal interview. **No. of freshman applications:** N/P. **Minimum admission requirements:** N/P. **Test required:** N/P. **Preferences:** N/P. "We are looking for students who desire an education that focuses on college prep academics, extracurricular activities, and Christian spiritual growth, and are putting all three areas into practice in their current life, both in and out of school. **What kind of student do you best serve?** "Those students who are on a quest for academic achievement, artistic beauty, and/or athletic distinction in a Christian context."

Costs
Latest tuition: $12,705 payable in full or in 11 payments using an outside agency. **Sibling discount:** For 1st, 2nd, and 3rd sibling. **Tuition increases:** Approx. 5.95%. **Other costs:** Approx. $300 for books, $700 other fees. **Percentage of students receiving financial aid: 5%. Financial aid deadline:** N/P. **Average grant:** $1,000. **Percentage of grants of half tuition or more:** N/P.

School's Mission Statement/Goals
"Valley Christian Schools' (VCS) mission is to provide a nurturing environment offering quality education supported by a strong foundation of Christian values in partnership with parents, equipping students to become leaders to serve God, to serve their families, and to positively impact their communities and the world."

Academic Program
Courses offered (AP=Advanced Placement, H=Honors, (AP)=AP option, (H)=Honors option): **Bible:** Christianity in Our Culture, Old Testament Survey, Old Testament Studies, New Testament Survey, New Testament Studies, Bible Doctrine, Apologetics, Applied Ethics, Biblical Interpretation, Psalms, Romans, Spiritual Disciplines, Biblical Leadership, Advanced Biblical Leadership, Community Outreach, Biblical Government; **Communications:** Introduction to Film and Video, TV News and Multimedia Studies, The Art of Filmmaking, Applied Filmmaking, Scriptwriting, Radio Broadcasting I-III, Yearbook, Journalism I-III; **Computer Science:** Computer Software Anthology, Server Scripting, AP Computer Science A, Robotics, Computer Science Internship Program, Typing/MS Apps; **Dance:** Charis Dance Company, Jazz Dance I-III (H), Tap Dance I-III, Hip Hop I-II; **Electives:** Student Government (ASB), Life Skills, Study Skills, Study Hall, Aides: Teacher, Office, and Library; **English:** English I-III (H), Shakespeare (online only), Early British Literature, Late British Literature, Dramatic Literature, Contemporary Authors, AP English Language & Composition; **Foreign Languages:** American Sign Language I-III, Mandarin I, French I-IV, Japanese I-IV (AP), Latin I-IV, Spanish I-IV (AP); **Math:** Algebra I, II (H), Geometry (H), Consumer Math, Finite Math, Trigonometry/Precalculus (H), Statistics (AP), Calculus AB, BC (AP); **Music:** Symphonic Band, Conservatory Wind Ensemble, Jazz Lab, Jazz Ensemble Honors, String Ensemble, Early Music Chamber Ensemble, Percussion Ensemble, Piano, Music Practicum, Vocal Ensemble, Chorus, Introduction to Music Technology, AP Music Theory, History and Music, Color Guard; **P.E.:** For girls, P.E., Strength and

Conditioning; for boys, P.E., Strength and Conditioning; **Science:** Biology (H/AP), Biotechnology, Anatomy and Physiology, Physical Science, Chemistry (H/AP), Physics (H/AP); **Social Science:** Global Studies I-II (H), U.S. History (AP), AP European History, AP Human Geography, U.S. Government (AP), Economics, AP Comparative Government, AP Microeconomics, History and Music; **Theatre:** Theatre I-II (H), Acting for Film, Technical Theatre I-II (H); **Visual Arts:** Art I-III, AP Studio Art, AP 2D Design Portfolio, AP Art History, Photo Design I-II. **Computer lab/training:** "Cutting-edge technology in the classrooms. The latest high tech classrooms are outfitted with both wired and wireless network access, the latest in computer hardware, and the most recent versions of industry standard software packages." **Grading:** A- F. **Graduation requirements:** 4 years of Bible, English; 3 years history, math; 2 years P.E., science, technology, electives; 1 year fine art, government/economics. **Average nightly homework (M-Th):** AP Classes: 5-6 hours/week; honors/upper-level math: 3-4 hours/week; regular classes: 2-3 hours/week. **Faculty:** 73; 58% women, 42% men; 41% hold master's degrees, 1% hold a doctorate. **Faculty selection/training:** "The principals interview candidates by telephone; promising candidates visit the campus and are interviewed by administrators; a final interview is conducted by the President/Superintendent." **Teacher/student ratio:** 17:1. **Percent of students enrolled in AP/exam pass rate:** 66%; pass rate N/P. **Senior class profile (mean):** N/P. **National Merit Scholarship Program:** 3 were National Merit Finalists, and 6 were Commended Scholars. **College enrollment (last class):** "Over 98%." (N/P 4-yr, 2-yr) Recent **(last 4 yrs) colleges:** (partial list) Academy of Art, American U, Arizona SU, Ashland U, Azusa Pacific, Babson, Barry, Baylor, Berklee C of Music, Bethany, Biola, Boise SU, Boston C, Boston U, Brown, Cal Poly (SLO, Pomona), Cal Baptist, Cal Lutheran, Chapman, Clark Atlanta U, C of the Holy Cross, C of William & Mary, Columbia, Concordia, Cornell, CSU (Bakersfield, Channel Islands, Chico, East Bay, Fresno, Fullerton, Long Beach, LA, Monterey Bay, Northridge, Sacramento, San Marcos, Sonoma, Stanislaus, SD, SF, Humboldt), Dallas Baptist, Dominican, Duke, Fairfield, Florida SU, Fordham, George Fox, George Washington, Harvard, Hillsdale, Iowa SU, Johns Hopkins, Lewis & Clark, Loyola Marymount, Lynchburg, Manhattan School of Music, Menlo C, Michigan SU, Multnomah Bible, NYU, Northeastern, Northern Arizona, Northwestern, Occidental, Ohio SU, Oklahoma Baptist, Oklahoma Christian, Oregon SU, Penn SU, Pepperdine, Princeton, SFAI, Santa Clara, Seattle Pacific, SMU, Spelman, Stanford, Syracuse, Texas A&M, Texas Tech, UC (Berkeley, Davis, Irvine, Merced, Riverside, SD, Santa Barbara, Santa Cruz, LA, SD), Notre Dame, U-Wisconsin, U-Washington, U-Tennessee, UOP, USF, U-Puget Sound, U-Portland, U-Oregon, U-Oklahoma, U-Minnesota, U-Arizona, U-British Columbia, U-Colorado, U-Delaware, U-Edinburgh, U-Florida, U-Idaho; U.S. Air Force Academy, U.S. Naval Academy, Vanguard, Wake Forest, Washington SU, Westminster, Westmont, Whitman, Whittier, Whitworth, Willamette, Williams, Yale.

Other Indicators the School is Accomplishing Its Goals
"The Foreign Language Department has added a 6th language, Mandarin. The Music Conservatory continues to expand, and a Theater Conservatory is in the works. The percentage of graduating students attending college is 98 percent."

Campus/Campus Life
Campus description: "The school's 54-acre South San Jose hilltop campus, constructed in 1999, includes a dance studio, a professional theatre and set building facility, an art studio, a working radio station that broadcasts 24 hours a day on the Internet, a television studio with professional-caliber editing and production facilities, six fully-equipped science labs, two band rehearsal rooms with practice studios and recording booths, an extensive library, and modern computer labs including three dedicated video and graphics processing labs, and two mobile labs, all with high speed Internet connections." **Library:** "24,069-volume collection and state-of-the-art research facilities." **Sports facilities:** "State-of-the-art athletic facilities include a baseball stadium; a football stadium with locker rooms, weight rooms and a press box with Internet connectivity; soccer and softball fields; tennis and basketball courts; dedicated wrestling room; an all-weather track; and an aquatics center with an outdoor 53-meter swimming pool." **Theater/Arts facilities:** "The Skyway Campus includes a dance studio, a 196-seat theatre with a proscenium-style performance space and a computer-operated Vortek rigging system for flying in and out set pieces, as well as a 1,620 square foot scene shop (which includes equipment for set construction, wood-working, metal-working, scenic painting, and more), an art studio, a working radio station that broadcasts 24 hours a day on the Internet, a television studio with professional-caliber editing and production facilities, and 3 music rehearsal rooms with practice studios." **Open/closed campus:** Closed. **Lunches:** On-site kitchen providing complete meals. **Bus service:** Shuttle service available as well as on-site parking. **Uniforms/dress code:** Yes. (N/P description) **Co-curricular activities/clubs:** "At Valley Christian High School, we believe extracurricular programs which include sports, music, speech, drama, debate, and other various clubs and activities are where young people learn lifelong lessons as important as those taught in the classroom. We offer several honor clubs such as a Math Honor Society, a Dance Honor Society, and several foreign language honor societies. We believe activities enrich a student's high school experience, and through a variety of activities and events, we desire to offer something for almost everyone." **Foreign exchange program/internships:** "Approximately 30 students attend VCHS each year on student visas from other countries. Exchange programs with other schools in other countries are in the formative stages. However, students have been supported and encouraged to pursue such options on their own." **Community service:** "The school provides a full offering

of service opportunities with a 20 hour per year minimum commitment." (N/P examples) **Typical freshman schedule:** Christianity in Culture/Old Testament Studies, English 9 (H), Global Studies 1 (H), Algebra 1/Geometry/Algebra 2 (H), P.E. or Biology (H), P.E. or Strength & Conditioning, foreign language/fine art/technology elective.

Student Support Services
Counselor/student ratio (not including college counseling): 1:4. **Counseling:** "College counseling begins the freshman year with a freshman FAST TRACK orientation that includes meeting with a student mentor and discussing the transition into high school. Families are given a 4-year plan presentation, and students take the PSAT. Counseling continues the sophomore year with students taking the PSAT, attending a Sophomore Parent Night, and having individual meetings with a counselor. Junior students take the PSAT, attend a Junior Parent Night where PSAT results are explained and college preparation is the focus, and also meet with counselors individually. During the summer, juniors may attend seminars that include College Essay and Application, Building a College Resume, and SAT Prep. Senior students meet with various college representatives in the fall, take the SAT's, and have individual meetings with a counselor. College application procedures are covered, and direct assistance with online applications is available. The counseling office consists of two full-time freshman counselors, three full-time college counselors, and a full-time support services counselor." **Learning Disabilities:** "The Student Support Services Program serves students that have been identified as having cognitive, medical, psychological, or physical conditions that may interfere with their academic performance. The goal of the Student Support Services Program is to support students with special needs using accommodations in the mainstream classroom."

Student Conduct and Health
Code of conduct: "Valley Christian High School treats discipline as a serious Biblical responsibility and outlines its expectations in the Student Handbook. We have rules with consequences, and we follow those guidelines when the need arises. However, our consequences for misbehavior do not come from a one-size-fits-all mindset. When rules are broken, effort is given to determine what the best approach will be for the individual student." **How school handles drugs/alcohol:** "Valley Christian Schools take a strong stand against substance abuse. Parental and student consent and agreement to follow a policy of substance abuse testing is a condition of completed enrollment or re-enrollment at VCHS. Students may be required to submit to substance abuse testing for 1) cause or individual suspicion, or 2) admission or re-enrollment if the principal suspects the student may have a history of substance abuse." **Prevention and awareness programs:** "The school has a semester-long required health curriculum component that is integrated into the P.E. requirement. This curriculum includes sub-

stance abuse, sex education, abstinence, nutrition, and mental health and well-being. Also, every two years VCHS juniors and seniors take part in the 'Every Fifteen Minutes' program which demonstrates the dangers of drinking and driving."

Summer Programs
Six week on-campus classes are offered in core subjects such as math, English, P.E. and foreign language. Eight week online courses in math, photography and MS-Application are also offered. Special seminars and workshops are offered during the summer as well.

Parent Involvement
Parent participation: "Parents are required to volunteer 10 hours per year which can be fulfilled in a variety of activities. All parents are invited to attend Town Hall meetings which take place twice per year. Parents are also encouraged to be part of the PTPF (Parent Teacher Prayer Fellowship) which meets monthly to pray for and encourage teachers. An ANGEL (Always Nearby Giving Encouragement and Love) network also exists which allows parents to adopt a teacher for the year." **Parent/teacher communication:** Progress reports are sent two times per year, and options to communicate with teachers are available via e-mail or telephone. Grades are available online to view anytime, and each teacher maintains an individual class webpage. **Parent education:** N/P. **Donations:** N/P.

Sports
VCHS fields 48 teams in the West Catholic Athletic League, Central Coast Section. Includes track and field; boys soccer, baseball, basketball, football, volleyball; girls soccer, basketball, swimming, softball.

What Sets the School Apart From Others:
"U.S. Department of Education No Child Left Behind Blue Ribbon Award for Academic Excellence, scoring in the top 10% of schools in the United States; 2002 & 2006 CIF Division IV School of the Year award winner."

How Parents/Students Characterize the School:
Parent Response(s): "My son is a freshman, and it's our first year at Valley. It's been the MOST amazing experience. Not only is it obviously clean, well kept, and huge, but the teachers/counselors and entire staff provide an exceptional educational experience for the kids. What a blessing to be a part of Valley." "Valley Christian is an amazing school that provides a great Christian setting for young men and women to grow academically, physically, and spiritually. Students at VCHS show lots of passion and motivation in succeeding in academics, sports, arts, and other activities." **Student Response(s):** "I really enjoyed learning from the many great teachers that Valley has, as well as teaming up with my peers to solve challenging problems in my classes. Since I

have taken eight AP courses throughout high school, it was necessary to learn how to problem-solve with others to help myself better learn and retain the knowledge I had gained. Valley also trained my spiritual being as well, causing me to evaluate my actions and make sure that in everything that I do I am trying to please the Savior, not the people around me. At the end of my four years, I can definitely say that I felt prepared to start a new journey in college." "I know from my experience that Valley has many caring teachers and administrators who strive to make Valley a better place each year. I am sure that Valley will continue to grow and become even a better school than it is now. I had a wonderful time in Valley and feel blessed that I was able to have such an awesome experience. Go Warriors!"

Woodside International School
1555 Irving Street
San Francisco, CA 94122
(415) 564-1063

John S. Edwards, MA, Headmaster
Janet McClelland, Director of Admissions, jmcclelland@wissf.com
Ariel Edwards, Outreach Coordinator, aedwards@wissf.com

General
Coed day high school with middle school. Nonsectarian. **Founded** in 1976, incorporated 2007. **Enrollment:** Approx. 80. **Average class size:** 14. **Accreditation:** WASC. **School year:** Sept.-June. **School day:** 8 a.m.-4:30 p.m. **Location:** In the Sunset District one block south of Golden Gate Park and two blocks east of 19th Avenue. The school is accessible by the N Judah streetcar and the 28 Muni bus.

Student Body
Geographic breakdown (counties): 86% from San Francisco; 11% from San Mateo; 1% from Marin; 1% from Alameda; 1% from Contra Costa. **Ethnicity:** 49% Caucasian (non-Latino); 33% Asian; 3% African-American; 3% Latino; 12% other. International students (I-20 status): 35%. Middle school: N/P. (#, % schools)

Admission
Applications due: Year-round enrollment; applications for the fall are due by March. **Application fee:** $50. **Application process:** Students are encouraged to spend at least a half day at the school, attending classes with a current student. Applicants need to submit a completed application, test scores, copy of transcripts, and at least one letter of recommendation. An interview is then scheduled. **No. of freshman applications:** N/P. **Minimum admission requirements:** "Each applicant is reviewed on an individual basis." **Test required:** N/P. **Preferences:**

"To maintain a diverse, college-bound student body." **"We are looking for** students who are motivated to improve themselves, to develop and share their individual talents in a small community designed to help prepare for college and life." **What kind of students do you best serve?** "Woodside International School's flexible, supportive, and challenging program and small size allow students of a wide range of abilities, personalities, interests, and backgrounds to succeed."

Costs
Latest tuition: $19,995 to $20,280 depending on payment plan. Some extended payment plans are available, as well as low-interest loans. **Sibling discount:** 15%. **Tuition increases:** 3-5%. **Other costs:** A registration fee of $245; foundation contribution of $560; other fees of approx. $160. **Percentage of students receiving financial aid:** 12%. **Financial aid deadline:** Due with application. **Average grant:** $2,000. **Percentage of half-tuition or more:** 4%.

School's Mission Statement/Goals
"Woodside International School is committed to each of its students.•
We support those who like to work independently, as well as those who need lots of guidance and support, those who set themselves high goals, and those who need inspiration and encouragement, those who march to the beat of their own drum. • We recognize that some students express themselves best in class, some in one-on-one dialogues, some in writing, and some in photography, music, or art. • We understand that the support and understanding of students' families are crucial to their wellbeing and success in school, and we take care to work with families by keeping them fully informed of their progress. We believe that every child can be academically successful. We provide a unique environment to achieve this success."

Academic Program
"Woodside provides a solid college preparatory curriculum with courses that are UC and CSU approved. The curriculum is government approved for admitting international students." **Courses offered** (AP=Advanced Placement, H=Honors, (AP)=AP option, (H)=Honors option): **English:** English I-IV, Creative Writing; **Math:** Algebra I, Geometry, Algebra II, Pre-Calculus, Calculus (AP); **Social Studies:** Geography, World History, U.S. History, Civics/Econ/Cal History; **Science:** General Science, Biology, Chemistry (AP), Physics, Anatomy; **Foreign Languages:** Spanish, Japanese, French, Mandarin; **Other:** Current Events, Philosophy, Advanced Philosophy; Parenting; **Arts:** Art, Music, Jazz/Rock Ensemble, Music Studio 101, Photography, Film Appreciation, Yearbook, Woodshop; **P.E.:** Basketball, Soccer, Kung Fu, Adventures P.E., Individual P.E.; Health Workshop; ESL. **Computer/ lab training:** N/P. **Grading:** A-F and effort and study skills. **Graduation requirements:** 240 units. **Average nightly homework (M-Th):** 1-2 hours, assignments online. **Faculty:** N/P. **Faculty ethnicity:** N/P. **Faculty**

selection/training: "Teachers are selected based on their college record, their degree of expertise in their field, their ability to work as part of a team of caring adults, and their commitment to the educational process. Teacher credentials are not required. The school encourages teachers to take refresher and other college courses to enhance their skills." **Teacher/student ratio:** 1:14. **Percentage of students enrolled in AP:** N/P. **Most recent senior class profile (mean):** N/P. **National Merit Scholarship Program:** 1 junior qualified. **College enrollment (last class):** N/P. **Recent (last 4 yrs) colleges:** "Most UC colleges, SFSU, and SJSU, Stanford, Mills C, Sarah Lawrence, USC, SFCC, Academy of Art, and Williams."

Other Indicators the School is Accomplishing its Goals

"The wide variety of students, which includes our international students, testifies to the enthusiasm felt by both parents and students that the school addresses their needs in a special way. The range of colleges that students are accepted into further underlies this."

Campus/Campus Life

Campus description: "Woodside International occupies two buildings in the Middle Sunset district of San Francisco in a neighborhood of residences and small businesses. The main building on Irving Street has eight classrooms, a computer lab, and a recreation room; the building across the street has four classrooms." **Library:** 12 computers; 10 periodical subscriptions; Internet access; open 8 a.m.-4:30 p.m. Students also use the public library one block away. **Sports facilities:** School uses Golden Gate Park and local basketball court. **Theater/Arts facilities:** None. **Open/closed campus:** Open. **Lunches:** No lunch program – vending machines and microwave ovens. Students use cafés and delis in the neighborhood. **Bus service:** Public. **Uniform/dress code:** None. **Co-curricular activities/clubs:** "Many students are involved in student activities and numerous extracurricular classes. In addition, the school has dances, community service projects, class field trips, cultural activities, Sports Day, guest speaker presentations, monthly school field trips, a snowboarding trip, and a camping trip." **Foreign exchange program/internships:** None. **Community service:** 120 required community service hours toward graduation, which may be fulfilled outside of school or during organized community service field trips, including to Glide Memorial Church soup kitchens, Point Reyes trail clean-up, food drives, and school cleaning etc. **Typical freshman schedule:** Six to eight 45 minute periods each of: Algebra I, freshman English, geography, general science or biology, foreign language, P.E., reading, philosophy, current events, and extracurricular classes such as art, music, or woodshop.

Student Support Services

Counselor/student ratio (not including college counselors): 1:20. **Counseling:** "The Headmaster, Assistant Headmaster, Dean of Students, and all of the teachers engage in counseling students. Parents are kept informed as needed. The college counselor meets students from 9th grade on and meets individually with all juniors and seniors. One-on-one counseling is always available by appointment." **Learning disabilities/differences:** "No special programs or learning specialist. However, the school's program is designed to accommodate learning differences. This has allowed the enrollment of some students who have diagnosed learning disabilities."

Student Conduct and Health

Code of conduct: "Standard." **How school handles drugs/alcohol:** "We prohibit the use of drugs/alcohol at or around the school and we educate students on the effects of drug/alcohol use and on self-esteem and prevention." **Prevention/awareness programs:** "The school has annual and semi-annual prevention programs and separate workshops on tobacco, drugs, and alcohol. Community teen AIDS prevention programs are offered with guest speakers. The school also holds workshops on self-esteem, abstinence, and safe sex. Discipline is handled case by case and is based on honesty, forgiveness, and self-improvement."

Summer Programs

The school offers a morning summer school program during the month of July (also open to non-WIS students) to work individually with teachers, make up a class, work ahead, and/or improve skills in specific areas. Students earn a semester's credit through intensive work in specific areas. ESL students can take an intensive 4-week program in all aspects of English. Students can apply to take more than 10 credits.

Parent Involvement

Parent participation: No required hours. **Parent/teacher communication:** "Progress reports every four weeks keep parents informed. The dates of these reports are on the calendar with reminders in the monthly newsletter. Conferences can be arranged at any time. Parents can also review students' assignments, which are posted weekly on the school's web-site." **Parent education:** "We encourage parent/teacher conferences whenever issues arise and provide advice and recommendations. We also can refer parents to professional counselors outside the school." **Donations:** "An annual contribution of $560 to the Wildshaw Foundation is requested."

Sports

"Students may also earn credit by enrolling in outside programs that can confirm attendance and participation. The school offers an Adventures P.E. program, which includes training and preparation for trips such as kayaking, mountain biking, cross-country skiing, surfing, snowboarding, scuba diving, rock-climbing and hiking."

What Sets School Apart From Others

"Its special qualities include: its willingness to accommodate the individual needs of its students, its smallness, its open lines of communication with parents and students, its diverse student body, and the flexibility and wide range of its programs."

How Parents/Students Characterize School

Parent response(s): "Woodside International School has just the right "chemistry" for teenagers. Classes are challenging, yet my son never has felt so overwhelmed that quitting ever became a solution. Most important for teenagers is encouragement and support." "Woodside International is a breath of fresh air! The program is truly student-centered; each student is treated as an individual; the administration is flexible and understanding; the teachers are friendly and engaging. We feel lucky to have found this gem in our backyard.""My son likes the variety in the curriculum, as well as class periods under an hour. He can remain focused and engaged on the material so much better. Easy access to the administration and teachers, plus assignments given on a weekly basis, really help with organization and time management. The regular, directed study periods help him keep up with his workload." "Our daughter has blossomed in her first year at Woodside International. She is passionate with her studies and shares with us what she has learned in the classroom, sometimes in long discussions. She has opened up to us more and seems a happier and more motivated student than she was last year." **Student response(s):** "We are uniquely profound individuals with a lot on our minds. We have unique tastes and interests. We accept all types of students. The teachers are liberal. They take time to help students. They listen to our problems and help us solve them. They do not look at teaching as a job. They look at it as a wonderful experience." "The classes are often centered around discussions and not just writing. My views are respected and so are other people's views. I have been exposed to many different ideas and views."

Woodside Priory High School

302 Portola Road
Portola Valley, CA 94028
(650) 851-8220
www.woodsidepriory.com

Timothy Molak, Head of School
Al Zappelli, Admissions Director, azappelli@woodsidepriory.com

General

Coed Catholic day and boarding school. Independent. Benedictine. Founded in 1957. Nonprofit. **Enrollment:** Approx. 253 day, 47 boarding. **Average class size:** 14-18. **Accreditation:** N/P. **School year:** N/P. **Location:** 30 minutes south of San Francisco.

Student Body: N/P.

Admission

Applications due: mid-January (call for date). **Application fee:** $60. **Application process:** Application, student interest and writing sample, recommendations, transcripts, HSPT, interview, shadow visit. **No. of freshman applications:** N/P. **Minimum admission requirements:** N/P. **Test required:** HSPT. **Preferences:** "We are looking for N/P" **What kind of student do you best serve?** N/P.

Costs

Latest tuition: $28,050 day, $38,950 boarding. **Sibling discount:** None. **Tuition increases:** N/P. **Other costs:** $400 deposit at campus store. **Percentage of students receiving financial aid:** 20%. **Financial aid deadline:** N/P. **Average grant:** N/P. **Percentage of grants of half tuition or more:** N/P.

School's Mission Statement/Goals

"Our mission is to assist students of promise in becoming lifelong learners who will productively serve a world in need of their gifts."

Academic Program

Courses offered (AP=Advanced Placement, H=Honors, (AP)=AP option, (H)=Honors option): 16 AP classes: Art History, Art Portfolio 2D and 3D, Biology, French, Calculus (AB and BC), Computer Science, Music Theory, Physics, Chemistry, Spanish Language, Economics, Spanish Literature, English, Statistics, Environmental Science, European History, U.S. History. **Computer lab/training:** N/P. **Grading:** N/P. **Graduation requirements:** 4 years: English; 3 years: science, theology, perform theology, and history; 2 years: foreign language; 1 year: performing arts, visual arts, P.E.; 1 semester: computer; Service Learning: significant community service experiences integrated into specific curricula, plus 10 hours of community service per year. **Average nightly homework (M-Th):** N/P. **Faculty:** "71% advanced degrees." (N/P #, gender, degrees) **Faculty ethnicity:** "15% persons of color." (N/P ethnicity) **Faculty selection/training:** N/P. **Teacher/student ratio:** 1:9. **Percentage of students enrolled in AP:** N/P; 86% scored 3 or higher, 75% scored 4 or 5. **Senior class profile (mean):** SAT Math 633, SAT Critical Reading 610, SAT Writing 605; GPA: N/P. **National Merit Scholarship Program:** 13% of 2007 Class Finalists. **College enrollment (last class):** N/P. **Recent (last 4 yrs) colleges:** SF Academy of Arts, U-Arkansas, UC (Riverside, Berkeley, Irvine, LA, Davis), Seattle U, Princeton, Rice, Saint Louis U, Stanford, Elon, Clark, Chapman, Colorado SU, C of Holy Cross, Cornell, Duke, U-Redlands, Gonzaga, U-Oregon, Loyola Marymount, Oberlin, USC, Willamette, U-Puget Sound, and USF.

Other Indicators the School is Accomplishing its Goals: N/P.

Campus/Campus Life
Campus description: 60 wooded acres, 30 miles south of San Francisco. Library: N/P. Sports facilities: N/P. Theater/Arts facilities: N/P. Open/closed campus: N/P. Lunches: N/P. Bus service: N/P. Uniforms/dress code: N/P. Co-curricular activities/clubs: N/P. Foreign exchange program/internships: N/P. Community service: N/P. Typical freshman schedule: World Literature, math, World History, foreign language, World Religions, Writing Lab, Computer, Basic Beliefs and Values, Hebrew Scripture.

Student Support Services
Counselor/student ratio (not including college counselors): N/P. Counseling: "Students have an advisory network that includes their teachers, the academic deans, and an academic advisor (boarding students also have a residential advisor). The counseling team, which is headed by the Director of Guidance and Counseling, includes the academic deans, the campus minister, the learning specialist, the Director of College Counseling, a personal counselor, and others as needed." Learning differences/disabilities: "An academic resource center open before, during, and after school. A full-time learning specialist and personal counselor staff the center."

Student Conduct and Health
Code of conduct: "All members of the Priory community are responsible for their own conduct and for contributing to the well-being of the community. This is an ongoing community-wide effort, explicitly discussed and modeled." How school handles drugs/alcohol: N/P. Prevention and awareness programs: N/P.

Summer Programs: N/P.

Parent Involvement: N/P .

Sports
Gofl; boys soccer, basketball, tennis, baseball, volleyball, track and field; girls volleyball, soccer, softball; cross-country, swimming, water polo.

What Sets School Apart From Others: N/P.

How Parents/Students Characterize School: N/P.

ADDITIONAL SCHOOLS

Carondelet High School
1133 Winton Drive
Concord, CA 94518
(925) 686-5353 *fax (925) 671-9429*
www.carondelet.net

Sr. Kathleen Lang, CSJ, President
Teresa Hurlbut, Ed.D. Principal
Kathy Harris, Director of Admissions, kharris@carondeleths.org

Girls Catholic day high school. Founded in 1965. Sponsored by the Sisters of St. Joseph of Carondelet. **Enrollment:** 800. **Accreditation:** WASC. **Latest tuition:** $12,250. SAT Math 532, SAT Critical Reading 546, SAT Writing 556. **College enrollment (last class):** 85% 4-year, 13% 2-year.

Redwood Day Upper School
3245 Sheffield Avenue
Oakland, CA 94602
(510) 534-0800
www.rdschool.org

Michael Riera, Ph.D., Head of School
Ray Wilson, Upper School Director
Katrina Lappin, Admission

General
Opening Fall 2009 with the 9th grade growing through Grade 12.

School's Mission Statement/Goals
"Redwood Day School, a K-12 program, prepares students for life and for college by recognizing and utilizing the latest research in brain development, learning, and developmental psychology. In our program (which will be UC approved) students will learn how to identify, research, and solve problems both as individuals and as part of a team. Furthermore, students will learn to plumb the depths of their strengths through rich programs in athletics, drama, service learning, studio arts, music, and leadership. A developmentally inspired, research based, college preparatory curriculum will include: • A shift in thinking from a traditional independent school to an interdependent school that is deeply connected to our community and beyond; • A move beyond Advanced Placement courses. Instead, academic depth will come from creative cross-curricular and project-based work; • A range of learning activities and classroom configurations to teach students how to learn in a variety of settings such as: individual

projects, small group projects, seminar classes, multiple teachers and internships; • A schedule that appreciates the pace of how students really learn and includes a start time in accordance with adolescent sleep patterns and requirements; • Self knowledge that accounts for each student's unique learning and leadership style; • Anintegrated curriculum that involves multiple studio classes, active service learning, and a health and wellness program; • Our Life Planning program will incorporate the development of our students' goals and aspirations as human beings with college placement."

St. Joseph Notre Dame High School

1011 Chestnut Street
Alameda, CA 94501
(510) 523-1526
www.sjnd.org

Simon Chiu, Principal
Julianne Berry, Director of Admission, jberry@sjnd.org

Coed Catholic day high school. Founded in 1881. Nonprofit. **Enrollment:** 470. **Average class size:** 26. **Accreditation:** WASC. **Student Body:** N/P. **Geographic breakdown (cities):** 40% Alameda, 35% Oakland, 20% San Leandro. **Ethnicity:** 27% Caucasian (non-Latino); 14% Filipino; 17% African-American; 17% Latino; 7% Asian; 16% multiethnic. **Applications due:** Early January. **Latest tuition:** $11,620. Registration fee $750 and technology fee $400. **Percentage of students receiving financial aid:** 30%.

St. Vincent de Paul High School

849 Keokuk Street
Petaluma, CA. 94952
(707) 763-1032 *fax (707) 763-9448*
www.svhs-pet.org

Dr. John Walker, Principal
JaZelle Clifford, Admissions

Coed Catholic day high school. Founded in 1962. **Enrollment:** 400. **Accreditation:** WASC. **Latest tuition:** $9,850; registration fee $425, building assessment $400. **SAT mean:** Math 566; Verbal 558; Writing 561.

Ursuline High School

90 Ursuline Road
Santa Rosa, CA 95403
(707) 524-1130 *fax (707) 542-0131*
www.ursulinehs.org

Julie Carver, Principal

Girls Catholic day high school. Founded in 1880. **Enrollment:** 367.
Accreditation: WASC. **Latest tuition:** $11,600.

APPENDIX

At parents' request, certain statistics from the schools' profiles are
compiled below. Because of space consideration, commonly used
short names are used. IHS is International High School, ICA is Immaculate Conception High School, O'Dowd is Bishop O'Dowd, etc.

Class Size

The Marin School	8
Orinda Academy	10
Kehillah Jewish High School	10-15
Bentley School	12
San Domenico Upper School	12
Sonoma Academy	12
East Bay Waldorf School	12-15
San Francisco Waldorf High School	12-15
The Bay School of San Francisco	13
The Urban School of San Francisco	13
Castilleja School	14
The College Preparatory School	14
Crystal Springs Uplands School	14
Convent of the Sacred Heart High School	14
Drew School	14
Woodside International School	14
Woodside Priory	14-18
The Athenian School	15
Contra Costa Christian Schools	15
Lick-Wilmerding High School	15
Marin Academy	15
The Head-Royce School	15
Jewish Community High School	15
Lisa Kampner Hebrew Academy High School	15
Menlo School	15
Mid-Peninsula High School	15

Sacred Heart Preparatory	15
San Francisco University High School	15
The International High School	15-18
Lycée Français La Pérouse	15-20
Pinewood School	15-20
The Branson School	16
Stuart Hall High School	16
Fremont Christian School	17
Immaculate Conception Academy	17
The Quarry Lane School	17
The Harker School	18
St. Elizabeth High School	18
Chinese Christian High School	20
St. Lawrence Academy	21
Berean Christian School	22
Mercy High School-San Francisco	22
The King's Academy	23
Marin Catholic High School	23
Cardinal Newman High School	24
Mercy High School-Burlingame	24
Moreau Catholic High School	24
Notre Dame High School	24
Archbishop Riordan High School	25
Bellarmine College Preparatory	25
Bishop O'Dowd High School	25
Cornerstone Academy	25
Holy Names High School	25
Valley Christian High School	25
Junipero Serra High School	25-26
Sacred Heart Cathedral Preparatory	26
St. Ignatius College Preparatory	26
St. Joseph Notre Dame	26
Salesian High School	26
Archbishop Mitty High School	27
Notre Dame High School	27
Presentation High School	28
Saint Francis High School	28
Saint Mary's College High School	28
De La Salle High School	30

N/P: Carondelet High School, St. Vincent de Paul High School, Ursuline High School.

School Size

Archbishop Mitty High School (San Jose)	1650
Saint Francis High School (Mountain View)	1600
Bellarmine College Prep (San Jose)	1550
St. Ignatius College Prep (San Francisc	1450
Sacred Heart Cathedral Preparatory (San Francisco)	1250
Valley Christian (San Jose)	1215
Bishop O'Dowd (Oakland)	1180
De La Salle High School (Concord)	1000
Junipero Serra High School (San Mateo)	990
Moreau Catholic High School (Hayward)	910
Carondelet High School (Concord)	800
Presentation High School (San Jose)	752
Marin Catholic High School (Kentfield)	730
Archbishop Riordan High School (San Francisco)	650
Notre Dame High School (Belmont)	630
Notre Dame High School (San Jose)	630
Saint Mary's College High School (Berkeley)	600
Salesian High School (Richmond)	585
The Harker School (San Jose)	563
Menlo School (Atherton)	540
The King's Academy (Sunnyvale)	530
Sacred Heart Preparatory (Atherton)	530
Mercy High School-Burlingame (Burlingame)	500
Mercy High School-San Francisco (San Francisco)	500
St. Joseph Notre Dame (Alameda)	470
Cardinal Newman High School (Santa Rosa)	430
Lick-Wilmerding High School (San Francisco)	430
Castilleja School (Palo Alto)	415
Berean Christian School (Walnut Creek)	400
Contra Costa Christian Schools (Walnut Creek)	400
Marin Academy (San Rafael)	400
St. Vincent de Paul High School (Petaluma)	400
San Francisco University High School (San Francisco)	389
Ursuline High School (Santa Rosa)	367
The College Preparatory School (Oakland)	350
Crystal Springs Uplands School (Hillsborough)	350
St. Lawrence Academy (Santa Clara)	350
The Urban School of San Francisco (San Francisco)	350
The Head-Royce School (Oakland)	340
The International High School (San Francisco)	328
The Branson School (Ross)	320
The Athenian School (Danville)	300
The Bay School of San Francisco (San Francisco)	300
Pinewood School (Los Altos Hills)	300
Woodside Priory (Portola Valley)	300
Holy Names High School (Oakland)	275
Immaculate Conception Academy (San Francisco)	265

Drew School (San Francisco)	250
St. Elizabeth High School (Oakland)	250
Bentley School (Layfayette)	225 to grow to 290
Chinese Christian High School (San Leandro)	225
Fremont Christian School (Fremont)	218
Convent of the Sacred Heart High School (San Francisco)	200
Sonoma Academy (Santa Rosa)	200
Stuart Hall High School (San Francisco)	165
Jewish Community High School of the Bay	155 to grow to 450
San Domenico Upper School (San Anselmo)	150
San Francisco Waldorf High School (San Francisco)	140
Mid-Peninsula High School (Menlo Park)	125
Orinda Academy (Orinda)	125
Kehillah Jewish High School (San Jose)	110 to grow to 250
Cornerstone Academy (San Francisco)	100
The Marin School (Sausalito)	100
Lisa Kampner Jewish Community HS (SF)	90
Woodside International School (San Francisco)	80
The Quarry Lane High School (Dublin)	50 to grow to 400
East Bay Waldorf School (El Sobrante)	43

N/P: Lycée Français La Pérouse

Total Costs/Tuition Only/ Other Costs

The Branson School	$33,315 /$31,315/$2,000
The Bay School	$32,400/$29,500/$2,900
Marin Academy	$31,870-$31,570/ $30,970/$600-$900
Lick-Wilmerding	$31,700 / $30,700/ $1,000***
Menlo School	$31,350/$30,800/$550
The Marin School	$31,000/$30,900/$100
Crystal Springs	$30,775 /$30,075/$700
The Harker School	$30,744/$21,574 /$29,894-$20,674/$775-$850
Castilleja School	$30,600-$30,500/$29,900/ $600-$700
Sonoma Academy	$30,150/$28,500/$1,650
Stuart Hall High School	$29,800-$29,500/$29,200/$300-$600
Convent	$29,750 /$29,200/$550
San Francisco University	$29,750
International High School	$29,670/$27,670/$2,000**
College Prep	$29,600/$28,600/$1,000
Urban	$29,400/$28,000/$1,400
Athenian	$28,520/$27,520/$1,000
Drew	$28,500 /$28,500/$0
Woodside Priory	$28,450/$28,050/$400
The Head-Royce School	$28,000 /$27,000/$1,000
Jewish Community High	$27,900-$27,800/$27,700/$100-$200
San Domenico	$27,300/$27,000/$300
Sacred Heart Preparatory	$26,885

Kehillah Jewish High School	$26,800 /$24,600/$2,200
Mid-Peninsula	$26,400/$25,000/$1,400
San Francisco Waldorf	$25,775/$24,700/$1,075
Bentley School (Lafayette)	$25,665-$25,365/$24,865/ $500-$800
Orinda Academy (Orinda)	$24,695/$23,995/$700
Pinewood School	$22,110/$21,210/$900
Woodside International School	$20,960/$19,995/$965
The Quarry Lane High School	$19,860/$18,460/$1,400
East Bay Waldorf School	$19,800 /$18,800/$1,000
Lycée Français La Pérouse	$19,670-$17,770 /$18,570-$16,670/$1,100***
Lisa Kampner Hebrew Aca.	$16,855/$15,900/$955
Mercy -Burlingame	$16,725-$16,325/$15,325/$1,000-$1,400
St. Ignatius	$16,500/$15,500/$1,000
Notre Dame-Belmont	$15,950-$15,550/$14,950/$600-$1,000
Bishop O'Dowd	$15,700-$13,600/$12,700/$900-$3,000*
Junipero Serra	$14,600 /$14,100/$500
Sacred Heart Cathedral	$14,400/$12,800/$1,600
Bellarmine	$14,250-$14,150/$13,800/$350-$450
Marin Catholic	$14,200 /$13,900/$300
Archbishop Riordan	$13,810/$12,960/ $850
Valley Christian	$13,705/$12,705/$1,000
Archbishop Mitty	$13,550 /$12,900/$650
De La Salle)	$13,500 /$13,200/$300
Saint Mary's	$12,940/$12,540/$400
St. Joseph	$12,770/$11,620/$1,150
Mercy-San Francisco	$12,725/$12,500/$225
Notre Dame	$12,650****
St. Lawrence	$12,380****/$11,480/$900****
Carondelet High School	$12,250+/$12,250/N/P
Saint Francis	$12,200
Holy Names	$12,150-$11,750 /$10,800/$950-$1,350
The King's Academy	$12,079-$9,296/$11,154-$8,371/$925
Moreau Catholic	$11,894/$11,544/$350
Cardinal Newman	$11,875 /$11,100/$775
Ursuline	$11,600****/$11,600
Salesian High School	$11,265****/10,540/$725****
Immaculate Conception	$11,260-$10,860/$9,900/$960-$1,360
Cornerstone Academy	$11,150 -$8,150/$10,550-$7,550/$600
St. Vincent de Paul	$10,675/$9,850/$825
Fremont Christian	$10,540/$10,260/$280
St. Elizabeth	$10,150-$10,000/$9,000/ $1000-$1150
Chinese Christian	$9,600-$9,200 /$8,350/$850-$1,250
Presentation	$9,485
Contra Costa Christian	$8,730+/$8730/ N/P
Berean Christian School	$8,175+/$8,000/$175+

*$2,900 one-time laptop fee
** $2,000 one-time new student fee

***$1000 one-time facilities use/or new student fee
**** Additional costs

Percentage of Students Receiving Financial Aid

Lisa Kampner Hebrew Academy High School (San Francisco)	88%
Immaculate Conception Academy (San Francisco)	65%
St. Elizabeth High School (Oakland)	51%
East Bay Waldorf School (El Sobrante)	47%
Mercy High School-San Francisco (San Francisco)	46%
Lick-Wilmerding High School (San Francisco)	42%
Kehillah Jewish High School (San Jose)	40%
Sonoma Academy (Santa Rosa)	40%
The Bay School of San Francisco (San Francisco)	38%
Drew School (San Francisco)	38%
San Francisco Waldorf High School (San Francisco)	37%
Holy Names High School (Oakland)	35%
Sacred Heart Preparatory (Atherton)	35%
San Domenico Upper School (San Anselmo)	35%
Stuart Hall High School (San Francisco)	35%
Archbishop Riordan High School (San Francisco)	32%
Jewish Community High School of the Bay (San Francisco)	31%
Convent of the Sacred Heart High School (San Francisco)	30%
St. Joseph Notre Dame (Alameda)	30%
Bentley School (Lafayette)	28%
Salesian High School (Richmond)	28%
Saint Mary's College High School (Berkeley)	27%
The Head-Royce School (Oakland)	25%
Lycée Français La Pérouse (San Francisco)	25%
Mid-Peninsula High School (Menlo Park)	25%
Notre Dame High School (Belmont)	25%
Sacred Heart Cathedral Preparatory (San Francisco)	25%
St. Lawrence Academy (Santa Clara)	25%
De La Salle High School (Concord)	24%
The College Preparatory School (Oakland)	23+%
The International High School (San Francisco)	23%
San Francisco University High School (San Francisco)	23%
Junipero Serra High School (San Mateo)	22%
The Urban School of San Francisco (San Francisco)	22%
Marin Academy (San Rafael)	21%
The Athenian School (Danville)	20%
Bellarmine College Preparatory (San Jose)	20%
Bishop O'Dowd High School (Oakland)	20%
Marin Catholic High School (Kentfield)	20%
Menlo School (Atherton)	20%
Mercy High School-Burlingame (Burlingame)	20%
Moreau Catholic High School (Hayward)	20%
Orinda Academy (Orinda)	20%

Woodside Priory (Portola Valley)	20%
Crystal Springs Uplands School (Hillsborough)	19%
St. Ignatius College Preparatory School (San Francisco)	19%
The Branson School (Ross)	17%
Archbishop Mitty High School (San Jose)	16%
Castilleja School (Palo Alto)	16%
Notre Dame High School (San Jose)	16%
The Marin School (Sausalito)	12%
Woodside International School (San Francisco)	12%
Saint Francis High School (Mountain View)	10+%
Berean Christian School (Walnut Creek)	10%
Chinese Christian High School (San Leandro)	10%
Chinese Christian School (San Leandro)	10%
Fremont Christian School (Fremont)	10%
The Harker School (San Jose)	10%
The King's Academy (Sunnyvale)	10%
The Quarry Lane High School (Dublin)	10%
Contra Costa Christian Schools (Walnut Creek)	5%
Valley Christian High School (San Jose)	5%
Pinewood School (Los Altos Hills)	1%

N/P: Cardinal Newman, Carondelet, Cornerstone Academy, Presentation, St. Joseph, St. Vincent de Paul, Ursuline

Percentage of Financial Aid Awards 1/2 Tuition+

Castilleja School (Palo Alto)	88%
The Branson School (Ross)	82%
The Athenian School (Danville)	79%
The Marin School (Sausalito)	78%
Marin Academy (San Rafael)	76%
The College Preparatory School (Oakland)	72%
Bentley School (Lafayette)	55%
Crystal Springs Uplands School (Hillsborough)	53%
Stuart Hall High School (San Francisco)	52%
The Head-Royce School (Oakland)	50%
Immaculate Conception Academy (San Francisco)	46%
Orinda Academy (Orinda)	45%
Bellarmine College Preparatory (San Jose)	42%
San Francisco Waldorf High School (San Francisco)	40%
Holy Names High School (Oakland)	18%
Sacred Heart Preparatory (Atherton)	18%
Mercy High School-San Francisco (San Francisco)	11%
De La Salle High School (Concord)	10%
Fremont Christian School (Fremont)	10%
Chinese Christian School (San Leandro)	8%
Pinewood School (Los Altos Hills)	8%
Junipero Serra High School (San Mateo)	8%

Woodside International School (San Francisco)	4%
Archbishop Riordan High School (San Francisco)	<1%
East Bay Waldorf School (El Sobrante)	0%
The King's Academy (Sunnyvale)	0%
Pinewood School (Los Altos Hills)	0%
St. Lawrence Academy (Sunnyvale)	0%

N/P: Mitty, The Bay School, Berean Christian, O'Dowd, Cardinal Newman, Carondelet, Contra Costa Christian, Convent, Cornerstone Academy, Drew, Harker, IHS, Jewish Community High School, Lisa Kampner Hebrew Academy, Kehillah Jewish High School, Lick-Wilmerding, Lycée Français La Pérouse, Marin Catholic, Menlo, Mercy-Burlingame, Mid-Peninsula, Moreau Catholic, Notre Dame (Belmont), Notre Dame (San Jose), Presentation High School, Quarry Lane, Sacred Heart Cathedral, St. Elizabeth, Saint Francis, St. Ignatius, St. Joseph, Saint Mary's, St. Vincent de Paul, Salesian, San Domenico, San Francisco University, Sonoma Academy, Urban, Ursuline, Valley Christian, Woodside Priory.

SAT Math Scores (Mean)

The College Preparatory School (Oakland)	715
The Harker School (San Jose)	712
Lick-Wilmerding High School (San Francisco)	680
San Francisco University High School (San Francisco)	677
Castilleja School (Palo Alto)	673
Menlo School (Atherton)	672
The Head-Royce School (Oakland)	668
Pinewood School (Los Altos Hills)	668
The Branson School (Ross)	664
The Athenian School (Danville)	651
Crystal Springs Uplands School (Hillsborough)	650-740 (mid 50%)
Marin Academy (San Rafael)	645
Woodside Priory (Portola Valley)	633
Chinese Christian High School (San Leandro)	621
The King's Academy (Sunnyvale)	620
San Domenico Upper School (San Anselmo)	614
The International High School (San Francisco)	610
St. Ignatius College Preparatory School (San Francisco)	605
Kehillah Jewish High School (San Jose)	598
The Bay School (San Francisco)	594
Sonoma Academy (Santa Rosa)	591
Stuart Hall High School (San Francisco)	591
De La Salle High School (Concord)	588
Saint Francis High School (Mountain View)	587
Sacred Heart Preparatory (Atherton)	584
Notre Dame High School (San Jose)	580
Jewish Community High School of the Bay (San Francisco)	578

San Francisco Waldorf High School (San Francisco)   575
Archbishop Mitty High School (San Jose)   570
Convent of the Sacred Heart High School (San Francisco   567
St. Vincent de Paul High School (Petaluma)   566
East Bay Waldorf School (El Sobrante)   565
Orinda Academy (Orinda)   559
Contra Costa Christian Schools (Walnut Creek)   548
Notre Dame High School (Belmont)   545
Mercy High School-Burlingame (Burlingame)   538
The Marin School (Sausalito)   529
Carondelet High School (Concord)   532
Mid-Peninsula High School (Menlo Park)   518
Archbishop Riordan High School (San Francisco)   497

N/P: Bellarmine, Bentley, Berean Christian, O'Dowd, Cardinal New-
man, Cornerstone Academy, Drew, Fremont Christian, Holy Names,
Immaculate Conception, Junipero Serra, Lisa Kampner Hebrew
Academy, Lycée Français La Pérouse, Marin Catholic, Mercy -San
Francisco, Moreau Catholic, Presentation, Quarry Lane, Sacred
Heart Cathedral, St. Elizabeth, St. Joseph, St. Lawrence, Saint
Mary's, Salesian, Urban, Ursuline, Valley Christian, Woodside Inter-
national.

SAT Critical Reading Scores (Mean)

The College Preparatory School (Oakland)   716
Castilleja School (Palo Alto)   701
The Harker School (San Jose)   688
Lick-Wilmerding High School (San Francisco)   685
San Francisco University High School (San Francisco)   677
Pinewood School (Los Altos Hills)   663
Menlo School (Atherton)   662
The Head-Royce School (Oakland)   651
Marin Academy (San Rafael)   650
The Branson School (Ross)   646
Sonoma Academy (Santa Rosa)   640
The International High School (San Francisco)   623
The Athenian School (Danville)   620
St. Ignatius College Preparatory School (San Francisco)   617
The Bay School (San Francisco)   614
Crystal Springs Uplands School (Hillsborough)   610-750 (mid 50%)
Woodside Priory (Portola Valley)   610
Kehillah Jewish High School (San Jose)   608
San Francisco Waldorf High School (San Francisco)   608
Convent of the Sacred Heart High School (San Francisco)   606
Jewish Community High School of the Bay (San Francisco)   605
Sacred Heart Preparatory (Atherton)   596
San Domenico Upper School (San Anselmo)   595

Stuart Hall High School (San Francisco)	591
The King's Academy (Sunnyvale)	588
Saint Francis High School (Mountain View)	581
Orinda Academy (Orinda)	578
De La Salle High School (Concord)	575
Chinese Christian High School (San Leandro)	574
East Bay Waldorf School (El Sobrante)	568
Mercy High School-Burlingame (Burlingame)	567
Archbishop Mitty High School (San Jose)	561
Notre Dame High School (San Jose)	560
St. Vincent de Paul High School (Petaluma)	558
Mid-Peninsula High School (Menlo Park)	556
Carondelet High School (Concord)	546
Contra Costa Christian Schools (Walnut Creek)	544
The Marin School (Sausalito)	539
Notre Dame High School (Belmont)	532
Archbishop Riordan High School (San Francisco)	502

N/P Bellarmine, Bentley, Berean Christian, O'Dowd, Cardinal Newman, Cornerstone Academy, Drew, Fremont Christian, Holy Names, Immaculate Conception, Junipero Serra, Lisa Kampner Hebrew Academy High School, Lycée Français La Pérouse, Marin Catholic, Mercy-San Francisco, Moreau Catholic, Presentation, Quarry Lane, Sacred Heart Cathedral, St. Elizabeth, St. Joseph, St. Lawrence, Saint Mary's, Salesian, Urban, Ursuline, Valley Christian, Woodside International.

SAT Writing Score (Mean)

The College Preparatory School (Oakland)	719
Castilleja School (Palo Alto)	706
The Harker School (San Jose)	702
Lick-Wilmerding High School (San Francisco)	687
San Francisco University High School (San Francisco)	682
Marin Academy (San Rafael)	675
The Branson School (Ross)	671
Pinewood School (Los Altos Hills)	668
The Head-Royce School (Oakland)	661
Menlo School (Atherton)	661
Sonoma Academy (Santa Rosa)	634
Convent of the Sacred Heart High School (San Francisco)	632
The Athenian School (Danville)	629
St. Ignatius College Preparatory School (San Francisco)	627
The Bay School (San Francisco)	624
The International High School (San Francisco)	620
Crystal Springs Uplands School (Hillsborough)	620-750 (mid 50%)
Sacred Heart Preparatory (Atherton)	616
Woodside Priory (Portola Valley)	605

San Domenico Upper School (San Anselmo)	604
Jewish Community High School of the Bay (San Francisco)	602
Kehillah Jewish High School (San Jose)	602
Saint Francis High School (Mountain View)	596
San Francisco Waldorf High School (San Francisco)	590
Stuart Hall High School (San Francisco)	583
The King's Academy (Sunnyvale)	581
Contra Costa Christian Schools (Walnut Creek)	576
Archbishop Mitty High School (San Jose)	575
Orinda Academy (Orinda)	572
East Bay Waldorf School (El Sobrante)	570
Notre Dame High School (San Jose)	570
Chinese Christian High School (San Leandro)	566
Notre Dame High School (Belmont)	560
De La Salle High School (Concord)	563
St. Vincent de Paul High School (Petaluma)	561
Carondelet High School (Concord)	556
Mid-Peninsula High School (Menlo Park)	520
The Marin School (Sausalito)	518
Archbishop Riordan High School (San Francisco)	508

N/P: Bellarmine, Bentley, Berean Christian, Bishop O'Dowd, Cardinal Newman, Cornerstone Academy, Drew, Fremont Christian, Holy Names, Immaculate Conception, Junipero Serra, Lisa Kampner Hebrew Academy, Lycée Français La Pérouse, Marin Catholic, Mercy-San Francisco, Moreau Catholic, Presentation, Quarry Lane, Sacred Heart Cathedral, St. Elizabeth, St. Joseph, St. Lawrence, Saint Mary's, Salesian, Urban, Ursuline, Valley Christian, Woodside International.

Percentage Students Enrolling in College Upon Graduation

The Bay School (San Francisco)	100%
Bellarmine College Preparatory (San Jose)	100%
Bentley School (Lafayette)	100%
The Branson School (Ross)	100%
Castilleja School (Palo Alto)	100%
Chinese Christian High School (San Leandro)	100%
The College Preparatory School (Oakland)	100%
Convent of the Sacred Heart High School (San Francisco)	100%
Crystal Springs Uplands School (Hillsborough)	100%
The Harker School (San Jose)	100%
The Head-Royce School (Oakland)	100%
Holy Names High School (Oakland)	100%
Immaculate Conception Academy (San Francisco)	100%
The International High School (San Francisco)	100%
Jewish Community High School of the Bay (San Francisco)	100%
Junipero Serra High School (San Mateo)	100%

Lisa Kampner Hebrew Academy High School (San Francisco) 100%
Kehillah Jewish High School (San Jose) 100%
The King's Academy (Sunnyvale) 100%
Lick-Wilmerding High School (San Francisco) 100%
Marin Academy (San Rafael) 100%
The Marin School (Sausalito) 100%
Mercy High School-Burlingame (Burlingame) 100%
Mercy High School-San Francisco (San Francisco) 100%
Notre Dame High School (Belmont) 100%
Notre Dame High School (San Jose) 100%
Pinewood School (Los Altos Hills) 100%
Presentation High School (San Jose) 100%
Sacred Heart Cathedral Preparatory (San Francisco) 100%
Sacred Heart Preparatory (Atherton) 100%
St. Ignatius College Preparatory School (San Francisco) 100%
Salesian High School (Richmond) 100%
San Domenico Upper School (San Anselmo) 100%
San Francisco University High School (San Francisco) 100%
Stuart Hall High School (San Francisco) 100%
Archbishop Mitty High School (San Jose) 99.7%
Saint Francis High School (Mountain View) 99.4%
Archbishop Riordan High School (San Francisco) 99%
Cornerstone Academy (San Francisco) 99%
St. Lawrence Academy (Santa Clara) 99%
Saint Mary's College High School (Berkeley) 99%
The Urban School of San Francisco (San Francisco) 99%
Bishop O'Dowd High School (Oakland) 98%
Carondelet High School (Concord) 98%
De La Salle High School (Concord) 98%
Drew School (San Francisco) 98%
Moreau Catholic High School (Hayward) 98%
St. Elizabeth High School (Oakland) 98%
Valley Christian High School 98%
Sonoma Academy (Santa Rosa) 96%
Fremont Christian School (Fremont) 95%
Marin Catholic High School (Kentfield) 95%
Orinda Academy (Orinda) 95%
San Francisco Waldorf High School (San Francisco) 95%
Cardinal Newman High School (Santa Rosa) 93%
Contra Costa Christian Schools (Walnut Creek) 93%
East Bay Waldorf School (El Sobrante) 92%
The Athenian School (Danville) 90-100%
Mid-Peninsula High School (Menlo Park) 90%

N/P: Berean Christian School, Lycée Français La Pérouse, Menlo School, The Quarry Lane High School, St. Joseph Notre Dame, St. Vincent de Paul High School, Ursuline High School, Woodside International School, Woodside Priory

Percentage of Graduates Enrolling in 4-year/2-year Colleges

Bentley School (Lafayette)	100%
The Branson School (Ross)	100%
Castilleja School (Palo Alto)	100%
The College Preparatory School (Oakland)	100%
Convent of the Sacred Heart High School (San Francisco)	100%
Crystal Springs Uplands School (Hillsborough)	100%
The Harker School (San Jose)	100%
The Head-Royce School (Oakland)	100%
Lick-Wilmerding High School (San Francisco)	100%
San Domenico Upper School (San Anselmo)	100%
San Francisco University High School (San Francisco)	100%
Marin Academy (San Rafael)	99%/1%
Saint Mary's College High School (Berkeley)	99%
The International High School (San Francisco)	98%/2%
Drew School (San Francisco)	98%
Bellarmine College Preparatory (San Jose)	95.2%/4.8%
The Bay School of San Francisco (San Francisco)	95%/5%
Marin Catholic High School (Kentfield)	95%
Pinewood School (Los Altos Hills)	95%/5%
Sacred Heart Preparatory (Atherton)	95-100%/ 0-5%
Saint Francis High School (Mountain View)	94.5%/4.9%
Notre Dame High School (San Jose)	94%/6%
St. Ignatius College Preparatory School (San Francisco)	94%/6%
Bishop O'Dowd High School (Oakland)	93%/5%
Sacred Heart Cathedral Preparatory (San Francisco)	92%/8%
The Marin School (Sausalito)	90%/10%
The Athenian School (Danville)	90-100%/0-10%
Cardinal Newman High School (Santa Rosa)	90%/3%
Chinese Christian High School (San Leandro)	90%/10%
The King's Academy (Sunnyvale)	88%/12%
Notre Dame High School (Belmont)	88% /12%
Presentation High School (San Jose)	87%/13%
De La Salle High School (Concord)	87%/11%
Mercy High School-Burlingame (Burlingame)	85%/15%
Carondelet High School (Concord)	85%/13%
Orinda Academy (Orinda)	84%
Holy Names High School (Oakland)	83%/17%
Immaculate Conception Academy (San Francisco)	82%/18%
Junipero Serra High School (San Mateo)	80%/20%
Moreau Catholic High School (Hayward)	77%/21%
East Bay Waldorf School (El Sobrante)	77%/15%
Salesian High School (Richmond)	75%/25%
Mercy High School-San Francisco (San Francisco)	70%/30%
Fremont Christian School (Fremont)	70%/25%
St. Elizabeth High School (Oakland)	62%/36%
Archbishop Riordan High School (San Francisco)	61%/38%

N/P: Mitty High School, Berean Christian, Contra Costa Christian, Cornerstone Academy, Jewish Community High School, Lisa Kampner Hebrew Academy, Kehillah Jewish High School, Lycée Français La Pérouse, Menlo, Mid-Peninsula, Quarry Lane High School, St. Joseph Notre Dame, St. Lawrence, Saint Mary's, St. Vincent de Paul, San Francisco Waldorf High School, Sonoma Academy, Stuart Hall, Urban, Ursuline, Valley Christian, Woodside International, Woodside Priory

OTHER PARENTING BOOKS PUBLISHED BY PINCE-NEZ PRESS

By Betsy Little and Paula Molligan:

Private Schools of San Francisco & Marin Counties (K-8)
Extensive information on private independent and parochial schools in San Francisco and Marin County and expert advice on the admissions process. ISBN 978-1-930074-02-6, $24.95

By other authors:

Finding a Preschool for Your Child in San Francisco & Marin
by Lori Rifkin Ph.D., Vera Obemeyer, Ph.D., Irene Byrne, M.A., and Melinda Venable. Profiles of public and private preschools, and discussions of how to choose a preschool. ISBN 978-1-930074-12-5, $23.95

Birthing: Choices You Have to Create the Best Birth Experience for You and Your Child
by Irene Byrne, M.A. Compiles the most current information from experts in the fields of midwifery, Lamaze, obstetrics, prenatal care, and much more regarding these choices and many more. It encourages women to carefully consider each option and to make their decisions free from pressure from advocates of any one approach and with the ultimate objective clearly focused on delivering a healthy baby. $19.95, ISBN 978-1-930074-06-4

Learning Disabilities from a Parent's Perspective: What You Need to Know to Understand, Help and Advocate for Your Child
by Kim E. Glenchur, MS, MBA
A comprehensive guide from a parent's point of view about how to help children with learning differences and disabilities. $23.95, 430 pages, ISBN 978-1-930074-07-1

Confessions of a Slacker Mom
by Muffy Mead-Ferro. A hilarious break from the pressure of parenting. Now published by Da Capo Press as ISBN 0-7382-0994-5.

Order at www.pince-nez.com.

LaVergne, TN USA
02 March 2011
218509LV00003B/111/P